DOCUMENTA MISSIONALIA - 19

(STUDIA MISSIONALIA - DOCUMENTA ET OPERA)
FACULTAS MISSIOLOGICA - PONT. UNIVERSITAS GREGORIANA

DHARMA, HINDU AND CHRISTIAN, ACCORDING TO ROBERTO DE NOBILI

Analysis of its meaning and its use in Hinduism and Christianity

SOOSAI AROKIASAMY, S. J.

EDITRICE PONTIFICIA UNIVERSITÀ GREGORIANA
ROMA 1986

IMPRIMI POTEST

Romae die 3 iunii 1986

R. P. URBANUS NAVARRETE, S.I.
Rector Universitatis

Con approvazione del Vicariato di Roma
in data 15 dicembre 1986

EDITRICE PONTIFICIA UNIVERSITÀ GREGORIANA
EDITRICE PONTIFICIO ISTITUTO BIBLICO
Piazza della Pilotta 35 - 00187 Roma, Italia

ACKNOWLEDGEMENT

It gives me great pleasure to express my deep and sincere gratitude to M. Dhavamony, S.J. for the assistance rendered to the author at various stages of the research done on de Nobili. I express my gratitude also to E. Hamel, S.J. for his inspirational help, E. Coffey, S.J. for his reading of the manuscript of the dissertation with painstaking care and all my friends who helped me in one way or another to complete this study. I cannot forget to express my debt of gratitude to the community of Collegio Bellarmino and the three Rectors I have had at the College for their understanding and support during my study. I would like to thank also Rex Pai, S.J., Provincial of India, for his encouragement for the publication of this work and my Rector and colleagues at Vidyajyoti, Delhi.

TRANSLITERATION OF SANSKRIT WORDS

(*Approximate English equivalents are given as far as possible*)

अ	a	ड	ḍ
आ	ā	ढ	ḍh
इ	i	ण	ṇ
ई	ī	त	t
उ	u	थ	th
ऊ	ū	द	d
ऋ	ṛ	ध	dh
ए	e	न	n
ऐ	ai	प	p
ओ	o	फ	ph
औ	au	ब	b
क	k	भ	bh
ख	kh	म	m
ग	g	य	y
घ	gh	र	r
ङ	ṅ	ल	l
च	c	व	v
छ	ch	श	ś
ज	j	ष	ṣ
झ	jh	स	s
ञ	ñ	ह	h
ट	ṭ	ः	ḥ
ठ	ṭh	ं	ṃ

A NOTE ON THE TAMIL TRANSLITERATION

Vowels	Consonants
அ — a	க — k
ஆ — ā	ச — c
இ — i	ட — ṭ
ஈ — ī	த — t
உ — u	ப — p
ஊ — ū	ற — ṟ
எ — e	ர — r
ஏ — ē	ங — ṅ
ஐ — ai	ஞ — ñ
ஒ — o	ண — ṇ
ஓ — ō	ன — ṉ
ஔ — au	ந — n
	ம — m
	ய — y
	ல — l
	ள — ḷ
	ழ — ḻ
	வ — v
	ஃ — ḵ

LETTERS BORROWED FROM SANSKRIT

ஜ	j
க்ஷ	cc
ஷ	ṣ
ஸ	s
ஹ	h

TABLE OF CONTENTS

Chapter Two
THE THEORY OF KARMA AND REBIRTH AND THE UNDERSTANDING OF THE HUMAN SOUL IN RELATION TO DHARMA

Chapter Three
DHARMA AND MORAL NORMS

Chapter Four
DHARMA AND SALVATION IN HINDUISM

PART TWO
DHARMA IN CHRISTIANITY

CHAPTER FIVE
THE CONCEPT OF RELIGION (*VĒTAM*)

Chapter Six
DHARMA AND SALVATION IN CHRISTIANITY

PART THREE

CHAPTER SEVEN
A SYNTHETIC SUMMARY

INTRODUCTION

In the choice of the topic "*Dharma*, Hindu and Christian, according to Roberto de Nobili" I had made a circuitous journey. I began with the idea of studying caste and ecclesial community in India in the sixteenth and seventeenth centuries from a moral-theological point of view. That would have taken me into history and sociology. Caste and caste system are indeed important expressions of *dharma* in Hinduism. Therefore a study of the concept of *dharma* in de Nobili was undertaken by me. *Dharma*, though a complex concept, includes in its meanings principally ethico-religious meanings which would be worth investigating from the point of view of moral theology.

We are aware of the different studies done on de Nobili.[1] Ours is not a study of theology of adaptation which Nicolas Tornese has done in a study of Robert de Nobili.[2] He has not used the Tamil works in his study. There is no attempt to study the concept of *Dharma* on the part of this author as present in de Nobili's method of adaptation. Again, ours is not a study of the mission method from a historical viewpoint.[3]

Tiliander Bror has done a study of Hindu and Christian terminology with reference to the Tamil area.[4] It is a study of both Catholic and Protestant missionary theologians concerning this matter. He has taken Robert de Nobili as the principal Catholic rep-

[1] We mention here studies done from the point of view of theology in fulfilment of academic degrees.

[2] Nicolas Tornese, *Roberto de Nobili*. Contributo al Dialogo coi non-Cristiani, Cagliari, 1973.

[3] Peter Bachmann, *Roberto Nobili*. Ein Missionsgeschichtlicher Beitrag zum Christlichen Dialog mit Hinduismus, Roma 1972.

[4] Tiliander Bror, *Christian and Hindu Terminology*. A Study in Their Mutual Relations with Special Reference to the Tamil Area, Uppsala, 1974.

resentative for his study of theological terms. He refers to the *Dharma* terminology in de Nobili just on one page. His examination of ethico-religious terms in de Nobili is very brief and incomplete. He doesn't consider de Nobili's knowledge of Hinduism in the examination of these terms. D. Yesudhas in his study examines de Nobili's attitude to Hinduism in general.[5] Nowhere does he treat of the idea of *Dharma* in de Nobili. He hasn't used the Latin treatises of de Nobili in his study.

The aim of our study is to investigate the concept of *Dharma* in Hinduism, as understood by de Nobili and his use of the concept in his writings to present Christianity to the Hindus and to the Indian Christians. Thus our study is distinct from that of others mentioned above, and this precisely constitutes the originality of the thesis.

Since the concept of *Dharma* is complex in Hinduism itself, a careful study of the concept in de Nobili's writings is needed to identify its different meanings. For this we adopt an analytical method. We do this in terms of socio-ethico-religious meanings of *Dharma*.

A word on the material used in our study. We base our study on the currently available published works of de Nobili in their original languages or in translations. De Nobili's treatises in Latin were his apologies for or *defensiones* of his method of evangelisation in Madurai. They give abundant evidence of his knowledge of *Dharma* in Hinduism and his attitude to it. So too his letters and those written by his collaborators. The letters used in this study are either in the original languages or in translations.

Tamil works of de Nobili edited by Fr S. Rajamanickam S.J. have been used in the study, and not those edited by M.C. Iyakappa Pillai (Trichinopoly, 1882 and 1907), since he says that he has changed words and usages which are no more current.[6] A problem exists concerning many Tamil works attributed to de Nobili. In this we have chosen to follow Rajamanickam's final list in his *The First Oriental Scholar*. It includes works of certain authorship because of internal evidence and the testimony of de Nobili himself and those which are attributed to him with high probability.

---

[5] D. Yesudhas, "Indigenization or Adaptation? A Brief Study of Roberto de Nobili's attitude to Hinduism". *Bangalore Theological Forum*, I (1967) pp. 39-52.

[6] S. Rajamanickam, S.J., *The First Oriental Scholar*, Tirunelveli 1972, p. 98. Cf. *Nānōpatēcam*, Mūnrām Kāṇṭam, ed. M.C. Iyakappa Pillai, Tiruchinopoly 1907, the title page.

The thesis breaks up into seven chapters in three parts. Part I is concerned with *dharma* in Hinduism. In part I, chapter I we examine *dharma* as ethos in a descriptive way. We examine social *dharma* under *varṇadharma* (*dharma* of the four classes) and that of *āśramadharma*. This includes social duties, virtues, religious duties. The idea of *svadharma* (duties of one's own class) the specific idea of caste dignity and 'losing of caste' are also discussed. We examine how the *dharma* of the classes is enforced and the idea of obligation that goes with it. Here we show how *dharma* is understood as law. We also examine how *dharma* can be understood in a general sense as the ways and customs of a country and of peoples. We then consider the place of tradition in Indian society. We examine moral virtues apart from the *dharma* of classes and that of the stages of life.

In chapter two, section one, we present the different views of the human soul in so far as they determine the understanding of *dharma* in its ethico-religious meaning. We also present de Nobili's objections to such views.

In section two of the same chapter, we review the theory of *karma* and rebirth as presented by de Nobili and his criticism of the theory from the point of view of moral action. In section three, we present de Nobili's functional interpretation of the myth of creation concerning division of society into four *varṇas* (classes) and his explanation of the order of society in terms of microcosm and macrocosm.

In chapter three, we examine the ethical norms in Hinduism and de Nobili's use of ethical norms with regard to Hindu *dharma*. First, we examine tradition as ethical norm, then the place of law-books in the enjoinment of duties as the source of obligation. Then we examine the relation of religious rituals to ethical *dharma*. We consider also the custom of commending a practice with the idea of merit and demerit and its relation to ethical norm. We then examine the justification of social *dharma* and the critical evaluation of social *dharma* according to the theory of *karma* and rebirth. We also consider *jus gentium* (the law of the nations) and the grounding of Hindu *dharma* in natural law. We refer here to the idea of the final end and *dharma* and the final end according to the materialists.

We consider the presence of *recta ratio* in Hinduism and its use by de Nobili. We then examine how de Nobili uses the notion of right order as an expression of right reason. We also examine how de Nobili uses the determinants (*fontes*) of morality, namely, object, end and circumstance in his critique of Hindu *dharma*.

In chapter four, we examine *dharma* in its relation to salvation in Hinduism. In this relation of *dharma* to salvation, we consider the Hindu notion of God and its relation to righteous conduct and salvation, and how de Nobili evaluates its positive and negative aspects. Here in particular we examine the Hindu notion of *Trimūrti* and the idea of *avatāra* (incarnation) in relation to *dharma*. We again examine the doctrine of *karma* and rebirth but from the point of view of the notion of sin, its removal and forgiveness and salvation. Then a critical evaluation is made of the Hindu notion of the intermediary heaven (*svarga*). Then we examine the final end of man which comes through *mokṣa*. A critical evaluation of the notion of heaven in different sects and of the different stages of the final bliss is made in relation to the ethico-religious meaning of *dharma*.

We then consider if the Hindu scriptures are utterances of God for the salvation of man and if Hinduism is a religion of salvation according to de Nobili. We present here de Nobili's explanation of popular cults. We consider then de Nobili's view of the salvation of non-Christians. We then examine de Nobili's understanding of the distinction of caste from religion in Hinduism itself.

In part II, we consider de Nobili's use of *dharma* in Christian theology. In chapter five, we examine de Nobili's definition of religion with reference to the ethico-religious meaning of *dharma*. We then consider how he presents the attributes of God and how he shows the nature of God as the nature of righteousness and as the foundation of all righteous teaching of religion. We consider also how de Nobili conceives God as the supreme Guru who becomes the visible Guru to teach the way of righteousness (*tarmaneṛi* or *tarmavali*) for the salvation of man. We show that de Nobili presents the Christian religion as *tarmaneṛi* (the way of righteousness). Its purpose and meaning (*artam*) as the revealed religion of God (*tēvōkkitta vētam*) is to declare *dharma* and *adharma* for the salvation of man. Definition of religion includes the idea that it is the way. The supreme meaning of religion consists in the *dharma* of love. In this connection we show how de Nobili rejects a caste notion of religion and also a nationalistic notion of it. Here we mention the difficulty de Nobili had in removing the use of the term parankis synonymous with Christians.

In chapter six, we consider the different uses of *dharma* in Christian theology. The meaning and purpose of incarnation (*avatāra*) of Christ is explained in terms of *dharma*. The passion and death of Christ are again explained in terms of *dharma*. We then examine the terminology of *dharma* in the explanation of virtuous conduct in Christianity as present in de Nobili's catechetical, apologetic and devotional writings. We show here how he uses the *dharma* terminology to signify different virtues, theological and moral, holy men and holiness. We also examine de Nobili's presentation of love (*bhakti*) as the highest virtue (*uttamatarmam*). We also consider how de Nobili presents the meaning of suffering in terms of *dharma*. We examine his presentation of the Ten Commandments. We then consider how de Nobili understands *āśramadharma* in Christianity, especially that of renunciation and that of married life. We examine how de Nobili uses the concept of *dharma* in his theology of grace and in the explanation of sin and its forgiveness. De Nobili's use of the concept of *dharma* in his explanation of the final salvation, namely, *mokṣa* is also considered. At the end of the chapter, we give some examples of de Nobili's use of *dharma* terminology in the explanation of different Christian ideas.

In part III, Chapter seven, we give a synthetic summary of *dharma* in Hinduism and Christianity and a theological evaluation of de Nobili's understanding of *dharma* in Hinduism and its use in Christianity in the light of the doctrine of the Vatican Council II. In Section one *dharma* in Hinduism is considered in its socio-ethico-religious meaning. In Section two, *dharma* is considered principally in its ethico-religious meaning in Christianity. In section three we show how de Nobili's approach to Hinduism and his method of presenting Christianity to the Hindus, in some way anticipates, though imperfectly, many of the points concerning the relation between Christianity and non-Christian religions which find a better development and a more perfect expression in the documents of the Second Vatican Council. De Nobili was one of the first Europeans to have known the concept of *dharma* in its polyvalent meaning. His undestanding of the *dharma* of the Hindus and his use of it in the presentation of Christianity are to be understood as one of the first 'encounters' of the two religions, Christianity and Hinduism.

PART ONE

CHAPTER ONE

DHARMA AS ETHOS

Dharma is a central and fundamental concept of Hinduism and its ethos. De Nobili shows a fair undestanding of this complex concept and comes to use it in his presentation of Christianity to the Hindus.[1] He was aware of the different meanings of the word *dharma*. He adopts these different meanings in his catechetical and apologetic works. Fr. Buccerio, once a companion and sympathiser of de Nobili, accused de Nobili of using the word *dharma* in two different meanings (virtue and duty of caste) at the same time.[2] De Nobili answers the objection: "Moreover it is to be noted that it is much on the lips (of men) regarding the point in Sanskrit discipline (or science) that one and the same word without change embraces different kinds of meanings. Thus, for example, the word *dharma* sometimes means virtue, similarly alms, sometimes qualities of body, besides customs of a region, also the obligatory duty of caste." [3] In the same

---

[1] DE NOBILI uses the word *dharma* as a Hindu would use it in his religious and ethical discourse. De Nobili could use it because he had understood its profound meaning. Since it is untranslatable, we shall use the word as such, but its different meanings will be made clear from the contexts of its use.

[2] Fr. Andrea Buccerio wrote his objections against de Nobili's *Informatio de quibusdam Moribus Nationis Indicae* (the text is given in Rajamanickam's *Roberto de Nobili on Indian Customs).* De Nobili in his answer to Buccerio written on 29-12-1615, refers to Buccerio's objection: "quod vox *dharma* quam semel stirpis officii functionem significare dixi alio in loco quasi mei immemor pro virtute acceperim," Cf. *Responsio quibusdam a P. Andrea Buccerio obiectis contra meam* informationem. 29-12-1615 (ARSI: Goa 51, f. 214). In the text of the thesis, all translations from Latin and Tamil and other languages into English are mine unless otherwise indicated. A summary of de Nobili's answer to Buccerio's objections is found in *Adaptation* by S. Rajamanickam, Palyamkottai, 1971, pp. 200-203. I must acknowledge here that I have profited by the translations of de Nobili's *Informatio*, as given in *Roberto de Nobili on Indian Customs*.

[3] *Responsio a quibusdam a P. A. Buccerio obiectis*. (ARSI Goa, 51, f. 214). "Insuper notandum est ex eo in grandana scientia multum esse in labiis quod una vox et eadem invaria-

place, de Nobili says that one must know not only the different meanings of a word but also use great prudence or care in rendering a word differently according to changes in meaning. First, we shall analyse the concept of *dharma* in Hinduism, as presented by de Nobili. In this chapter we will survey *dharma* as ethos.[4]

A. DHARMA IN THE SENSE OF OBJECTIVE DUTIES

a. *Varṇadharma*

We shall consider first duties in the context of society. The duties of society arise according to the division of society into classes, and they are called *varṇadharma* (duties of classes). De Nobili refers to this phrase from Manu in his treatise, *Informatio quebusdam moribus nationis Indicae.*[5] In this treatise de Nobili speaks of the division of Indian society into four grades of civil functions:

> The state of Indians is divided into four grades of civil functions and similarly of civil nobility as it is very well known to those who deal with them closely and as it is explained in the eighteen volumes of *smṛti*[6] in which all the arrangement of

---

ta vox amplectat significationum genera v.g. vox haec (*dharma*) aliquando virtutem, significat itidem eleemosinas, quandoque corporis complexiones, preterea regionis consuetudinem, stirpis insuper debitum officium significat."

Cf. *Āttuma Nirṇayam*, Tuticorin, 1967, p. 44. In this work de Nobili uses *dharma* in the sense of quality of body or nature or disposition (cf. above: "*darma*... quandoque corporis complexiones"). The treatise *Āttuma Nirṇayam* will be hereafter referred to as A.N. Cf. Ibid. p. 49.

[4] Cf. P. HAECKER, "Dharma in Hinduism", *ZRM* 49 (1965) p. 99. He says that the Hindu idea of *dharma* is radically empirical. Here we discuss *dharma* in the aspect of ethos. Cf. ch. 3 for the ethical aspect of *dharma*.

[5] This treatise will be referred to hereafter in the thesis as I.C. (reference to *Roberto de Nobili on Indian Customs*, ed. S. Rajamanickam, S.J., Palayamkottai, 1972). The Latin text is found in this book in the 2nd part with its own pagination. Our pagination refers to that of the Latin text. Cf. ibid., p. 57. The phrase quoted from Manu is: "Varṇa dharma niyamo'bi prapaincam". *Varṇa dharma* means "variarum stirpium officium".

[6] *Smṛti* means "that which is remembered". The *smṛti* scriptures rank next to the *vedas* (the *Śruti*) in authority. The works expressly called *smṛti* are law-books called *Dharma śāstras* to which de Nobili refers. Cf. T. P. Mahadevan: *Outlines of Hinduism*, Bombay 1960, pp. 31-32. (Hereafter simply as Mahadevan). Cf. R. C. Zaehner: *Hinduism*, 1962, pp. 9-10. (Hereafter referred to as Zaehner). *Vedas* as *śruti* is the highest authority for, and source of, *dharma*.

laws which concern the order of citizens, government and the lists of castes has been abridged.[7] Of these *smṛti* law books, *Manu* enjoys the highest authority.[8]

De Nobili principally depends on *smṛtis* for his understanding of *dharma* of different castes of *varṇas*. He cites a text from *Manu* which in de Nobili's interpretation runs as follows:

> The office of Brahmin is wisdom, that of *Ksatryas* or Kings is protection, that of merchants is trade, that of Śudras i.e. Plebeians is service.[9]

We shall now examine each of the four *varṇas* and their respective duties (*dharma*).

i. *Dharma of Brahmins*:

Here de Nobili tries to show the *dharma* (duty) of Brahmins is that of knowledge and that they are a class of wise men (*sapientium*). He points out that the word Brahmin is derived from the verb 'Brahmate' which means 'to know' according to the Brahmins themselves.[10] This etymology is not scientifically acceptable.

All work of teaching belongs to them, especially of the noble sciences such as Logic, Philosophy, Theology, all of which are the works of Brahmins. De Nobili says that the teaching of all sciences is their proper office.[11] He also observes that it does not mean that all

---

[7] I.C. p. 2. "Indorum Respublica distinguitur primo quatuor gradibus civilium munerum, atque adeo civilis nobilitatis ut est iis qui apud hos intime verasantur notissimum et explicatur in decem et octo voluminibus *Smruti*, in quibus omnis legum dispositio quantum attinet ad ordinem civium, gubernationem rationesque stirpium redacta est".

[8] Ibid.

[9] Ibid. p. 7. "Id est Brahmanis officium sapientia, Xactrieris sive Regii officium servare populos, Mercatoris officium mercatura, Siudreris hoc est Plebeii officium famulatus esto."

[10] I.C. p. 3. "Primus gradus est Sapientum, quod Brahmanes vocant a verbo ut ipsi dicunt 'Brahmate' quot est scire". The derivation of Brahman from *Brahmate* is incorrect. It is derived from *brih* which means 'to grow'. The literal meaning of *brahman* is 'growth' or 'expansion' or 'evolution'. Cf. MONIER MONIER-WILLIAMS: *A Sanskrit-English Dictionary* (new edition by E. Leumann and C. Capeller et alii) Oxford 1974, p. 737. It will be referred to in the thesis as M.-Williams.

[11] Ibid. "Ad quem ordinem spectat omnis tractatio scientiarum praesertim nobilium, qualis est Logica, Philosophia, Theologia quae omnis Brahmanis sunt...".

treat of all subjects, since the subjects are so vast and many. Some become experts in many subjects, others in a few. Thus some become doctors of speculative sciences like philosophy and theology, others doctors of Law, others as *dharmaśāstris*, i.e., Doctors of Moral Science.[12] If the duty of Brahmins is that of *Jñāna* it does not mean, says de Nobili, that "it is the specific business of Brahmin to deal with those laws which treat in part of idols, except in so far as in this land they appear to belong to scientific knowledge, since to Brahmin belongs all learning." [13] According to de Nobili, the proper word for wisdom, *Jñāna* "is said to be the sum total of the Brahmin's duty, it does not comprise the laws nor the knowledge of these false gods (when it is taken in its specific sense); but it means wisdom which consists in sciences, or rather the knowledge of those things supplied by the light of nature about all things, but particularly about God one and unique, whereas the science of laws is distinguished from *Jñāna* and they call it *Karma.*"[14] Thus de Nobili understands that the office of Brahmins is *Jñāna* in a broader sense in support of which he cites a text from *smṛti* whose meaning he interprets:

> In comparison with ignorant persons those excel who are well-versed in the sciences, among the scientists, those excel who attain wisdom, among the latter, those distinguish themselves who make progress in this field every day more profoundly and widely.[15]

Then De Nobili goes on to examine the concept of the perfect Brahmin which concerns the moral qualities which he must cultivate. These qualities belong to the real meaning of Brahmin.

---

[12] Ibid.

[13] I.C. p. 10. "... non esse proprium Brahmanis leges hace in quibus ex parte de idolis agitur tractare, nisi quatenus in hac regione et hac pertinere videntur ad scientiam cum ad Brahmanem spectet omnis eruditio".

[14] Ibid. "Imo *Jñānam* quae vox proprie sapientiam significat et dicitur esse summa officii Brahmanis non includit leges, neque notitiam horum falsorum deorum (cum proprie accipitur) sed significat sapientiam quae consistit in scientiis seu potius notitiam horum luminis naturae circa omnia et praecipue circa Deum unum atque unicum; scientiam vero legum contradistinguunt a *Jñānam* et vocant *Karmam*".

[15] Ibid. "prae idiotis praecellunt ii qui sapientiam assequuntur, inter hos, illi sese extollunt, qui in hac intimius, et universalius proficiunt."

De Nobili cites a passage from *Parāśara Smṛti* which he translates as follows: "assiduous work, a bridling of the passions, compassion, liberality, truthfulness, virtue, discipline, a compliant disposition, science, wisdom, a readiness to embrace what others say truly — all these elements enter into the definition of Brahmin." [16] That is, these elements go to make the *lakṣaṇa* (characteristics) of the Brahmin. Here in the above text the word *dharma* is used for virtue.[17] Since the above-mentioned elements make the qualities of Brahmin, they are understood to be the duties of Brahmins. De Nobili explains also how the different elements mark the progress of one in the pursuit of wisdom.

The following is a comment of de Nobili on the above text:

> First appears the instrument of self-restraint and of moral virtues because without them no one can attain wisdom... or rather as they consider it to be the part that is conducive to perfect wisdom.[18]

This comment of de Nobili is significant in so far as it indicates *finis* of moral virtues. The different elements of *Brahmana lakṣaṇa* are the ways of preparing and disposing oneself for perfect wisdom. These elements of self-control and moral virtues have thus the meaning of instrument or means of *jñānam*. Brahmin is expected to strive for true wisdom in this moral way. Later we shall discuss this point in the section on the relation of *dharma* to salvation. Continuing his discussion of the true Brahmin, de Nobili cites a text from *smṛti* (*Manu*, I, 97) which along with another verse from the same book (I, 96) appears to be the definition of the perfect Brahmin. De Nobili renders their meaning as follows:

> Among the Brahmins, those should be said to excel and to be perfect who are truly wise and proficient in the sciences;

---

[16] I.C. p. 9. "Id est studiosus labor, continentia, pietas, liberalitas, veritas, virtus, disciplina, facilitas, scientia, sapientia, eius quod alii vere dicunt amplexatio haec omnia sunt Brahmanis definitio.

[17] Ibid. p. 8.

[18] I.C. p. 9: "Ubi notandum est enucleate poni totum progressum sapientis ut scilicet primo componet instrumentum continentiae et virtutum moralium, vel quia sine his sapientiam consequi nemo potest ut Auctor ipse docuit primo ethi. i., vel qui putant haec esse partem dispositivam perfectae sapientiae, ut mox dicetur".

among those who are well-versed in sciences, those who add to the knowledge of acting with virtue or prudence; among these, such men as actually behave virtuously, finally among those who behave virtuously those are perfect men who contemplate the true God.[19]

This is Manu's concept of the perfect Brahmin. De Nobili points out here that this goal of a perfect Brahmin has also been mentioned by St. Thomas and others. They hold that the happiness of the perfect sage in this life lies primarily in the contemplation of God and secondarily and by way of preparation to it in the use of speculative sciences, the practical intellect and the moral virtues. Thus the function of a true Brahmin is not pursuit of wisdom taken in a purely secular sense but also it is the quest of *jñānam* of God. The *dharma* of true or perfect Brahmin is in principle open to all in so far as it concerns the knowledge of the one true God. We already mentioned the distinction between *jñānam* and *karma* made by de Nobili.[20] By *karma* he means the laws governing the worship of gods. At the same time, he recognises that *karma* contains things which are partly acceptable.[21]

De Nobili takes pains to explain the *dharma* of *jñānam* though it belongs to a particular class because he sees its importance for conveying the *jñānam* of the Gospel. De Nobili continues his expla-

[19] I.C. p. 9. "Inter Brahmanes ii dicendi sunt excellere et esse perfecti qui vere sapientes sunt et scientias callent, inter scientes ii qui addunt scientiam agendi cum virtute seu prudentia, inter hos ii qui reipsa agunt cum virtute, inter agentes cum virtute ii perfecti sunt qui Deum verum contemplantur". The Sanskrit expression for the last category of people is *Brahma Vadinah*, i.e., they are knowers of the Brahman which de Nobili translates as God. Cf. BÜHLER: The Laws of Manu, the *Sacred Books of the East*, ed. Max Müller, vol. XXV, Oxford 1886, p. 25. This work will be referred to as Bühler in the thesis. In this connection, de Nobili comments on the use of the word Brahma for God. Brahma with the final short vowel does not mean any limited and false God, but the one true God who is spiritual and who can be known by the light of natural reason. I.C. p. 9. "Haec enim vox *Brahma* ultima brevi non significat Deum aliquem determinatum et falsum sed Deum in Communi, et usu fere applicatur etiam ad significandum illum verum Deum unicum et immaterialem qui lumine naturae cognosci potest."

[20] *Karma* is the aspect of Hinduism which Goncalo Fernandes treats in Tratado Pe Goncalo Fernandes Trancoso Sobre o Hinduismo, ed. Wicki, Lisboa, 1978. Cf. f.n. 2 of this chapter.

[21] I.C. p. 10. "Hae leges non totae malae sunt, sunt aggregatio verarum et falsarum sentetiarum, sacrorum et civilium praeceptorum."

nation of the true Brahmin. He again appeals to the *Smṛti* of Manu and sums up Manu as follows:

> Let the man who is versed in the sciences concerning the world, i.e. the natural sciences, in the science of laws, in the science about God, be honoured greatly.[22]

De Nobili quotes this text to show that a true Brahmin is not just a specialist in *karma* alone but also in natural sciences and, above all, sciences about God. He also quotes a saying "Vedapatho Nirarthakah," which means that if one knows solely the laws (*karma*), it is not of much use. Indeed, Brahmins are devoted to such a variety of innumerable laws that one cannot say their knowledge of the laws is only knowledge of these particular laws (*karma*).[23] Identification of Brahmin with teachers of superstitious laws, de Nobili rejects. He considers the duty of wisdom of the Brahmins in a broader sense, that is, they can devote themselves to different sciences: social, philosophical, religious, etc., as is clear from the different sciences with which they deal.[24] He speaks of the four castes as "four grades of civil offices".[25] The Brahmin class by its *ratio* and *officium* is a class of wise men.[26] Besides, the Brahmins are the wise men of India with the supposition that in every country there are wise men.[27] The duty of Brahmins is, moreover, a hereditary profession.[28] If wisdom were wanting in a Brahmin, the name of Brahmin would apply to him only equivocally. According to Manu, just as an elephant carved out of wood is called the elephant, and just as the skin of an animal is called the animal, so too a Brahmin without knowledge is called a Brahmin.[29]

---

[22] Ibid.: "Id est scientias ad mundum pertinentes, hoc est naturales scientiam legum, scientiam de Deo si quis consecutus sit illud maxime honorato". (M. 2, 117). This is about the honour to be paid to the teacher by the student. Cf. Bühler, p. 51.

[23] I.C. pp. 10-11.

[24] Ibid. p. 3.

[25] Ibid. p. 2.

[26] Ibid. p. 6.

[27] Ibid. p. 6.

[28] Ibid.

[29] Ibid. p. 7. "Id est sicut ex ligno elephas dicitur, sicut pellis alius cujusvis brutae animantis animal nominatur, ita Brahman qui sine disciplina est Brahman vocatur" Cf. M, 2, 157.

The commentator on the passage of Manu says why the law does not consider those who neglect sciences Brahmins. They do not live up to their office, i.e., the duty of their class (*officium suae stirpis*).[30] De Nobili goes on to show that Brahmins in order to be Brahmins must be learned. Thus with reference to *pariṣad* or *sabha* (the Assembly), of the learned Brahmins, says de Nobili, unlearned Brahmins even if they were a thousand in number would not make the *pariṣad.*[31] This is the authority of Manu. The duty of the Brahmin class is *tractatio sapientiae* (*jñānam*). Now according to the same testimony, de Nobili continues, *tractatio scientiarum* is forbidden to other castes.[32] Yet, de Nobili is aware that the other two castes, namely, royal families (*Kṣatryas*) and merchant class (*Vaiśyas*) can attend lectures in sciences as granted to them according to *Parāśara Smṛti*.[33] It means that the learning is open to the higher classes, that is, the twice-born (*dvijas*). However, de Nobili tries to show that learning sciences and teaching them is the proper office of the Brahmin class.

Such a function is not conceded to any other class, not even to the class of the Rajas.[34] De Nobili goes on to say in the same place that *Vaiśyas* do not practically learn sciences, though they can, whereas *Śudras* or Plebeians are forbidden to learn even the Grantha (*Sanskrit*) alphabet.[35] The duty of one class cannot be done by another class. That is *varṇadharma*. The Brahmin class cannot as-

---

[30] Ibid. "... quia hujusmodi homines secundum officium suae stirpis non vivunt". *Gradus* is rendered as order and *stirps* as class by Rajamanickam.

[31] Ibid. p. 8. "Id est eorum qui nomen tantum Brahmanis substentant (scilicet indoctorum de quibus ibi loquitur) Pariciat i.e. insignium virorum congregatio nulla est quamvis mille Brahmanes congregantur".

[32] Ibid. "... coeteribus stirpibus interdicitur tractatio scientiarum". Cf. P. DAHMEN: *Robert De Nobili l'Apôtre des Brahmes*, Premierè Apologie 1610, Paris 1931, p. 93. De Nobili speaks of the rule forbidding Brahmins to teach the scriptures to those who are not Brahmins. "Bracmanibus nefas esse hujusmodi libros alios docere, qui Bracmanes non sunt, quod putant maximum peccatum". Hereafter this book containing de Nobili's first defense of his method will be referred to as Pr. Ap. (Premierè Apologie).

[33] I.C. p. 8. Cf. also J. BERTRAND: *La Mission du Maduré* tome II, Paris 1848, p. 90. De Nobili in a letter (22 Nov. 1610) to his Provincial says that *Vaiśyas* and *Śudras* are excluded from the study of higher sciences. (References to this work will be made under the name Bertrand II).

[33] I.C. p. 8.

[35] Ibid.

sume the duties of other classes. If Brahmins neglect the office of learning and take up the duties assigned to other classes, they will not have the dignity which is due to them despite their present wealth. According to Manu, these people should be removed from the grade of Brahmins. They are to be considered degenerate.

We shall now examine the duties of the other three classes, namely *Kṣatryas* (Kings), *Vaiśyas* (merchants) and *Śudras* (Plebeians).

ii. *Dharma of Kṣatryas*

The second of the four classes is that of kings or chiefs or bearing arms belongs to them primarily. They are called Rajas or *Kṣatryas.*[36] De Nobili says that they liberate people from fear.[37] They use the phrase *kṣatat tryānte* meaning liberating people from fear. The office and duty of *Kṣatryas* are spoken of elsewhere and also in Manu. De Nobili refers to the verse of Manu which he translates:

> Not to flee in battle, to protect the people, to listen to the words of the wise are the three (duties) in which the activity of Rajas (their), good and excellence are contained.[38]

De Nobili explaining the etymology of *Kṣatrya* says that *Kṣatrya* has to do with 'liberating people from fear' (*kṣatat tryānte*). He sees in this phrase the original meaning and also a clue to the duty and function of *Kṣatryas*. Again, speaking of the office of Brahmins, he quotes Manu in which the phrase which sums up the duty of the Rajas is "*tapah kṣatraysya rakṣṇam*", i.e., the duty of *Kṣatryas* is Protection (*rakṣṇam*).[39] A further description of the duty of kings is given in terms of victory and bravery. De Nobili quotes Manu in which the phrase that refers to the *Kṣatryas* is this "*Kṣatriyānāmtu*

---

[36] I.C. p. 3.

[37] Ibid. "... quasi ut ipsi explicant Ksatat tryante, id est a metu populos liberantes". *Kṣatra* means power; *Kṣatriya* is the one who rules. De Nobili's etymology does not seem to be correct. Cf. *Ñānōpatēcam Kāṇṭam* III, Tuticorin 1968, p. 8. (The great catechism of de Nobili is in five parts (*Kāṇṭams*). References to the first three parts will be made simply as *Kāṇṭam* and its number), p. 8. The same phrase occurs here: "catātē iti cattiriya" (as written in Tamil).

[38] I.C. "id est in proelio non fugere, populos servare, sapientum dicta audire tria sunt, in quibus Regiorum actio, bonum et excellentia continentur".

[39] Ibid p. 7. De Nobili renders *tapah* as 'duty' instead of 'austerity'.

Vīryataḥ", that is, "the highest perfection of kings, is victory".[40] It is the purpose and benefit of *Kṣatryas*. However, it is granted to the *Kṣatryas* also the privilege of learning sciences according to *Parāśara smṛti.*[41] Another important aspect of *Kṣatryas* is to see to it that *varṇadharma* in society is observed and preserved. They must punish those who violate them. The order of caste hierarchy must not be disturbed.[42]

iii. *Dharma of Vaiśyas*

It is the third class of "the free-born merchants who apply themselves, namely, to (the acquisition of) wealth by dealing in apparel, gems and other articles of the same kind, to trade in which is considered honourable, which contributes to the vigour and the good of the state." [43] Once again de Nobili explains the duty of this class by giving the etymological meaning of the word *Vaiśya*. The Sanskrit word *Vaiśya* comes from *visati* which means 'to enter upon'. It means the acquisition of riches.[44] This style of life is the *dharma* of *Vaiśyas*. By practising their *dharma*, they contribute to the common good of the State. They are allowed to trade in that which is honourable.[45] There is a further definition of the function of the *Vaiśyas* in Manu (9, 329) to which de Nobili refers. He gives the meaning of the text as follows:

> To know, to deal out, appraise precious stones, pearls, coral ware, metals, clothing even perfumes and condiments, as well as to know their prices and values, all this pertains to this class (i.e., the *Vaiśyas*).[46]

[40] Ibid. "Summitas Regii est victoria."

[41] Ibid. p. 8.

[42] Ibid. p. 5.

[43] Ibid. p. 3. "Tertius gradus est ingenuorum Mercatorum, qui nimirum contrectandae pecuniae vestibus, gemmis et aliis eiusdem generis, in quibus honesta mercatura exerceri potest in reipublicae nervum et commodum operant..."

[44] Ibid. p. 3. "... Grandane Vaixeres appellant a verbo, Visati quod est ingredi, quo significant rerum, seu divitiarum consecutionem".

[45] Ibid. "... in quibus mercatura exerceri potest".

[46] Ibid. p. 4. "Preciosos lapillos, uniones, corallia, metalla, variam vestem, odores ipsos et sapores, haec omnia eorumque precia, et valores nosse merit iudicare ad hunc pertinent (intellige Vaixerem)".

De Nobili shows that *Vaiśyas* can engage in agriculture (M. 1, 90).[47] The whole purpose of these diverse competences or skills of the *Vaiśyas* is that they should busy themselves "in all these things and by lending out money, distribute the wealth justly acquired to all men." [48] Thus the goal of the *dharma* of the *Vaiśyas* is to contribute to the material prosperity of the State through just and honest commerce.

iv. *Dharma of Śudras*

The fourth is the class of those who are engaged in servile works. They are called, according to the meaning of the word *Śudra* which is derived from *śōcati* which means "to be with sadness or to work with irksomeness",[49] and their condition deprives them of the dignity which the other three higher classes enjoy, and they are condemned to lifelong hard labour. Their duty is to be at the service of the other three classes. Their condition is one of work as is clear from the word *śōcati*. They cannot aspire to the dignity of the higher classes nor to their offices. De Nobili quotes a text from Manu (1, 91) and gives the meaning as follows:

> On the *Śudras* or Plebeians has been enjoined this single duty that they serve without envy the good of the higher orders which we have enumerated.[50]

In the text of Manu (11, 236) which de Nobili quotes, the *tapa*, i.e. duty of *Śudras* is *sevanam* (service).[51] The Sanskrit phrase which de Nobili quotes runs like this: *Tapah śudrasya sevanam*. De Nobili re-

---

[47] Cf. BÜHLER: p. 24. " The *Vaiśya* to tend cattle, to bestow gifts, to offer sacrifices, to study (the *Veda*), to trade, to lend money, and to cultivate land."

[48] I.C. p. 4. "Finis autem huius multiplicis peritiae dicitur in loco supra citato esse in his omnibus in rebus negotiationem exercendo, pecuniam locando, cum iustitia coactos divitias omnibus hominibus elargiri".

[49] Ibid. p. 4. "Quartus gradus est hominum servitia quae vocant officia exercentium, quos Siudres vocant a verbo (ut aiunt) socati id est cum tristitia esse vel laborare cum molestia quippe hi expertes eius dignitatis quam habent tres gradus superiores ipsi in perpetuo molestoque versantur."

[50] Ibid. p. 4. "id est Siudreribus vel Plebeiis illud unum officium constitutum est, in commodum superiorum, quos ennumeravimus ordinum sine invidia famulari".

[51] Ibid. p. 7.

nders its meaning as follows: "The office of *Śudras* or of Plebeians is to be service".[52] They are forbidden even to learn the *Grantha* (Sanskrit) letters.[53] It is not their duty nor is it their ornament. Rather it will make them repulsive according to a Sanskrit text which de Nobili renders as follows:

> There are four kinds of objects (contact) from which one must keep away, from a horse recently washed (said to be most ferocious in that state), from an elephant that is excited by sexual urge, from a plebeian who has learnt the alphabet.[54]

The reason is their duty or office (*tapah*) is service (*sevanam*). Moreover, this duty is re-inforced by the expression of what is most desirable for this goal. If the *Śudras* were to be servants, they should enjoy a long life.

Concerning the *Śudras*, the text says: "the highest quality of the Plebeians is prolongation to a long life." [55] They must live long in order to serve. De Nobili observes that there is a great diversity and divisions of groups among them.[56] They could be broadly divided into another six orders or groups. The important point to be noted here is that they have specific duties to perform.

v. *Obligation and Varṇadharma*

De Nobili here observes that Indian society differs greatly from others, "that men have so divided the functions and attribute nobility of civil grade not by merit but they transmit by birth."[57] In order to understand the concept of obligations of each class one must ap-

[52] Ibid. p. 7. "Siudreis hoc est Plebeii officium famulatus esto". Here de Nobili renders *tapah* as *officium* whereas it means austerity. Bühler, p. 478. He translates it as 'austerity'.

[53] Ibid. p. 8.

[54] Ibid. p. 8. "id est a quatuor generibus rerum longissime fugiendum est, ab equo recens loto (quem aiunt esse perferocem), ab elephante libidine acto, a tauro eodem motu libidinis moto, a Plebeio homine qui characteres didicerit".

[55] Ibid. p. 7. "Śudranameva janmatah".

[56] Ibid. p. 4.

[57] Ibid. p. 5. "Porro Indorum Respublica a coeteribus rebus publicis hoc maxime differt, quod hi ut officia, sic homines diviserunt, civilisque gradus nobilitati non meritis tribuunt, sed generatione transmittunt". This is what makes for *jāti* though de Nobili uses this word only rarely in his Latin works. He does not make a clear distinction between *varṇa* and *jāti*.

preciate this difference of Indian society where classes are fixed by generation, and not by merit. That one cannot pass from one caste to another and that each caste must perform its duties which go to make up the caste *dharma*. Caste duties are not flexible and varying activities according to each one but they are established and fixed according to Scriptures and tradition and have the binding character of law. De Nobili shows an appreciation of this nature of the functions of different castes. Moreover, he observes that there are as many castes as there are functions, since the functions are not assigned according to merit but transmitted by birth.[58] De Nobili remarks that according to the degree of nobility of each office, they are considered nobler or less noble. This concept of greater or lesser nobility attached to each office is a factor that helps enforce the caste obligations. De Nobili has understood this factor and shows how it operates. It is not simply a factor of discrimination but *dharma* with a purpose. Thus he says:

> If anyone from a higher caste descends to the duties of a lower caste he is said to fall from his class and grade of nobility and to become like others who belong to the lower grade by birth.[59]

That one by doing the duties of a lower caste falls from one's own caste ensures the observance of caste duties and is a measure of its strictness of observance. This applies to Brahmins as mentioned in Manu (10, 92) [60] as well as to other castes. De Nobili mentions here *paradharma* (duties of a caste other than one's own) and *svadharma* (duties of one's own caste). It is an important point of *varṇadharma* that each one does his own duty (*svadharma*). Doing the duty of another (*paradharma*) is a violation of *varṇadharma*. De Nobili considers *svadharma* to be the duty proper to one's own caste and does not speak of *svadharma* as individual duty proper to one's nature.

---

[58] Ibid. p. 5. "Ex quo fit ut quot sit in India officiorum discrimina tot sunt discrimina gentium, sive stirpium, quae pro mensura nobilitatis officii cui addicti sunt, nobiliores ipsi vel ignobiliores censentur".

[59] Ibid. "Quare si quis ex superiore stirpe ad inferioris stirpis officia descendat, cadere dicitur genere et gradu nobilitatis fierique talis, quales sunt caeteri qui inferiori gradu nati sunt."

[60] Ibid.

De Nobili quotes Manu (10, 97) whose meaning he renders as follows:

> If someone flinches from his own duty out of intemperate greed and spends his life (doing) the duty alien to (his) caste, let him be removed from his grade.[61]

Svadharma is the positive expression of what one must do, and *paradharma* is the negative expression of what one must not do. Thus *paradharma* and *svadharma* govern the relation between castes. It also means that one cannot abandon *svadharma* and perform *paradharma*. If one performs *paradharma* out of greed, he should be punished by striking him off from the grade of his caste to which he belongs. Punishment is not only an expression of the enforcement of the law of the castes but also an expression of how one understands the force of law. This is made clear in another way. Thus if one of a lower class takes up the duties of a higher caste, the king must intervene. He should have him beaten and expelled from the kingdom. This is what is prescribed in Manu (10, 96). De Nobili sums up the meaning of the text as follows:

> If a member of an inferior order usurps the function of a superior order, let the king have him beaten and expelled.[62]

In the texts of Manu (10,17; 10,96), the violation of caste duties is attributed to 'intemperate cupidity' and 'usurpation'. That means that violation of caste duties not only goes against the established order of society, but springs from morally reprehensible motives. The king must see to it that each caste performs its own *dharma*. This is the *dharma* of the king. It may happen, by the neglect of the kings, that some of the lower castes enter the higher castes. If so, they do not acquire the dignity and honour of the higher classes nor the public estimation of nobility.[63]

---

[61] Ibid. "Id est si quis intemperanti cupiditate suum officium fastidiens alieno stirpis officio vitam traducat, statim eum gradu deiicito". Cf. the *Bhagavad-Gitā*, 3,35., 18,47. These two verses of the *Gitā* praise the performance of one's own duty.

[62] I.C. p. 5. "Id est, inferioris stirpis cum sit superioris gradus officium sibi usurpet, eum rex fustibus caesum statim expellito".

[63] Ibid. The negligence of Rajas in maintaining the law of castes implies that they have a duty to maintain it.

As for customs and manners of city life, what has been said above about the *dharma* of each caste, applies to them. In the matter of manners of dress, eating, cleanliness and other things concerning the care of the body, there is also a higher or a lower level of refinement according to the castes. The social usages according to the caste rank enjoy a higher or lower dignity.[64] For instance, greater refinement is found among Brahmins.

vi. *Losing of Caste and Caste Dignity*

De Nobili pays attention to the idea of 'losing caste' and caste dignity present in the caste hierarchy. We shall first examine how he explains the nobility of Brahmins. De Nobili shows that in Indian society Brahmins are the highest in rank in the caste hierarchy and dignity and not *Kṣatryas*. Of this Goncalo Fernandes does not have a correct appreciation.[65] He argues that de Nobili seems to go about his new ways of contacting all caste Hindus without the royal placet. But de Nobili from the very beginning understood that the Brahmins occupied the highest place in the hierarchy. Their dignity derives from their function which is the office of wisdom. Brahmins claim that they posses wisdom by hereditary right and through very ancient and permanent tradition. When de Nobili says that Brahmins have certain privileges owing to their nobility, he attributes them to the nobility of wisdom in support of which he quotes St. Gregory Nazianzen: "I consider that erudition (knowledge) among all human goods ranks first." [66]

---

[64] De Nobili draws attention to the concept of dignity attached to each caste and office which is natural to them. De Nobili is sensitive to this aspect which is his merit in understanding the specific difference of Indian society and its concept of *dharma* from western society.

[65] Pr. Ap. 204. Goncalo Fernandes complains that de Nobili has not obtained the royal permission. He little realised that in Indian caste hierarchy, Brahmins occupied the first place unlike other countries. In the list of castes, Brahmins come first. Here the principle "cuius regio, eius religio" does not automatically hold. Cf. I.C. p. 14.

Ibid. p. 13. When De Nobili says "sed ne videar parvi facere virum aliquem, quia audio etiam in controversiam vocasse...", he refers to Fernandes who holds that the function of Brahmins is priesthood which de Nobili shows to be lower in dignity.

[66] I.C. p. 13. The words of Gregory are, "arbitror eruditionem inter humana bona primum locum tenere". De Nobili also quotes another passage from Manu which he interprets as "quatuor res excellentiam habent, inter homines Brahmanes, inter lumina sol, inter membra caput, inter virtues veritas". He gives another text from Manu (I, 96): "Inter res creatas viv-

Therefore, the nobility of Brahmins is due to their office of wisdom, and there is no other reason given for their nobility than this: that they are the noblest of all men because they exercise the noblest office of dealing with wisdom and teaching all men sciences.[67] This is what is suggested in their books.[68] It is for this reason too that the other castes are asked to show reverence towards Brahmins. It is for the same reason that even Rajas must show reverence first to the Brahmins, i.e., *namaskāra* (Salutation).[69] Hence it is said that Brahmins are at the top and their head.[70] That de Nobili has understood that the Brahmins are at the top of the caste hierarchy is also significant from the point of view of *varṇadharma* peculiar to India. When de Nobili says that it is entirely false that Brahmins are "absolutely inferior to the Rajas in honour and position,"[71] he means Brahmins as a caste are superior to Rajas in the caste hierarchy, though the office of *Kṣatryas* is important in the matter of public administration, for that is the office given to them[72] which is alien to Brahmins.

De Nobili goes on to meet another objection concerning the of-

---

entes, inter viventes animantes, inter animantes homines, inter homines Brahmanes nobilissimi sunt."

[67] Ibid. "Ratio vero quae in his libris, aliisque multis insinuatur aut apte traditur est, quia genus Brahmanum sortium est tractatio sapientiae quae est omnium nobilissima, et munus docendi omnes mortales."

[68] Especially the Books of *smṛti*, particularly *Manu, Parāśara, Apastamba Sūtra, Apastamba Grihya sūtra*.

[69] I.C. pp. 13-14.

[70] Ibid. De Nobili translates the Sanskrit phrase "Varnanam Bramano guruh" as "Brahman est stirpium culmen et caput". Here de Nobili takes the word '*guruh*' in the sense of 'excellent' or 'superior', since in the text he refers to it in which it is also said "ignem esse formarum gurum i.e. nobilissimum et maritum esse uxoris gurum i.e. superiorem". That of all the elements fire is excellent, of the wife the husband superior. So too Brahmins are among the *varṇas guruh*, and their excellence, as *Manu* has shown, consists in treating of wisdom.

[71] Ibid. p. 14. "si vero dicat in publicis locis et conventibus et demum absolute Brahmanes inferiores esse Ragiis honore et loco, omnino falsum est". Here de Nobili points out that Brahmin in question is not any particular Brahmin but every Brahmin ("de omni Brahmane").

[72] Ibid. Here de Nobili argues according to the *varṇadharma* of the caste in question, i.e., of the Rajas. The public affairs of the state belong to them. "... hoc totum pertinere ad gradum secundum nempe Ragiorum et esse alienum a Brahmanibus..." De Nobili criticises the view that considers the office of public affairs the highest, ignorant of the rank and dignity of the four castes according to *varṇadharma*.

fice of Brahmins. De facto there are Brahmins who are ignorant and take up the duties of lower classes. Yet they are not inglorious. They become governors and princes in the courts of kings.[73] This seems to go against *varṇadharma* which de Nobili follows in his explanation of caste duties. Hence he has to explain this difficulty.

If Brahmins neglecting their duty of sciences acquire wealth and undertake 'alien duties', they will not enjoy the dignity of true Brahmins.[74] De Nobili goes on to show with the authority of Manu (10,83; 3,152; 10,92) that if they undertake other duties like acquiring wealth which belongs to the third order of *Vaiśyas* or become princes, which is the duty of the second order, they will be considered degenerate. That is the law of Manu. *Parāśara Śmṛti* too considers such duties done by Brahmins indecent or improper.[75] If a Brahmin undertakes trade of *Vaiśyas* or royal position of the 2nd grade, all of which are higher castes, even this is insufficient to remove a Brahmin from his caste.[76] Brahmins are not allowed to rule except that they be devoted to letters. He also quotes from the *Yajur Veda* which says that ruling is not proper for Brahmins.[77]

Since Brahmins are expected to devote themselves to wisdom, they cannot work to acquire wealth as the *Vaiśyas* do. They can, therefore, receive alms, the reception of which is regulated by law.[78] The two conditions prescribed in civil law for receiving alms are that they are poor and wise men. Without these conditions, they may not

---

[73] Ibid. p. 11. "... quamplurimi Brahmanes sunt, qui non solum nihil sciut sed et inferiorum stirpium munera obeunt, neque tamen sunt inglorii, imo quidem eorum Gubernatores Provinciarum sunt, et Principies in aulis Regum".

[74] Ibid. Note the alien offices are expressed as *paradharma*, cf. also ibid. p. 5 where de Nobili quotes Manu on *paradharma* and *svadharma* (10,97).

[75] Ibid. pp. 11-12.

[76] Ibid. p. 12, "Imo alii inter ea quae sufficiunt ad movendum aliquem a Brahmanum stirpe numeratur mercatura quae pertinet ad tertium gradum et in aula Regum versari aut militare quae est proprium secundi gradus". De Nobili also quotes Manu (3, 64) which he translated as: "Id est artes fabriles exercere, mercaturam facere, ad Plebeiorum mores descendere, pastoralia agere, vectaria victum quaerere, regi famulatum gerere officia sunt, quae si Brahmen exerceat, gradus movendus est".

[77] Ibid. p. 12. *Yajur Veda* was well-known in Madurai at the time of de Nobili.

[78] Ibid. p. 60. Here de Nobili tries to show against the view of G. Fernandes that Brahmins receive alms not because they are priests, but because they are poor men devoted to wisdom which Manu regulates.

accept alms.[79] The *smṛti* law-book says "Though a Brahman has aptness to receive alms, let him completely abstain from it. If he has accepted it, let him know that he received the remuneration of a Brahmin." [80] De Nobili explains further the right of Brahmins to receive alms in terms of *Varṇadharma*. A poor Brahmin's aptness (*congruitas*) lies truly in his office of treating wisdom. In general, the reason for receiving alms is that one is poor.[81] With regard to Brahmins, the rule is stringently stated.

> Therefore, let him who lacks knowledge take great care not to receive anything (from others). If he accepts even the smallest thing (gift), he is loaded with evils as a cow holds fast to the filth in which it is sunk.[82]

A Brahmin who is diligent in learning (*atapah*) and who is ignorant (*anādhiyānah*) does not deserve to collect alms, as though sunk into water together with the one who gives alms, with a stone tied to his neck.[83] Almsgiving is recommended only to the wise Brahmin. By giving alms to an ignorant Brahmin, one loses merit.[84]

De Nobili in his treatise *Narratio* explains the law of the castes and their obligation on the social level.[85] The stringency of religious

---

[79] Ibid. "Dico igitur Brahmanes eleemosynas hoc solo titulo accipere, quod pauperes sapientes sunt, quia utrumque praecipitur in eorum civili lege, ut videlicet ne accipiant nisi pauperes sint, et nisi sapientes sint."

[80] Ibid. Nobili quotes Manu (4, 186) "Brahman etsi congruitatem ad accipiendum habeat negocium accipiendi prorsus abiiciat, si acceperit Brahmanis remunerationem accepisse se sciat."

[81] Ibid. p. 60. "Quare alibi in communi statuunt rationem eleemosynae pauperum esse..."

[82] Ibid. p. 61. "Quamobrem sapientia carens a quacumque re accipienda magnopere caveat si vel minutissimum quid accipit, quasi vacca quae in coeno demersa hereat, malis prematur".

[83] Ibid. p. 60. De Nobili quotes another text from Manu (4, 190). "Si quis Braman neque laborans in discendo sapientiam neque sapiens cupiditate ductus de accipiendo eleemosynas cogitet, quasi si alligato ad collum lapide demergatum una cum eleemosynas dante demergitur."

[84] Ibid. p. 61, in the enforcement of law, the idea of merit is also used.

[85] *Narratio Fundamentorum quibus Madurensis Missionis Institutum caeptum Est, Hucusque consistit*. This is the full Latin title of the treatise. It will be referred to hereafter in the thesis as *Narratio*, p. 112. The text is found in *Adaptation* ed. S. Rajamanickam, Palayamkottai, 1971. The Latin text and the English translation are found there side by side. Our pagination refers to the Latin text. This is the treatise in which de Nobili enumerates the principles of

affiliation is not so strong as that of caste rules. If one changes one's sect, one is not punished for it by the magistrates, but if one were to abandon one's caste customs, one would suffer severe consequences. Caste customs are inviolable. It has been established (statutum) that no one can change his order of caste, and must remain in the caste of his ancestors. That means, e.g., *Kṣatryas* cannot become Brahmins nor *Vaiśyas* [86], whereas the different castes can follow different religious persuasions. Such caste laws are strict with regard to marriage. If one abandons the law of the caste and marries a low caste woman, he must eat the remains of a Plebeian's food. Similar punishment is meted out if one is drunk.[87]

In connection with the punishments due to violation of caste rules, we shall consider the idea of 'losing caste'. In the foregoing pages we explained the stringency of caste rules and the idea of the dignity which each caste enjoyed. We also explained how the sense of caste dignity helped prevent violation of caste rules. It was precisely this caste dignity which created such a strong sense of shame that one would not like to lose it at any cost. 'Losing caste' came to mean losing one's caste dignity and rank. De Nobili was quite aware of this aspect of the consequences of violating caste rules. This was not merely a sociological fact but something explained and given as punishment against caste violation in the *smṛtis*[88], especially, in texts

---

Madurai Mission. "Cum hi populi unum habeant civilem cultum, religionem vero multiplicem, ex eo nascitur, quod desertores alicuius religionis, vel religionis stemmatis non animadvertant, poenam infligendo, unicuique enim hucusque liberum est eam amplexari religionem, quae sibi bona videtur, cultus vero et civilis mos, quem uti quam maxime aestimant determinatus est unicuique stirpi, et rigorose ab unaquaque familia servandus: in qua re minime est liberum pro suo arbitrio vivere, sed majorum irregradabili praescripto civilem propriae stirpis cultum tenetur unusquisque servare. Nam ex una stirpe ad alium gradum facere nefas est." I have also profited by the English translation of the text as given in Adaptation. Cf. bibliography on this work.

[86] *Ibid. p. 112. We do not enter into the thorny question of de Nobili's interpretation of the thread, kudumi* (tuft of hair) worn by Brahmins and others, etc. as religious symbols. Our interest here is that de Nobili was aware of the inexorable law of the castes and their obligation. Cf. J. Neuner, ed, *Religious Hinduism*, Allahabad, 1964, p. 114 on the notion of caste. Cf. also I.C. p. 5.

[87] *Narratio* pp. 112, 114.

[88] I.C. p. 11. Cf. J.A. DUBOIS: *Moeurs, Institutions et Ceremonies de Peuples de l'Inde*. Tome I, Paris 1825, pp. 36-44. He testifies to the rigours of the misfortune of losing one's caste. This work will be referred to as Dubois.

which describe debasement of one who violates caste *dharma*. It is, therefore, understood to be part of *varṇadharma* of society. This is what de Nobili says on this point:

> There is a singular characteristic (I might say) of this nation among all the other nations, that they punish most severely those who reject the ancestral customs which are merely civil.[89]

At the same time, de Nobili was aware that caste customs had the force of law because they were enjoined by the code of Manu and so accepted in practice.[90] The caste customs dictated the insignia of each group, their manners, dress, etc. They too had the force of law. As for caste violations, de Nobili realised that not only the legal aspect of punishments due to them but also the peculiar idea of 'losing caste', are too severe for any one.[91] Yet he was aware of the exaggerations of caste pride.[92]

De Nobili notes another aspect of the sanctions against caste violations. Though it is common law (*praeceptum*) of all classes of India,[93] the sanctions are more severe towards the first three noble castes, i.e. Brahmins, Rajas and merchants than for *Śudras*.

The king has a great responsibility in preventing any violation of

---

[89] I.C. p. 110. "... illud huic nationi inter caeteras nationes omnes (quod dicam) singulare est, quod eos qui mores patrios qui mere politici sunt abiiciunt severissime puniunt".

[90] Ibid. p. 110. "Sunt enim unicuique gradui civium et praecipuum officium ita praecipua insignia habitusque vestis, et praecipua mores, et cultus politici quos qui non retinent gradu moventur, ut est usu notissimum, et praecipitur in libro Manu Smrti versu qui incipit Silpena Vyavaharena (Manu 3, 64), etc."

[91] Ibid. De Nobili says concerning losing caste: "Amissio vero gradus gravissimum est inter hos homines malum quod multi liberter ipsa morte redimerent, et redimunt saepe! Statim enim atque quis e stirpis ordinis motus est omnis honoris et patriae dignitatis fit expers, eiicitur ab omnibus si intra eum gradum haberi solent conventibus, ab omni civium et cognatorum consortio mandatur, ab ipsorum domesticorum consuetudine convituque secernitur." De Nobili's point is that Indian Christians should not be allowed to suffer this. He was also aware of the difference of Indian customs and manners from those of Europe Ibid. p. 60. The customs "sunt enim valde ab europeis moribus dissidentes, ut mirandum non sit, eos qui ex Europae cultu de cultu Indico Judicium ferre volunt in has et his similes consecutione prolabi." Cf. also de Nobili's answer to Buccerio in AHSI (1970) p. 263, "But as these Hindus make much more of social position and rank than of religion, they punish those who give up their social and political insignia but not those who abandon their religion." They suffer even exile.

[92] Ibid. Without contact with other civilizations, they consider their own to surpass all others in refinement.

[93] Ibid. p. 110.

caste rules and customs. In support of this de Nobili cites Manu (8,46):

> Regarding the customs received from the ancestors, as it were by hand, which in every region the three noble castes called the twice-born retain, let the king watch with the greatest care lest anything contradictory to them be introduced.[94]

De Nobili who considers the thread of the higher castes social in significance says if a Brahmin or a prince or a merchant is deprived of the thread, he falls from the grade of nobles and is considered a Plebeian.[95] De Nobili also discusses a notion that Brahmins enjoy immunity from capital punishment.[96] Here de Nobili explains how this immunity is not absolute. We note that there are also punishments meted out to Brahmins and they are severe precisely because they enjoy greater nobility.[97] They are subject to capital punishment for certain crimes known as *atatai*. According to another book,[98] de

---

[94] Ibid. pp. 110-111. "I.e. quos mores a maioribus acceptos quasi per manus in unaquaque regione tres nobiles stirpes qui Duigenae vocant retinent, his ne quid repugnans introducatur magnopere videat Rex."

Bühler, pp. 261-262. He translates it as follows: "What may have been practised by the virtuous, by such twice-born men as are devoted to the law, that he shall establish as law, if it be not opposed to the (customs of) countries, families, and castes (*jāti*)." In the f. n. 46, Bühler adds a different understanding of the verse by commentator Medh: "what has been practised by the virtuous and by twice-born men... he shall establish as law for countries, families, and castes, if it is not opposed (to texts of *śruti* and *smṛti*)."

[95] *Narratio*, p. 116. "... quod cum Brahman, vel vir regius, vel mercator in poenam linea privatur, et a nobilium cadit ordine, in plerumque adscribitur numerum..."

[96] I.C. p. 5. It is said that when Brahmins commit crime, they are not killed. Goncalo Fernandes thinks that they enjoy immunity from capital punishment.

[97] Ibid. p. 51. Goncalo Fernandes thinks that because Brahmins enjoy immunity from capital punishment, they must be priests. De Nobili answers the objection by saying that it is only relative punishment. In de Nobili's view, being priest is not higher in dignity than being wise men. But even wise men are not free from punishment, especially from capital punishment. De Nobili mentions the crime called *atatai* which deserves capital punishment according to Manu (8, 350) which de Nobili translates: "sive sit magister sive sit puer, sive sit senex, sive sit Brahman quam maxime sapiens, hi omnes si sint rei criminum *atatai*, sine solemnitatibus fori, sine consilio interficiendi sunt." In Skt, the word used is *atatayin*. It means literally "one who has (the bow) drawn to take another's life", i.e., an assaulter, a murderer. In later legal literature it means also ravishers, incendiaries and thieves.

[98] Ibid. De Nobili mentions the book called *Scanda Prahasa* a *smṛti* book. The name of the book is written as de Nobili gives it.

Nobili also enumerates the crimes which demand death punishment for people like those who are ungrateful in serious matters, people who desert their parents in their old age. Similarly, to a Brahmin who drinks *suram*,[99] or steals a large sum of money from the king, the punishment prescribed is death.[100] At the same time, de Nobili is aware that in meting out punishments Brahmins are handled with greater mildness, which is founded on their dignity of wisdom, the cause of their nobility.[101] He also remarks that Brahmins in drawing up the civil laws, also instituted them with a view to their favour and dignity.[102]

De Nobili being in favour of admitting castes among Christians has to be understood against the background of the Hindu caste system, its offices, dignity and severe punishments sanctioned against violations, all of which had the binding character of law and which were understood as *dharma*.

vii. *Varṇadharma, the Thread and Its Social Significance*

It is by the conferral of the thread that one who is like *Śudra* is constituted the twice-born (*dvijah*).

> By generation one is born plebeian, by the ceremony of the thread one is born Brahmin.[103]

Here de Nobili understands by *dvijah* Brahmin. He explains later in the same treatise that kings and merchants (*Kṣatryas* and *Vaiśyas*) are also the twice-born.[104] Of the two births of *dvijah*, one is natural, the other is into civil society.[105] It is by the thread that one is constituted in his grade. De Nobili refers to the formula of investiture of the thread. It is the same formula for all the twice-born.

---

99 *Suram* is a drink prepared from the juice of the fruit of the palm tree. Cf. I.C. p. 51.

100 Ibid. De Nobili refers to *Siatatapam Smṛti*. (De Nobili writes the name in this way).

101 Ibid. p. 52.

102 Ibid. p. 52. Cf. also G. H. MEES, *Dharma and Society*, S-Gavenhage, 1935, pp. 16-17.

103 I.C. p. 66. "Generatione nascitur Plebeius, collatione lineae nascitur Brahman".

104 Ibid. p. 68. "... etiam Regii et mercatores vocantur vulgo quemadmodum Brahmanes dvijah...".

105 Ibid.

> I by the investiture of the thread declare and constitute you (in the particular grade).[106]

De Nobili comments on the Sanskrit word *samskarisye*. It means both 'to declare' and 'to constitute'.[107] Therefore before the investiture of the thread, Brahmins, Rajas and Merchants are not allowed to exercise their proper office. Before the investiture, they are like *Śudras* in civil dignity.

De Nobili then goes on to speak of the appropriate times when the thread could be given. Thus if a Brahmin boy shows eagerness for learning at an early age and if he is capable of wisdom, Manu allows that he can be given the thread at the age of five.[108] Similarly, the thread can be given to a young prince if he has already the spirit of fortitude and valour at the age of six, so too a *Vaiśya* boy can be given the thread at the age of eight, though generally it is given to the Brahmin boy at the age of eight, to the prince at eleven, to the merchant boy at twelve. The text from Manu which de Nobili quotes assigns the years five, six, eight to Brahmin, *Kṣatrya* and *Vaiśya* respectively for the investiture of the thread.[109]

De Nobili also speaks of the material used for the thread for the twice-born castes. The office of Brahmin is signified by cotton used for the thread; the thread made of hempen (*Sana*) signifies the office of the kings and the thread made of fibres of Vica signifies the office of merchants.[110] Since the thread is a sign of the caste, it must be

---

[106] Ibid. "Ego te lineae collatione declaro et constituo." The Sansk. formula cf. p. 66. "tvam upanayana Karmana samskarisye".

[107] Ibid. p. 66.

[108] Ibid. p. 68. "According to Manu", "... Brahmani qui sit sapientiae capax, et sapientiae decus adamare incipiat concedit jactum lineae quinto aetatis anno, statim idem pro portione concedit Regio qui fortitudinis et bellicae virtutis spiritum jam habeat, ut nimirum linaem accipiat anno sexto et mercatori anno octavo, communiter enim iacitur linea Brahmani anno octavo, Regi 11°, Mercatori 12°." Cf. also Pr. Ap. p. 120. Here even the months are assigned. Thus cf. pp. 120-121: For Brahmins the month of April and May, for Rajas June and July, for Merchants October and November.

[109] I.C. p. 68. "Brahmani qui jam sapientiae decus adamet quinto anno lineae jactus concessus est, Regio quia jam fortitudinis laudem cupiat anno 6°, Mercatori qui jam ad divitias anhelet anno octavo."

[110] Ibid. p. 67. "Nam sicut per lineam ex gossippio declaratur officium Brahmanis, ita per lineam ex Xana declaratur officium mercatoris." cf. also Pr. Ap. p. 119.

made of different materials respectively. This is prescribed in Manu (11,44) which de Nobili renders as follows:

> Let the thread of the Brahmin be formed from thrice twisted cotton thread, for kings let it be prepared from hemp, for merchants let it be from the fibres of Vica plant.[111]

Thus de Nobili shows how the thread is a sign of different castes by analysing the formula of the ceremony, the age at which it is to be worn and the material out of which it has to be made according to different castes. In this he also shows that the thread has an acceptable social purpose.

viii. *Varṇadharma As Applied to Religious Duties of Sacrifices*

We shall consider how *varṇadharma* comes to be expressed in religious duties. De Nobili is aware of the religious duties being regulated according to caste. Thus there are sacrifices and ceremonies which cannot be performed at all by Plebeians, and there are those ceremonies proper to Plebeians, which cannot be performed at all by the higher castes (*Brahmins, Kṣatryas* and *Vaiśyas*). These are prescribed and established and have the force of law.[112] For example, there are sacrifices common to all the higher castes, i.e., the Twice-born.[113] The sacrifices are forbidden to Plebeians. Besides, the time for the sacrifice differs according to the three castes, and it is prescribed. Thus Brahmins perform it in April and May, the royal families in June and July and *Vaiśyas* in October and November.[114]

---

[111] I.C. p. 67. "Brahmanum linea ter in se reducta ex gossipio sit, Regiis ex Siana, Vaisieribus seu Mercatoribus ex Vica." Cf. Pr. Ap. p. 119. Where the same text of Manu (2, 44) is given, though de Nobili's rendering of the text is from that he gives in I.C. p. 67.

[112] *Narratio*, p. 114. "... quod in hac Indica republica non solum stirpium gradus irrefragabili praescrito, inter se divisi sunt, sed familiis nobilium virorum quaedam sunt propria sacrificia, et ceremoniae, quae a Plebeio peragi minime possunt, sicut nec a nobilibus confici possunt sacrificia, quae ex maiorum praescripto, plebeis sunt gentilia..." One of the earliest meanings of *dharma* is sacrifice or cult act. Cf. Unto Tähtinen, *Indian Philosophy of Value*, Turku 1968, p. 69.

[113] *Narratio* p. 114. "Brachmanes, regii viri, et mercatores sacrificium peragunt quod vocant Eghiam." Cf. also I.C. p. 43. Here the sacrifice is referred to as *Egnam*. Probably it is *yajña*.

[114] *Narratio* p. 114.

The horse sacrifice is performed by kings alone.[115] De Nobili tries to show that sacrificial duties are regulated according to the social status of the *varṇas* and that social division of castes is not for the sake of priestly function.[116]

The three higher castes and *Śudras* have their own sacrifices. Therefore, if one is degraded from one's caste, he may not perform sacrifices proper to him. Being deprived of the caste thread deprives one also of the right to perform sacrifices proper to one's caste. Similarly, a noble deprived of the thread may not eat with nobles. He may not perform the sacrifice, proper to *Śudras*. This is also a punishment for the violation of caste rules or *varṇadharma*. According to de Nobili deprivation of the right to perform particular sac rifices because one is degraded from one's caste will not affect those who reject sacrifices, though they lose their caste dignity.

In this connection one must mention the caste deities.[117] Each caste offers sacrifices to its deities who are known as *Kulatēvar*. Every caste has its own deity to whom certain sacrifices can be offered. These any one can perform. The *homam* sacrifice is offered to *Agni* (the fire god). It is not reserved to Brahmins alone, contrary to another opinion.[118] De Nobili says that it is common to Brahmins, *Rajas, Vaiśyas*, and *Śudras*. There is another sacrifice which all the three castes perform in August at the New Moon or at the full moon.[119]

Besides, de Nobili points out the rule that neither a Brahmin, nor *Kṣatrya*, nor a *Vaiśya* can offer *homan* sacrifice for another, but only for himself. If he offers it for another, he suffers degradation of his caste status. In this connection De Nobili quotes a text from Manu which he translates:

---

[115] Ibid. p. 116. *Aśvamedha* - the horse sacrifice.

[116] Ibid. p. 116. "... quod cum Brachman, vel vir regius, vel mercator in poenam linea privatur, et a nobilium cadit ordine, in Plebeiorumque adscribitur in numerum, non nisi quae sunt plebeis gentilica sacrificia peragere potest, et non nobilium, quippe qui nobilitate privatus."

[117] I.C. p. 40. Also Pr. Ap. p. 166.

[118] I.C. The contrary opinion is that of Goncalo Fernandes. De Nobili quotes the skt. text from the *Yajur veda* which he renders as follows: "eo anni tempore cui nomen est *vasanta* i.e. mense Aprilis et Martii, *homan* igni Brahmanes peragant; mense Junii et Julii *homan* peragant Regiae familiae, mense Augusti et Octobris, peragant mercatores."

[119] Ibid.. pp. 40-41.

> If a Brahmin greedy of money should perform the *homan* sacrifice for a *Śudra*, that is, for a Plebeian, let the Brahmin be a *Śudra*, let the *Śudra* be a Brahmin.[120]

De Nobili remarks that this rule applies not only to *Śudras* and Brahmins but also to other castes. Besides *homam* could be performed also by *Śudras* according to the precepts of Agamas[121] and also because the text of Manu speaks of the four castes. There are sacrifices which only *Śudras* offer, e.g., to *Aienar* (guardian deity of the village), *Viren, Pidari, Badrakali* (the deities of the lower castes).

In the rules governing sacrifices according to different castes, de Nobili tries to show and explain that the religious duties are not the basis of the four castes, but rather the latter regulate the sacrifices.[122] Since every class performs sacrifices, there cannot be a priestly class in an exclusive sense. De Nobili's argument is that Brahmins cannot be called a priestly class in an exclusive sense since every class performs its own sacrifices. Our point here is that *varṇadharma* regulates also the duties of sacrifice. They are enforced as laws. Violation has sanctions against it. De Nobili explains *varṇadharma* in this way.

There are some other customs which have to do with caste behaviour which are also prescribed. Professions will regulate one's belonging to a particular caste. For example, certain types of professionals cannot be included in Brahmin castes according to Manu (3,152):

> Physicians, temple priests, meat venders, managers of shops of mechandise must be expelled from the families of Brahmins.[123]

[120] Ibid. p. 41. "Si quis Brahman pecuniae avidus pro Siudrene i.e. plebeio Homan peregerit Brahman Siudren esto, Siudren Brahman esto." Manu 9.24, comes close to this. The exact text is not identifiable.

[121] Ibid. p. 42. *Agamas* are Śaivite Scriptures. De Nobili quotes a passage from an *Agama* in Tamil which he renders: "Is qui natus sit ex aliquo ordinum Brahmanum, scilicet, Regiorum, Mercatorum, Siudrenum seu Plebeiorum, qui irae motus temperabit, qui operationem ignis hoc est homan recte conficiant, qui ritus et preces absque ullo errore possideat, qui multa pietate praeditus sit servato Rudrenis dixi seu ritu jure magister dici potest..."

[122] Ibid. p. 44. "... si sacerdotis nomen sumatur in priori sensu, nullum hominem Idolatram esse in India cuiusvis generis sit qui sacerdos non sit, quippe in eo sensu unusquisque sacrificat, quem morem olim viguisse apud nostrates Idolatras nemo ignoraverit, qui in historiarum libris omnino rudis non sit."

[123] Ibid. p. 46. "Medici, sacerdotes, carnes vendentes, tabernis mercium praesidentes ex

It is also said that Brahmins may not even look at public priests or those who belong to a lower grade or come near them or touch them. It is prescribed that they must look at the sun or take a bath, if they fail in this regard.[124]

b. *Stages of Life (Aśramadharma)*

We shall now consider *dharma* according to *āśramas* (stages of life). De Nobili is aware of the stages of life according to Hinduism when he speaks of the stages of student, married life and renunciation.[125] Nowhere does he systematically present the four stages of life. There is no mention of *Vanaprastha*. He speaks more clearly of *varṇadharma* of the four castes.

i. *The Stage of Studentship (Brahmacārya)*

De Nobili discusses the custom of wearing the tuft of hair according to Manu as mentioned in the part called *Brahmacārya Karman.*[126] He refers to the section in Manu which speaks of the *dharma* of *brahmacārya.*[127] He cites Manu (2, 117) about honouring the man (teacher) of knowledge. He refers to *Taittiriya Upaniṣad*.

The student regards his teacher with love. The origin of knowledge according to *Taittiriya Upaniad* (I, 3, 3,) which de Nobili cites is this: There should be a teacher to whom a student must listen.[128] De Nobili mentions the duty of gratitude of the student to his teacher as mentioned by the same *Upaniṣad* (I, II, I). The student must offer money to his teacher with love for his livelihood.[129] De

---

Brahmanum familiis expellendi sunt." Cf. Bühler, p. 103. The categories of people mentioned here must be avoided at sacrifices offered to the gods and whereas de Nobili says that these must be expelled from brahmin families.

[124] Ibid. They are rules of purity prescribed in the *smṛtis*, here according to the *Parāśara smṛti* corresponding to the four classes.

[125] N.C.C. (Cf. bibliography) pp. 34-35: De Nobili speaks of *sannyāsa āśrama* and *brahmacārya āśrama* in the same true religion. De Nobili speaks of the *āśramas* of *sannyāsa* and *vivāka* (marriage). Ibid, p. 124. Here de Nobili speaks of *āśramas* in relation to Christianity.

[126] Pr. Ap. p. 112; also I.C. p. 80.

[127] I.C. p. 10 where de Nobili refers to the honour to be paid to the man of knowledge. In Manu, it refers to the respect the student must show to his teacher.

[128] Ibid. p. 61.

[129] Ibid.

Nobili refers to the section of the *Upaniṣad* in which an exhortation to the departing student on his duties of virtue and study is given.[130]

The young Brahmin before marriage must remain chaste and practise some austerities. He must not sleep on a cot but on the floor, must not use sandal paste and chew betel leaves with arecanut.[131]

Before the initiation into the stage of student the Brahmin boy should not undertake study.[132] After the investiture of the thread he can begin his study. He is considered Plebeian until he receives the thread and after this he begins his studies. Till then, he is not expected to learn even the Sanskrit grammar called *Śabda*. But de Nobili understands the investiture of the thread to be rather initiation into caste duties. One who has received the thread is expected thereafter to observe caste rules and rules of cleanliness. A noble or a *Vaiśya* is constituted *Kṣatryas* or merchant with the reception of the thread. Thus they are initiated into social life.[133].

ii. *The Stage of the Householder* (Grhastha)

De Nobili faces a special difficulty with regard to *sannyāsa āśrama* existing among the Hindus according to which one enters this *āśrama* after having been married and begotten children. The Hindus say that without being married one cannot enter *sannyāsa* and that one enters it normally in one's old age.[133] Besides, according to their tradition, one must marry a young virgin, and a young woman must

---

[130] Ibid. p. 34. Cf. Mahadevan, pp. 76-77.

[131] Pr. Ap. p. 136. Dahmen refers to 'the Apastambas Aphorisms on the Sacred Law' (*The Sacred Books of the East*, Oxford 1896) vol. II, pp. 7-8: The text in French: "L'étudiant doit toujours occuper un siège ou une couche plus basse que celle de son maitre... Il n'usera pas de parfum. Il gardera la chasteté."

[132] Ibid. p. 66; *Narratio*, p. 106. "... puerum Bracmanem ante lineae collationem a Plebeio propter eamdem causam differre minime putant linea vero insignitus potest litteris navare operam (sine linea enim, nec grandanam grammatica, quam ipsi xabdam, vocant, addiscere fas est) caeteraque ad munditiem, et politicum pertinentia morem servare tenetur." Cf. above in his chapter *varṇdharma* and the thread. Here *śabda* is written as *xabdam*.

[133] *Narratio*, p. 106. "... ita puer lineae collatione stirpis Brachmanum esse, sive regiorum virorum, vel mercatorum, etc. exprimitur." De Nobili further says that "lineae stemma in puero sacrum minime est, sed politicum redolet cultum".

[134] *Kāṇṭam* II Tuticorin, 1966, p. 232. De Nobili says, however, that one cannot say that renunciation in old age cannot be virtuous. Cf. ibid. p. 233.

not die as a virgin, i.e., unmarried.[135] The Christian teachers spread the contrary idea of *sannyā*sa for young men without passing through the married state. The accusation against them is that "The Christian teacher is to blame for spreading something which does not obtain in the country..."[136] Our point is that de Nobili was aware of the different idea of the stage of *sannyāsa* of the Hindus, but he does recognise *sannyāsa* and *vivāka* as legitimate *āśramas* though not in the way the Hindus understand the four *āśramas* of *brahmacārya, gṛhastha*, *vanaprastha* and *sannyāsa*, one stage succeeding another.

iii. *The Stage of Renunciation (Sannyāsa)*

Among the four stages, *sannyā*sa is of particular interest to de Nobili because it signifies renunciation. Though he rejects the idea that every one should get married first before entering *sannyāsa*, he does not reject the idea of *sannyāsa* in its goodness. He finds a definition of *sannyāsin* in the Sanskrit glossary called *Nighantu* which he renders:

> *Sannyāsin* is one who makes perfect abnegation and renunciation of all things.[137]

Besides, de Nobili says that in Tamil poems the idea of *sannyāsa* is expressed in three words *ponnācai* desire of land and *peṇṇācai*, i.e. desire of gold, *maṇṇācai*, i.e. desire of woman. *Sannyāsin* is one who renounces these three desires. He should be without gold, without his own land, be a wanderer and be without a woman.[138] It is for this reason de Nobili accepts this concept of *sannyāsa* which is even symbolised by the colour of the dress-saffron (*cāvi*) which *sannyāsins* wear.[139] It is the concept of renunciation one must appreciate when

---

135 Ibid. p. 232.

136 Ibid. p. 239. That which does not exist in India is the practice that young men can enter permanently into *sannyāsa* without getting married, for here *sannyāsa āśrama* comes after one has been *grahasthya* (householder) as a married man. There are exceptions. Śankara is believed to have entered *sannyāsa* in his youth; in modern times Vivekananda.

137 Pr. Ap. p. 59. "perfecte abnegationem et rescindentiam omnium faciens ille est *Sanias*.

138 Ibid. p. 59. It is also popular expression of renunciation of three things, desire of wealth, desire of kingdom and desire of woman, a succinct expression of total renunciation as becomes a *sannyāsin*.

139 Ibid. pp. 110-111. "Qua vestes et vestium color, quibus ego utor, nullam, nec

one of the twice-born becomes a *sannyāsin*. A *sannyāsin* must renounce, as the name itself suggests, worldly honours and marks of dignity. Hence one renounces the thread and the tuft of hair which de Nobili interprets to be marks of social dignity.[140] In the *āśrama* of *sannyāsa*, one gives up the marks of social dignity belonging to the other *āśramas*. Besides, de Nobili does not accept the sequence of the four *āśramas* in the sense that they are stages of spiritual progress in one's life. De Nobili says that it is certain doctrine (*cittāntam*) that the husband who is a priest (*dīkṣita*) if he embraces renunciation (*sannyāsa*) perfectly, will reach *mokṣa* without going to the intermediate *svarga*.[141]

c. *Deśācāra (usage of a region) and Kuladharma (customs of a family or a tribe)*

De Nobili accepts the principle that it is proper to follow the customs and manners of a country where one lives. For this he finds a support in Hindu scriptures and also in the tradition of the Church.[142] When he accepts the principle of conforming oneself to *deśācāram*, he does so not only to avoid the aversion of the

---

primariam nec secundariam prae se ferunt religionis alicuius vel sectae cultum sed tantum castitatem, paupertatis et carentiam propriae regionis..." Cf. Ibid. p. 111. "If anyone who is chaste or a virgin, and has knowledge of the true God and lives without departing from spiritual doctrine, such a man should wear the dress of the colour called *cavi*" (saffron). This is according to the collection of poems called *Ziruva Siyam* (which is not identifiable). Cf. A.N. p. 616. Buccerio in a letter to Fr General (3 Oct. 1610) writing of Fr. de Nobili says that the house of the *aiyyar* (i.e. de Nobili) is called *maṭam* and that it is how the houses of the renouncers are called. The renouncers (*sannyāsins*) profess chastity and do not chew betel which excites the passions of the flesh and inclines man to evil. Cf. Bertrand II p. 5. Laerzio in his letter to Fr General (20 Nov. 1609) says that chastity is a virtue much admired by the Indians.

140 Pr. Ap. p. 59. "Cum propter devotionem et pietatem brachmanes Saniassi fiunt, et mundum cum honore contemnunt, curumbii et lineam abscindunt", cf. also p. 123. Without entering into the question of the controversy of the social interpretation of these things, we note here that de Nobili discusses it with reference to *sannyāsa āśrama dharma*.

141 A.N. p. 376. It is *nivṛtti* (the way of withdrawal) for the attainment of *mokṣa*. *Pravṛitti* is the way of action. De Nobili doesn't use this classification explicity, but the two ways of *dharma* are present in his explanation of *dharma*.

142 Pr. Ap. p. 106. De Nobili quotes from the *smṛti* which he translates: "Unusquisque in regione, in qua vivit, ad illius more sex antiquitate protractos se effingere justum est." (cf. M. 2, 18). He also refers to the *Decretalium Gregorii* which gives instructions to clerics to adapt to the customs of the people to whom one preaches. Cf. ibid. pp. 105, 106.

people [143] but also because he perceived that the Hindus considered them binding on the members of the community. Among the *deśācārams*, he includes those that concern the manner of life, of dress, food, etc. [144] The criterion against their acceptability is that they are clearly sinful. [145] Otherwise *deśācārams*, as such, should be accepted, since such practices are *dharma* for the people of a country. De Nobili uses his negative criterion for some cases which are accepted as *deśācāram*. Thus he is critical of the view that one woman can have many husbands, or that one woman can act as a wife to all the brothers of her husband or that one man can have many wives. It is said that "these two kinds of practices (polyandry and polygamy) are *deśācāram and kuladharma*". [146] They do not recognise they are disorderly and sinful. De Nobili is critical of the reason given for calling these *ācārams* proper to a country as *dharma*. The argument is that these customs come down to them from generation to generation and that therefore they must be retained. [147] With the exception of sinful practices, de Nobili admits all caste observances and civil customs. Thus he says in his treatise *Kaṭavuḷ Nirṇayam* "without violating the social manners belonging to caste customs, avoiding only sins..." [148] Discussing the custom of wearing the tuft of hair on the head, [149] de Nobili describes it as a sign of caste of the twice-born. [150]

---

[143] Pr. Ap. p. 106. The *Gautamasmṛti* says: "The customs (*dharma*) of countries (*deśa*), castes (*jāti*) and families (*kula*), which are not opposed to the Vedic scriptures are authoritative and binding (11.22)." Quoted in U. TÄHTINEN: *The Philosophy of Values*, p. 70. This is another meaning of *dharma*. Cf. Mees, op. cit. p. 9. Monier-Williams, op. cit. p. 500.

[144] Pr. Ap. pp. 105-106. Cf. also de Nobili's *Tūṣṇa Tikkāram* (hereafter referred to as T.T.), pp. 493-508.

[145] T.T. p. 493, also pp. 391-393.

[146] Ibid. pp. 391, 394: "They consider them as patrimony coming from their ancestors."

[147] Ibid. pp. 391-394.

[148] *Kaṭavuḷ Nirnayam* is found in the book *Nittiya Cīvana Callāpam*. Tuticorin 1964, p. 121. The first book will be known hereafter as K.N.

[149] It is called *kuṭumi* in Tamil. De Nobili writes it as *corumbi* or *coruminum*.

[150] I.C. p. 80. De Nobili translates *dharmatah* as *discrimen stirpis*, following one of the commentators.

Cf. W. CALAND: Roberto de Nobili and the Sanskrit language and literature in *Acta Orientalia* 3 (1926), p. 41. Caland has identified the text as M. 11,35. Cf. Bühler, p. 36, on the interpretation *dharmatah*. De Nobili follows probably the commentators Narada and Nandini who explain *dharmatah* by "according to the law of the family instead of for the sake of

"The use of the tuft of hair is proper to the twice-born, namely of the Brahmins, Rajas and merchants..." [151] According to the same testimony, *Śudras* are excluded from the twice-born. The tuft of hair is the sign of all the twice-born castes. What is of interest to us here is that *dharma* is used in the sense of distinctive caste or family mark, thus referring to a matter of social order and grade of castes and families, which must be retained as such. De Nobili recognises the acceptability of such a custom of keeping tuft of hair on the head in so far as it serves a social pupose of distinguishing different castes. Hence the tuft of hair as *kuladharma* is a legitimate custom.[152] De Nobili argues to show that *deśācāram* and *kuladharma* are legitimate, and that they serve a social purpose. He shows that this is the understanding of social and family rules and customs in the *smṛti* books. He refers to a popular saying concerning *deśācāra* and *kuladharma*:

> On account of the variety of regions, there are different honours coming from civil customs. A prudent man must conform his way of acting to the custom of the region where he now lives, corresponding to his class and civil grade which he has left.[153]

The saying makes two points: First, it speaks of the acceptable honours (*honestates*) of the different regions; and secondly it concerns the obligation one has to conform to those of the region in which he lives. De Nobili refers to a text of Manu which he renders as follows:

> The way of acting said to be in agreement with that of a prudent man is that which men in the region where he is, be they of his own class or of the first or of the middle grade retain as handed down from ancestors.[153]

---

spiritual merit." Hereafter all references to Caland's article will be simply referred to as Caland. Cf. also Pr. Ap. p. 112. Cf. I.C. p. 81. *Kuladharmah* as a sign of the family referred to in a text from *Apastamba Grhya sūtra*. (16.6.7.). Cf. Caland, p. 41.

151 I.C. p. 80 "usus corumi proprius est Dvigiatinorum, i.e. Brahmanum, Regiorum, et mercatorum..."

152 "Legitimate' in the sense that it does not violate any moral principle or contradict any truth of faith.

153 I.C. p. 113. "Pro varietate regionum varias esse morum civilium honestates, virumque

The popular saying *deśācāram kuladharmam* means that each one must consider the customs of a region where he lives as customs of one's own caste, that is, one's own *kuladharma.*[155] De Nobili explains how people understand *deśācāram* to be of obligation:

> One should be so disposed as not only to adopt the manners of the region but to make them his very own, and so to say, hereditary and inborn.[156]

Manu asks the king to see to it that no one goes against the customs of the Nobility.[157] The law is not uniform, and it is modified according to the region.

From all this, therefore, one understands that the Indians have the idea that every one whatever he is, must live and adopt the customs similar to his rank and nobility. They also judge foreigners according to their *deśācāram*. Here they conceive society divided into four classes. They expect a foreigner to fit into one of the four classes and observe corresponding customs or *dharma*. *Varṇadharma* is, therefore, a concept of society in the frame work of which they judge other peoples. At the same time, they consider their society

---

prudentem in eo stirpis genere et gradu civili quem sortitus est ad eius regionis in qua degit consuetudinem suum agendi morem formare debere." De Nobili does not quote the saying but only sums up its meaning.

[154] I.C. p. 113. "Ille modus agendi prudenti viro consentaneus dicitur quem in ea regione in qua est sui ordinis homines sive primi, sive mediae sortis sint a maioribus acceptum retinent."

[155] Ibid. "Desa acarh Kuladharmah i.e. civilis mos uniuscuiusque regionis aequipollet propriae consuetudinis stirpis". Manu (1,108) says that the traditional custom is the highest *dharma* (*ācārah paramo dharmah*). Cf. V.S. Sukthankar: *On the Meaning of the Mahabharata*, Bombay 1957, p. 79. Ibid. *Dharma* means also something which has its origin in orthodox traditional custom (*ācāraprabhavodharmah*).

Bühler, p. 31. Manu (2,12) defines *dharma*: "The Veda, the sacred tradition, the customs of virtuous men, and one's own pleasure, they declare to be visibly the fourfold means of defining the sacred law."

Tähtinen, op. cit., p. 71. The source or authority of *dharma* is fivefold: "The Vedic scriptures (*śruti*), the sacred law (*smṛti*), the practices of the good (*sadācāra*), whatever is agreeable (*priya*) to one's own self (*svatman*), and the desire (*kāma*) which has arisen out of wholesome resolve (*samayaksaṅkalpa*) all these are traditionally known to be the sources of dharma." (*Yājñavalkya smṛti* I,1,7).

[156] I.C. p. 113.

[157] Ibid. "... ne quid patitur rex introduci contra morem nobilium." This is the *dharma* of the *kings*.

open to others.[158] De Nobili views critically in his treatise *Tūṣaṇa Tikkāram*, some of the observances which are considered good by the Hindus.[159] This he does according to the criterion of right reason. It is also in some way criticism of ritual morality. One considers that to add to food red-coloured greens, pumpkin, etc. will lead to great sin. To ruin another, to have hatred for another, to desire another's wife, to worship created realities are not considered sins. De Nobili criticises many other customs which are observed as of obligation without regard for their moral rightness. This is what Hindus think according to de Nobili:

> Through tradition handed down from generation to generation (sin) may not appear to be sin.[160]

Thus they consider killing the scorpion that stings and killing the cobra that kills great sin. So too *sati* is considered a virtue according to tradition.[161] Likewise, touching a *Caṇḍāla* (an outcast) or looking at him at mid day is sinful. These are *ācārams* coming down to them from generation to generation and therefore they are considered right. We shall discuss later in the 2nd part of this chapter the moral argument of this problem. What we note here is that the social and religious observances have the force of law. They form the *dharma* of a country. The criterion of acceptability of the usages and customs is that they do not refer to idolatrous practices and that they are good and legitimate according to natural law.[162]

---

[158] Ibid. "Atque ex hac persuasione, et lege inferunt isti quasi necessaria consecutione nullum hominem externum nobilem et ingenuum esse, atque adeo nec suo convicto dignum nisi qui iis moribus utatur, quibus inter ipsos nobiles viri utuntur."

[159] T.T. pp. 50-51.

[160] Ibid. p. 51.

[161] *Sati* is the custom of widowed wife dying on the funeral pyre of her husband. The word means 'true woman'. The custom of committing *sati* (more accurately, the custom of becoming a *sati*), has been banned by law in 1829. Cf. on *sati* (suttee in Anglo-Indian form) Kane, *History of Dharmaśāstras*, Vol. 2, no. 1, Pune, 1941, pp. 624-636.

[162] Sukthankar, op. cit., p. 79. The *Mīmāmsā* writers define *dharma*: "any matter enjoined by the Veda with a view to attaining any useful purpose ("Vedena prayojanam uddisya vidhiyamano 'rtho dharmah - Mīmāmsanya prohasa" 3).

B. *Dharma as Virtue*

So far we considered the duties of behaviour in society and functions and duties of sacrifices, all flowing from *varṇāśramadharma*. We shall now consider *dharma* as virtue.

i. *Virtues of a Perfect Brahmin*

We shall first examine the virtues recommended to Brahmins. De Nobili in defining a true Brahmin stresses the point of virtues recommended to them.[163] The virtues recommended are: diligent work, self-restraint, compassion, almsgiving, generosity, truthfulness, and righteousness.

These virtues stand in the order of increasing importance leading finally to wisdom.[164] They are not only virtues of a perfect Brahmin but also those of a perfect wise man in general. This means that they are open to all.[165] De Nobili refers to St Thomas with regard to the bliss of a perfect wise man in this life. The opinion expressed by Thomas is that beatitude in this life consists primarily, though imperfectly, in contemplation of God and, secondarily, and by way of disposing oneself, it consists in the use of speculative sciences and the practical reason and in the use of moral virtues.[166] In the opinion of Christian theologians, moral virtues stand in this relation to God and are open to all. De Nobili perceives such a relation of virtue to God present in Hinduism.[167] The virtues recommended to Brahmins are, indeed, open to all.

ii. *Truthfulness* (satya)

Another virtue that gets a high rating in de Nobili's evaluation is the virtue of truthfulness (*satyam*). He sees such a rating present in

---

[163] I.C. pp. 8-9.

[164] Ibid. pp. 9-10.

[165] Ibid. p. 11.

[166] Ibid. pp. 9-10. "... perfectionem et felicitatem perfecti sapientis in hac vita, ut est imperfecte comprehensor primario et quasi essentialiter consistere in contemplatione. Dei, secundario et dispositive in uso scientiarum speculativarum et in ratione practici intellectus, et demum in usu moralium virtutum..." Cf. S. Th. 1,2, q.3, a.5 and 2,2, q.180, a.2.

[167] Ibid. pp. 9-10.

Hinduism itself. He quotes a verse from Manu which speaks of the nobility of Brahmins and which at the same time shows the importance attached to the virtue of *satyam*. It is the most perfect of all *dharmas*. The text runs as follows:

> Four things have excellence, among men Brahmins, among lights the sun, among the members (of the body) the head, among virtues truthfulness.[168]

Here *satyam* is said to be excellent and to be perfect. When de Nobili speaks of wearing the thread, he says that they understood the thread to be the symbol of wisdom. In this connection be quotes a *smṛti* passage which says:

> There is no virtue better than truthfulness, no evil worse than untruth. The world was created by this virtue, and therefore no virtue is greater than truth.[169]

Here againt the excellence of the *dharma* of truth is affirmed. Its opposition to untruth as a great evil is also stressed. Besides, it is said that God creates the world by the power of this *dharma* or it is the cause of creation of the world.

There is another text concerning virtues which de Nobili says he found in an *Araṇyaka*. He says that it speaks of truth, 'truthfulness, virtue to be practised, act of giving thanks, rendering the like good for the like good done.'[170] In this list, truth occurs in the first place. It is remarkable that the books of *māyāvādins* which one might reject as those of idolators speak of virtues which are acceptable.

---

[168] Ibid. p. 13. "Id est quatuor res excellentiam habent, inter homines Brahmanes, inter lumina sol, inter membra caput, inter virtutes veritas".

[169] Ibid. p. 75. "Veritate nulla virtus melior, falsitate nullum malum peius quippe hac virtute mundus creatus est, ergo veritate nulla virtus maior". This text is from Kalidasa's *Kumara Sambava*, II.

[170] Ibid. p. 34. "ubi de veritate, de veracitate, de virtute exercenda, de gratiarum actione, de paris pari beneficio redditione". De Nobili refers to Taitt. Up. beginning with "siksam vyakhyaṡyamah" (1,2,2,). De Nobili has high appreciation of the moral ideas present in this *Upaniṣad*, as in the *Śikṡa Valli*, esp. 1,9,1; 1,11,1-6; 1.12.1). Moreover, de Nobili distinguishes between truth (*veritas*) and truthfulness (*veracitas*) according to the text of *Araṇyaka* referred to. Cf. G. Gispert-Sauch, *Bliss in the Upaniṣads*, New Delhi 1977, pp. 20-23. Taitt. Up. belongs to the black *Yajur Veda*. Ibid. p. 21, Taitt. Up. forms 7,8,9 chapters of Taitt. *Araṇyaka*.

iii. *Non-Violence* (Ahiṁsā)

Another virtue praised by Hindus is *ahiṁsā* (non-injury to living beings). As regards this virtue, de Nobili rejects the Hindu understanding of it. He is not so much critical of the virtue itself as the motives for the recommendation of this virtue. The virtue is recommended like this:

"*Ahiṁsā* is the supreme *dharma*, *adharmam* is the torture of living beings."[171]

De Nobili says that this saying is current among the Hindus. He says that for Hindus to kill a man and animals wilfully is sin of the same nature.[172] Because they accept the opinion that in each body the same soul exists.[173]

Therefore, it means that a human soul exists in plants. Man uses greens for eating and cuts plants. These things are necessary for human life, but according to this opinion there is always sin. Hence works of expiation (*prāyascittas*) are prescribed. De Nobili then sharply criticises this view:

"If we approve of the idea the human soul dwells in the bodies of animals and in greens, then if any one eats this food according to his caste, both *Śudras* and Brahmins would commit murder." [174]

De Nobili could not approve a doctrine which says that the soul in all bodies are of the same nature without any differences.[175] De Nobili would not approve of the torture of animals but he would find it equally unacceptable that killing man and animals are sins of the same nature. Hence it is understandable that de Nobili rejects *ahiṁsā* based on such an understanding of the soul and its manner of existence.

iv. *The Buddhist Titles of Moral Heroes*

When treating of virtues, we cannot omit what de Nobili says of Buddhists, though they are *nāsticas*.[176] He calls them the most fam-

[171] A.N. p. 264. De Nobili probably refers to a popular saying on *ahiṁsā*, cf. P.V. KANE: *History of Dharmaśāstras*, Poona, Vol. I, 1930, p. 3. He remarks that "ahiṁsā paramo dharmah" makes the definition of *dharma* one-sided.

[172] A.N. p. 264.

[173] Ibid.

[174] A.N. pp. 264-265.

[175] Ibid. p. 265.

[176] I.C. p. 27. In so far as they do not accept the authority of the *Vedas* of the Hindus.

ous and the most ancient.[177] He considers them the most famous because of their excellent moral traditions and moral heroes.

De Nobili mentions first their moral heroes who are known by their title for their moral virtues and other perfections.[178] There are those who are men of all wisdom. De Nobili shows this by the meaning of the term. The second group has a title which means they are the dwellers in the temple of knowledge. *Buddhers* are those who consider all the things of the world to be nothing. The fourth group are the *dharmarājas*. They are kings adorned with every kind of virtue. The fifth group are known by the title *Tatagatvah* which means men possessing truth and intelligence. The sixth title refers to men who are abounding in all goodness or virtues. The seventh title mentioned means having six perfections in an excellent degree. De Nobili then lists six qualities or perfections.[179] They are fortitude, ornament or grace, wisdom, freedom from perturbation of soul. After this, de Nobili continues with the rest of the titles.[180] The men of the eighth title are those who are victorious over greed and lust. The men of ninth title are those who have conquered the world. The men of the tenth title are the victorious men.

After this, de Nobili continues with the twelfth title which is of greater importance for our study of *dharma*.[181] It is given to men remarkable for ten virtues. The moral virtues mentioned are continence, patience, good character, fortitude, contemplation, mature counsel, strength, counsel to do a work in the right way, and rever-

---

Hence they are called *nāsticas* It is *Buddha Matam*. We treat of the Buddhists to show that de Nobili appreciates properly moral values wherever they are found. Though they are *nāsticas*, they have the concept of *dharma*. Cf. Haecker, art, cit. p. 93.

177 I.C. p. 27 de Nobili's opinion that Buddhists are the most ancient is disputable. Cf. ibid. p. 29.

178 Ibid. pp. 27-28.

Ibid. p. 27. *Sarva Jñānam* = *Sarvagnen*, ibid. "omnem sapientiam possidetes", *Sugatrers* = "in intelligentiae asilo versantes", *Buddhers* "omnia quae in mundo sunt pro nihilo habentes", *Dharmarājas* = "Omni virtutum genere Reges", *Tatagatavah* = "veritatem et intelligentiam possidentes", *Samanda-bhadren* = "omnibus virtutibus bonitate pollentes". *Bagavani* = "sex laudes in eccellenti gradu habentes."

179 Ibid. p. 27.

180 Ibid. *Malagit* "cupidinis et luxuriae victores". *Logagit* = "mundi victores". *Ginaa* (Jina) = "victores", *Siadabignaa* (*Sadabhijna*) = "sex praeclaros sensus habentes.

181 Ibid. p. 28. De Nobili lists here the Buddhist virtues. *Dasiabalam* is explained by de Nobili as follows: "decem virtutibus insigniti".

ence.[182] After this de Nobili continues with the enumeration of the rest of the titles.[183] The thirteenth title means "those who consider all one, for they say all things are vanity".[184] The fourteenth title is explained as follows: "Those who are free and without master or princes of masters or without doctors among masters".[185] The fifteenth title is *Munindra* which means "the first among the renouncers of human things."[186] De Nobili's purpose in giving all these titles is to show how illustrious these men of the Buddhist sect are. Most of the titles speak of moral virtues and show the things they value. They are *Buddhers* who hold the things of the world for nothing.

Dharmarājas are kings who possess all virtues, *Samantabhadra* who abound in all virtues and goodness, *Malajit*, those who have overcome cupidity and lust, *Jina* those who are victors in the sense of having conquered all evil desires, *Lokajit* those who have conquered the world, those who have ten qualities (*daśabala*), most of which are moral qualities and perfections. The titles of *Munindra* and *Muni* and *Vināyaka* are also titles of moral heroes, of those who have renounced everything and who are free. *Muni* is interpreted by de Nobili as meaning 'erudite men'.[187] Then there are men who have six praises. Of these, some are moral perfections like fortitude, freedom from perturbation of soul.[188] The great fame of Buddhist sects rests on their estimation of these titles of moral perfection and of virtues. Besides, since they are a sect of *Nāsticas*, de Nobili feels more secure with the discussion of moral virtues and perfections without their being contaminated by idolatrous beliefs.[189] Most of

---

[182] Ibid. p. 28. The Buddhist words for the ten virtues: *Danti, santi (xanti), Silam, Viriam, dhyana, Sandhi, Balam, Upaia, Pranidi*. (The words as written by de Nobili).

[183] Ibid. p. 28.

[184] *Aduaiaa (advaya) vadi* means "Omnia unum facientes, dicunt enim omnia vana esse". Ibid. p. 28.

[185] Ibid. p. 28. "*Vianaiacaa* = liberi et sine domino, vel dominorum principes, vel Doctores."

[186] Ibid. p. 28. "*Munidra* i.e. Primarii inter abiectores rerum humanarum."

[187] *Muni* generally means men who have renounced. One could question de Nobili's interpretation as '*eruditi*'.

[188] Ibid. p. 27. *Viriyam, Vairagya*.

[189] Ibid. p. 29. We get an inkling into it when de Nobili remarks that idol worshippers (*māyāvādins*) introduced their laws and idol worship.

the perfections concern the idea of renunciation, self-conquest of desires.[190] De Nobili recognises the value of *tapah* (penance), *dāna* (almsgiving), *dhyana* (meditation) and *japa* (prayer) just as he recognises the value of renunciation and chastity of *sannyāsa.*[191].

v. *Value of Virtuous Practices*

De Nobili would accept, e.g. almsgiving and austerity as good in themselves, for almsgiving alleviates the sufferings of the poor; by austerity one controls passions. He is also aware that they can be defiled if done for one's own glory or for wrong reasons.[192] Thus to fast in order to save is miserliness, to perform austerity and almsgiving and prayer for the sake of created realities is a disorder. What is of interest to us is that de Nobili recognises austerity, almsgiving as practised by the Hindus as virtuous. Concerning austerity he says:

> All are agreed that austerity is virtuous.[193]

Austerity, almsgiving, etc. have their moral justification apart from belief of religious merit or forgiveness of sin. Austerity implies a certain asceticism and control of body and mind which remove causes of sin.[194] The right way of such practices for a follower of another religion consists in performing them for the sake of one true God whom one knows by the natural light of reason.[195] Now we would like to comment on two expressions: *tapōtānam* and *tarmatānam.*[196] These expressions exist in Hinduism concerning almsgiving and austerity. *Tapodānam* means merit-giving actions and *dharmadānam* means the same.[197]

---

[190] Ibid. pp. 27-28. Cf. the words *Buddhas, Advaya vadi, Munindra* which express renunciation; conquest of passions is expressed by words like *Malajit, Lokajit, Vianāyaka*.

[191] Cf. the meaning of *sannyāsa* explained above in this chapter. Cf. *Narratio*, p. 208. N. Godhino s.j., defending de Nobili's method takes note of the meaning of dress of *sannyāsins* which symbolises renunciation and chastity.

[192] Cf. T.T. p. 413; cf. ibid. p. 281: "Austerity is virtuous, to spoil it is sinful."

[193] Ibid. p. 281, cf. also p. 231.

[194] Ibid. p. 412.

[195] Ibid. p. 414.

[196] Ibid. Cf. pp. 412 and 423 for the expression *tapōtānam* (skt. *tapodāna*) and cf. p. 418 for the expression *tarmatānam* (skt. *dharmadāna*).

[197] *Dharmadāna* means 'alms from a sense of duty'. Cf. A.A. MACDONELL: *A Practical*

Dharma means also good works such as almsgiving. It is used as synonymous with almsgiving.[198]

One of the meanings of *dharma* is religious rite or ordinance.[197] De Nobili uses dharma in this sense when he says that when one changes one's sect and joins another sect, he fulfils *dharmas* (*tarmankaḷai*) like *cātakaraṇam* and *nāmakaraṇam* (*nāmakarṇa*) with prayers proper to them.[198]

Sanskrit Dictionary, Oxford 1954, p. 130. De Nobili uses it in the sense of virtuous or meritorious actions like the expression *tapodāna*.

[198] 26 Serm. p. 46. Cf. also *Responsio quibusdam a P.A. Buccerio*, (ARSI Goa, 51, f. 214). One of the meanings of *dharma* de Nobili gives here is alms (*eleemosynae*).

[199] KANE, *History of Dharmaśāstras*, Vol. I, p. 1.

[200] T.T. pp. 360, 336: Here de Nobili mentions *tarmankaḶ* in the sense of religious rites or ceremonies. 'To fulfil the rites (*tarmankaḷai*) with their prayers' refers to the rites of the different sects. Cf. Monnier-Williams, p. 417. *Cātakaraṇam* (skt. *jātakarman* is "a birth-ceremony consisting in touching a newly-born child's tongue thrice with ghee after appropriate prayers"). *Nāmakaraṇam* is the ceremony of naming a child after birth.

CHAPTER TWO

THE THEORY OF KARMA AND REBIRTH AND THE UNDERSTANDING OF THE HUMAN SOUL IN RELATION TO DHARMA

So far we considered *dharma* in the sense of duties and virtue as de Nobili found it in Hinduism. We shall now consider the doctrine of *pūrvajanma*, *karma* and *punarjanma* which explain the basic structure of the concept of *dharma* in Hinduism.[1] Our consideration has two parts: the first consideration of the nature of the soul and the second consideration of the ethical part which explains *pūrvajanma*, *karma* and *punarjanma* in terms of the ethical behaviour of man.

SECTION ONE

a. *The nature of the soul of man* (Ātma):

De Nobili examines the different views held by Hindus concerning the soul of man. One of them reads like this:

> Some hold the view that there are two kinds of souls, *Paramātma* and *jivātma* in man and that *Paramātma* endowed with intelligence is in all, that he is God and that *jīvātmas* are many.[2]

---

[1] *Pūrvajanma* = previous state of existence or previous birth, *karma* = the result of good or bad actions in a previous birth.
Punarjanmam = rebirth.

[2] *Punar Jenma Accēpam* (Refutation of Rebirth), ed. S. Rajamanickam, Tuticorin, 1963, pp. 8-9. This work of de Nobili will be referred to hereafter in the thesis as P.J.A. De Nobili mentions the different opinions on the soul without mentioning the names of the sects which

De Nobili explains the existence of the same soul in all living beings in the work Āttuma Nir*ṇayam*. He says:

> They would say that in innumerable living beings the soul is one. Therefore they would say the soul which is endowed with knowledge and which is indestructible and eternal exists in the house of the body like a man who lives in a house.[3]

That the soul exists in the body as one lives in a house is explained further as follows:

> So too they say that the soul which is now in the house of the body existed in dog, jackal, donkey and all the other animals in former times and that it will happen in future. Besides this, the soul as it lives in the bodies of all kinds of animals, will exist in the house (of bodies) of all kinds of trees, plants and grass.[4]

This is the explanation of the soul in a new birth. It would mean that the qualities of intelligence and liberty would exist in animals and in plants and even in inanimate beings.

Among other erroneous opinions concerning the metaphysical constitution of man, some say that:

> i. "God who is the form of all goodness lives in the world as a human soul with a body." [5]
>
> ii. Others say that:
> "the soul (of man) is a part of God." [6]

iii. Still others say: "There are in man a gross body and an inner organ which is a subtle body." It is also said that in the inner organs

---

hold them. We present them here as he does. *Paramātmā* is the Supreme Soul. *Jīvātma* is the individual soul.

[3] A.N. p. 261.

[4] Ibid. pp. 261-262, 19-20. Cf. P.J.A. Appendix, A Letter of Father Leitão to Father Provincial (Madurai, 26th Sept. 1609), p. 8. Fr Leitao, a companion of de Nobili mentions this idea as he heard it from de Nobili. He mentions the idea that "the soul is like a rider on horseback or like a bird in a cage."

[5] A.N. pp. 129-130. De Nobili gives seven different views. We present here his summary.

[6] Ibid. p. 129.

of mind (*manacu*), intellect (*putti*), consciousness (*cittam*) and the ego-principle (*akankāram*) the image of the Supreme Soul, the Absolute will be reflected just as in different pots of water the image of the sun is seen reflected, and that the reflected image is being endowed with knowledge and that it is the Supreme Soul (*paramāttuma*) and that the inner organs are the individual soul (*cīvāttuma*).[7]

iv. Another opinion is this: They "do not agree that in the soul is God, but say that it is existing without beginning along with God." [8] The Saivite doctrine goes in this line. Their doctrine of *pati* (Lord), *pacu* (the soul, lit. cattle) and *pācam* (lit. cord, here *karma*) is explained as follows:

> Some say that *pati, pacu* and *pācam* which are God, soul and body with bonds of karma exist eternally, and that the soul is always bound to bodies which are cords...[9]

v. Here is another opinion which says that "all human souls were created by God at the beginning of the world" and that "according as each soul showed love or no love towards God, they in later times joining with different bodies live in the world." [10]

vi. De Nobili mentions another view:

> Some others established the view that father and mother just as they help the generation of the human body, are also the cause of the human soul.[11]

vii. One more view de Nobili mentions is this: Some hold that the soul is "a regular assemblage of elements." [12] These views are important for the understanding of *dharma* in Hinduism. In de Nobili's view they will weaken or destroy the meaning of *dharma* in its moral content and its relation to salvation.

---

[7] Ibid. pp. 129-130. De Nobili uses *stūlacarīram* for the gross body and *linkacarīram* for the subtle body. Mahadevan, op. cit., p. 170 for the internal organs (*antakaraṇa*) of *manas*, buddhi, citta and *ahankāra*.

[8] Ibid. p. 130.

[9] P.J.A., p. 1.

[10] A.N. p. 130.

[11] Ibid. p. 130.

[12] Ibid.

b. *De Nobili's objections to the Hindu view on the human soul*

We shall briefly consider here how de Nobili answers the difficulties arising from these beliefs. De Nobili answers first the objection by saying that God who is a Being by Himself and the form of all good cannot be the soul of man. He says:

> Since it was shown that the soul is the form of the body, it is not wrong to say that its half and incomplete being forms the complete being together with the body. If this is so, only the ignorant and the foolish would say that the soul is the all-good Supreme Being.[13]

De Nobili in showing the difference between God and the human soul stresses two points: first the metaphysical nature of the human soul which as an incomplete principle forms together with the body the complete human being; and secondly that God who is all good cannot be the incomplete and limited human soul, since one cannot attribute imperfection to God. That God is the form of all goodness is the truth to which de Nobili constantly appeals in refuting the Hindu theories of God. If one were to say that God were man's soul, it would amount to saying that "God who is infinite goodness would suffer from ignorance and weakness." [14] Therefore God cannot be the form (*māttirai*) of man: To give God the form of a human being would involve many imperfections, such as ignorance, enmity and lust in God. That is to say, God who is all good becomes the principal cause of such sins.[15] Besides, such a doctrine would negate the meaning of repairing and forgiving of sin.[16] It would mean God punished Himself for sin. The important point is that God and man are different in nature (*cupāvacurūpam*).

---

[13] Ibid. p. 131. De Nobili refutes this belief with the Christian doctrine of the human soul and body which he explains in the first two lessons of this treatise (pp. 6-42). De Nobili uses *māttirai* (*skt. mātra*) to signify the form which the human soul is for the human body. De Nobili uses here Thomistic metaphysics which is Aristotelian.

[14] Ibid. p. 131.

[15] Ibid. pp. 131-132.

[16] Since sin is an offence against God who is different from man and who is all-good, to ask for forgiveness becomes meaningless with the above doctrine. De Nobili refutes all these Hindu ideas of the human soul with the Christian doctrine that God is one, independent from man and creation and that He is all-perfect.

The opinion that the human soul is part (*amśa*) of God cannot be accepted. If there are parts in God, they can separate themselves from God: it would mean that God continually suffers changes.

> ... Since continually parts are born from the Being, by such separation of parts, changes and differences come to befall the Being.[17]

Approval of this doctrine would mean that:

> if the soul is part of the Supreme Being it must be the form of the qualities of wisdom, power like the Supreme Being.[18]

Besides, it would amount to positing moral faults in God.[19] God cannot be the reflection of Himself in the inner organs of man, since the reflected image is a created reality.[20] Being a created reality, it is limited. A limited being derogates from the infinite perfection of God.[21]

> Besides, since God is infinite knowledge, if we say that the reflection of such infinite knowledge is in man, then there would be no room for ignorance and such errors in man.[22]

So too when we say that the reflection of God who is all good can be created, we make God present to our interior senses and thus make him a limited being for:

> the image of a thing is where the thing is not. Thus the objects of the five senses are not in the senses, but since the images are present in the senses, the sense through the image of the thing perceives the object.[23]

---

[17] Ibid. p. 133.

[18] Ibid.

[19] Ibid. pp. 133-134.

[20] Ibid. p. 135. De Nobili argues according to the nature of God who is Being by Himself. Reflection is posterior to the being itself. "As the sun is not present in the pot of water nor man in the mirror, (but) in the pot of water and in the mirror only images of the sun and of man are seen." Cf. pp. 135-136.

[21] Ibid. p. 136.

[22] Ibid. p. 137.

[23] Ibid.

If so, God who is infinite cannot be present in the inner organ. De Nobili rejects the view that "the inner organ cannot have knowledge by its own nature...".[24] According to this view, only the reflection of God makes the inner organ capable of knowing whereas:

> knowledge which is a living act inheres in the being from which it proceeds and makes that being intelligent.[25]

Therefore, the view which makes the reflected image of God the principle of knowing removes the intrinsic principle of man's knowing. If man does not have the principle of knowing in himself, he cannot be said to be the agent of knowledge and of responsible acts.

De Nobili then examines the view of those who want to show that the soul (of man) is without beginning (*anāti*) like God. They say that "*pati, pacu* and *pācam* which have been determined to be God, soul and *karma*, these three together, should be eternal." [26] De Nobili wants to counter the view that the soul and body bound with *karma* are co-eternal with God. It means that if the soul is beginningless, it took a body after infinite time. According to their view (*matam*) *karma* preceded. But *karma* will not result without a body. If so, one cannot say that after infinite time it assumed a body. [27] Besides, since God is the complete Lord of all beings because He created them, it would mean He had not created souls, and therefore not the Lord or Creator in the full sense of the word.[28] As man is a complete being with body and soul together, the view that God created souls without a body or bodies without a soul cannot be accepted.[29]

Another opinion that de Nobili rejects is that father and mother are the cause of the birth of the human soul. Since human soul does not require intrinsically a body for its existence or any other material thing, God alone is its cause.[30] Then de Nobili goes on to meet the

---

[24] Ibid.

[25] Ibid. p. 138.

[26] Ibid. p. 140. Cf. also p. 143. The body is the result of *karma*. Also P.J.A. p. 1.

[27] A.N. p. 143. De Nobili says also that we know from revealed religion that the soul of man is not without beginning.

[28] Ibid. p. 146.

[29] Ibid. p. 150.

[30] Ibid. pp. 151-152.

opinion of the materialists on the nature of the human soul, which says that "the human soul is a collection of elements" (*pūtiyankaḷ*).[31] This view has serious consequences for moral actions of man, and hence de Nobili shows it to be untenable. This is how he does it:

> That is to say, the substance brought about by the collection is called inanimate substance (*caṭapatārtam*) and body; if so, if it were said that the collection of elements were the soul, one must accept the error that there is no difference in nature between inanimate substance which has no action of its own, and soul which is the cause of different actions.[32]

It would mean that "the human soul would require (or desire) a body for itself to exist..."[33] It also means that with the death of man, the human soul is destroyed:

> if we were to say that through the death of man, the soul were destroyed, one must say that the efforts of austerity and other righteous actions would be fruitless.[34]

Such a doctrine implies that there is no future life. If there is no future life or life hereafter, there would be no reason for man to renounce honour, riches and pleasures and practise austerity and other virtues.[35] Besides, on the occasion of the performance of rites for the dead[36] one performs austerity, prayer, almsgiving and other *dharmas* (virtuous deeds) for the dead. But such *dharmas* would avail nothing if the human soul were an assemblage of elements. Hence de Nobili asks:

> If after the death of a man the human soul is destroyed and if

---

[31] Ibid. p. 153. Cf. I.C. p. 31. De Nobili speaks of *lokāyatas* (materialists) here, cf. also N.C.C. pp. 40-41. *Pūtiyankaḷ* is *bhūta* in skt. Cf. N.V. Banerjee, *The Spirit of Indian Philosophy*, London 1975, p. 136.

[32] A.N. p. 153.

[33] Ibid.

[34] Ibid. Cf. Banerjee, op. cit., p. 137.

[35] A.N. pp. 153-154. Cf. also N.C.C. p. 47. A materialist (*lokāyata*) who does not believe in the immortality of the soul considers that to ruin others for his own good is justice (*nīti*) and righteousness (*tarmam*).

[36] De Nobili uses the word *tivacam* for *śraddha* (the ceremony for the dead). *Tivacam* means 'day'. Here it is used for the day of *śraddha*.

> it does not exist, why should one perform the ceremony of *tivacam*, the *dharmas* of prayer, austerity and almsgiving.[37]

De Nobili's criticism that *dharmas* like prayer, austerity, almsgiving and such other virtuous deeds will not have any meaning if the human soul is destroyed with death, means that he accepts the value of such good actions as practised by Hindus. They are good actions wasted, since they are done towards some one who does not exist.

Another view is that human soul which is not dependant for its being on a body can according to the almighty will of God become dependent on a body for its being.[38] It is also said that God can make the soul of an animal which is dependent on a body for its being, by His infinite power independent of a body for its being.[39] Here only the divine power is used as an argument to make the human soul depend on the body intrinsically for its being. It would mean a change of nature itself. This has consequences for the understanding of *dharma* according to the Christian view point which de Nobili wants to explain to the Hindus in his works.

> If we say human soul depended for its being on body, when such a soul is separated from the body, we must accept the fact that the soul will be destroyed. Therefore we must also accept that for such a human soul there is no hell or heaven.[40]

Besides the human soul capable of knowledge could offend God and yet not be punished for it. This, says de Nobili, is against reason and divine justice.[41] In his view if the human soul were destroyed, the whole meaning of *dharma* would be destroyed. Moreover, a human being who has faith in and love for God and who does many meritorious actions (*mōccacātaka puṇṇiyankaḷ*) would go unrewarded. The view holding that the human soul which depends on body for its being will open the way to all sin and lead to the atheistic doctrine (*nāstika matam*).[42].

---

[37] A.N. p. 154.

[38] Ibid. pp. 164-165.

[39] Ibid. p. 164.

[40] Ibid. p. 173.

[41] Ibid.

[42] Ibid. pp. 173-174. N.C.C. pp. 40-48, on the sect of the materialists where the same point is explained.

We shall now examine the view of the human soul present in the doctrine of *karma* and rebirth. It is stated like this:

> Those who accept rebirth say that the soul is not the form of the body, that it exists in the body like the one who dwells in a house (or) like a bird in a cage.[43]

This is the first point of the view. Concerning the nature of the soul, there is another point which goes like this:

> They say only this that the soul which is in all bodies, is of one kind and that there are no souls of different nature; this is the second idea accepted by those who believe in rebirth.[44]

Since the soul exists in the house of the body, it can exist in different bodies, in bodies of animals and of plants.[45] It can exist even in inanimate things. That the soul exists in the body as in a house or in a cage does not explain the unity of body and soul that man is. It is known from experience that

> the soul is united with the body, and the body grows... that the body along with the soul goes hither and tither and not otherwise. Thus since the soul is in the body, the body performs different functions and we see this. Whereas if you and I are in a house, the house is not seen to do any action. Hence it must be said that there is a great difference between the way every one lives in one's house and the way the soul is in the body.[46]

The idea of a soul existing in the body as one lives in a house posits two complete beings, which is not the case of body and soul func-

---

[43] P.J.A. pp. 9-10. Also ibid., Appendix, p. 8, where the letter of Fr Leitão to the Provincial (26 Sept. 1609) mentions the same point. Here the soul is compared to a rider on horseback. Cf. also Bertrand, II, p. 7. Laerzio quotes de Nobili on the same point. Here the soul is also compared to a chick in the shell of an egg, a view like that of the Platonists. Also A.N. pp. 19-20.

[44] P.J.A. p. 10

[45] A.N. pp. 261-262. Here de Nobili does not take into consideration the view that holds the existence of the gross body and the subtle body with its inner organs of *manas, buddhi, citta* and *ahankāra*.

[46] P.J.A. p. 16.

tioning together as one being in man.[47] Besides, one easily leaves one's house and returns to it as one wishes. But the soul cannot do likewise. On the contrary, we see that the body is destroyed once the soul leaves the body.[48] Therefore the unity of body and soul is to be accepted. Moreover, the idea that a human soul can enter different bodies of animals or plants or inanimate beings is also rejected by de Nobili [49] for this would mean that there is only a difference of body between an animal of one species and that of another and that there is only a difference of body between man and dog.[50] It would mean also that:

> one must accept that the intellect and mind with its spiritual liberty and the glory that comes to man from them, such things together are present in dog, donkey and other animals. Besides one must also accept that such glories as knowledge are present in trees, plants and grasses and in stones and in similar inanimate beings.[51]

There are no reaons for this view nor signs of the presence of such things in plants, animals and stones. Besides, it would mean that since, human soul could be present in goats, chicken and other animals and plants, whenever man drives out the soul from 'houses' of these things, he would be commiting the crime of murder.[52] Above all sacrifice (*ekkiyam*) which is considered virtuous involves sacrifice of animals. If so, it involves the sin of murder.[53] Moreover, for the reason that the soul is present in plants and animals, *ahiṁsā* is recommended as the great *dharma*.[54] Since the same soul can exist in the several bodies of animals and plants, the ordinary activities of man like cutting of plants, eating of greens would involve the crime of murder. Because the human soul is present in plants and animals,

---

47 Ibid.

48 A.N. p. 262.

49 Ibid.

50 Ibid.

51 A.N. p. 263.

52 Ibid. p. 264. The Skt. *yajña* is written as *ekkiyam* in Tamil by de Nobili. The same form of *yajña* occurs in *Tratado Pe Goncalo Fernandes Trancoso sobre o Hinduismo*, ed. Wicki, Lisboa, 1973.

53 Ibid. p. 264.

54 Ibid.

it would mean one should prescribe the sacrifice of *homam*, prayer, almsgiving which are normally prescribed for the soul that it may reach a good state when it leaves the body of man for plants and animals. But this is not done.[55] Here de Nobili tries to show that such an inconsistency will result if one accepts the doctrine of rebirth. De Nobili says that the plants, animals and man have different kinds of souls which are different in their nature.[56] If so, the human soul cannot be the soul of plants and animals. Nor is it a complete being existing in the body as in a house. This is how de Nobili answers the difficulties regarding the nature of the human soul arising from belief in rebirth.

SECTION TWO

a. *The Doctrine of Karma and Rebirth and Dharma*

We shall examine the doctrine of *karma* and rebirth in relation to the meaning of *dharma*. De Nobili says that the doctrine of *karma* and rebirth is accepted by all sects except the materialists. He says that though they are divided into countless and contradictory opinions, they are agreed upon one thing, namely, rebirth.[57] The following doctrine is considered the first and the principal foundation of rebirth:

> We see among men that men are in different castes. Thus we see Brahmins who are great, Vellalas and other *śudras*, parayas and others in alien castes who live in the world. Besides, among men some are kings and rich men, others who serve other men and who are poor. Still others undergo suffering and diseases whereas some others have good health and enjoyments as their lot... Thus all differences... seen in animals and all other creatures are said to come from sin and virtue done (previously).[58]

---

[55] Ibid. p. 264.

[56] Ibid. pp. 266-267.

[57] P.J.A. p. 7.

[58] Ibid. p. 10. Cf. also A.N. p. 210, "all fortune or prosperity must be the fruit of each one's virtue. Moreover, disease and misfortune all this are in the form of punishment..."

Those who believe in rebirth go on to explain as follows:

> All that is seen in the world can be divided into good *karma* and bad *karma*, good *karma* being the fruit of virtue and bad *karma* the punishment of sin. If this is accepted, royal states and such lordships, riches, grains, enjoyments of body and pleasures, such things are said to be good *karma*. Poverty and disease and other such pains, sufferings and insults and humiliating lowliness, if they are considered, have to be given the name of bad *karma*.[59]

De Nobili then goes on to explain how virtue leads to the fruit of good *karma*.

> If they (men) are born with these fortunes, it cannot be considered that they practised virtue in this birth to deserve them. Hence there was a previous birth in which they performed good deeds in order to enjoy the fruit justly; thus they are said to be born with the above-mentioned fortunes.[60]

This way all that is seen in the world can somehow be explained in terms of good and bad *karma*. If one did not accept this view, one would have to say that one would enjoy the fruits of virtue without practising virtue: "If one were to speak like this, it would amount to saying that without the cause of the result the result came to be." [61] De Nobili refers to the view that one can suffer disease and pains only through sin and that one cannot suffer disease and pain without sin.[62] De Nobili rejects this karmic view of suffering.

God enters this scheme of *karma* and rebirth and regulates justly the results of *karma*. God sees to it that those who did bad acts in a previous state of life enjoy the results of bad *karma* (deeds) in this life. Since God is perfectly just, the opinion that he gives wages to one who did not work will not be according to just order.[63] This is

---

[59] P.J.A. p. 11. Here *karma* means result of the activity of man. In the passage quoted, *nalvinai* and *tīvinai* are used in the sense of good *karma* and bad *karma* respectively. In *Kāṇṭam* III, p. 469 *nalvinai* and *tīvinai* are used in the sense of morally good acts and morally bad acts. Cf. Bror, pp. 155, 158.

[60] P.J.A. p. 11.

[61] Ibid.

[62] Ibid. p. 73.

[63] Ibid. p. 12.

how the role of God in the scheme of *karma* and rebirth is explained. De Nobili continuing his exposé of the doctrine of *karma* and rebirth explains how this works out in the case of those whom we see commit sins and who in the middle of their life begin enjoying fortunes and lordly honours.

> We see that many in this life after having committed many sins, right in the middle of their lives receive countless good things such as riches, kingship and such lordly things. Since these (latter) are the fruits of virtue, it has to be said that they received these good things on account of the virtues they performed. Hence we have to accept that such men in ancient times had another birth in which they performed virtues the fruits of which they enjoy as pleasures and fortunes in this life.[64]

Here de Nobili says that those who accept the scripture of *Pūrvamīmāṁsā* hold that the world goes on only according to the law of *karma* and that it does not go on according to the command of God.[65] If God's role in the law of *karma* is admitted, He is said to give each man the fruits of his *karma*.

> If this is not accepted, it would mean that God gave the fruits which He gives through virtue to virtuous men to sinners who committed numberless sins. This we could say of those who suffer poverty, suffering and misfortunes. Whatever is bad *karma*, it is punishment for sin committed.[66]

Material prosperity, physical, social and sensible enjoyments are interpreted to be the fruits of virtue and material poverty, physical suffering and diseases are understood to be the fruits of sins. God is the just distributor of the fruits of *karma* to every man.

De Nobili continues with the explanation of *karma* and God's role in it on the conditions of men:

---

[64] Ibid. p. 12. De Nobili works out this argument in order to show the fallacy therein.

[65] Ibid. p. 72. The text says that *Uttaramīmāṁsā* holds this view, whereas it is *Pūrvamīmāṁsa* that holds this view. Cf. I.C. pp. 25-26. Here de Nobili says that the *Mīmāṁsā* school (*Pūrvamīmāṁsā*) denies that there is an author (*autor* or efficient cause) of the world.

[66] P.J.A. p. 12.

> That many men are born in poverty, afflicted with disease and suffering, without honour and as aliens is punishment due to sin committed by them. Now even a foolish man would not say that to undergo this punishment which is bad result, any sin was committed by them in this birth. Hence, that in order that those who are born with such misfortunes and punishments may undergo punishments for the sins committed in a previous state of life which they had before in ancient times, we must accept that God who is just ordained that they be born in this life with the above-mentioned misfortunes.[67]

De Nobili continuing further with their explanation of God's role in the scheme of *karma* and rebirth says this:

> If one does not accept this, one who has not committed a single sin suffers the punishment that comes from sin committed which is due to a sinner. If one considers all this carefully, it is not consonant with the infinite grace of God.[68]

De Nobili explains how *karma* works out with respect to those whom we see practise virtues and yet in the middle of their lives suffer misfortunes. He explains *karma* also with reference to those who are seen to commit sin and in the middle of their life enjoy fortune. Virtuous men suffering misfortune in the middle of their life implies a former birth:

> While they spend their time in doing great virtues, they lose the fortunes and riches after they have enjoyed them for a short period and experience poverty, disease and such sufferings in the middle (of their lives). If we consider the misfortune that befell such men, one could only say that it is an evil result and punishment. Therefore that it came through sin is a matter of truth.[69]

---

[67] Ibid. pp. 12-13. Ibid., Appendix, p. 1. According to Leitão, de Nobili says that God's holiness means that He is infinitely just. He cannot reward unless he finds some merit. Nor can He punish unless He finds some fault.

[68] Ibid. p. 13.

[69] Ibid.

De Nobili tries to show how the Hindu theory of *karma* can explain every part of one's life. "Since the above-mentioned virtuous men do not commit sin and ceaselessly walk in the way of virtue and (thus) do not commit serious sin, there is no cause for their suffering of punishment seen in this life."[70] Therefore in ancient times, they must have had another birth:

> In it they performed virtue for a short time and for some other time they spent their lives in committing serious sin. Hence in this life after enjoying for a short time riches and fortunes, they underwent the suffering of poverty and other misfortunes for some time. Thus it could be said that they would enjoy the fruit of virtue performed in previous birth and the fruit of sin in this life.[71]

Besides these reasons given by those who accept the theory of *karma* and rebirth, they say that this belief has been taught by the *purāṇas.*[72]

b. *Critique of the Theory of Karma*

We shall now examine how de Nobili refutes the idea that physical sufferings and poverty and such evils are the fruit and punishment of sin and that material prosperity and sense enjoyments are the fruit of virtue. De Nobili takes the example of a low-born man who is utterly poor and who suffers from different diseases and sores. He is continually despised by men. The reason for such a state is the law of *karma.*[73] One considers it just like a king in the world who imprisons a thief. So too God punishes man for the sin he committed in a previous birth by locking him in another body. Hence the view:

> The perfectly just one (God) locks in the prison of the body of humiliation and blame the wicked soul which committed sin in

---

[70] Ibid. p. 13.

[71] Ibid. pp. 13-14.

[72] Ibid. p. 14. *Purāṇa* belongs to the class of Hindu scriptures called *smṛti*. Cf. I.C. p. 19 on the definition of *Purāṇas* as those poetical works celebrating the deeds of gods, of which the chief and the most ancient ones are eighteen *purāṇas*.

[73] A.N. pp. 211-212.

> a previous birth. The evil soul is in such a body so that through this suffering it may be rid of all sins committed by it.[74]

Besides the idea that God executes the punishment, here is the idea that being imprisoned in a new body with sufferings and diseases is a way of ridding oneself of sins. De Nobili rejects this idea. He argues especially against the idea of body being a prison for the soul for the sin committed in a previous life. This is how he reasons:

> If the body of a low-born man with all its misfortunes were a prison for the bad soul to suffer punishments, one must say that a wicked soul is bound with such a body by necessity. In such a body the state of the soul is against its own will. This one must accept. Since this state is against the will (of the soul), it must ceaselessly desire to release itself from the the prison of the body.[75]

If so, the soul would greatly desire the ruin of that which is like prison and rejoice over it. Morever, it should work towards it [76]. Therefore one could expect to discover these qualities to be present in the wicked soul imprisoned in the body whereas one finds the opposite qualities in the soul of a lowborn man [77]. Besides man is afraid of the separation of the body from the soul. The soul is not perceived to desire release. On the contrary, it rejoices in existing together with the body. The idea of separation of the soul from the body can cause sadness to man [78]. If a man of low caste has a lowly body with all its misery as punishment for sin, he must perceive it and long for the release of his soul from such a body whereas he desires its perpetuation which will make the thing worse for him. God has nothing to do with condemning of the soul to the prison of the body. Therefore

> it cannot be accepted that the Lord ordained disease and other

---

[74] Ibid. p. 212.

[75] Ibid. p. 212.

[76] Ibid. pp. 212-213.

[77] Ibid. p. 213.

[78] Ibid.

> misfortunes only that man may suffer the punishment for the sins committed in a previous life [79].

This exclusive punishment view of suffering based on the idea of previous state of birth *(pūrvajanma)* de Nobili rejects.

c. *Freedom and Determinism in the Theory of Karma and Rebirth*

The idea of suffering punishments for sins committed in a previous birth is open to contradictions in a moral sense since it implies some form of determinism. De Nobili argues against this. The theory of rebirth starts from the interpretation of present facts. For example we see a man who is profligate and loose in his conduct with women. According to the view of *karma* and rebirth, God punishes such a man in this way for his sins of a previous birth [80]. This would destroy the meaning of virtue. De Nobili critically examines the determination of man according to *karma*, determinism resulting from it and the popular concept of fate *(lātalipi* = lit. writing on the skull) derived also from the theory of *karma.* De Nobili sums up the different expressions of the limitation of freedom due to *karma* [81]. First, according to the *karma* of each one, God has written certain letters on the cranium of every man which God Himself cannot wipe out [82]. Hence it points to its being determined. Secondly:

> in every one there is a quality like a stimulator for every one to do this or that by necessity in this life. They (the Hindus) teach that it came to each man as a result of deeds done in a previous birth. They say it is called *purvacenmavācanai* (impression of a previous birth or effect) or *pūrvacenmacamskāram*

---

[79] Ibid. pp. 215-216.

[80] Ibid. p. 217.

[81] Ibid. pp. 67-68.

[82] Ibid. p. 67. De Nobili presents this view as held by popular belief. We mention it here insofar as it is seen to be derived from the theory of *karma* and rebirth. Cf. P.J.A. Appendix p. 2. Here de Nobili says that God when He puts a soul in a body, writes on the forehead of man, according to the merits and demerits of each six things: death, span of life, prosperity, unhappiness, infirmity and health. Cf. Mahadevan, p. 57. He says that the popular identification of *karma* with fate is mistaken. *Karma* does not mean fatality. De Nobili as an apologist for Christianity meets the popular view.

> (impression left by previous birth) or *pirāktana* (lit. the former).[83]

Since it is at work in man, man does different things by necessity. Moreover they say:

> Besides the writing on the head, *pirāktanam*, such things which come through actions done in a previous birth are sufficient (for man) to do this or that.[84]

The third view is that the Lord exists and that he sees to it that each one receives the fruit of his *karma* in this life.[85] This view is important since it refers to man having no freedom.

> Some say that the Lord exists in the world and that such a Lord controls man and other things like dolls and that it is He who does all things and experiences all things. Hence the foolish men say that it is He who falls into sin.[86]

These views remove the freedom of man and destroy the concept of virtue which in so far as it is a human act, must be a free act. Hence, "man though he is endowed with his own power to perform his actions, while so doing, is not able to will or not to will this or that action. He does this action or that only driven by fate or such things."[87]

De Nobili then examines the problem of whether actions done

---

[83] Ibid. p. 68. *Pūrvacenmavācanai* is the Tamil form of skt. *Pūrvajanmavāsana*. Cf. M. Williams, p. 947. *Vāsana* means "impression of anything remaining unconsciously in the mind, the present consciousness of past perceptions, knowledge derived from memory." (*Saṁkhya*). The effect or impression of previous birth remaining in the mind. *Pūrvacenmacamskāram* is the Tamil form of skt. *Pūrvajanma samskāra*. M. Williams, p. 1120, for *samskāra*. It is "the faculty of memory, mental impression or recollection, impression on the mind of acts done in a former state of existence." *Pirāktanam* is the Tamil form of skt. *prāktana*. It means simply 'former, prior, preceding.' Here it means the impression of a previous life. M. Williams, p. 704. The impression of a previous life becomes an inner stimulator (*prērakan*) for man to act in a particular way. Cf. Mahadevan, p. 59. He explains how the impression of an action of a previous birth affects the character of a man in the present life.

[84] P.J.A.

[85] Ibid.

[86] Ibid. p. 68.

[87] Ibid. p. 69.

in a previous birth are virtuous actions done in freedom. There are two ways of understanding the actions done in a former life. A virtuous action done in a former existence is done either owing to previous *karma* or it is done freely without any cause of previous *karma*. If the former, it is not virtue since it is done by necessity through *karma* or if the latter, man can choose to practise virtue or choose not to practise it. If we admit the first interpretation that one performs virtue owing to *karma*, then if one is born a king, he is born in such a condition for an action which is not properly virtue, for virtue is to be done in freedom.[88] De Nobili shows in this way the contradiction present in the *karma* explanation of one being a king or of being in a lowly state.

> Therefore when we say that some one is born king now because he performed in a previous birth austerity and other similar actions, it must also be said that for such a person to be born a king, actions done by him are not the cause, he is born a king because he did actions which were not virtues. Therefore being a king which is the result of virtue, it could be said, came for such a person who did not do virtue and that consequently every one can enjoy all other fortunes without having done virtue previously.[89]

Here de Nobili explains one of the basic elements of virtue, namely, freedom. He does it in a way that any man who thinks can understand.

> If the king against my will forces me to give my wealth to every one, there is no doubt no one will call this the virtue of almsgiving. Or if the king forces me to starve, who would say that such a fast is *dharma* performed by me.[90]

Thus de Nobili gives examples to show that any *dharma* performed under compulsion could not be called virtue. Hence if one were to say that God who is just gave the reward of virtue to these actions which are not *dharma*, it would not be in keeping with the just or-

---

[88] P.J.A. p. 43.
[89] Ibid.; A.N. pp. 226-227.
[99] A.N. p. 227.

der.[91] Prayer, austerity and sacrifice are virtuous actions. If these are done without freedom as the theory of *karma* implies, then virtue cannot be commended for practice.

De Nobili then considers the element of knowledge in virtue and sin. If a sinner does not know the sins committed in a previous existence, he cannot really repent of them, even though sufferings in this life are supposed to be punishment for sin, for repairing of sin means turning one's will from sin: "One cannot consider that one's sin is removed and that one has become acceptable to the all good if one does not turn away one's will from sin."[92] Thus the two basic elements of moral action, freedom and knowledge are difficult to explain in the theory of *karma* and rebirth.

Another element implied in the theory of *karma* that makes moral responsibility difficult to explain is that "the soul is not the form of the body and that the soul exists in the body as in a house..." [93] If one accepts this view concerning the relation of the soul to body, it means for the sins committed by man in a particular body, another body will be inflicted with sufferings and disease and punishment.[94] That the soul passes from body to body according to *karma* raises difficulties concerning the basic elements of moral action, namely, knowing and willing.

De Nobili explains the elements of knowledge and freedom from the example of a king who administers justice in his kingdom. If a king punishes a thief, it is for the acts of theft done in this life, and not for acts of theft in a previous life. This meting out of justice by the king is sufficient to explain the punishment the thief undergoes.[95] It explains one's responsibility for one's actions without positing a previous state of existence and *karma*.

De Nobili argues against the theory of *karma* in another way. The evil action of a previous birth affects the character of a man. *Samskāra* or *vāsana* of previous birth affects man's character. De Nobili considers it a weakness of the theory of *karma*. The weakness is that the present evil state of a man such as that of being a robber

---

[91] Ibid.

[92] Ibid. p. 221.

[93] Ibid. pp. 308-309.

[94] Ibid. p. 309.

[95] Ibid. p. 216.

inclined to sin is a punishment for sin committed in a previous birth. Thus an evil condition inclining man to sin is a punishment for sin. In this way sin will not be removed. Instead punishment for sin will lead to more sin. This implication of the theory of *karma* de Nobili rejects.[96] Moreover, God cannot ordain a state of man conducive to sin as punishment for sin.

De Nobili makes out another argument against the theory of *karma* from what Hindus believe about it. He argues:

> ... whatever deeds done by man in this birth are only proportionate to whatever deeds done in a previous birth and not otherwise. Thus the man who had a previous birth will perform deeds which are proportionate to the deeds performed in that birth. This is what one has to say. Or else, one must say that a man does only a few deeds which correspond to the deeds of the previous state of life and that he does many other deeds *de novo* which do not come from the *karma* of previous birth.[97]

Implicit in this argument is the fact that the Hindus admit such deeds which man does in this life. De Nobili goes on to show the want of logic in the *karma* explanation of human actions which are supposed to be in part owing to *karma* of a previous state of existence and in part *de novo*:

> A certain person did twenty thousand deeds and died. What must be considered is this. One must accept that either all these twenty thousand deeds he did on account of the deeds he did in a previous birth or that one must say that this person did half of his actions, i.e., ten thousand deeds *de novo.*[98]

That means the second half of his actions have no cause in a previous birth. De Nobili, therefore, argues that the explanation accepted concerning one half of man's actions must also be accepted for the other half of his actions.[99] When one explanation is sufficient for the

---

[96] Ibid. p. 217.
[97] Ibid. p. 268.
[98] Ibid. p. 269.
[99] Ibid.

actions of man, there is no need to bring in the theory of *karma* to explain them. If one were to hold the view that man performs deeds in this life only corresponding to those of a previous life, it means that man does not do any action *de novo*, except as a result of deeds of the previous life.[100] This argument brings in quantification of virtue and sin. If one accepts this view, one admits determinism and loss of freedom which take away the meaning of all moral progress.

> One who was a virtuous man in a previous birth will only be a virtuous man in this life, in the subsequent births and for all time. As for an evil man, if he was a thief in a previous life it cannot but happen that he will be only a thief in this birth, in the next birth and always so.[101]

If one practised virtuous deeds (*tarmakiriyai*) in a previous state of existence, he will always, i.e., in all births do only virtuous deeds and be a virtuous man. So too a sinner will always be a sinner in all births. Thus one is condemned for ever to be a virtuous man or a sinner.[102] In this view virtue and sin are understood differently. An action done as a result of virtue in a previous birth is called virtue.[103]. So too sin is understood as an action done as a result of sin done in a previous birth. De Nobili means to say that accepting this one-to-one correspondence theory of *karma* is open to such an unacceptable definition of virtue and sin.

From the point of view of the psychology of moral action, a difficulty arises from the belief that the human soul can exist in animals or in plants. According to this belief, human soul in animals is incapable of knowing its sins, and therefore incapable of repenting of them. Besides this criticism, de Nobili criticises another point. One does not know the sins of a previous birth. Knowledge of the sin of a previous state of existence falls outside the personal imputability for one's sins.[104] De Nobili argues according to the meaning of repentance which means one should feel sorry for one's sins and give up the will to sin. This is a personal act with the knowledge of one's

---

100 Ibid. p. 270.

101 Ibid.

102 Ibid. pp. 270-271.

103 Ibid. p. 271.

104 Ibid. p. 222.

sins and acceptance of responsibility for them. One would not be capable of the personal act of repentance, if one were born an animal.

> If the erroneous point that a sinner is born as dog or other such animals, trees or stone is accepted, he cannot in such births know the sins committed by him and repent of them...[105]

Another argument de Nobili proposes from the point of view of the psychology of moral action against the theory of *karma* and rebirth concerns the chain of births in which one is excepted to remove one's sins. De Nobili says that this would encourage sin, since one may postpone repairing of sin to any number of births. Thus it would not be a perfect means of removing sin.[106]

If the theory of *karma* and belief in fate (*viti, lāṭalipi*) is accepted, then the good utterances on *dharma* in good scriptures will be futile.

> Since sinners would commit sin by necessity through the fixed rule of fate, virtuous utterances such as 'give up sin and before death comes to you perform virtue' written in scripture and other good books addressed to sinners, one must consider only futile utterances and unjust teachings.[107]

Moreover, the holy men, the teachers and saints would be to no purpose. Their principal work is to tell sinners "give up the path of unrighteousness of sin and walk in the perfect way of great righteousness." [108] But if man were to commit sin by necessity through the fixed rule of fate, then these counsels of *dharma* would become futile. On the one hand, such great men are needed for the world; on the other, with the admission of *karma* and fate, they are not at all needed for the world.[109]

---

[105] Ibid. p. 222.

[106] P.J.A. p. 75.

[107] A.N. p. 81. Here 'virtuous utterances' are called *tarmavākkiyankaḷ* (skt. *dharmavākyas*).

[108] Ibid.

[109] Ibid. p. 81. The original expression for 'unrighteousness of sin' is *pāvattinuṭaya atarmam*.

De Nobili rejects the prior state of existence according to the ways of human cognition. The *karma* of a previous birth is not accessible to the way of direct knowledge or perception (*pirattiyaccam*). Nor is it known through inferential knowledge (*anumānapiramāṇam*) as one would know the existence of fire from the sign (*anumānam*) of smoke.[110] If such a knowledge is not available, one turns to the *purāṇas* which speak of *karma* and rebirth. This evidence [111] is quite weak, since in the *purāṇas* one finds mutually contradictory things, and also things contrary to evident truth.[112] Among the learned men (*vittiyápạrākar*) all do not approve of all the *purāṇas*. Rather they approve of some things in them and reject others. Hence de Nobili says that the theory of *karma* is an error against reason.

d. *Relation Between Virtue and Prosperity and Sin and Suffering*

One principal difficulty de Nobili meets with in the theory of *karma* from the point of ethics is the close cause-and-effect relation between sin and suffering, virtue and prosperity.[113] Here we want to stress two points in connection with the karmic explanation of prosperity and suffering. i. That "through sin and virtue alone prosperity and suffering come to man who lives in the world" [114] is unacceptable, since it implies God doesn't rule the world with just order. This explanation does not include the possibility of suffering for the sake of righteousness without its being the result of sin committed in a previous birth, as it is stressed in Christianity. ii. If God were to reward materially for virtues, one would be making God party to a view which is not moral. In this connection, we may note what de Nobili says on the purpose of freedom. Freedom is needed for the salvation of man. God gave man the faculty of free-will concerning his choice of virtue and sin. Therefore the purpose of freedom in-

110 Ibid. p. 70. A.C. Danto., *Mysticism and Morality*, New York, 1972, pp. 41-42. He points out the difficulty of proving the existence of *karma*.

111 Evidence coming from word written or spoken is called *śabdapramāṇa* (testimony).

112 A.N. pp. 70-71. De Nobili gives the example of Saivites and Vaiṣṇavites. The former reject the *purāṇas* of Vaiṣṇavites, since they speak of Viṣṇu as the Supreme Being, and Vaisnavites reject the *purāṇas* of Saivites since they speak of Rudra as God.

113 P.J.A. p. 14.

114 Ibid. p. 74.

115 A.N. p. 87.

tended by God cannot be the enjoyment of long life and kingdom, since they can be obstacles to salvation and to the orderly conduct of the world.[115]

e. *The Theory of Karma and Origin of Castes*

We consider here de Nobili's interpretation of the existence of different castes in the world which was one of the principal reasons given for the proposal of the theory of karma.[116]

De Nobili refers to the myth of creation of the four *varṇas* (classes), *Brahmaṇas* (or Brahmins), *Kṣatryas, Vaiśyas* and *Śudras* from Brahma at the beginning of the world, as mentioned in the puranic tradition. He says this is how it is written in the *purāṇas:*

> Brahma generated from his head the first Brahmin, from his arm, thigh and feet, kings, *vaiśyas* and *Śudras* respectively...[117]

De Nobili says that in the *Yajur Veda*, in the sixth part, it is written: "When nothing existed, all things were created." [118] If this is the case, there was no world before creation and no men. It means that the Brahmins generated by Brahma were the first Brahmins without a previous state of existence. *Kṣatryas* thus generated by Brahama were the first *Kṣatryas* without previous birth. Such is the case with the first *Vaiśyas* and the first *Śudras* as generated from Brahma. To say then that these first men have a previous state of existence is unfounded. There could be no *karma* of a previous birth for them.[119] If on the contrary, one were to admit that Brahmins, *Kṣatryas, Vaiśyas* and *Śudras* were created in their respective conditions because of *karma* of previous birth, it would imply a self-contradiction that God created these men first and yet that they were not the first men.[120]

De Nobili explains the condition of men in different conditions created at the beginning without *karma*.

---

[116] P.J.A. p. 10.

[117] Ibid. p. 67, also ibid. p. 50. Here too de Nobili mentions the common belief concerning the origin of castes. Cf. Puruṣa sukta of Rg Veda.

[118] Ibid. Cf. I.C. p. 56. Here too the origin of castes is spoken in like manner.

[119] P.J.A. pp. 67-68.

[129] Ibid. p. 50.

If one considers the Brahmins created from the head of Brahma, one cannot say that they had another life before they were generated by Brahma, since they were the first Brahmins. As they had no previous birth, one cannot say that virtue done in that is the cause of their being born Brahmins.[121] Of the disease they suffered and the death they underwent while they lived on earth, there is no reason to consider the sin committed (in previous birth) to be the cause. In this manner, one cannot say that for the birth of their children and grand children as Brahmins, the virtue done by them was the cause.[122]

De Nobili applies the same argument to the origin of the low caste from the feet of Brahma. Thus *parayas* are not low-born because of sins committed in a previous birth.[123] Therefore Brahmins and men of low castes who live in the present life are in their respective conditions without previous birth and their good and bad deeds.[124] In the same way it could be said that men enjoy health or suffer sickness without a previous birth.[125]

Continuing his explanation of creation, de Nobili says that plants and animals too were created without previous birth. "Without a previous life in the world, man, animals and plants and inanimate things such as stone were created." [126] Implicit in the argument is the idea that plants and animals in the world were created owing to *karma*, since one could be born animal or plant on account of one's bad *karma*.[127]

The social nature of castes and their duties have their own sufficient reason, and therefore there is no need to bring in other explanations like that of *karma*. The karmic explanation of the world will involve the fallacy of *processus in infinitum*.

In the tradition of man, in order that one does not accept

---

[121] Ibid. p. 68. Cf. A.N. pp. 76-77. De Nobili explains the same point here.

[122] P.J.A.

[123] Ibid. p. 68.

[124] Ibid. p. 69.

[125] A.N. p. 275.

[126] P.J.A. p. 69.

[127] Ibid. p. 8, cf. ibid. Appendix, p. 2.

> the fault of *processus in infinitum*, one must admit that the Lord created some men at the very beginning".[128]

If the idea of creation is not admitted, then one will fall into the fault of *processus in infinitum* concerning former births and *karma*.

After explaining these arguments against the theory of *karma*, de Nobili goes on to explain the social purpose of the division of society into castes for which the theory of *karma* is not necessary. The world of men compared to a body must have different members for different functions. This is how de Nobili explains the purpose of men being in different conditions:

> For the well-being of the body, leg and head are necessary; without them the body cannot exist. If this is the case, it is doubtless a meaningless thing to say that a body can exist without leg and head. In like manner for the well-being of the body of the world, it is evident that there should be men of lowly condition and great men who are like leg and head respectively in the world. That men are in such different conditions is needed for the well-being of the world. If so, to say there was a circumstance in which men in such conditions did not exist would amount to saying that a body could exist without leg and head.[129]

In this manner de Nobili explains the social purpose of men being in different conditions. That there should be different states is an evident truth of social existence for de Nobili.[139] This is the order (*kiramam*) of the world which must exist and be maintained steadily. De Nobili considers that belief in previous birth, *karma* and rebirth could weaken this due order of the world. He argues against the theory on the basis of the free actions admitted by it.[131] The follow-

---

[128] A.N. p. 76. *Anavastai tōṣam* means here *processus in infinitum*. Ibid. p. 599. Fr Beschi renders the expression *anavastai tōṣam* of de Nobili as *processus in infinitum*.

[129] Ibid. p. 229. P.J.A. Append. p. 9.

[130] P.J.A. p. 54. Belief in *karma* would mean that without men in low castes, who are the feet of the body of the world, the world existed. It would be an error.

[131] In a former state of existence, actions are newly and freely done. De Nobili takes up this part of *karma* theory and shows that the logical consequence of the admission of free actions is that it could nullify the order of the world. Cf. also A.N. p. 229.

ers of this belief claim that those who are kings etc., did meritorious acts of virtue with free will in a previous birth. They also affirm that their present fortunes are the fruit of real virtues performed in a previous birth.[132] De Nobili takes up their statement that "those who now enjoy the fortunes of kingdom, etc., did in previous births true virtuous acts without compulsion and free will." [133] De Nobili argues from this that they had free will:

> If one considers the virtues performed by each one by his own free will in a previous birth, one must accept (the possibility) that each need not do such virtuous deeds. If one admits that each man need not do such virtues, it would amount to saying that those who are in the state of kings, etc., need not be in the world.[134]

Then de Nobili takes up the case of those socially low who are said to be in this condition because they commited sin by their own free will in a previous birth.

> That is to say, one should say either that the actions done by necessity, and therefore no sins, were punishment or that in a previous birth the sinner by his own free will did sin. If so, we can admit that the sinner need not commit such sins. If we admit that no sin occurs, it must also be accepted that those who serve and those socially low need not be in the world.[135]

De Nobili argues that the order of the world should not be made to depend on the free actions of men done in a previous birth which take away the ground of stability of the world order and previsibility.[136]

---

132 A.N. p. 228.

133 Ibid.

134 Ibid., P.J.A. p. 54.

135 A.N. p. 229.

136 *Liberum arbitrium* of men in previous birth cannot be the foundation of world order or order of human society. If it were subject to the free choices of men in the previous birth, the stability of world order or that of society would be destroyed. Cf. P.J.A. p. 54. A.C. Danto, op. cit. p. 32. "It is dismal to reflect that there must always be enough people whose *karma* is evil if any work is to be done."

To account for the difference of conditions of men, visible cause must be accepted. De Nobili argues that if cause and effect are both seen to be immediately evident, one need not accept that which is not seen.[137] Thus if one suffers capital punishment, it is due to his crime in the present life, which is a sufficient reason to explain the punishment. That is how justice is administered in the world.[138]

f. *Functional interpretation of the Myth of Creation*

De Nobili refers to the *māyāvādins* who tend to interpret the myth of the creation of the classes of men in a literal way.[139] But he goes on to explain the meaning of the myth in a functional sense. When they say that Brahmins and the other *varṇas* arise from different parts of God, they mean to establish the different functions of *varṇas*. De Nobili says that he finds that people (here in India) are accustomed to employing frequently allegories by way of commentary. He finds that they explain the duties of the four *varṇas* in this way through the use of allegory as a sort of commentary.[140] De Nobili explains the functional meaning of the origin of castes from God in this way:

> And so they narrated that God created the Brahmins from the face or head which is the seat of wisdom, the kings from the shoulder which is the sinewy centre of fortitude, the merchants from the thigh which is the symbol of fecundity, the plebeians from the feet, who placed under the others support the rest of the body.[141]

---

137 P.J.A. p. 56.

138 A.N. p. 216.

139 I.C. pp. 56, 58. The argument de Nobili faces here is that because Brahmins are born from the head or face of Brahma, they should be priests. If this were accepted, it would make all the four castes priests, holy men and gods.

140 Ibid. p. 56. "Ut enim apto commento (quippe solent hi frequenter huiusmodi allegoriis uti) ut (inquam) scito invento explicarent officia quatuor civilium ordinum..." Cf. *Raguali d'Alcune Missione Fatte Dalli Padri della Compagnia di Giesu Nell India Orietali*, Roma 1615, p. 110. The same fable of creation of castes is mentioned here.

141 I.C. pp. 56-57. "... dixerunt Deum creare Brahmanes ex facie seu ex capite quod est sedes sapientiae, Reges ex humero qui nervus est fortitudinis, mercatores ex faemore quod est symbolum feacunditatis, Plebeios ex pedibus, qui reliquum corpus subditi substentant."

This is the functional meaning attached to the origin of castes from the different parts of God. De Nobili finds support for this interpretation in Manu. He says that Manu himself resorted to the symbolic manner of speaking when he wanted to speak of the diversity of creation. He quotes Manu (1, 31) and translates it thus:

> Contemplating the beauty of the world, God created the Brahmins, the kings, the merchants and the plebeians from head, from shoulder, from thigh and from feet respectively.[142]

De Nobili sees in this the beauty of orderly functions. In the text the word 'world' (*lokam*) means according to a commentary "assembly of men." [143] When it is said "God contemplated the beauty of the world", it means He contemplated the beauty of the community of men. Manu himself explains what he means by the creation of different castes from head, from arm, from thigh, from feet for the sake of the beauty of the world.[144] He notes that men discharge different functions, some as head, some as arm, some as thigh and some as feet as it were of the body and that this concerns the beautiful constitution of the world.[145] Manu explains this in a verse clearly:

> With a view to protecting the world which he (God) was creat-

---

[142] Ibid. p. 57. "Id est, mundi pulchritudinem intuitus Deus ex facie, ex humero, ex femore, ex pedibus, Brahmanes, Reges, Mercatores, Plebeios creavit..." The text is from Manu 1, 31. Cf. Bühler, pp. 13-14. "But for the sake of prosperity of the worlds, he caused Brahmana, the Kśatrya, the Vaiśya, and the Śudra to proceed from his mouth, his arms, his thighs, and his feet."

Biihler cf. f. n. 31 on pp. 13-14. Bühler says the commentator Nārāyna explains *lokavivriddhyartham* to mean "for the sake of the prosperity of the worlds" by *varṇair lokarakshanasamvardhanartham* which means "to protect the world by means of the castes and to make it prosperous." Other commentators like Kulluka, Govindaraja interpret the phrase to mean "in order that (the inhabitants) of the world might multiply." One can meaningfully remember the etymology of *dharma* (*dhr* = to bear, to support) here. The purpose of social *dharma* is *lokasangraha*.

[143] I.C. p. 57. "... ubi notat commentum ibi dici Mundum, ipsam hominum congregationem."

[144] Ibid.

[145] Ibid. "Quid autem intelligat Manu per hoc quod dicit originem stirpium fuisse ex capite, ex humero, etc. propter mundi pulchritudinem explicat ipsemet distinctius in alio versu, quod nimirum ad mundi pulchram constitutionem pertineat, ut ratione officii quod exercent quaedam stirpes caput, quaedam humeros quaedam femur, quaedam pedes huius quasi corporis representent."

> ing, he assigned different duties to different castes, some as the head, some as the shoulder, some as the thigh and some as the feet.[146]

Commenting on the verse, the commentator confirms the same view by saying that Manu wanted to explain in the first place "the office of different castes"[147] and thus establish *dharma* (office or duty) of the different castes. The word referring to the world in the verse is *prapañcam* which means the "congregation of men" (the aggregate of men).[148] De Nobili translates the word for the world in the verse of Manu as *Universitas*. The commentator continues further that the symbols of the head, the arm, the thigh and the feet refer to the highness or lowliness of the *varṇas* and their offices. This again shows that the myth of creation of the *varṇas* from God concerns the explanation of social function, and not the actual creation of men from different parts of God. The text that de Nobili quotes from the commentator runs like this:

> He (Manu) says that Brahmins, kings, merchants and Plebeians are as it were the head, the arm, the thigh, and the feet and that Brahmins are the head. Therefore he says that it is clear from this that different nobility or obscurity results from the function of the castes.[149]

Thus the presentation of the origin of castes is allegorical, and it refers to the social *dharma* and the varying degrees of dignity attached to each *varṇa* on account of office.

---

[146] Ibid. "i.e. Universitati quam creabat prospiciens diversum officium, diversis stirpibus tribuit, ut quaedam veluti caput, quaedam humeri, quaedam femur quaedam pedes essent." (M, I, 87). Bühler, p. 24. He in his translation (M.I. 87) refers to the castes as having arisen from head, shoulder, thighs and feet. But de Nobili understands the head, the shoulder, thighs and feet as referring to the different functions of the four castes. They are the allegory of their functions. Cf. P.J.A. Append. p. 9. De Nobili says that Divine Providence has put different men in different conditions for the preservation and good government of society.

[147] I.C. The skt. phrase is "varṇa dharma niyamo 'bi prapañcam" which he translates as "variarum stirpium officium."

[148] Ibid. p. 57.

[149] Ibid. p. 57. i.e. quod ait esse Brahmanes, Reges, Mercatores et Plebeios veluti caput et humerum, et foemur, et pedes, caput vero esse Brahmanes, etc. ideo dicit ut ex eo appareat varia ex officio stirpium nobilitas, aut obscuritas."

De Nobili says that the functional interpretation of the origin of castes is also found in the law-book of the *māyāvādins* called Yajur,[150] which is almost the same as that found in *Manu smṛti.* De Nobili gives its meaning as follows:

> The world (it is the assembly of mortal men) was created by God in such a way that the head of the world should be Brahmins, the shoulder the kings, the thigh the merchants, etc. as above.[151]

The same author continues with his account of creation: "From him (namely from God) came forth *Virāta*. *Virāta* is the very *puruṣa* (which term means man)."[152] That the first man is *puruṣa* is further interpreted to mean "the assembly of men." [153] The commentary on the word *puruṣa* goes like this:

> The word *puruṣa* means the very assembly of men, namely, all those who had been and all those who will be.[153]

De Nobili quotes another text from the same author which also points out the functional interpretation of the myth of creation of castes from God. The author asks:

> Which is the face in this *puruṣa* or universal assembly of men? Which the shoulder? Which the thigh? Which the feet?" [155]

---

[150] Ibid. p. 58. De Nobili gives the references as *Egesu primo Arana*. So far de Nobili gave argument from *smṛti*, especially Manu for the functional interpretation. Here he refers to the testimony of the *Veda*, to the *Yajur-veda* in particular. *Egesu* is the *Yajur veda* and *Arana* is the *Aranyaka*.

[151] Ibid. p. 58. "Nimirum mundum esse creatum a Deo (hoc est mortalium congregationem) ita ut mundi caput sint Brahmanes, humerus Reges, femur mercatores, etc., ut supra."

[152] Ibid. p. 58. "ab ipso (scilicet Deo) processit Viratha, Viratha autem est ipse Puruscen (quae vox hominem significat)."

[153] Ibid. "totam hominum multitudinem."

[154] Ibid. p. 59. "Puruscen vox est ipsa hominum universitas omnes scilicet qui fuerunt erunt."

[155] Ibid."Huius Puruscenis seu universitatis hominum facies quae est? qui sunt humeri? quod femur? qui pedes?"

To this question he himself gives the answer as follows:

> The Brahmin is his face, the king is his shoulder, the merchant
> is his thigh, finally the plebeians are his feet.[156]

From all this evidence de Nobili shows that the allegory of creation
of the four *varṇas* from God serves only to explain the division of
office and dignity men have in society like the members of a human
body.[157]

g. *The Order of Civil Society and the Division of Classes*

De Nobili explains the order of civil society on the analogy of
the human body with its different members, all working together for
the good of the whole body. That men are in different conditions
and that God created them is explained with the idea of the world
as macrocosm and the human body as microcosm by him.[158] He
says that the saying that "all that is present in the microcosm (*piṇṭam*) is present in macrocosm (*aṇṭam*) and that all that is present in
macrocosm" is present in microcosm is commonly accepted among
the people in India.[159] De Nobili says that the meaning of the saying
is that it is the order conformable to the intelligence of God who
rules the world.[160] He explains further by giving the meaning of *aṇṭam* and *piṇṭam*. "The name *piṇṭam* applies to the body of man; the
world has the name of *aṇṭam*." [161] Therefore "the meaning of the
saying that "all that is present in *piṇṭam*" is that all that is present in
the small world of the body is also present in the big body of the
world." [162] De Nobili sums up the meaning of the analogy of microcosm and macrocosm:

> Thus just as different members are needed for the well-being
> of the small world (*piṇṭam*), so too for the perfect operation of

---

[156] Ibid. "Brahmen est illius facies, Rex est eius humerus, mercator est femur, Plebei denique pedes sunt."

[157] Ibid. p. 59.

[158] Cf. A.N. pp. 287-290. For the idea of microcosm and macrocosm. Cf. also P.J.A. pp.
55-56, 82-84.

[159] P.J.A. p. 82.

[160] Ibid.

[161] Ibid.

[162] Ibid. p. 82, A.N. p. 287.

> the big body (*anṭam*), there should necessarily be the different members, i.e., men in different states.[163]

This is how the idea of a well-ordered society and its efficient fuctioning is explained on the analogy of the human body. If this order were wanting, men in the world would not be able to live.[164]

Then de Nobili says that no one would dare ask God, the Creator of the human body, why he has created and ordained the head, eyes, mouth, hands and feet in such diverse manners and positions.[165] He explains the purpose of different positions of the different members of the body in the form of an address of God to the above-mentioned question:

> O foolish man, how can the body function well if in the body (*piṇṭam*) which is like a microcosm, the different members in different positions of above and below and with many differences do not exist? It does not. Hence my will for the well-being of the body is the cause of the different members of the body like microcosm, to be in different positions of high and low.[166]

The same purpose of God one can undestand with regard to the big body-*anṭam* (the world):

> Just as for the microcosm of the body the head is needed, so too for the body of the macrocosm, there should be kings and such men in high position. For the well-being of the microcosm of the body, there should be eyes. In like manner, for the well-being of the body of the macrocosm, there should necessarily be without fail Brahmins and other learned men and spiritual men who are the eyes. Moreover, for the proper well-being of the microcosm of the body without any deficiency, it must possess mouth. So too for the perfect well-being of the macrocosm, great souls who correspond to the mouth must exist in the world.[167]

---

163 A.N. p. 287, P.J.A. Appendix p. 9.

164 P.J.A. p. 83

165 Ibid.

166 Ibid. p. 83.

167 A.N. pp. 287-288. In explaining the different conditions of men, de Nobili is not fol-

Continuing the explanation of the image of the microcosm and macrocosm, de Nobili says that since the spiritual masters teach ignorant men the way of righteous conduct for salvation, they correspond to the mouth in the human body.[168] If in the body of the world the spiritual teachers (*gurus*) are the mouth because they teach the way of righteous conduct for salvation, there should be disciples to hear the teachers:

> Moreover, just as for the microcosms of the body an ear is necessary, there should also be disciples who are the ears and who will hear the teaching (of the gurus).[169]

According to the same image of microcosm and macrocosm, the farmers and others who serve and many others who do numberless jobs are needed for the life of the world.[170] In the same way, like the leg for the body, for the proper functioning of the world, those of low castes are needed. Without them, the world cannot go on.[171]

De Nobili then tries to answer an objection. One could ask God: "Lord, why do you make so many members in the body which is a microcosm?" [172] Or one could ask: "if head is the perfect member and the eye also a good member, why didn't you make throughout the body the perfect member and eyes?" [173] The answer is this: "If the whole body is the head, where is the leg for walking? If the whole body is the eye, where are the hands which do different works for the sake of one's livelihood?" [174] If the members of the

---

lowing the hierarchy of the different *varṇas* as present in the allegory of creation. Here he says that the kings are like the head of the macrocosm and that Brahmins and wise men are the eyes, whereas in the myth of creation of *varṇas* Brahmins are the head and kings are the arm. We point out here that the idea of microcosm and macrocosm is not particularly Indian. It is also a Stoic concept. Cf. M. Spaneut, *Permanence du Stoicism*, Gembloux 1973, pp. 185-186.

[168] De Nobili is careful to stress the role of spiritual masters (*gurus*) in teaching the way of salvation to God. Cf. also P.J.A. p. 83.

[169] A.N. p. 288. Though de Nobili explained the origin of castes from God as an allegory of social functions and different states of nobility, he prefers the image of microcosm and macrocosm, since it is more flexible to explain the many different functions of men in society.

[170] Ibid.

[171] Ibid. De Nobili's explanation does not bear on the social discrimination of the low castes but on the mutual interdependence of different functions in society for its well-being.

[172] Ibid. p. 289.

[173] Ibid. p. 288.

[174] Ibid.

body are not in different positions, some above, some below, the body cannot carry on its work. So too in the big body of the world, men are in different conditions, some in the position of kings, some as servants, some rich, some poor.[175] If one were to ask why God created men in such different conditions, the answer would run like this:

> It is clear that kings who are like the head are in a higher condition like the perfect member (head). But if all like the head are kings, where are the farmers who cultivate crops and those who do other such works for the life of the world? If we consider Brahmins, the learned and spiritual masters who are like the eyes, we say that such men are perfect men, high in the social status and worthy of respect of men. But if all of us are Brahmins and the learned, there won't be men of low caste in lowly state, who are like the leg that is meant for walking on earth for the life of all, in the world.[176]

Therefore, if men do not exist in different conditions, the world which is like a human body would not survive.

In the above explanation of different conditions of men in the world on the analogy of microcosm and macrocosm, the cause is shown to be the order of the world which is required for the harmonious functioning of the world. It is not to be found in the intrinsic constitution of man owing to *karma* of a previous state of existence. This also means that men being in different conditions is a matter of convention or agreement of men (*lōkacankētam*) in the world. Hence that men are in different conditions is not to be attributed to difference in the nature of men. One could speak of different species (*cātis*) among plants and animals. But castes (*cātis*) among men are not to be understood in like manner. In the former they differ in nature. But castes among men have nothing to do with difference in nature, since all men are of the same nature. The difference in conditions of men in society is entirely due to convention (*lōkacankētam*):

> Since all men have souls of the same nature and bodies of the

---

[175] Ibid.

[176] Ibid. pp. 289-290, P.J.A. PP. 83-84. The same idea is expressed here.

> same nature, castes are said to be entirely due to convention of men in the world.[177]

That there are different castes among men for the sake of order in the world and that it is due to convention or agreement of men are also in conformity with God's will. One could also object to God's partiality in creating some in high state and others in low state. As an answer to this objection, the theory of *karma* is proposed to account for different conditions of nobility and lowliness of men in the world.[178] Since the theory of *karma* is unacceptable, de Nobili refers to the order of human society (*lōkakiramam*) and interdependence. This requires that men be in different conditions. If equal social dignity is sought after by all men out of envy, human society will not go on just as the leg and hands which fail to do their work will lead to the ruin of the body and their own destruction.[179]

The interdependence is further explained as follows. The work of one member of the body helps the other members and thus the whole body. De Nobili uses the example of stomach. If hands and legs were to say that they would not work for the stomach, they themselves would die for each member has a particular function redounding to the good of the other members and of the whole body.[180] This analogy applies to the big body of human society. Thus:

> Those who carry palanquin, the farmers who cultivate and others who do different menial works are like the members hands and feet and that these work so that benefit comes to those rulers who are like the stomach.[181]

After this de Nobili goes on to say:

> When we consider those who serve mutually and those who

[177] A.N. p. 267. *Kāṇṭam II*, p. 15. Here de Nobili discusses the idea of species among angels. Each angel is a species (*cāti*) by itself. But *cātis* (castes) among men are different from the classes (*cātis*) among angels, since the former is based on convention of men. *Cāti* is the Tamil form of skt.-*Jāti*.

[178] A.N. p. 291.

[179] Ibid. pp. 291, 293.

[180] Ibid. p. 293.

[181] Ibid. pp. 293-294.

> mutually receive services, it is clear among them that one lives through (the help) of another.[182]

The kings receive taxes, etc. from farmers and other citizens. In turn, the farmers and citizens receive aid and protection and have justice meted out to them in a fair way.

> Therefore, that men in different conditions like different members (of a body) doing different jobs work for kings and lords who are inactive like the stomach is the order required for the going-on of the world and the means of special good for everyone. Because of this order one cannot impute partiality to God, nor can it be said that such order came through sin and virtue performed in a previous birth.[183]

If this order is the explanation, one cannot say that God who is the father of all men, condemned some to a low state and gave others a higher status.

---

[182] Ibid. p. 294.
[183] Ibid. pp. 296-297.

CHAPTER THREE

DHARMA AND MORAL NORMS

We have so far considered *dharma* in the sense of objective duties and virtues in different spheres of human behaviour - social, ethical and religious. We shall examine the normative grounding of *dharma* in Hinduism [1] and de Nobili's critique of it.

a. *Moral Standards*

i. *Tradition*

De Nobili in his critique of *dharma* in Hinduism shows that tradition imposes many of the duties and observances. Men observe them because it is a tradition handed down from generation to generation. Thus if a tradition is long-standing, it becomes a legitimate custom or observance. One is convinced that a long-standing tradition which one's ancestors have been observing from time immemorial must be good. There is a kind of norm in this for knowing what is good.[2] But tradition cannot be an unambiguous criterion of knowing what is morally good and bad. De Nobili gives an example. That a woman who is married behaves like a wife to the brothers of her husband is considered right or legitimate because it has been observed from time immemorial. Such is the case with polygamy.[3]

---

[1] Haecker, art. cit. p. 99. Though the Hindu idea of *dharma* is basically empirical, ethically normative questions are not entirely absent. Cf. the discussion on 'final end' in this chapter. Cf. Tähtinen, op. cit., pp. 75-76 on the same point.

[2] I.C. p. 113. Manu (2,18) whom de Nobili quotes has this idea: "The custom handed down in regular succession (since time immemorial) among the (four chief) castes (*varṇa*) and the mixed (races) of that country, is called the conduct of the virtuous men." Cf. Bühler, p. 32.

[3] T.T. p. 391. Cf. ibid. p. 50.

The legitimation of such customs is seen in the idea that it is observance proper to a country (*deśa ācāra*) and observance and duty proper to a clan or family (*kuladharma*).[4] De Nobili admits that a duty or an observance of a clan or of a family in a region could be legitimate and right. Therefore, he respects in general the *dharma* of a region or of a family or a clan. In his first defence of his method of adaptation, he speaks of the principle of adapting oneself to the customs of people or of a country in support of which he quotes not only Christian authority [5] but also the authority of *smṛti*. The latter text he quotes, runs as follows:

> That every one must adapt himself in the country where one lives to its customs which are handed on from ancient times is proper.[6]

This is one of the sources of *dharma* mentioned by Manu.[7] De Nobili recognises this principle while defending the legitimacy of wearing the tuft of hair on the head. He quotes from the *Apastamba Sūtra* which says that the tuft of hair is to be worn on the head according to the fact that one is head or chief of the family and that it is a distinctive mark of the family.[8] This observance belongs to *kuladharma*. De Nobili understands the legitimacy of *kuladharma* and *deśa ācāra* according to certain criteria. His criteria of acceptability and therefore of legitimacy of customs of countries and families are in terms of teleological ethics. Hence de Nobili always examines the purpose (*finis*) of an observance or of what is called *dharma*. His criteria of legitimacy and acceptability move on two levels: First, an observance is socially meaningful or it has some purpose. Secondly,

---

[4] Ibid. p. 391.

[5] Pr. Ap. pp. 105-106. De Nobili cites *Decretalia Gregorii IX* which speaks of the need for adaptation. Cf. *Narratio*, p. 36. Here he recognises that social customs of long-standing can have the force of law.

[6] Pr. Ap. p. 106. "Unisquisque in regione, in qua vivit ad illius mores ex antiquitate protractos se effingere justum est." Cf. I.C. p. 113 where the text is from Manu (2,18). It is probably the same text that is cited in Pr. Ap. here.

[7] Manu (1,108) says that the traditional custom is the highest *dharma* (*ācārah paramo dharmah*). Cf. V.S. Sukthankar: *On the Meaning of Mahābhārata*, p. 79. Ibid. *Dharma* is that which has its origin in orthodox custom.

[8] I.C. p. 81. "Iuxta caput seu ducem familiae coruminum in capite relinquatur. Atque adeo his familiis coruminum sit peculiaris familiae proprium signum."

it does not involve sin nor does it go against right reason, i.e., what is observed is morally right. It is according to these criteria that de Nobili examines the observances and customs of countries and families and also observances in the sphere of religion which, moreover, have their own criterion of true religion.

De Nobili proceeds in this manner with regard to the rules of purity and defilement. He finds these rules with regard to lower classes legitimate in so far as they have an anthropological meaning. He explains it as follows: a matter like this, and many others are founded on the estimation of men. Here in India to stand before the king with bare head would be considered an insult to him.[9] De Nobili says that no one can directly find out on what such customs are based, especially if one cannot find their author or their purpose.[10] He says that it is tradition which presumably comes from antiquity, a habit which confirms it and a certain inclination of the soul which helps observe it.[11] Here he gives an example of a tradition which is authorless and whose purpose is not clear. One cannot stand before a prince with bare head, for it would be an insult to the king. In the customs according to which the higher classes take a bath after coming into contact with men of lower classes [12], their purpose and author are not to be found. These customs start with certain ideas of cleanliness and men's estimation which in the course of time becomes a tradition if observed over a period of many generations. Habit and the inclination of men confirm their regular practice. De Nobili argues that it is legitimate, since every country has such customs. For legitimacy thus understood in an anthropological sense, the only positive moral criterion is that it is according to the order of right reason and true religion. De Nobili uses these criteria with regard to certain customs which are unacceptable and which are otherwise justified on the grounds of tradition alone:

Thus they (the Hindus) consider killing a scorpion and the

---

[9] *Narratio*, pp. 168-170. "... hanc, et quam plures alias civiles consuetudines fundari in hominum existimatione. Quam enim immunditiem contraxerunt manus chirothecis contectae, ut aqua illa purgemus antequam comedamus? ... In India vero ante regem discoperto capite sistere nefas est?"

[10] Ibid. p. 170. "Si auctorem vel finem quaeras, non invenies."

[11] Ibid. p. 170.

[12] Ibid. p. 169.

> cobra that kills a man by its bite a great sin whereas they consider asking women to accept *sati* and pushing them into fire a virtue. They consider touching an outcast and seeing him at midday a sin and regard desiring a woman other than one's own as normal.[13]

The reason for such a consideration is that they have been observed as long-standing traditions. One could refer to the custom of temple prostitution which is considered virtue.[14] These customs and observances are not merely social, for in this sense they could be legitimate. Since they are described as sin and virtue, they come under the criteria of morality and have to be judged accordingly. De Nobili considers that they have not used the criterion of right reason and the definition of sin and virtue. He notes that they consider observances which are not sin to be sin; those that are sins are considered to be virtue by them. No moral criterion is adduced for their justification. Desiring a woman other than one's own wife is considered virtuous unquestioningly. This is a case where tradition alone is not sufficient to decide what is virtue and what is sin, since through tradition what is not sin appears as sin and what is clearly a sin appears as virtue. In these cases one does not pay attention to the order of right reason.[15] Unless one uses this further criterion besides that of tradition, one does not have the guarantee of knowing right and wrong. Tradition could be a source of knowledge of right and wrong and a criterion only in a relative sense, since tradition itself needs to be justified by the further criterion of right reason. One cannot always judge correctly that something is morally good or bad simply because it is an accepted tradition.

ii. *Obligation through Prescription in the Law-Books and Scriptures*

We shall now consider how de Nobili understands the prescription of duties and observances through the law-books and scriptures

---

13 T.T. p. 51, I.C. p. 48. *Parāśara Smṛti* prescribes expiations for Brahmins for touching or looking at a *Caṇḍāla*. Kane Vol. I, p. 193. He says that *Parāśara Smṛti* eulogises the practice of Suttee.

14 T.T. p. 391.

15 Ibid. pp. 390-391. De Nobili uses the phrase *niyāya kiramam* for 'the order of right reason.'

of the Hindus. The laws concerning social and religious duties and observances with their rituals are found in different books. For social and civil duties, the principal source for de Nobili is the Laws of *Manu, Āpastamba Sūtra* and *smṛti* books of this kind.[16] Generally all the books that deal with social and civil duties are called *dharmaśāstras* whose meaning is moral science and science of principles of behaviour.[17] De Nobili quotes abundantly from Manu. In this connection, de Nobili notes that these *dharmaśāstras* do not consider the theoretical questions of morality. He says that theoretical questions of ethics are discussed in the section called Philosophy. De Nobili has in mind *Cintāmaṇi* of Gangeśa.[18] He says that it corresponds to natural philosophy. We shall consider how de Nobili understands prescription of social and civil duties through such law-books, and how the ritual observances come to be interpreted through the sacred books of the Hindus. We begin with the prescription of duties enjoined by *dharmaśāstras*.

De Nobili argues in general that the Scriptures could be a legitimate source of the knowledge of duties and a normative guide, though in a relative sense. He remarks that *dharmaśāstras* also called *nīti śāstra* means 'science of civil law.'[19] *Dharmaśāstras* have collected civil duties and observances which are found scattered in different law-books. The important point is that these laws are accepted

---

[16] De Nobili explains the *dharma* of the Hindus principally from the *smṛti* sources but he is also aware that the *Veda* is the first source of *dharma*. According to Manu (2,6) the whole of the *Veda* is the source of *dharma*. De Nobili draws upon sections of the *Yajur Veda* (e.g. on the origin of the four castes) Cf. I.C. p. 58; on the gift to be given to one's teacher, ibid. p. 61. Cf. Caland, pp. 40, 43, 45-46 for texts of the *Vedas* cited or alluded to by de Nobili. De Nobili draws mostly on *Manu Smṛti* which enjoys the highest authority on civil laws, customs and duties of castes. Besides, he draws upon other law-books such as *Apastamba gṛhyasutra, Paraśara Smṛti, purāṇas* and *kāvyas*.

[17] I.C. p. 26. "Octava Disciplina est quam vocant Dharmaśāstram, cuius vocis interpretatio est scientia de moribus.

[18] Ibid. Since *dharmaśāstras* do not deal with theoretical questions of ethics, one is likely to say that there is no section of ethics in the Hindu Scriptures. De Nobili refers to Gangesa's *Cintāmaṇi*, part 3 which is partly metaphysics and partly moral philosophy. Ibid. p. 23. *Cintamaṇi* referred to by de Nobili is *Tattvacinṭāmaṇi* of Gangeśa. Cf. Caland, R. De Nobilis Bekendheit met het Sanskrit en met de sanskrit-Teksten," *Verslagen en Mededeelingen der K.Ak. van Wetenschappen*, 5e Reeks, Reel 3, Amsterdam, 1918, p. 333.

[19] This refers to *Manu dharmaśāstra*. Cf. I.C. p. 26.

as binding and as having the force of law.[20] The *dharmaśāstras* contain the division of castes and the assignment of duties according to castes, different manners and points of behaviour and those things that pertain to the administration of the city and the kingdom.[21] They have the same force of law, and all are expected to obey them. De Nobili also perceives the means to enforce the laws and observances given in *dharmaśāstras*. Brahmins are expected to be experts in these matters, especially in *dharmaśāstras*, and to help kings know the laws, since the kings are to see to the observance of the laws prescribed. This means that what has been enjoined in the law-books has a binding force which Brahmins are expected to make known to the kings, of which neither Brahmins nor kings are the authors. The same authority and binding force apply to the rules concerning monastic life, civil virtue of ordinary citizens and the economic (household) life. *Dharmaśāstras* prescribe them.[22] They are the source of law and also of moral behaviour.

The prescription of duties and virtues through the *dharmaśāstras* also involve sanctions and punishments for violations. Thus for example if a Brahmin looks upon a common priest (a non-Brahmin), an act of expiation is prescribed.[23] So too the punishment of death is given for the crime of murder to any one, young or old, teacher or Brahmin according to the law of Manu.[24] Our purpose in referring

---

[20] I.C. "*Vim legis*". Bühler, p. 27. Manu (1,108): "The rule of conduct is transcendent law whether it be taught in the revealed texts or in the sacred tradition; hence a twice-born man who possesses regard for himself, should be always careful to (follow) it."

[21] I.C. "Itaque et divisiones officiorum et stirpium, et eorum varii mores et cultus, et demum quidquid ad civitatis et regni gubernationem pertinent in his libris continetur. Cf. also Pr. Ap. p. 119.

[22] I.C. p. 26. "... in iisque peritos Brahmanes cum quid decernere volunt Reges audiunt." Also ibid. "Verum quidem est multa etiam in his libri praecipi quae pertinent tum ad monasticam hoc est privatorum hominum civilem virtutem, tum ad oeconomicam."

[23] Ibid. p. 46. "Si quis publicos deorum sacerdotes vel in ipso meridie aspexerit solem aspicito." P.V. Kane: *History of Dharmaśāstras* vol. II, part I, 1941, p. 109. Kane remarks that in modern times people call *Brāhmaṇas* a priestly caste. This is not accurate. "All Brahmanas never were nor are priests." According to him temple priests are comparatively a later institution. They were generally looked down upon in ancient times. They are regarded as inferior even in these times.

[24] I.C. p. 51. Cf. Bühler, p. 315. According to Manu (8,350) "one may slay without hesitation an assassin who approaches (with murderous intent), whether (he be one's) teacher, a child, or an aged man, or a *Brāhmaṇa* deeply versed in the Vedas." Cf. I.C. p. 51. De Nobili

to these texts is to show that what is enjoined in the law-books is accepted to have the force of law.

Sometimes the idea of sacredness of books helps enforce a law or a practice. For example, de Nobili refers to the sect of idolators (*māyāvādins*). They attribute divine authorship to their books in order to ensure observance and respect.[25] De Nobili is aware of such a practice among the ancients in the West. Minos drew up laws for Cretans from the cave of Jupiter. Lycurgus made Apollo of Delphi the author of the law he gave to Spartans.[26] De Nobili explains how this tradition arose in the East and the West of giving divine authorship of the law-books, or of making laws sacred in order to ensure obedience to them. But de Nobili's criterion as to whether a law is right or wrong is not the sacredness of the law of the scriptures which prescribe the law but their purpose. If the purpose of the law concerns the good of society and if it is in conformity with right reason, or if it is in consonance with true religion, then it can be accepted. Sacredness by itself is not a clear criterion, since in the name of sacredness morally unacceptable practices could be enjoined. Nor is sacredness to be understood with regard to pagan customs a sure criterion of their badness.[27] In this context, against the objection that pagan customs which go with the authority of pagan religion are *ipso facto* wrong, de Nobili says that pagan customs need not necessarily be wrong, since they deal with many social and civil matters and even with things that are compatible with true religion.[28] This confirms de Nobili's view that something is not bad because it is of gentile or of pagan origin or religion. There need to be further criteria of right reason and true religion.

Though de Nobili understands the idea that scriptures alone are insufficient as a criterion of rightness, he, however, resorts to the

---

refers to *Scanda Prahasa* in which the type of crimes called *Atatai* are enumerated: ingratitude in a grave matter, desertion of one's parents in their old age, acceptance of stipend by Brahmins.

[25] I.C. p. 36.

[26] Ibid.

[27] De Nobili is reacting against the idea that whatever is 'pagan' must be wrong. The content of pagan customs must be further examined to determine if they are wrong in a moral sense or against true religion.

[28] I.C. p. 36. "Fateor, sed quid- an idcirco non etiam profana mereque civilia agunt? an non pleraque docent de moribus, an non multa, verae religioni consentanea et nostris hominibus praecipiunt..."

Hindu scriptures to show if they are good or bad. He says that it is on the scriptures written in Sanskrit one draws for the meaning and definition of (Hindu) words and ideas.[29] He does not reject the Hindu scriptures or any pagan books for the simple reason they are gentile scriptures. Moreover, he says that in different religions, there are some right utterances (*tarmavākkiyankaḷ*) together with prescription of some morally unacceptable observances. Therefore, one cannot appeal to them. They err in the matter of forbidding sin. De Nobili, in his apologetic for Christianity stresses the weak points of the *purāṇas* which have stories that are not so edifying.[30] If this is the case, the written scriptures cannot be always an unerring source of morality. Since what is prescribed in their books is a mixture of good and bad things, one should not consider the things prescribed by them bad by the very fact that they are found in pagan scriptures. De Nobili's argument goes like this: Something found in pagan scriptures by itself cannot be the criterion of goodness or badness. The goodness or badness of a thing prescribed has to be judged according to its nature and right reason.[31] This could be exemplified in the case of the utterance recommending *ahiṁsā*. *Ahiṁsā* is called the highest *dharma* and the torture of living beings *adharma.*[32] Just because an utterance like this exists, one cannot be sure that it leads to correct understanding of *dharma* and *adharma*. The first part of the saying does not bring out the difficulty but the second part does for hurting any living being is *adharma*. This is not to deny the possibility of such statement serving as norms of action, but we are interested in the foundation of moral norms. *Ahiṁsā* as recommended by this utterance, i.e., non-injury to all living beings will make human life impossible, though de Nobili would accept this rule in its proper human significance. Therefore one cannot rest satisfied with

---

[29] T.T. p. 77.

[30] Ibid. cf. appendix, pp. I-X. The editor appends certain stories which have their source in the *purāṇas*. Ibid. p. 11. De Nobili says he read them in the *grantam*. (Expurgated passages in the Appendix.)

[31] Pr. Ap. p. 124. De Nobili answering G. Fernandes' objection against pagan customs prescribed in their books says: "Nec refert quod in eorum legibus huiusmodi insignia gestari praecipiantur, quia in illis permixte, et quae ad stirpem perinent, et quae ad venerationem Deorum sunt instituta, praecipiuntur. Quare utrum aliquid bonum sit, vel malum, non ideo quod in lege continetur, vel praecipitur, est diiudicandum..."

[32] A.N. p. 264.

utterances from scriptures as norms of *dharma*. Scriptures can be a help to a correct knowledge of *dharma* only in a relative sense, for sometimes they could prescribe something which is not in conformity with right reason.

iii. *Religious Rituals and Ethical Dharma*

We could mention another way of normative thinking which is very weak in its reasoning. De Nobili refers to its presence.[33] Thus one refers to the double string tied to the sacrificial post to justify one's marrying two wives. The sacrificial post and the two cords on it have nothing in common with a husband and two wives. One could see a posteriori a symbolic expression of a man with two wives. De Nobili rejects such an argument.

Daily actions are surrounded with rituals. There are no actions one does without reciting a prayer (*mantra*).[34] When all actions are surrounded by ritual religion, one is not quite sure of the righteousness or wrongness of many of these actions. Reason must help detect their purpose and discren its goodness or badness. De Nobili perceives a human meaning in many of the actions before they are ritualised as in the case of actions like eating, bathing, etc.[35] One need not reject such actions because they are ritualised nor consider them wrong. Besides, that something is ritualised (in Hinduism) cannot by itself be a criterion of knowing right and wrong, for de Nobili finds many of its ritual practices have elements that are acceptable and others unacceptable.

iv. *Merit and Dharma*

We shall consider another element which usually goes with enjoining of duties and observances. It is the element of merit or reward promised for the performance of duties and practices. It is at-

---

33 *Kāṇṭam* II, p. 88, T.T. pp. 80-81. Here also de Nobili mentions actions associated with religious rituals which are not worthy of moral praise.

33 I.C. p. 102. De Nobili mentions a Tamil saying which means: "Without prayer no action is done." Ibid. pp. 99-102. De Nobili mentions the different *mantras* to be recited on different occasions.

35 Pr. Ap. pp. 100-104, I.C. p. 102.

tached to social customs as well as to ritual observances. Giving of alms to a wise Brahmin is meritorious. If one gives alms to an ignorant Brahmin, one loses the reward of alms.[36] It is how an observance like this is enjoined. It is a way of encouraging Brahmins to be faithful to their *dharma* of wisdom. Those who give alms are encouraged to do so by way of gratitude and respect.[37] Both punishment and reward are supposed to help men follow the prescribed duties and practices. De Nobili understands certain apparently ritual practices to which merit is said to be attached in this way: One can keep some of the practices for the social purpose that goes with them, as is the case with the thread that the twice-born wear.[38] It is said that the wearing of the thread brings reward in the next world. The reward or merit attached to a practice could be either understood as reward for next life or as a way of recommending a practice. With regard to the thread, de Nobili does not accept the idea of reward for the next life but he accepts it for the social significance it has. He understands it as a way of recommending a good practice.[39] As regards the criterion to judge if a practice is good or bad, that something is recommended for practice alone cannot suffice. One must look for other grounds in the nature of the practice itself and its purpose. Giving of alms to a wise Brahmin helps the order of society. Wearing of the thread helps distinguish castes. Commendation of such practices are based on such good social purposes. De Nobili explains the meaning of merit in this way. He says it is a constant custom of the Indian writers to praise very much a practice they love and cherish and to propose it to men that from such a practice one derives bliss and happiness, even forgiveness of sins and beatitude in the next life.[40] Thus the author of a treatise of philosophy says that

[36] I.C. p. 61. "Imo saepius nullius meriti fore dicunt eam eleemosynam quae datur Bramani non sapienti." De Nobili quotes a text from a *purāṇa*: "Sicut olim (loquitur cum deo Visnu) sine te arcus, sagitta, currus, equus in incassum recidit mihi quando cum uno homine pugnavi, item perdit eleemosynam qui tribuit Brahmani non sapienti."

[37] Ibid.

[38] Pr. Ap. p. 103, cf. also *Narratio*, p. 158.

[39] *Narratio*, p. 143. One praises writing of books and begetting of children.

[40] Ibid. p. 140. "Perpetuus mos est huius gentis Indicae scriptorum virorum, ut disciplinam illam, vel rem, quam quisque adamat et colit, maxime laudet et ad sidera evehat, ita non solum omnibus eam proponat verum etiam generis nobilitatem, et felicitatem, ex ea nasci et quod caput est, peccatorum veniam et beatitudinis supremae donum ab illa pendere plenis buccis praedicent." Cf. ibid. p. 150.

he wrote the treatise to extricate men from sin.[41] One says that merit and riches are attached to the study of mathematics.[42] In this manner the importance of such sciences is expressed. In a similar manner they say that a Sanskrit word correctly used and understood could bring one all the pleasures of *svarga*.[43]

On all this de Nobili remarks that men here follow this manner of speaking concerning anything however inferior and social customs.[44] Because they use hyperbolic language to praise such things and attach merit to them, they need not be bad in themselves; in so far as they concern civil practices which have their own legitimate purposes, they are good. If there is a primary anthropological or social meaning or purpose in practice or custom or a duty enjoined, then even if there is a superstitious meaning attached to it, the latter meaning does not take away the prior anthropological or social meaning. According to de Nobili a legitimate human meaning or a social purpose becomes a criterion to judge the goodness or badness of different customs and observances among the Hindus. Thus if milk is considered the good of the gods or the ambrosia, it is not a superstitious thing in itself.[45] One could say the same of many other things to which superstitious meanings have been added later. For de Nobili, the legitimate social and human meaning which we could call *humanum* is the criterion which he applies to many practices of the Hindus to judge if they are acceptable or not.[46] Thus that something is commended is not always a criterion of goodness though it could be one, provided there are further arguments based on right reason and true religion. One must first make the judgement on the intrinsic nature of a practice before one considers the aspect of its being recommended. Practices recommended with merit and praises need to be questioned as to their intrinsic nature and moral reason.

---

[41] Ibid. p. 140.

[42] Ibid.

[43] Ibid. p. 142. *Svarga* is a place of the gods, and it satisfies all desires. It is a place of one's good *karma*. It is still within the cycle of births, and the final release (*mokṣa*).

[44] Ibid.

[45] Ibid. p. 150.

[46] Ibid. p. 166. De Nobili speaks of the custom of baths in the same way.

v. *Moral Examples and Dharma*

We shall consider the role of holy men (*mahātmas*) with reference to the knowledge of *dharma*. In de Nobili's understanding of the role of holy men, sages and ascetics, there are two aspects: i. their positive role and ii. the negative aspect. De Nobili's critique is that they alone are not a sufficient help to know right and wrong.

First of all it is to be noted that the Hindus attach great importance to holy men, sages and ascetics.[47] They would readily accept good and righteous words such as "Before death give up sin and do that which is righteous" (*tarmam*),[48] which is supposed to be uttered not only by good scriptures but also by spiritual teachers and sages. It is the duty of such holy men. Such a role of holy men, spiritual masters and sages, the Hindus would readily accept. For them they could be a source of knowledge of *dharma*, and their words and actions could be accepted as a standard of right action. Besides, the scriptures are said to have been written by sages and ascetics. They are a collection of opinions by such men. It is said that the wise men of the East uttered them.[49] The authority of sages and ascetics behind the scriptures could be a guide to the knowledge of *dharma* in so far as the sages and the seers are men of virtue and men who have renounced the world. Yet this by itself cannot always be an unfailing source of knowledge of *dharma*, since scriptures contradict

---

[47] A.N. p. 81. While speaking of fate de Nobili refers to the role of sages and ascetics. Cf. Haecker, art. cit., p. 97 on his critical comment on Kumarila's definition of *dharma*, esp, on the *sadhu*. Cf. ibid. p. 98.

[48] Ibid. Cf. also T.T. p. 81. De Nobili says here that some appeal to the authority of holy men (*mahātmas*) who hate and disapprove of unrighteous behaviour.

[49] I.C. p. 35. "Haec omnia dixerunt prudentes orientales". This is de Nobili's understanding of the phrase "iti pracina yogyopasva". It is a phrase from Taitt. Up. I.6.2. Cf. Radhakrishnan, *The Principal Upanishads*, p. 534. He translates "iti pracinayogyopasva" as "Thus do thou contemplate, O Pracinayogya." De Nobili says that the section in the *Upanisad* (*Taittiriya*) after saying many things about God, concludes with this phrase. Similarly, de Nobili translates "iti rsir avocat" as "quidem vir ex iis qui renunciarunt rebus humanis ita dixit." Cf. I.C. p. 35. In Taitt. Up. I.7.1. the phrase *rsir avocat* occurs. Cf. Radhakrishnan, op. cit., pp. 534-535. De Nobili also refers to the phrase from Taitt. Up. (I.10.1) "Iti trisankor vedanuvacanam", which he translates: "haec omnia vir cui nomen Triscianco locutus est." Radhakrishnan translates it as "Such is Trisanku's recitation on the Veda-knowledge." Cf. *The Principal Upanishads*, p. 537. De Nobili mentions the name of Visvamitra and Vyasa, the sages to whom some scriptures are attributed. I.C. p. 35. Cf. Manu 2,12, on the customs of the virtuous (*sadācāra*) being one of the definitions of *dharma* (*dharmasya lakṣaṇam*).

each other in many things. Of course, they treat of many things social and moral in a way that is acceptable.[50] In practice one can appeal to the sages for certain wrong things. De Nobili refers to such cases and shows that even the sages cannot always be reliable guides. They generally hate and disapprove of morally wrong behaviour. Therefore one may rest assured that among all the things approved by them, there is nothing reproachable.[51] However, one cannot always rely on them unquestioningly. De Nobili refers to some practices during sacrifices which the sages or ascetics do not seem to disapprove.[52] One sometimes appeals to what sages did in ancient times, since, for instance, in ancient times sages married many women, one could marry many women.[53] This being the case, appeal to the authority of great sages or to their authorship of scriptures or to the approval or non-approval of practices by them, or their own example is not in all cases reliable. Though one could generally rely on them, yet one must make a further judgment on a practice or an action according to right reason (and true religion) to know if it is right or wrong. One justifies polygamy on the ground that in ancient times great sages married many women.[54] For polyandry one gives a similar argument. From the fact that Tiraupati was a wife to the five brothers of Pāṇṭavar shows that a woman could have many husbands.[55] Such being the case, this type of argument can be confirmatory of something whose moral rightness is known on the ground of right reason. Examples must be judged good or bad. If good ones, they confirm and inspire; otherwise no.

b. *Dharma of Society* (*Samājadharma*)

Concerning the moral standard that applies to society as a whole, de Nobili not only critically examines it with reference to the concept of tradition and that of prescription in the law-books, but also

---

[50] I.C. p. 36. "Appareat 2° leges has non omnino esse damnandas, sed posse retineri quatenus morales sensus, aut civilia tractant."

[51] T.T. p. 81.

[52] Ibid. pp. 81-82. De Nobili has in mind immoral behaviour in rituals as in the case of *Śakti pūja*. Cf. ibid. Appendix, p. i.

[53] Cf. Manu 2,6. The customs of holy men is one of the sources of *dharma*.

[54] A.N. p. 89.

[55] *Kāṇṭam* II, p. 89.

tries to ground it in the very nature of society, its goal and order. *Dharma* of society is founded on the order of the world (*lōkakiramam*). This concept of the order of society is explained in terms of different castes and their duties by means of the myth of creation,[56] the analogy of the human body[57] and the idea of microcosm and macrocosm.[58] The order of the world means that men should perform different functions and help each other, thus working towards the good of society like the members of the human body. It looks to, and is ordained towards the development or progress of the world in interdependence just as members of the human body work together for the good of the whole body.[59] The *dharma* of society is founded in this order (*lōkakiramam*), and its goal is the common good of society. These two aspects ground the normative nature of *dharma* of society. The concept of the order of society is connected with another idea of consensus or agreement of men (*lōkacankētam*) obviously in view of the common good. Men perceive and accept that men need to be in different conditions to perform different works for the orderly progress of the world and its universal good. Now we may say that what traditions propose, and what law-books enjoin, concerning society as *dharma* of society are not always by themselves sufficient to justify its moral bindingness, since what they enjoin could either be wrong in a moral sense or irrelevant to a new situation and may not help maintain the order of society and serve the common good. The *dharma* of society needs to be grounded in, and justified by, the further criterion of the order of the world and common good which are permanent requirements of society. That they are permanent requirements is hinted at by the analogy of microcosm and macrocosm. At the same time, the idea that the order of the world is based on the agreement or convention of men points out the relative nature of the order (the concrete or the particular order) of the world or society insofar as men have to judge and agree upon the particular form of this world order. The order of the world which consists in men being in different conditions is not fixed by the very nature of every man in a deterministic

---

[56] I.C. p. 56.

[57] A.N. pp. 287ff.

[58] Ibid.

[59] Ibid. pp. 292-298.

way, as it would be according to the theory of *karma*, whereas the order of society is the object of the agreement or consensus or convention of men [60] and therefore subject to the control of reason, and it is not the inevitable effect of the inexorable and impersonal law of *karma*. Hence it is in conformity with right reason. At the same time, social customs approved by the consent of their users come to have force of law and are binding on all.[61]

c. *Jus Gentium (the law of the nations)*

In our consideration of de Nobili's understanding of Hindu *dharma*, we note that he recognises *jus gentium.*[62] This recognition of *jus gentium* is recognition of Hindu *dharma* in its social and moral aspects. He shows that the law of the Hindus with regard to these aspects is as legitimate and valid as *jus gentium* which people in the West accept, as it is reasonable. The laws of Indians [63] do not differ from the laws of other nations, since they have many things in common and since they concern social matters which have the force of law. They are obligatory on all like many other civil laws contained in the *smṛti* collection.[64] These laws are social or truly based on natural law and retained unpolluted.[65] Practices and actions based on the purposes of society and true to the nature of man go to constitute the laws of a country along with many other practices which

---

[60] Ibid. p. 267.

[61] *Narratio*, p. 36. "Diuturni mores consensu approbati utentium, legem imitantur."

[62] I.C. p. 107. St Thomas cites the definition of *ius gentium* given by Gaius iurisconsultus in S. Th. 2,2, q. 57, a. 3. "Quod naturalis ratio inter omnes homines constituit, id apud omnes gentes custoditur, vocaturque ius gentium." Cf. E.B.F. Midgley: *The Natural Law Tradition and the Theory of International Relations*, London 1975. He discusses the law of nations according to Vitoria and Suarez, cf. pp. 83-90. Also p. 87. Both agree that *jus gentium* is a true law. As St Thomas (cf. above) quoting Gaius says that it is the law which natural reason constitutes among all peoples. It is to be judged good according to the legitimate and useful purpose it serves among men. Cf. Mees, op. cit., pp. 8, 15-16. *Dharma* was understood also as international law.

[63] I.C. pp. 36-37. Here de Nobili discusses the law-books of *māyāvādins*.

[64] *Narratio*, p. 36.

[65] I.C. p. 107. "Sed omnia prorsus haec insignia et actiones vel civiles vel naturales sincere et impollute retinent." Also ibid. "...res de qua agitur naturae vel gentium iure bonum habet et legitimum usum."

could be superstitious. But we can accept *jus gentium* in all those aspects based on the nature of society and insofar as it has a legitimate good in view.

d. *Recta Ratio*

Acceptance of *jus gentium* goes also with recognition of *recta ratio* as the criterion of morality. De Nobili goes about his interpretation of Hindu customs and manners with the understanding that they are led by the light of reason (*lumen naturale*).[66] The expression *lumen naturale* means not only the faculty of knowing but also reason insofar as it knows right and wrong or it becomes the criterion of knowing right and wrong, i.e., *recta ratio*. It is in this sense that *jñānis* (the wise men) are said to know and teach by *lumen naturale* good works and moral virtues and the avoidance of sin.[67] De Nobili's clear recognition of *recta ratio* by which pagans can know and practise virtues is based on the Council of Trent, Thomas, Soto and the constant teaching of Christian theologians.[68] Along with the recognition of *lumen naturale* or *recta ratio* by which pagans are led, that men even before justification can posit morally good acts will guide de Nobili in his interpretation of *dharma* in Hinduism. He mentions that the Church always used this criterion with regard to different nations. If the customs of the nations were not contrary to reason, the Church kept them.[69] De Nobili does find that pagans (here Hindus) judge good and bad through *ratio* or *lumen naturale*. So too do they know virtue and sin through right reason. De Nobili finds that many points of the Hindu customs and

[66] *Narratio*, p. 8. "... lumen naturale, quo solo illi ducuntur." Ibid. p. 90. *Jñānis* "solum unum esse fatentur Deum naturali lumine notum" and "ex naturali lumine notum" and "ex naturali lumine bona opera, moralesque virtutes docent amplexendas, peccataque fugienda."

[67] Ibid. p. 90.

[68] Pr. Ap. pp. 90-91. The Council of Trent in the 6th session in the Ist canon says: "Non est asserendum neque dicendum, opera omnia seu infedelium seu peccatorum fidelium, quae vel ante fidem vel ante gratiam praevenientem quacumque ratione facta sint, esse peccata, aeterna morte ac damnatione punienda, ea praesertim, quae secundum humanam iustitiae regulam non solum non vituperantur sed etiam iure meritoque laudantur." Cf. Concilii Tridentini Actorum, Tomus quintus, ed. Stephenus Ehses. Freiburg, 1911, p. 823. Cf. S. Th. 2,2, q. 10, a.4. De Nobili refers to Soto, the Dominican theologian, esp. his work *De natura et Gratia.*

[69] *Narratio*, p. 42, "rationi consonum."

manners (therefore of its *dharma*) are in conformity with right reason but some others incompatible with it. In this connection, we mention his discovery of the principle of right reason in Hinduism in a particular formulation concerning the definition of sin.

The definition of sin that he found runs as follows:

> Piramāṇikkapparittiyāka, appiramāṇikkaccuvikāram pāvam.[70]
>
> Giving up that which is according to the manner of right reason and just order and adopting that which is contrary to the way of right reason and just order is sin.

De Nobili adds a remark on the saying that it is like a saying of those who follow the revealed religion (Christianity). It is a saying written by the learned men of India.[71] De Nobili then goes on to give the meaning of the key-words of the *sūtra*. *Piramāṇikkam* is derived from *piramāṇam* (skt. *pramāṇa*). Therefore de Nobili explains the meaning of *piramāṇam* like this: "The way of reason and the order of justice is *piramāṇam*." [72] Then de Nobili applies it to the way of salvation as taught by God who is the form of justice. The way of salvation is the faultless way of virtue. Therefore it is *piramāṇam*.[73]

Piramāṇam as it is the way of reason and the right order of justice becomes a standard of right behaviour. All actions, words and thoughts which are in accord with *piramāṇam* thus understood share the character of *piramāṇam* and are called *piramāṇikkam* (skt. *pramāṇika*).[74] Therefore, *piramāṇam* is a normative term. *Piramāṇikkam* means that which is of the nature of, and in accord with, *piramāṇam*, and it refers to the content of morality. It is important to notice the distinction between the two words. *Piramāṇikkam* refers to actions, words and thoughts which are in conformity with, and pertain to, *piramāṇam*. *Appiramāṇikkam* refers to actions, words and

---

[70] T.T. p. 400. De Nobili doesn't give the source but gives only the Sanskrit text and explains it.

[71] Ibid.

[72] Ibid. "Niyāyamuḷḷa mēraiyum nītiyuḷḷa kiramamum piramāṇamākum." (The text in Tamil). Here *nīti* does not mean the virtue of justice but moral righteousness.

[73] Ibid. *Neṛi* is the Tamil word for the 'way' used often in ethico-religious sense.

[74] Ibid.

thoughts which are not in conformity with *piramāṇam*, and are contrary to *piramāṇikkam*.[75] De Nobili continuing his explanation says that God has given to man the right understanding and has taught through religion what sinless actions, words and thoughts are and the way of perfect virtue. If one rejects all these and freely accepts the contrary actions, words and thoughts, then one commits sin. Here de Nobili makes the three expressions of *piramāṇikkam*, i.e., deeds, words and thoughts also the content of true religion.[76]

We shall not pursue further this point of the relation between religion and morality. We are interested at this stage in the role of right reason and its meaning. The saying under study here means that all actions, words and thoughts which are not *piramāṇikkam* become *appiramāṇikkam* and therefore also sin insofar as they go against what God has taught. What God has taught is in conformity with right reason. Or we could say that sin is both against right reason and religion. Sin is contrary to right reason and to the command of perfect virtue by God. Therefore, de Nobili says that sin is unjust (*aniyāyam*).[77] He explains the meaning of *piramāṇikkapparittiyākam* as "giving up the established way of justice",[78] and *appiramāṇikkaccuvikāram* as "adopting that which is against reason" (*aniyāyam*).[79] *Appiramāṇikkam* are unjust deeds, words and desires which are not in accord with "the way of reason and the order of justice" which is the meaning of *piramāṇam*. If so, *appiramāṇikkapparittiyākam* means "giving up that which is unrighteous" and *piramāṇikkacuvikāram*" adopting the way of justice." [80] These two phrases are definitions of virtues in its negative and positive aspects.

De Nobili uses right reason thus understood in his critique of *dharma* in Hinduism. De Nobili applies, for example, this criterion to the action of Rāma killing Rāvana. It is considered a great crime. De Nobili considers this a wrong judgement, for if God punishes wicked men, it is according to justice.[81] Therefore he says:

---

[75] Ibid. p. 400.

[76] Ibid.

[77] Ibid. p. 401.

[78] Ibid. p. 404.

[79] Ibid.

[80] Ibid.

[81] N.C.C. p. 65.

> An action that is done according to justice can only be *dharma* and not sin. Besides this, all sin can be said to be not in conformity with perfect justice and therefore be called an action against reason.[82]

Here de Nobili uses the words *nīti* and *aniyāyam*. An action of justice or righteousness (*nīti*) is *tarmam*. The way of justice or righteousness (*tarmavali*) is said to be in conformity with right understanding (*niyāya putti*).[83] An action that is not in conformity with justice is said to be against reason (*aniyāyam*). These words are expressions of *recta ratio*. *Nīti* though it could mean the virtue of justice which consists in rendering each one his due, here signifies moral righteousness and therefore that which is according to right reason. Justice (*nīti*) is always according to right reason (*niyāyam*) and that which is against justice is always against reason (*aniyāyam*). Another expression used in relation to *recta ratio* is *putti* (skt. *buddhi*). It means in general understanding or intelligence. De Nobili uses this expression also in the moral sense of right understanding in the subject. Thus, for example, he says:

> Virtue is an observance that is in conformity with right understanding (*putti*); sin is conduct that is not in conformity with right understanding.[84]

De Nobili commenting on understanding of man says that it can become weak owing to greed, traditional habits and many other reasons, and so be unable to judge sin and virtue. Such weak understanding can fail frequently in the matter of determining sin and virtu.[85]

We shall now consider two elements of right reason, knowledge and freedom. First knowledge. If there is no knowledge, there is no room for *recta ratio*. The moral deeds, words and thoughts as

---

[82] T.T. p. 404. *Aniyāyam* is the opposite of *niyāyam* (skt. *nyaya*).

[83] P.J.A. p. 47.

[84] T.T. pp. 51-52. This text shows that it seems to correspond to *recta ratio*.

[85] Ibid. p. 52. In de Nobili one does not find the modern expression *manacātci* (conscience) here. It is difficult to pinpoint any constant expression for conscience. Here *putti* appears to correspond to the subjective aspect of reason, i.e., conscience, since it is said to judge sin and virtue and to fail, since it is weakened by greed, etc. Cf. ibid. p. 413.

piramāṇikkam or as *appiramāṇikkam* are possible only if there is knowledge on the part of man.[86] *Piramāṇikkam* and *appiramāṇikkam* are moral actions and human acts. They stand for righteous and unrighteous acts. They imply the activity of knowledge which is a perfect activity.[87] De Nobili defines the perfect activity of knowledge as follows:

> The knowing act concerns the knowledge of that which is just, of that which is according to reason, of that which is virtue, of that which is sin, and, of the punishment for sin and reward for virtue.[88]

The spiritual activity of knowledge as defined above belongs to the spiritual nature of man.[89] Activities of this nature are absent in animals and plants. Hence these latter beings are not capable of virtue and sin. The doctrine of *karma* and rebirth according to which man could be born plant and animal makes all moral activities impossible, and it does not help us understand the righteous and the unrighteous.

We shall now consider the element of freedom present in, and necessary for, the understanding of righteous acts and unrighteous acts. Righteous deeds or unrighteous deeds are possible only if there is freedom.[90] Only through freedom there is renunciation of the righteous deeds and the adoption of the unrighteous deeds which is sin or adoption of the righteous deeds and renunciation of the unrighteous deeds which is virtue. Freedom is called 'power from within' (*cuvātantiriyam*, skt *svatantra*) as opposed to 'power from without' (*paratantiriyam*, skt *paratantra*).[91] This meaning of freedom alone is insufficient. The freedom of man which principally concerns virtue and sin goes always with knowledge of good and bad in a moral sense (i.e. *piramāṇikkam* and *appiramāṇikkam*). It is the power from within to choose that which is righteous or that which is unrighteous. Without freedom the order of right reason is unintelligi-

86 Ibid. pp. 400-401.

87 A.N. p. 31.

88 Ibid. p. 32.

89 Ibid.

90 T.T. pp. 400-401.

91 A.N. p. 51.

ble. Thus if that which is righteous is done by necessity, which is implied in the theory of *karma* and rebirth, then there is no sin for sin comes about when one consents freely and with knowledge to the unrighteous. If God were to punish a man for sin committed under necessity, it would disrupt the order of right reason.[92] If good deeds like prayer, worship are not done in freedom, they cannot be said to be virtuous deeds.[93] Freedom is a constitutive element of virtue and sin, and it goes to constitute human acts together with the element of knowledge. Free activity is an activity of the faculty of free will (*cuvātantiriya manacu*). The principal consequence of freedom with regard to virtue and sin is responsibility for one's actions. If a king by force makes a man give alms, such alms does not deserve the name of the virtue of almsgiving. A fast undertaken through force or under compulsion is not virtuous.[94] De Nobili gives another example:

> If a man who has no will to adore the one Lord, adores God under compulsion, no foolish man would say such adoration is virtue.[95]

Without the element of freedom to choose to do virtue or to choose to reject it, one cannot understand virtue. A good action done without freedom is no virtue, a wrong action done without freedom is no sin. De Nobili's argument against theory of *karma* and rebirth is based on the point that it means want of freedom which is a constitutive element of virtue and sin as human acts.[96]

De Nobili explains another aspect of freedom in this connection, namely, the purpose of freedom. He says:

> God has given the power of freedom to man in the matter of sin and virtue.[97]

---

92 Ibid. pp. 79-80.

93 Ibid. p. 227.

94 Ibid.

95 Ibid.

96 Ibid. pp. 226-230. For this argument cf. also P.J.A. pp. 52-53, where de Nobili explains actions done under compulsion cannot be either virtue or sin.

97 A.N. p. 87. This point touches the concept of reward and punishment in morality. If moral actions are understood as being ordained to produce directly non-moral benefits or material ones, then it would cut at the root of the moral meaning of virtue.

If this is so, one asks why God doesn't give such power of freedom to man that he may enjoy long life, kingdom and such prosperous things.[98] God has given the power of freedom to man because it is needed for salvation. He gave it only for the matter of virtue and sin:

> Freedom for enjoying long life, kingdom and other fortunes is contrary to man's salvation and to the orderly conduct of the world.[99]

If so, one can conclude that God didn't give freedom for the sake of long life, kingdom, etc. The object of freedom concerns the human acts of virtue and sin. In religion, the object of freedom is salvation. Moreover, de Nobili remarks that what is an obstacle to the growth of virtue (therefore it means sin) is not in man according to his nature. It is not written into the specific human nature, for that would mean determination of man's nature to sin, which would mean determinism. An obstacle to the growth of virtue is a result of one's own desire to have it.[100] If God created a nature to commit sin, then there will be sin by necessity, whereas it is not the case. Sin is the result of the free desire of man. This idea goes against the theory of *karma* and rebirth according to which one would have obstacles to virtue in one's own nature in the form of *karma*.

e. *The Idea of Right Order* (*karma*)

We shall now consider the concept of right order which is abundantly present in de Nobili's understanding and critique of *dharma*. The word *kiramam* (skt. *karma*) meaning order appears frequently when de Nobili speaks of moral order. At the same time, the word by itself means regular order without any moral meaning. It acquires moral meaning only in a moral context. Thus de Nobili explaining the morality of marriage, uses the expressions of *kiramam*

---

98 Ibid.

99 Ibid.

100 T.T. p. 442. "The qualities which are obstacle to the growth of the crop of virtue do not exist in man according to nature but are defects that man has caused in himself by his own desires..."

(order) and *akkiramam* (disorder).[101] He uses the argument of right order to approve of monogamy and moral disorder to reject polygamy. De Nobili explains how the expressions *kiramam* and *akkiramam* pass from their non-moral meaning to moral signification. He says that "all that is disorder cannot clearly be shown to be serious sin." [102] Thus, for example, if a man walks with head down and legs upwards he cannot be said to commit a serious sin. If one were to wear a cap on the feet instead of on the head, one would call his action disorder. One uses the expression disorder (*akkiramam*) of actions wihch are not evident moral wrongs.[103] Hence there is difficulty in using this word in moral discourse, and it is indeed widely used. Hence if *akkiramam* and *kiramam* are to be used in a moral sense, one could ask what should be the criterion of this use. Disorder in its general sense is an evil or an undesirable thing. The question is: When does it become a moral disorder and therefore morally deserving of condemnation? One could understand a disorder committed in the matter of marriage to be no sin.[104] De Nobili therefore explains the criterion for moral disorder that it is "disorder in a grave matter." [105] Continuing his explanation, de Nobili says:

> Though every disorder need not be said to be sin, it has to be said that disorder done in a grave matter is said to be sin.[106]

In a grave matter, an important good or a serious harm could result. If one were to prevent or place an obstacle to the important good directly, it is something serious against reason.[107] De Nobili exemplifies this in the case of wilful abortion, contraceptive union or infanticide to cover a shameful union. These are disorders in a serious matter. Hence they become serious moral wrongs.[108] De Nobili argues according to the understanding that marriage is meant for the

---

[101] *Kāṇṭam* II, pp. 81-90.

[102] Ibid. p. 90.

[103] Ibid. pp. 90-91.

[104] Ibid. p. 91.

[105] Ibid.

[106] Ibid. In contemporary moral discourse, such a definition of moral disorder would not be adequate.

[107] Ibid. pp. 91-92.

[108] Ibid. pp. 92-93.

procreation and increase of the human race for the good of the world. Therefore, he says that the above disorders become direct obstacles to the progress of the world.[109] The concept of order expresses the objective order of things and of men. In the case of men, especially, in marriage, the objective order is that marital union is for procreation. If it takes place according to this order, then it is order (*kiramam*). If not, it is disorder.

We have seen that de Nobili considers order in a serious matter to be moral order. Therefore moral order is founded on the objective order of things. In the definition of *piramāṇam* as "the way of reason and the order of justice",[110] there are two elements: i. the mode of reason and ii. the order of justice. According to the latter *piramāṇam* is just or right order. It is in this moral sense de Nobili uses the word *kiramam*. Order in a moral sense is expressed by two terms: *nītikiramam* (order of righteousness) [111] and *niyāya* (or *ñāya*) *kiramam* (just order or order according to reason).[112] For example, de Nobili uses the idea of order when he explains the way a king rules his kindgdom. If the king punishes the one who commits serious crimes by capital punishment, it is *dharma* of faultless order.[113] Therefore order in its moral meaning must be founded on righteousness or justice and reason. Punishment of a criminal is according to the order due to society, and it serves the common good of society.

De Nobili explains the meaning of virtue with reference to just order as follows:

> All actions done in violation of just order can only be said to be disorder. Such action will be unjustly called virtue only by ignorant men.[114]

A (moral) disorder can never be called virtue, since it has the nature (*pirakiruti*) of sin. Mere subjective consideration would not make

---

109 Ibid. p. 93.

110 T.T. p. 400.

111 Ibid. p. 400. *Nītiyuḷḷa kiramam* means 'order in keeping with justice.'

112 A.N. p. 255. It means order compatible with reason.

113 Ibid. Here *Tarumam* (*dharma*) means the act of justice or punishment. It is one of the meanings of *dharma*. Cf. Monier-Williams, p. 510.

114 T.T. p. 427.

what by its nature is sin virtue.[115] Virtue must also be just order.[116] Thus de Nobili explains virtue in terms of just order. It is the order of reason. Any action that goes against the just order of reason cannot be virtue.[117] From this it follows that just order of reason is a criterion of moral actions. Through this criterion one judges an action to be sin or virtue, moral order or disorder. De Nobili uses the idea of just order to judge if certain practices are virtuous or sinful. Thus just order of worship of God consists in its being offered to the true God. Building of temples for the purpose of worship of the true God is according to just order, whereas building of temples in honour of those who are not God is moral disorder.[118] Here the moral sense of order and disorder is grounded in the concept of one true God. When de Nobili uses the term *kiramam* in a moral sense, he also gives the supporting argument or reason that goes with it. He explains order and disorder in a moral sense with another example. This is the reasoning: If one makes the gift of food (to the poor) and builds inns for the purpose of relieving the suffering for the sake of God, it is in accord with right order. If kings and nobles, on the contrary, do such actions for the sake of fame, then such actions fall outside the just order of helping the suffering.[119] De Nobili says that right order concerning these acts of almsgiving and relieving the suffering is that they are done for the sake of God. Performing meritorious actions for the sake of God alone is the right order of these acts.[120] Thus this consideration becomes a criterion of right order.

We may mention other uses of order with regard to *dharma* and *adharma*. *Dharma* is that which is according to right order. *Adharma* is that which is against right order.[121] De Nobili explains this idea of

---

[115] Ibid. *Pirakiruti* is the Tamil form of skt. *prakrti*.

[116] Ibid.

[117] Ibid.

[118] Ibid. pp. 428-429.

[119] Ibid. pp. 429-490.

[120] Ibid. pp. 411-412. De Nobili gives the example of a woman decorating herself for the sake of her husband, which is according to just order (*ñāya kiramam*). If she were to decorate herself for the sake of another man besides her husband, she would violate the just order.

[121] Ibid. p. 428. De Nobili adds the phrase "since such and such a thing is according to order" to his moral arguments. He supposes that order (*kiramam*), just order (*ñāya kiramam*) are accessible to reason and to any thinking man.

order and disorder as intelligible to any thinking man, since all men are guided by reason concerning moral good and evil. De Nobili constantly alludes to it.[122]

De Nobili in his critique of *dharma* of society uses the concept of order. That there should be different functions in society is required by the order of the world (*lōkakiramam*). That there should be kings for the good of the world is just order which means that it is good.[123] It is according to the manner of the world and for the common good.[124] Such an order is good in a moral sense, and therefore it goes with moral obligation, and it can be said to be just order (*ñāyakiramam*).[125]

f. *The Final End and Dharma*

De Nobili's interpretation of *dharma* is also based on the ethics of the final end of man. We shall discuss this aspect of *dharma* in particular in relation to salvation in Hinduism in the next chapter. Here we point out the final end as a principle of *dharma* present in Hinduism in some way. While speaking of the part of Indian scriptures called *Ciṇtāmaṇi*, de Nobili says that the third part of it has a section that deals with moral philosophy in the discussion of which one finds the most celebrated question concerning *finis operis* which has interested philosophers of all times. It treats, especially the end of good and wicked men, or the question whether the natural beatitude of man consists in contemplation alone or also in action.[126] De Nobili refers to the idea of last end of the present life consisting in wisdom. While speaking of the office of Brahmins as consisting in wisdom, he comments on a text from Manu (2,146), drawing attention to the word *śāśvatam* in the text which means 'incorruptible good' or 'beatitude' by which the author (Manu) wanted to affirm that beatitude of the present life lies in wisdom.[127] Thus de

---

[122] P.J.A. p. 45. What de Nobili says of the function of kings as being good order applies equally to the functions of the other classes of men in society.

[123] Ibid.

[124] Ibid. p. 55. Cf. the analogy of *aṇṭam* (macrocosm) and *piṇṭam* (microcosm).

[125] Ibid.

[126] I.C. p. 23. The role of final end is a central point in Thomistic ethics. Cf. E. Gilson: *Saint Thomas, Moraliste*, 1974, pp. 23-24.

[127] Ibid. p. 56. "Vox sasvatam quod significat bonum incorruptibile et beatitudinem,

Nobili sees the perspective of last end present in the thought of *dharma* in Hinduism. To the same idea de Nobili refers when he says that the perfection and happiness of the perfectly wise men lies primarily in the contemplation of God though the wise man may understand it imperfectly.[128] De Nobili understands this to be natural beatitude in this life. He doesn't relate the last end spoken of here to the next life in terms of salvation.

In this connection, we must mention another important observation de Nobili makes. All efforts of the study of man and the practice of virtues are a preparation for the end of wisdom. Thus they acquire the role of making one dispose oneself for this end. Their purpose is expressed as *ratio dispositiva.*[129] This means that moral life, the practice of virtues prepares a man for the wisdom of God.[130]

We can also mention in this context the doctrine of the materialists according to whom man is an assemblage of elements. This understanding of man will destroy the meaning of *dharma*, since there is no final end of beatitude after death, as man comes to an end through death and destruction of the soul.[131]

> If we say that the human soul is destroyed through death, to strive after austerity and other deeds of virtue must be said to be fruitless.[132]

That means that the denial of an after-life strikes at the root of the ethic of the last end and therefore of the meaning of *dharma*. Thus the reason of all moral actions is destroyed. If there is no next world (here the last end of heaven or *mokṣa*), it will be extremely difficult

---

quasi simul definiat hic autor beatitudinem huius vitae in sapientia consistere, quod ex eodem autore." Here *beatitudo* is an expression of the final end. Cf. Mahadevan, op. cit., p. 66. In Hinduism, there is a scheme of goals for human life (*puruśarthas: artha, kama, dharma* and *moksa*). It helps us understand the meaning of ends of human actions.

[128] I.C. pp. 9-10. "Cum aiunt perfectionem et felicitatem hominis in hac vita, ut est imperfecte comprehensor primario et quasi essentialiter consistere in contemplationem Dei..."

[129] Ibid. p. 12.

[130] This idea of de Nobili bears on the question of a non-Christian's moral rectitude.

[131] A.N. pp. 153-154.

[132] Ibid. p. 153.

to show a weighty reason for actions such as renunciation of all things (*carvaparittiyākam*) and practice of different virtues.[133]

g. *Springs (fontes) of morality*

De Nobili makes a general remark on gentile customs. If one wants to judge the ends, intentions and circumstances which qualify the morality of such customs, one must have a scientific knowledge of these customs.[134] Here de Nobili applies the determinants (*fontes*) of morality, which he bases on St Thomas, to a critique of *dharma* in Hinduism.

Concerning *dharma*, we examine here the determinants of morality, namely, object, end (*finis*) and circumstances.[135] As regards the first spring of morality, namely, object, de Nobili recognises the objective nature of morality in the sense that *obiectum* qualifies morality when he says that there are actions which are by their nature or in themselves bad.[136] For example, acts of worship of false gods are by their very nature morally bad. We may also refer to our discussion on moral order and the objectivity of moral order. De Nobili says that moral disorder is a disorder in a grave matter.[137] The grave matter (*obiectum*) qualifies the morality of an action. Similarly, he says a moral disorder can never be called virtue, since its nature (*pirakiruti*) is that of sin.[138]

De Nobili refers to St Thomas (S.Th. I,2, q.20, a.I) where St Thomas says that exterior acts can be said to be good in two ways: i.

---

133 Ibid. pp. 153-154.

134 Pr. Ap. p. 91. "4 um noto istorum ethnicorum non omnium operum seu insignium finem reperiri in D. Th. nec in aliis scholasticis, ut sunt fines et intentiones cur Curumbi lineam et alia huiusmodi gestant." He also says: "Ex quo colligo non posse rationabiliter ab aliquo iudicari utrum huiusmodi opera sint bona vel mala, nisi opus fideliter et exacte istorum ethnicorum pervolvens examinaverint." De Nobili adds "3um noto non esse damnanda istorum ethnicorum opera, seu insignia nisi finis propter quem fiant seu instituta sint recte cognoscetur."

135 M. Zalba, *Theologiae Moralis Summa*, Matriti 1952, p. 170-201, on springs of morality in Thomistic ethics, pp. 122-143. Cf. also J. Fuchs, *Theologia Moralis Generalis*, pars altera (ad usum privatum auditorum), Romae 1968/69, pp. 66-69.

136 Pr. Ap. p. 94. He uses the expression *per se male*. Cf. I.C. p. 106.

137 Pr. Ap. p. 94. Cf. also T.T. pp. 428-429.

138 *Kāṇṭam* II p. 91.

according to the genus of the acts and according to the circumstances in themselves considered, and ii. the other way according to which something is said to be good or bad from the ordination to the end. The end (*finis*) is the proper object of the will. The reason of goodness or badness which exterior acts have is from the ordination to the end and is found first in the act of the will. From this, goodness or badness flows into the exterior acts.[139] De Nobili refers to the second mode in which exterior acts have their goodness or badness.[140] The first mode according to which some exterior acts can be considered good or bad according to the genus and circumstances considered in themselves refer to the object of moral acts which de Nobili doesn't consider here.

The end in view of the agent (*finis operantis*) goes to qualify the morality of human acts. De Nobili states it as follows: "All actions according to intention can be said to be right and wrong" (*tarmātarmam*).[141] De Nobili illustrates this principle. If a woman decorates herself for the sake of her husband which is in keeping with right order, then what she does is *dharma*. But if on the contrary, she decorates herself for the sake of another man, then what she does is *adharma*.[142] Thus the end in view (*finis operantis*) or intention (*eṇṇikkai*) makes the act of the woman good or bad.

Circumstances are said to be one of the three springs of morality. De Nobili mentions this determinant element of morality but says it becomes one with *finis operis* or obiectum. This is what he says:

---

[139] S. Th. I,2, q.20, a. 1. About the second mode to which de Nobili refers this is what St Thomas says: "Alio modo dicitur aliquid esse bonum vel malum ex ordine ad finem: sicut dare elemosynas propter inanem gloriam, dicitur esse malum. Cum autem finis sit proprium obiectum voluntatis, manifestum est quod ista ratio boni vel mali quam habet actus exterior ex ordine ad finem, per prius invenitur in actu voluntatis, et ex eo derivatur ad actum exteriore exteriorem."

[140] Pr. Ap. 90. De Nobili states the principle from St Thomas as follows: "Ium noto operationem quamlibet seu actum externum vel signum non habere ex se bonitatem, vel malitiam sed tantum per dominationem extrinsecam ab actu voluntatis, si videlicet spectetur aliquid in operis exsecutione, tunc enim, ut suppono ex D. Th. I^{a}2^{ae} q.20, art. 1, aut primus actus exterior sequitur voluntatis bonitatem, quae eius principium ex quo derivatur (sic) ad actum exteriorem hominis, vel malitiam."

[141] T.T. p. 411. The Tamil word for intention (*finis operantis*) is *eṇṇikkai.*

[142] Ibid. pp. 411-412. This example reminds one of the examples given by St Thomas (I,2, q.20, a.I). Giving of alms with fulfilment of due circumstances is good but giving of alms for the sake of vain glory is bad. Cf. also Pr. Ap. p. 94. Good acts in themselves can become bad, e.g. baths when taken to show forth false cults.

> I do call the end (*finem*) not only the primary or the formal object (of an action) but all the circumstances which are essential, for the end is one together with circumstances.[143]

Essential circumstances enter the definition of *finis operis* or *obiectum*. De Nobili says that this is the view of St. Thomas.[144] He applies these determinants or springs of morality, especially *obiectum* and *finis operantis* to gentile customs. There are certain customs which are by themselves bad which can badly be intended or willed as such, like the veneration of false gods. When it is willed as such, it is said that this action bad in itself is badly intended.[145] Here the object (*finis operis*) and the intention (*finis operantis*) coincide. But sometimes actions which are good in themselves (*ex se bona*) or indifferent such as marriage, ablutions of the body, wearing of caste symbols and practices of this kind which, if they are done with impious ceremonies of false adorations, become bad because of the new intention. De Nobili says that such things are sinful solely with regard to the mode (*quoad modum*) and not with regard to substance (*non quoad substantiam*).[146] Here *quoad substantiam* refers to the *obiectum* (*finis operis*), which can specify the morality of an action. *Quoad modum* can refer to circumstances which modify the object and determine the morality of human actions or refer to intention of the agent (*finis operantis*) which determines the morality of an action.

---

143 Pr. Ap. p. 91. "3 um noto non esse domnanda istorum ethnicorum opera, seu insignia nisi finis propter quem fiant seu instituta sint recte cognoscatur. Finem voco non solum primarium seu formale obiectum sed circumstantias omnes quas vocant essentiales ex quibus dicam, unus integretur seu confletur finis, induunt tales circumstantiae rationem finis."

144 S. Th. I,2, q.18, a.3 in C. "Sicut ens dicitur secundum substantiam et secundum accidens, ita et bonum attribuitur alicui et secundum esse suum essentiale, et secundum esse accidentale, tam in rebus naturalibus, quam in actionibus moralibus." In the same article St Thomas says this on the determination of morality by circumstances. In moral actions: "nam plenitudo bonitatis eius non tota consistit in sua specie, sed aliquid additur ex his quae adveniunt tanquam accidentia quaedam. Et huiusmodi sunt circumstantiae debitae. Unde si aliquid desit quod requiratur ad debitas circumstantias, erit actio mala."

145 Pr. Ap. p. 94.

146 Ibid. Cf. I.C. pp. 105-106; here too de Nobili asks if an action or a practice is by itself good or by itself meant for adoration of false gods. Similarly, he says here that a thing may be good *quoad substantiam*, but bad *quoad modum*. Here de Nobili refers to theologians who teach (e.g. S. Th. 2,2, q. 3, a. 3.). Cf. also *Narratio*, p. 132.

Thus de Nobili uses the determinants of morality to judge the goodness or badness of gentile customs and practices. 'Pagan' (*gentilicum*) is not by itself a criterion of moral badness. 'Pagan' is not to be easily equated with something superstitious, since according to St. Augustine whom St. Thomas quotes, something is superstitious which has been instituted by men for the cult of idols or to the cult of a created being or a part of a creature as God.[147] De Nobili examines the pagan customs if they are by their very nature bad (as superstitions in the meaning defined above) or good or indifferent or if they become bad only through use (here a new intention) or circumstances.[148]

---

[147] Pr. Ap. p. 95. St Thomas cites St Augustine from *De Doctrina Christiana* in S. Th. 2,2, q. 94 a. I in C. "Superstitiosum (here de Nobili adds: de idolatria loquitur) est quidquid institutum ab hominibus est ad facienda vel colenda idola vel pertinens ad colendum sicut Deum creaturam, vel partem ullam creaturae."

[148] Ibid. pp. 95-96.

CHAPTER FOUR

DHARMA AND SALVATION IN HINDUISM

a. *Concept of God and Dharma*

De Nobili considers it important that one has a correct notion of God for the understanding of *dharma* in relation to salvation. This is reflected in his critique of the Hindu concept of God. De Nobili accepts all that is positive about God as found in Hinduism and works out his criticism of the negative elements with reference to *dharma* in its moral and religious meaning of salvation.

i. *One God and His attributes*

He recognises first the existence of the science of God called *adhyātmika śāstra.*[1] It treats of God and theological matters. De Nobili pertinently remarks that among Brahmins there are many schools of theology on account of the variety of religious sects among them. He mentions the school of *Jñānis* whose theology is known as *Vedānta.*[2] Its meaning is the 'end of knowledge'. In this school, the part called *Vivacanaciotpattiam* which treats of one true God known by the light of reason.[3] But it is to be noted that this

[1] I.C. p. 24. "Sexta Disciplina est quam vocant *Adiatmicam* i.e. scientiam de Deo seu theologiam. Haec apud Brahmanes una non est sed multiplex pro varietate sectarum ad religionem pertinentium. R. De Smet, 'Roberto de Nobili and Vedanta', *Vidyajyoti*, 40 (1976), p. 364 on *Adhyātmika śāstra*. It treats of the Supreme Spirit.

[2] I.C. p. 24. "Istorum theologia *Vedānta* nominatur cuius vociș significatio est finis scientiae." The school of spiritual masters (*Jñānis*) is one of the three well-known schools of *Adhyātmika.* Ibid, pp. 24-25. The other two schools are the school of Buddhists and the school which contains 4 parts one of which is *Mīmāṁsā.*

[3] De Smet, art. cit., p. 264. He notes the difficulty about the correct reading of the word. Cf. ibid. f.n. 2. He writes it as *Vivacanayotpadyam*.

notion of the Absolute is monistic.[4] In *Satva Vivegam* [5] and in its commentary called *Advi Tipichei*,[6] the oneness of God and soul is inculcated. The third part is called *Beda Ticcaram* which means removal of multiplicity in God and soul.[7] De Nobili is in agreement with the idea that God is one who can be known by reason; but he is also aware of a notion of God among the Vedantins according to which in God there is something like a material substance called *māyā* from which God creates all things. This substance is two fold. From one, God creates souls and from another bodies, since the Vedantins hold the principle that 'nothing can come out of nothing." [8] They also speak of the one soul common to all beings (*paramātma*) and another individual soul (*jīvātma*) dependent on the former, which is also immortal.[9] Such is the doctrine of the Vedantins about the Ultimate Reality. What is of interest to us is that de Nobili shows an appreciation of the doctrine of the school of *Jñānis* in so far as they speak of one God and reject the multiplicity of gods though he cannot agree with all points of the Vedanta doctrine, for instance, the doctrine of *māyā* and the idea of the same soul in all beings. De Nobili is quite appreciative of their rejection of sacrifices to gods. Some of them go so far as to say that sacrifice cannot be

---

[4] De Nobili calls the Absolute (*Brahman*) of the Vedantins God. This term would refer to Iśvara in the Vedanta. De Nobili seems to ignore this distinction of the Vedantins and calls *Brahman* simply God. Cf. Zaehner, *Hinduism*, p. 73. The *Advaita* (non-dualism) of Śankara is that there is only one reality that is *Brahman*.

[5] Pr. Ap. Introduction, p. 47. Caland identifies it as *Tattvavivekam*. Cf. I.C. p. 25. "Satva Vivegam cuius explicatio est supremae veritatis inquisitio...".

[6] Ibid. Caland identifies it as *Advaitadīpika*. I.C. p. 25. It is written here as *Advi tipichei* which means: "cuius notio est lucerna veritatis...".

[7] Pr. Ap. Introduction, p. 47. According to Caland again it is *Vedasāra*. In I.C. p. 25, it is written as *Beda Ticcaram*. This latter name is in agreement with the meaning of the name given by de Nobili. "Beda ticcaram, cuius vocis explicatio est remotio multiplicitatis in Deo et anima." In these three parts of the Vedānta (*Advaitadipika* or *Advi tipichei, Tattvavivekam* or *Satva vivegam* and *Beda ticcaram* or *Vedasāra*), according to the testimony of de Nobili, almost all the absolute divine attributes are explained.

[8] I.C. p. 25. "Alii tamen praeter ea quae de vero Deo dicta sunt fingunt in Deo quandam materiam quam appellant *Maiam* ex qua Deum creare omnia aiunt, quam duplicem faciunt, unam ex qua eius creat animas, alteram ex qua corpore, mordicus enim defendunt ex nihilo nihil fieri". Cf. Dubois, I, p. 82. He gives the skt. form of "ex nihilo nihil fit" as "abavanabavanasti." He says that Advaita holds this view. The Christian concept of creation 'ex nihilo sui et subiecti' is not present in Hinduism.

[9] I.C. pp. 24-25, 30. *Jñānis* reject plurality of gods.

offered even to the one true God and that He should be worshipped only in spirit. They reject sacrifices done to different idols by idolators, be they Brahmins or others, as being useless for the attainment of glory (salvation).[10] He quotes a vedic text on the rejection of sacrifices which he translates:

> Not from sacrifices nor from the happiness of children, nor from riches, nor from free distribution of wealth do men obtain beatitude.[11]

This is why they are called *Jñānis* (spiritual masters). De Nobili then mentions the sect of *māyāvādins* whose books contain a variety of opinions including oneness of God. De Nobili is careful to comment on the word for God, since there are many names of gods. The word for the one true God, unique and immaterial who can be known by the light of reason is *Brahma* with the final short vowel. Hence *Brahma* thus written is not any particular God.[12] The Saivites teach that there are three fundamental realities which are eternal and that God (*pati*) is one.[13]

The concept of one true God is also understood as one universal cause of the world which view is a correct opinion held among the *māyāvādins.*[14] The school of *Jñānis* which rejects plurality of gods and idolatry holds that there is one universal cause of all things which can be shown clearly by production and order of the world. De Nobili quotes a poem from *Cittiyār* in support of this idea.[15]

---

[10] Ibid. pp. 24, 30.

[11] Ibid. p. 31 on the rejection of sacrifices by *Jñānis* as a means for attaining salvation. De Nobili quotes from *Taittiriya Araṇyaka* (of the *Yajur Veda*), 10,10. 3a. Cf. De Smet, art. cit., p. 367. The skt. text: "Na karmana na prajaya dhanena tyagenaike (na) amrtatvam anasur." (as quoted by de Nobili, I.C. p. 31). Cf. ibid. p. 10. De Nobili alludes to the division of the Veda into *Karma-kāṇda* (ritual section) and *Jñāna-kāṇda* (knowledge section). Cf. T.M. Mahadevan, op. cit., p. 31. There is a third division of the Veda *Upāsana-kāṇda* (meditation section) which de Nobili doesn't mention though he quotes from it (e.g. *Araṇyaka*).

[12] I.C. p. 9. "Haec enim vox Brahma ultima brevi non significat deum aliquem determinatum et falsum sed Deum in communi, et usu fere applicatur etiam ad significandum illum verum Deum unicum et immaterialem qui lumine naturae cognosci potest."

[13] A.N. p. 140. "*Pati, pacu pacam*, these are one God, soul and *karma*."

[14] I.C. p. 34. Also ibid. p. 25: Among the attributes of God mentioned by the works of *Jñānis*, that He is the cause of all is also mentioned.

[15] Ibid. p. 30. "Dicunt enim unam omnium rerum universalem quam et esse et unam esse

What is to be noted here is that the idea of one God who is the universal cause of all is present at least in some schools of the Hindus. De Nobili refers to a *smṛti* text in which it is said that by the virtue of truth the world was created.[16] In Kalidasa's *Kumārasambhava* II, it is said: "Thou contemplatest this world with thy soul and thus by the soul thou createst the world." [17] This idea of God as creator by knowledge is a point acceptable to de Nobili. This preserves the simplicity of God, since he creates by knowledge.

We shall now consider the attributes of God. According to the poem of *Cittiyār* referred to above, God is one (*unus*), beginning and end (*principium et finis*), self-existent by himself (*aptus ex sese*), existing in himself (*in se manens*), eternal, blissful (*beatus*), form of intelligence (*intellectionis figurae*).[18] De Nobili speaking of the school of *Jñānis* says that in the three parts, *Vivacanciotpattiam, Satva Vivegam* and *Beda Ticcarem*, almost all the divine attributes are explained, namely, that he is a being by himself, that he is eternal, that he is incorporeal, that he is naturally good, that he exists everywhere and that he is the cause of all.[19] He adds that all this they assert by the light of reason.[20] De Nobili mentions the *Araṇyaka* law-book which speaks of many things of God which Christians can accept. It speaks of the nature of God like this: God "by his very nature is good" (*ṛtam*).[21] De Nobili takes *ṛtam* in the

---

maxime ostendunt ex mundi fabrica et ordine." The verse from *Cittiyār* de Nobili renders as follows: "Id est mundus ex tribus generibus, masculino, foeminino, et neutro in qui cum ordine quidem oriantur, quaedam permaneant, quaedam corrumpantur, causa istorum debet esse unus, qui sit expers principii, et finis aptu ex sese, et in se manens, aeternus, beatus, intellectionis figura." Cf. Dhavamony, *Love of God*, pp. 225-226. *Cittiyār* is known as *Sivajñāna Cittiyār* The poem of *Cittiyār* reflects the idea of creation present in the first of the twelve *sūtras* said to have originated from the *Raurava Āgama*. Cf. Dhavamony, op. cit. pp. 327, 330.

[16] Ibid. p. 75. "Veritate nulla virtus melior, falsitate nullum malum peius quippe hac virtute mundus creatus est, ergo veritate nulla virtus maior."

[17] Ibid. pp. 75-76. "Tu mundum hunc tua anima contemplaris et sic anima mundum producis."

[18] Ibid. p. 30.

[19] Ibid. p. 25. "Atqui in his tribus partibus omnia divina attributa absoluta explicant, nimirum quod sit ens a se, quod sit aeternum, quod incorporeum, quod naturaliter bonum, quod ubique existat, quod sit omnium causa."

[20] Ibid.

[21] Ibid. p. 34. "Rtam tva bhagah i.e. ex sua ipsius natura bonus." Cf. De Smet, art. cit., p. 368.

He identifies it as a text from *Taittiriya Upaniṣad* (1, 4, 3) which is a constitutive part of

sense of goodness. Then he refers to another text which says that "God is infinite knowledge." [22] Then it is said that God "is spiritual in form."[23] De Nobili commenting on the phrase *ākāca carīram piramam* says that they understand it to mean only that God has a body of *ākācam* (ether) and that they do not think that it could mean that God is *acarīrī* (incorporeal).[24] De Nobili gives here another text on the nature of God which says: "Thou, say I, art God and brightness itself, thee God I say to be true, thee I say to be truth." [25] These attributes of God are significant in relation to virtue and salvation. Though the Hindus have not known the nature of God perfectly, they have determined a few attributes. Thus "that God is one being" (*oru vastu*) and that he is "truth, knowledge and the infinite" and that he is " in the form of knowledge and bliss" is spoken by them.[26] De Nobili remarks here that one needs to know well the determination of the divine attributes though this alone by itself is not sufficient for salvation. But one must note also the positive aspects spoken of the nature of God. It is said that God is clarity in the sense of light, *ṛtam* in the sense of being good and truthful and *satyam*, i.e., truth. Moreover, de Nobili says that the Hindus re-

---

Taittiriya Araṇyaka. The text runs as follows: "tam tva bhaga." De Nobili's text has *ṛtam* instead of *tam*. Cf. Radhakrishnan, *The Principal Upaniṣạds*, p. 631. The full phrase runs as follows: "tam tva bhaga pravisani svah" which is rendered by Radhakrishnan: "Into thee thyself, O Gracious Lord, enter into me. Hail."

[22] I.C. "Jnanam anantam Brahma, i.e. infinita intellectio." Cf. Tait. Up. 2.1.1. Radhakrishnan, op. cit. p. 541, He translates "jnanam anantam brahma" as "Brahman as knowledge and as the infinite." In the verse of Taitt. Up. *satyam* precedes *jnanam*. In *Kāṇṭam* II, p. 187, de Nobili gives the phrase "cattiya ñanam anantam Piruma" (as written by him in Tamil).

[23] I.C. p. 34. "Akaśa śariram Brahma, i.e., Aereae, hoc est spirituali figurae." Generally, says de Nobili, the spiritual being the opposite of body is expressed by the negative term *asariram* meaning *incorporeum*. De Nobili takes *ākāśa śariram* to mean *incorporeum*. Cf. Taitt. Up. 1, 6, 2.

[24] *Kāṇṭam* II, p. 188. This is also from Taitt. Up. 1, 6.2.

[25] I.C. p. 34. "tvam eva pratyaksam Brahma vadisyami, rtam vadisyami, satyam vadisyami." De Nobili translates it as: "Tu inquam Deus et ipsa claritas, te Deum dico ipsam claritatem, verum te dico, veritatem te dico." The text is from the invocation of the first *Sikśa Vallī* of the Taitt. Up. (1, 1, 1).Radhakrishnan, the *Principal Upanisạds*, p. 527. He translates the verse as follows: "Thou indeed, art the visible (perceptible Brahman). Of thee indeed, the perceptible Brahman, will I speak of the right. I will speak of the true..." De Nobili translates *ṛtam* and *satyam* as qualifying Brahman.

[26] *Kāṇṭam* II, pp. 186-187. "Cattiya ñānam anantam piruma" from Taitt. Up. 2.1.1. The other phrase is "*cittānanta curūpi.*" Cf. Gispert-Sauch, op. cit., pp. 37-44.

fer to God as one who rewards the good in the words: "One who knows this God attains to glory." [27] This is not an absolute attribute of God in himself but expression of God's attribute of goodness in relation to man in terms of *dharma* and salvation. The good (those who know the true God) God rewards with glory (of the Supreme), that is to say, they reach the Supreme. So far we considered that de Nobili did appreciate the positive aspects of the Hindu notion of God. He is also critical of their weak points.

ii. *De Nobili's Critique of the Hindu Understanding of God*

We shall now consider de Nobili's critique of the points which are against the unicity of God. First we note here de Nobili's appreciation of the point of the sect of *Jñānis* in so far as they reject the plurality of gods and sacrifices which are made to idols, which *māyāvādins* accept.[28] Among the *Jñānis* or the Vedantins, the view that in God there exists a material principle called *māyā* from which God creates all things would destroy the simplicity of God's spiritual nature.[29] The sect of idolators admit plurality of gods [30] and defend their views according to their books of which, says de Nobili, there are four parts called *Bhatta*, *Prabhacaram, Siastratipichei* and *Mimamxei (Mimāṁsā)*.[31] These books propose many reasons for the existence of many gods and the need of sacrifices to be performed for them. The last part of *Mīmāṁsā* says that there is no author (or efficient cause) of the world.[32] *Lokāyatas* (the materialists) consider the elements, moon and the sun respectively to be God and *māyāvādins* spirits and incorporeal bodies to be God; Vamer attribute divinity and supreme honour to *Śakti.*[33]

---

[27] I.C. p. 35. "Denique verus remunerator bonorum iis verbis *Brahmavid apnoti param* i.e. Deus hunc sciens gloriam consequetur." The phrase *Brahmavid apnoti param* is from Taitt. Up. 2.1.1. Cf. Radhakrishnan, *The Principal Upaniṣads*, p. 641. He translates it as "The knower of Brahman reaches the Supreme." Cf. Gispert-Sauch, op. cit., p. 37.

[28] I.C. p. 24.

[29] Ibid. p. 25.

[30] Ibid. p. 31.

[31] Ibid. p. 25. Transliteration of the 4 parts is as given by de Nobili.

[32] Ibid. pp. 25-26.

[33] Ibid. p. 31. Here we may mention the sect *Sigivageres* who consider everything visible to be God. It is difficult to identify this sect.

One could fall into an error like this: since in God there is no limit to His knowledge and power, it could be said there is no one who could put a limit to the number of gods.[34] There is another objection to the concept of God among the Hindus. It is said "One God has different kinds of form" (*rūpam*).[35] Correct knowledge of God is a serious matter for salvation. It is said:

> One cannot even think and say that God who is without difference (*vikāram*), who is the form of perfect bliss and knowledge and who is the cause of all and one Being is the form of each of all the created beings.[36]

Therefore, to conceive of God as being the forms of created beings would make men conceive God as something that would be to their liking.[37] If God were to be the form of created things, it could be said that He could be the form of an ignorant sinner. Such an identification of the form of God with man and other created things would render the religious act of worship (*namaskāram*) meaningless.[38]

We shall next consider de Nobili's criticism of admitting sinful conduct in God. If sinful conduct were to be found in God, it would have two consequences for the practice of *dharma* among men: i. One would find it difficult to know what is evil. ii. One would not have fear of wrong (*atarmam*) or shame.[39] Since deeds which are apparently sinful are attributed to God, one would admit easily the fallacious argument of the saying: "yatta rācāttattāp piraca." It means that "citizens must follow the way of the king."[40] Therefore the attribution of sinful deeds to the King of kings, means, God makes people who are His citizens think that they too can behave in a similar fashion. This criticism goes mainly against *līlās*

---

[34] *Kāṇṭam* I, pp. 21-22. The argument of the perfections of God is to be understood in a qualitative sense. That God is all-powerful, that he is all-knowing, implies that He is unique.

[35] T.T. p. 261.

[36] Ibid. p. 261.

[37] Ibid. p. 259.

[38] Ibid. pp. 261-262. The idea that God takes all forms of created things, in de Nobili's opinion, would remove the clear distinction of God from created reality on which the relation of worship of God by man is based. Otherwise, man would worship himself.

[39] *Kāṇṭam* II, p. 197. In skt. *yathā rājah, tathā prajāh*.

[40] Ibid. De Nobili says that this saying has been written in the books of the Hindus.

attributed to God. Besides such deeds, even if taught by the *purāṇas* are judged to be against reason. When man performs such deeds, he cannot do them without disturbance of his conscience. The experience of sin goes with shame and fear. The fear and shame are weakened by the sinful deeds in God as mentioned in the teachings of the religions here.[41] De Nobili's criticism is directed against the puranic concept of God which speaks of sinful deeds of gods. For instance, it is mentioned in the books of the *purāṇas* what Rudra is like, how Viṣṇu behaved and the deeds of Brahma, all of which one would mistakenly come to accept and approve of. But such deeds being contrary to righteousness (*tarmam*), one cannot approve of them in God who is the form of all goodness.[42] Gods are said to collaborate in a kind of black magic for the ruin of one another,[43] gods who want offerings which go with shameful observances,[44] gods who want human sacrifice which is to be done according to castes,[45] gods who make man commit suicide like *sati*, dying in the meeting of rivers (*cankam*)[46], such things make one think that these gods worshipped here are subject to sin, and that they live outside of *dharma* and that they are enemies of God.[47] Moreover, if one examines such things, one will find them to be not only against reason but also against the will of kindness (*tarmacittam*) of God. They will in no way help towards salvation. De Nobili is also critical of making kings long dead gods, especially those who are known to have done sinful deeds. One must examine if there are true signs (*laccaṇam*) of divinity in them.[48] We observe here that de Nobili is using highly polemical language in his criticism of popular Hinduism.

[41] Ibid. pp. 197-198. Here *manacu* (skt. *manas*) is used in the sense of conscience.

[42] *Kāṇṭam* I, p. 45, also pp. 45-49. Here de Nobili shows how gods are responsible for actions which go against the nature of God.

[43] Ibid. p. 46.

[44] Ibid. pp. 47-48.

[45] Ibid. p. 48. It is said that for Brahma, a Brahmin must be sacrificed, for the god called Cupacu, a Śudra must be sacrificed. Thus division of castes governs the human sacrifice to different gods. The hierarchy of castes is not only among gods but also among devils. Cf. *Kāṇṭam* II, p. 153. *Piruma rāccaci* (the demon of Brahma) and *cattiriya picācu* (the demon of the *Ksatriya* caste).

[46] Ibid. pp. 48-49.

[47] Ibid. pp. 49-50, cf. also T.T. p. 67.

[48] *Kāṇṭam* II, pp. 173-174.

Next de Nobili directs his criticism against the worship of created realities. One worships created things such as the sun, stars, fire and animals. In the order of created things, they are below the level of man. De Nobili considers worship of beings below the level of man a disorder. It is against the just order of things.[49] Worship done to such beings becomes a serious wrong if one attributes divinity to them and worships them for that reason. De Nobili then explains two kinds of salutation: social (*laukīka*) and divine (*teyvīka*). The former obtains among men in daily social intercourse. The latter is directed to God.[50] The social salutation is rendered according to the presence of deserving qualities in men. Therefore it is according to reason.[51] But if salutation is done in the form of worship or sacrifice, incense to created things, then it is no more social salutation, since one expects from it the removal of sin and blessings for the soul. It is divine worship addressed to created realities, which therefore is a serious wrong.[52] De Nobili attributes all this to ignorance of men with regard to God, especially as manifested in the worship of created things and men to the machinations of the fallen angel.[53] He also explains how such worship of beings other than God to be worship of the devil. He gives a phenomenology of this religious worship. He says that the sentiment of wonder (*āccariyam*), desire of benefit (*pirayōcanam*) and fear (*payam*) are the reasons for such a worship through sacrifices which ought to be offered only to God[54] De Nobili gives this explanation of the worship of gods as seen in popular Hinduism. These sentiments are the dominant motives in the subjective attitudes of worship of the gods and of created realities. The wrong concept of God makes man direct his worship either to beings less than God as against the obligation of man to

---

[49] Ibid. I, pp. 74-75.

[50] Ibid. p. 73.

[51] Ibid. p. 74.

[52] Ibid. pp. 79-80.

[53] M.V. pp. 25-26. Cf. Bibliography, *Mantira Vyakiyānam* is 4th part of de Nobilis' catechism.

[54] *Kānṭam* II, p. 142. Cf. also N.C.C. pp. 56, 61-63, 71-75. Here de Nobili gives four reasons for the origin of the worship of different idols, which go to explain popular religion. They are i. power (Tam. *valumai*), ii. sorrow (*tukkam*), iii. wonder (*aticayam*) and iv. love (*cinēkam*). These four reasons concern the idea of making men God. Cf. also KP pp. 41-43, where the author says that the fallen angel inspires fear and love for it and makes men worship men. Cf. bibliography on this.

worship one true God for his salvation, or it makes him think of sinful deeds in God which cuts at the root of the meaning of God being the source of *dharma* (righteousness) and renders meaningless the demand of the way of righteousness required for salvation.

Similarly, the motive of love invests the authors of the scriptures with the name of gods.[55] Thus the name of Mahadeva (lit. the great God) came to the author of the *āgama* scripture.[56] In the same one would call the one who wrote *bhaṣyam* (commentary) in *Śabda śāstra*, divine incarnation (*avatāra*). The author of the *Bhagavad-Gītā* is said to be God. Besides those who are adept in different *śāstras* are called great seers (*maharṣis*). They were offered worship which is meant for God alone. This is the case with *Vyasarṣi*. The twelve Aḷvārs of Vaiṣṇavism, Śaṅkarārya of *māyāvādins*, many others who enjoyed the status of *ācāryas* (teachers) though not called gods receive the worship which is usually offered to God.[57] This is the criticism of de Nobili directed against the particular aspect of Hinduism which makes men gods in some way.

In this connection we shall consider how de Nobili meets the objection that sinful deeds as some of the *līlās* done by God in his *avatāra* do not affect God.

If one asks how sinful deeds do not affect God, one bases one's answer on the omnipotence of God. He is capable of preventing sin from affecting Him. De Nobili criticises the admission of moral wrongs in God on the basis of His power. He examines the notion of power in relation to sin and its avoidance. De Nobili says that men could commit sin comes from weakness rather than from power or strength.[58] The correct moral language is that we say that one is able to avoid sin or that one is unable or too weak to avoid sin. De Nobili explains the human meaning of power. Thus we do not say that man is endowed with power to fall and die, as if it were perfection of man. It is no perfection of his power but his weakness. If a man were never to fall and so die, that would be a perfection of his

---

[55] N.C.C. pp. 74-75.

[56] N.C.C. p. 74. De Nobili considers the author of the *āgamas* to be only man, whereas the Saivites believe that the *Śiva āgamas* were revealed by Śiva himself. Cf. Dhavamony, *Love of God*, p. 4. Mahadeva is a name for Rudra-Śiva.

[57] N.C.C. pp. 74-75.

[58] T.T. p. 93.

strength. Therefore we must hold this concerning God: Because He is the form of infinite strength or power, He is unable to fall into ignorance and other sins or imperfections, which speaks of the perfection of His power. But to say that God is able to fall into sin could mean only weakness in God, which is an error.[59]

Another argument is adduced on the admission of sinful deeds in God by the Hindus. According to this God and man are not equal. Therefore man may not do what God does.[60] De Nobili admits that with regard to matters pertaining to the realm of God, man who is not equal to God cannot be said to do what God did. For example, God created the world and governs it. Man cannot be said to do this.[61] De Nobili goes on to say that if we consider the matter of *dharma*, deeds of righteousness must be found in God in a more eminent way than they are found in the righteousness of man.[62]

Continuing the same argument, de Nobili answers another objection coming from the Hindus who say that "there is nothing impossible for God who is all powerful." [63] It is said that however improperly God behaves, he is able to 'digest' it. This is explained with the help of a simile. It is the image of a worm in the fire. The worm that falls into fire is burnt by it, but the fire itself doesn't rot from contact with the worm. In the same way through the unbecoming actions of God, no evil can come to Him.[64] De Nobili takes up the saying "to fire can a worm cling?" to explain the truth that wrong which is compared to a worm, cannot befall God who is the form of all goodness. It is an error to say that wrong (which is like a worm) befell God and got consumed. That would mean a contradiction of God's being which is goodness. It would be like darkness and light existing together at the same time in the same being. This

---

[59] Ibid. pp. 93-94.

[60] Ibid. pp. 139-140.

[61] Ibid. p. 139. What is to be noted here is that de Nobili distinguishes the moral concept of sin from the non-moral concept of power.

[62] Ibid. pp. 139-140.

[63] *Kāṇṭam* II, pp. 42, 43.

[64] Ibid. The concept of power by itself, that is, by its semantic meaning does not refer to a moral idea of perfection. The concept of power must be further referred to a moral perfection. Though in God all perfections are interconvertible, yet we maintain the semantic distinction between power as non-moral idea and a moral perfection, e.g., justice.

would be an impossibility.[65] Moral wrong in God is a contradiction, i.e., the existence of His nature and its non-existence at the same time.[66] The above-mentioned simile of worm in the fire is based on the non-moral concept of power, whereas sinful deeds must be excluded from God by His very nature, since they contradict the divine nature which is infinite goodness. Sin is the non-existence of goodness. This criticism of de Nobili holds good concerning some of the *līlās* in particular.

iii. *The Concept of Trimūrti and its Refutation*

We shall now consider de Nobili's critique of the concept of *trimūrti* in Hinduism. Among the sect of idolators who hold the idea of *trimūrti*, de Nobili mentions four sects, namely, *Māyāvādins*, *Śaivites, Vaiṣṇavites* and *Tattvavādins.*[67] *Māyāvādins* hold that *Brahma, Viṣṇu* and *Rudra* to be equal though they attribute to each a different function. The first creates all things in the world; the second rules the world; the third destroys it.[68] They also worship many other gods who are either sons of these gods or their servants or heroes.[69] Śaivites hold Rudra to be the supreme God of the three gods and consider the other two to be minor gods. To Rudra they assign different names according to his function.[70] Vaiṇṣavites make Viṇṣu the supreme God of the three and make the other two gods subservient to Viṇṣu.[71] *Tattvavādins* consider Viṇṣu to be supreme but differ from Vaiṇṣavites in certain things.[72] In all this, de Nobili

[65] *Kāṇṭam* I, pp. 42-43.

[66] Ibid. pp. 43-44.

[67] I.C. p. 31.

[68] Ibid., *Kāṇṭam* II, p. 188.

[69] I.C. p. 31. "Prima est Maiavadarum, qui tres deos aequales faciunt Brumma, Visnu, Rudhren apud hos summa imperii sit, ita tamen ut primus creet omnia quae in mundo sunt, secundus gubernet, tertius destruat. Alios vero deos quos multos colunt partim horum filios, partim famulos, partim heroas faciunt." Cf. *Kāṇṭam* II, p. 189. Cf. Bertrand II, p. 257. Antonio Vico, companion of de Nobili, says that the perfections of God have been corrupted into the idea of *trimūrti*.

[70] I.C. p. 31. "Xaiverum qui ex tribus illis unum eligunt Rudrenem quem faciunt supremum deum, reliquos vero duos aliosque deos minores; quidam asserunt esse Rudrenem variis nominibus appelatum prout varia gessit." Cf. also *Kāṇṭam* II, pp. 191-192.

[71] I.C. p. 31. "... Vaisnavanorum qui simili modo tantum e tribus illis sibi elegerunt pro Deo nimirum Visnu, cui caeteros omnes deos subiiciunt..." Cf. also *Kāṇṭam* II, pp. 190-191.

[72] I.C. p. 31.

though appreciative of the valid and correct points concerning God and his nature which one can know by the light of reason, considers that one cannot without the light of faith, help admitting errors in one's determination of the attributes of God.[73] He, therefore, shows that the concept of *trimūrti* is not compatible with the nature of God. Some hold that *trimūrti* are equal and that among them the summit of sovereignty exists.[74] But what is said in the books of the *purāṇas* on the manner of the activities makes us think that they cannot be God; for it is said that Rudra cut the head of Brahma, that he stabbed Viṇṣu, that Brahma and Viṇṣu discussed among them. These and many other deeds of *trimūrti* do not show forth the glorious attributes of God. De Nobili says that such things are sung by clever poets in the style of epics.[75] These deeds of behaviour of *trimūrti* cannot be accepted as reasonable signs of the one supreme God.[76] De Nobili rejects the idea of making Viṇṣu the Supreme Being, since in the *purāṇas* "many things incompatible with reason and understanding" are told.[77] Besides *avatāras* (incarnations) of Viṣṇu as fish, boar, etc., that he consented to sentiments of anger and lust, go against the very nature of God. These things show that "in Viṣṇu there is no nature of the Supreme Being."[78] So too Rudra cannot be God in so far as those who hold Rudra to be God narrate things of him that would contradict the nature of God. Thus he is spoken of as having five faces and three eyes and that he carried his wife on his head.[79] Attribution of such unbecoming things to God is done by those who do not know the nature of God. Thus it is said that God is in man-woman form and that He is the cause of man by being of like form of man. De Nobili rejects this idea of God.[80]

He observes that there are things they say of God which could be correctly understood, which however they understand wrongly.

---

[73] Ibid. p. 25. "... quamquam suus cuique error non deerit, utpote fidei deficiente luce."

[74] *Kāṇṭam* II, p. 189. "Some consider that these *trimūrtis* are one supreme Being."

[75] Ibid. pp. 189-190.

[76] Ibid. p. 190.

[77] Ibid. pp. 190-191.

[78] Ibid.

[79] Ibid. pp. 191-192.

[80] *Kāṇṭam* I, pp. 39-40. The Christian concept of God is opposed to this. In the Judaeo-Christian concept of God, the anthropomorphic form of God is rejected from the very beginning. Cf. 26 Serm. pp. 11-12. God is not *anurūpakraṇam* (the cause of like form).

Thus when they say God is *ākācacarīri*, they consider Him to have a body of ether and fail to consider Him to be incorporeal (*ācarīri*).[81] Similarly, it is said that God is "carkka stiti pirattiyapakaraketu" which means that God is the cause of creation, protection and destruction.[82] Then there is a sentence which expresses this pointedly: "The Lord is *tiriyampakan.*[83]. They understand *tiriyampakan* only in the sense that "God is one who has three eyes of the moon, the sun and the fire." [84] De Nobili's objection is that people here understand these utterances in a material sense which goes against the nature of God.

In the matter of God's government of the world, one attributes carelessness to Him:

> Some say that the Lord of all who is the Supreme Being ordained the charge of governing the world to the *trimūrtis*. Thus they say that God has no care for the world in entrusting the government of the world, creation, maintenance and destruction, one to each of the *mūrtis.*[85]

This derogates from the nature of God and from the truth that He has care for the world. This de Nobili attributes to ignorance.

Another opinion on the nature of God is that

> There are three qualities, namely, *cātvika*, *tāmaca* and *rācaca* produced in God.[86]

This introduces multiplicity and imperfection in God. De Nobili says that many authors of sacred scriptures are of the opinion that Hari, Hara and Brahma, the *trimūrtis* are not God. Rather according to the followers of the school of *Māyāvādins, catvika, racaca* and *tamaca* are only qualities (*guṇas*) which originate from God.[87]

---

[81] *Kāṇṭam* II, p. 188.

[82] Ibid. It is skt. phrase written in Tamil.

[83] Ibid.

[84] Ibid.

[85] Ibid. p. 189.

[86] Ibid. Cf. Zaehner, *Hinduism*, p. 69. *Cātmika* is the Tamil form of the skt. *sattva* which literally means 'the quality of being', *rajas* the skt. form written in Tamil as *rācaca* means 'the quality of energy' and *tāmaca* (the skt form is *tamas*) means the 'quality of darkness.' The usual translation of these three *guṇas* is 'goodness, energy and darkness.'

[87] *Kāṇṭam* III, p. 5.

De Nobili in his rejection of the concept of *trimūrti* finds support in Indian authors themselves, as we mentioned above. He says that Vartakari and Śaṅkara and Manikkavacakar are of the opinion that the *trimūrtis* are not the Supreme Being and that by serving them no benefit will accrue to anyone.[88] Vartakari says that no benefit will come to anyone from service to Hari, Hara and Brahma, and that those who do so deceive themselves.[89] That they are are not God, that Hari Hara and Brahma did not know what God was, such things have been written by the authors of the *purāṇas.*[90]

De Nobili's objection to the concept of *trimūrti* is based not only on the concept of one God as such, but also on the idea of equating *trimūrti* with the Christian Trinity.[91] In order to answer the latter objection he examines the meaning of the word *mūrti. Mūrti* means sometimes body. If it does not mean body in certain contexts, it means nature and form.[92] If one considers these two meanings, says de Nobili, only an ignorant man would use *trimūrti* of God, for that would mean there are in God either three bodies or three natures.[93]

iv. *De Nobili's Critique of God-language in Hinduism*

De Nobili finds the God-language of the Hindus inadequate. We shall consider this point here below.

Our author recognises the partially correct definition of God's nature in some of its aspects, of which he gives some examples: the ideas of one God, of God being infinite knowledge, truth and bliss, of God being spiritual, God being the one universal cause of all.[94] According to him what obtains here is that many thinking men without the knowledge of revealed religion spoke of the mysteries of

---

[88] Ibid. pp. 5-6. Vartakari is probably Bhartrihari, poet and grammarian (of 7th A.D.). Cf. Monier-Williams, p. 748.

[89] *KāṇṬam* III, p. 5.

[90] Ibid. pp. 5-6.

[91] Ibid. p. 5.

[92] Ibid. p. 4.

[93] Ibid. Cf. A.A. Macdonell, *A Practical Sanskrit Dictionary*, p. 232. He gives the following meanings: i. solid body, material form, body. ii. manifestation, incarnation, embodiment; iii. person, frame, figure, appearance, iv. image, statue.

[94] *Kāṇṭam* II, pp. 186-187.

God, each according to his own thinking.[95] De Nobili recalls the story of four blind men on the form of an elephant by touch. Each one of them touched a part of the body of the elephant and asserted that the form of the whole elephant was the part each one had touched.[96] De Nobili says that some in the matter of the definition of God didn't go beyond ordinary experience of touch and spoke of God, the Supreme Being as if He were like a king one sees on earth and attributed many *līlās* to Him.[97] Many wrote of God who is above the mind and word of man merely from sensible experience of touch.[98] Yet de Nobili grants the possibility of knowing all the matters of divine mysteries required for salvation, at least in some vague way (*appirakāca mēraiyāi*) to a non-Christian. At the same time, in his view this knowledge by itself is not sufficient for salvation without the supernatural act of charity.[99]

De Nobili then examines critically the God-language of the Hindus. Some when they speak of the glorious (*makimaikaḷ*) of God, employ imprecise or unclear words and do not declare the meaning with understanding. De Nobili says that even if we admit that one or two can discover the meaning concealed by such words, many others begin to admit of qualities which do not exist in God. The reason for this is the imprecise words used of God by them.[100] De Nobili gives the example of the saying "ākāca carīra piramam" the meaning of which is understood as God having a material (though ethereal) body rather than as God being spiritual or incorporeal. Another saying is about the three functions of creation, protection and destruction of which God is the cause. This is expressed as God being *tiriyampakan* which means that God is three-eyed. The expression is understood literally rather than symbolically. So too they draw a circle to show that God is without beginning and end and say that God is five-faced which is meant to show that the five faces are the signs of the five actions (*pancakirittiyankaḷ*) by which the supreme power manifests itself.[101] These sayings, says de Nobili, do not help in any

---

[95] Ibid. p. 186.

[96] Ibid. pp. 193-194.

[97] Ibid. pp. 193-195.

[98] Ibid. p. 196.

[99] Ibid. p. 187.

[100] Ibid. pp. 187-188.

[101] *Pancakirittiyankaḷ* (skt. *pancakritya*) refers to the five actions by which the supreme

way to declare God's perfections clearly (*pirakācikka*).[102] The moral effect of imprecise language is ignorance concerning God's nature which is an obstacle to a saving knowledge of God. De Nobili is also aware of the inadequacy and imperfection of human language in general concerning the discourse on God and his nature. Yet we can speak of God only in human terms. If we do so, we must use them of the true God without attributing the imperfections that go with them. One must use human terms of God only analogically. [103] One must always think of the meaning that befits God eminently.

De Nobili makes another observation on the use of terms for God.[104] In general a word can have two meanings. Thus a word that names a thing is given to it because its meaning comes from a particular cause. Such a meaning is called *yokārtam.*[105] The word *pankaca* (skt *pankaja*), for example, means 'born from mud'. It is its *yokārtam*. But convention of men has come to apply it to the particular flower called lotus. Thus by convention of men *pankaca* has come to mean only lotus flower. This meaning of *pankacam* is known as *rūttiyārtam*. Through *rūttiyārtam*, often *yokārtam* disappears. So too, according to *yokārtam* the words Brahma, Viṣṇu, Śiva, Vinayaka could be used of God. But these words through convention of men, i.e. through the use in different *purāṇas* have come to have a *rūttiyārtam* through which their acceptable *yokārtam* has disappeared. The *rūttiyārtam* of these words in the *purāṇas* make them inapt to use of God. Hence, the principle is that we use names of God which bring out the true perfections of God.[106]

---

power manifests itself: *sṛṣṭi, sthiti, saṃhāra, tirobhāva* an *anugraha-karaṇa*. Cf. Monier-Williams, p. 575.

[102] *Kāṇṭam* II, p. 186. De Nobili says that these terms could be understood correctly. The correct meaning is not understood by people in general. God-language could be acceptably symbolic in the manner of *signum-signatum*; but without further explanation, one is likely to take them in a literal sense.

[103] Ibid. pp. 31-32, 96. It is with this idea of analogy de Nobili interprets *ākāca carira piramam* to mean 'God is spiritual', cf. ibid. p. 188. Also I.C. p. 34.

[104] *Kāṇṭam* III, pp. 10-12.

[105] *Yoga* and *rudhi* are the technical language of grammarians and rhetoricians, later borrowed by the naiyayikas (logicians), the two ways in which the meaning of words come to us: either by etymology from the root-meaning of the component parts of the word «*yōga* = connection), or by the actual usage of people (*rudhi* = increase, growth). Cf. *Kasika Vrtti* on Panini 1.2.55; Gangeśa, *Tattvacintamaṇi*, book IV, *Śakti vivadah*.

[106] *Kāṇṭam* III, pp. 13-14.

After the discussion of the kinds of meaning a term can have, de Nobili proposes a set of names for God that are descriptive names which do not arise from ignorance or wrong concept of God's incarnation.[107] Here are some of the names he proposes: *parāparavastu* (Supreme Being), *Carvēcura* (the Lord of all), *kartan* (the Creator or Lord), *cuvāmi* (the Lord), One who is the first cause (*ātikāraṇam*) of the world.[108] De Nobili uses phrases descriptive of the attributes or functions of God like the following: One who is the form of all goodness (*cakala nanmai curūpi*), one who exists by Himself. They are not synonyms but they speak of the different perfections of God.[109]

The important point to be noted here is that man needs to know God rightly so that he worships the only true God and thus disposes himself to be saved. False ideas of God lead to idolatory and to morally wrong practices in the name of God. In religious Hinduism, the concept of God is mixed with many erroneous conceptions, especially in the *purāṇas* which would create difficulties in the practice of *dharma*. De Nobili's critique concerns precisely these points. God's nature and all that He is said to do is relevant to *dharma* and its practice by man for salvation.

v. *Avatāra (Incarnation) and Dharma*

De Nobili is fully aware of the difference in the understanding of the nature of *avatāra* in Hinduism and Christianity.[110] He therefore designates the Christian idea of incarnation as *manuṣa avatāram* and the Hindu *avatāras* as *tēva avatāram.*[111] According to the Christ-

[107] Brahma, Viṣṇu and Śiva are said to perform acts according to the *Puraṇas*, which do not befit God's perfections. Some other names like Nīlakaṇṭan come from the story that Rudra swallowed the poison of *kalākalam*. Cf. *Kāṇṭam* III, pp. 12-13, for such names.

[108] *Kāṇṭam* III, p. 14. Cf. Dubois, tome II, p. 503. *Parā-paravastu* is the name given to the One Supreme Being by Jainas.

[109] Kāṇṭam III, p. 14.

[110] T.T. pp. 158-159. Cf. Dhavamony, 'Hindu Incarnations', *Studia Missionalia* 21(1972), p. 130. *Avatāra* is principally a *Vaiṣṇavite* idea. "*Avatāra* means 'descent' especially of a deity upon earth and the Vaiṣṇavas have made this idea their own by integrating this into their religious view of God." Cf. Bror, *Christian and Hindu Terminology*, pp. 95-96. Here Bror briefly comments on the use of *avatāra* by de Nobili. De Nobili is somewhat sparing in the use of *avatāra* for Christ's incarnation. He uses it in T.T. pp. 117, 122, 127. Cf. Zaehner, p. 91, on the Hindu notion of *avatāra*.

[111] T.T. pp. 133, 160, also pp. 105, 130.

ian concept, God assumes (*parikkirakam ceytal*) human nature. Hence the name *manuṣa avatāram*. God assumes human nature which is body and soul together as one reality.[112] In the *tēva avatāra* of the Hindus, God did not assume human nature which is the unity of body and soul. It is said that He assumed only the human body.[113] De Nobili argues that since true man is the unity of body and soul, the body without the human soul can only be said to be inanimate being or a corpse. It cannot be man. If God were to assume the human body, says de Nobili, such *avatāra* could then be said to be only incarnation in inanimate matter (*jaṭa avatāram*) or incarnation in a dead body. Therefore such an *avatāra* can never be said to be human incarnation. Besides, this kind of *avatāra* would mean that divine nature would be, as it were, the form of the body, thus being an incomplete principle. This would also mean that God derives benefit from the body which would contradict the idea that He is all-good.[114] De Nobili rejects the idea of subtle body with spiritual activities.[115]

The same idea of *avatāra* would involve another contradiction. It is said that God assumed only a human body. If so, the body being unable to commit acts of anger, lust and other such deeds, it has to be said that God Himself who assumed the human body performed such acts in His human nature. From this one must conclude that ignorance came to exist in God who is said to be the form of infinite knowledge.[116] "They say that by acceptance of the body, ignorance and other defects may come to exist in God." [117] That would mean that God who is infinite knowledge can be ruined by a

---

[112] The Concept of man being unity of body and soul as one being, of which the soul is the form of the body, de Nobili explains in A.N. pp. 236-243, 245-248.

[113] T.T. p. 158.

[114] Ibid. p. 158.

[115] A.N. pp. 41, 129-130. De Nobili criticises the Hindu belief of human *avatāra* as *avatāra* in inanimate substance (*jaṭa avatāra*) though he is aware of the Hindu view that there is an inner subtle body (*linka carīram*) as inner organ as opposed to the gross body (*stūla carīram*) which includes the organs (*antakaraṇankaḷ*) of mind (*manacu*), intellect (*putti*), consciousness or knowledge (*cittam*) and the ego-principle (*akamkāram*) and that they go with the individual soul (*cīvāttuma*). The inner organs of the subtle body are mentioned here according to de Nobili's list.

[116] T.T. pp. 158-159. The actions of anger, lust of God are references to the *purāṇas* where such things are said of God in His *avatāra*.

[117] Ibid. p. 159.

lowly body and that He consented to it.[118] Again, since it is said that God assumed only human body and offered worship to idols, it could mean either that God in His divine nature offered worship to another being or that He offered it to Himself.[119] Such an idea creates difficulties concerning understanding of God's *avatāra*. We may also observe here that the body cannot be a moral agent.[120] From the point of view of attribution of moral responsibility such a concept of *avatāra* would create difficulties. Since the body cannot be a moral agent or subject, sinful deeds and *līlās* have to be attributed to God. Such a difficulty arises from what de Nobili calls *jaṭa avatāram* (God's assumption of only the body without assumption of human nature).

De Nobili is severely critical of making or considering men *avatāra*. Many poets, says he, desiring their own interests praised and sang of kings as God and as *avatāras*. They composed many poetical works on them and sang in such praises of them that God Himself took *avatāra* in the world and took the form of different kings and enjoyed many different pleasures which are objectionable from a moral viewpoint.[121] This is how de Nobili explains how kings come to be considered God and *avatāra* to save the world.[122] Those who died long ago come to be worshipped in temples with sacrifices. In the course of time, they come to be considered God and *avatāra*.[123] Besides, clever poets who heaped praises on kings said that their books were revealed by God and uttered by many great sages and seers.[124] The chief moral reason against considering kings to be *avatāras* is that one sees in them errors and sinful deeds.

Another idea of the Hindu notion of *avatāra* different from that of Christianity is that God took many and different *avatāras* in forms

---

[118] Ibid.

[119] Ibid.

[120] The Hindu idea of subtle body would mean that to such a body moral acts can belong.

[121] *Kāṇṭam* II, p. 33, cf. T.T. p. 129. De Nobili says that when poets sing of lords as *avatāra*, they do so in the manner of epics (*kāviyarīti*). Cf. also ibid. pp. 103-104.

[122] N.C.C. p. 57. De Nobili calls kings or men made *avatāras tēva avatāra*. T.T. pp. 105, 130. In N.C.C. he uses of the Hindu *avatāra*, *manuṣa avatāra*, p. 57. Also cf. T.T. p. 117.

[123] *Kāṇṭam* II, p. 177.

[124] N.C.C. p. 57.

both human and non-human.[125] Vaiṣṇavites admit human *avatāras*.[126] As we mentioned above, de Nobili calls human *avatāras* *tēva avatāras*. He also mentions non-human *avatāras* along with human *avatāras*. Thus God is said to have had the *avatāras* of a boar, a fish, a tortoise and that of man-lion.[127] De Nobili's critique of the Hindu *avatāras* is always according to the criteria of the nature and attributes of God (*kaṭavuḷ nirṇayam*), of righteous conduct (*dharma*) and salvation. He understands that the Hindu idea of many *avatāras* in different forms in contrast to the Christian idea of one unique *avatāra* is a problem. He rejects the idea of many *avatāras*.[128] He says that just as one sun is enough for daylight and just as there is no need for ten suns for the same purpose, so too one *avatāra* would be sufficient for the salvation of man. Moreover, the nature of different *avatāras* would imply change in God. Divine nature should not be mixed with human nature.[129] When it is said that God as man-lion killed Ranian and drank his blood, that He became the *avatāra* of a boar, tortoise, etc., such *avatāras* show that He is weak and imperfect.[130]

---

125 Dhavamony, "Hindu Incarnations", p. 129. In this article he notes the different kinds of *avatāra*. There is the complete (*pūrṇa*) *avatāra* like that of Rama, Kriṣṇa or man-lion. The other kind of *avatāra* is a major partial incarnation (*amśa avatāra*) in which part of the deity becomes incarnate such as fish, tortoise, etc. There are minor partial incarnations (*kāla avatāra*), in which the deity is not so much present as in the major ones. *Śakti avatāra* (incarnation in might, *kārya avatāra* (which is only temporary of a purpose) such as that of holy men into whom divine virtues are infused. It is said there are ten principal *avatāra* of Viṣṇu. Cf. ibid. p. 130. KP, p. 81. Here the ten *avatāras* are mentioned. Cf. also T.T. p. 116.

126 T.T. p. 98. De Nobili says "without stopping with only human *avatāra* such religions say that God became boar, fish, tortoise, half-lion and half-man and many other erroneous things in this matter" (incarnation). Cf. T.T. p. 103. Among human *avatāras*, Rama, Kṛṣṇa and Vama (dwarf) are *pūrṇa avatāras*. De Nobili refers to Rama and Kriṣṇa. *Cf. Appendix of T.T.* pp. I-II, at the end. KP, p. 81. It is said that God took Rama *avatāra* to kill Ravana and that he took Vama *avatāra* to kill the king Mapali. The man-lion *avatāra* is also mentioned here. Cf. Dhavamony, Hindu Incarnations, p. 129. T.T. pp. 98, 117, also appendix, p. i. The man-lion *avatāra* of Viṣṇu is for the purpose of killing Ranian (Hiranyakasipu) to save his son (Prahlada). Cf. also ibid. p. 103 for different *avatāras*. Cf. Bror, op. cit. p. 96. He says that de Nobili has "failed to see the cosmological implications in the various myths describing *avatāras* in human animal forms."

127 T.T. pp. 98, 117.

128 Ibid. pp. 128-129.

129 Ibid. p. 98.

130 Ibid. p. 103.

Concerning the purpose of *avatāra*, de Nobili makes this one negative criticism: That God performed the marvel of *avatāra* for petty reasons and in a way that is not fitting to His nature.[131] The examples of petty reasons are that He took *avatāra* to kill some robbers, to kill Ranian, to show Himself as fire, to find the top and the bottom of a pillar (*linkam*), *avatāras* such as boar, fish, tortoise, etc. cannot be said to be *avatāra* for the saving of the world. It is said that the latter *avatāras* have the purpose of saving the world.[132] These *avatāras* have petty reasons and take place in a way that does not befit God's glorious nature. Besides, these erroneous opinions, one does not consider it objectionable to accept that sin can befall God in His human *avatāra*. *Līlās* attributed, especially to kṛṣṇa *avatāra* and many other deeds of Viṣṇu in his different *avatāras* are against *dharma* in the sense of righteousness, and they cannot be explained away.[132] Of course, one would say that such *avatāras* are described in the books of the *purāṇas*, which have been revealed by seers and sages.[134] De Nobili counters this objection. That such *avatāras* have been declared by seers and sages does not make them true *avatāras.* It is important that *avatāras* are compatible with God's nature and manifest His glory. *Avatāra* should never go against the perfect order of His nature and *dharma*. If God who as the Lord rules all things in perfect order did such a great marvel of incarnation for petty reasons, it would mean that the Lord failed in the perfect order.[135] Incarnation for petty reasons and *līlās* cannot help the salvation of man. God who is the form of righteousness must give all that is the form of righteousness as His teaching [136] for the salvation

---

[131] Ibid. p. 117. Cf. also ibid. appendix p. i.

[132] Ibid. pp. 117, 122. Also ibid. appendix p. i.

[133] Bror, op. cit. p. 96. He says that de Nobili doesn't mention Kṛṣṇa *avatāra*. But he does. Cf. T.T. Appendix, p. vii. Cf. Bertrand, II, p. 236. Vico says that de Nobili referred to the idea of the loves of Kṛṣṇa as 'sports', since they were against God's perfections and would not edify men.

[134] N.C.C. pp. 57-58.

[135] T.T. pp. 117, 122. That God becomes *avatāra* to kill Ravana, Ranian and to protect Prahlada are small favours. Here de Nobili concentrates on the puranic concept of *avatāra*, for according to him *mokṣa* (heaven, here salvation), alone is the good above all goods. The motive of salvation is not absent in Hinduism. Cf. Dhavamony, Hindu Incarnations, pp. 153-160, on the commentary on the verse of the B. Gita 4, 9 by Śankara, Ramanuja and Madhava.

[136] T.T. p. 118.

of the world. Therefore God's *avatāra* should be in conformity with the dignity of His nature, should involve no errors either concerning His nature or concerning the nature of *dharma* and should help man unto salvation.[137] As for the purpose of *avatāra* in Hinduism de Nobili says that the reasons given by it are not serious and that they are not necessary.[138] Besides, *līlās* attributed to *avatāras* which include sinful deeds will not create the desire for *dharma* in the heart of man.[139] They will not help man obtain forgiveness of sin. If *avatāra* is meant for the salvation of man, then it must show the way to heaven which consists in virtuous conduct and give teaching of righteousness.

b. *Salvation and Dharma*

i. *The Theory of Karma, Rebirth and Salvation*

We shall now briefly consider de Nobili's critique of the theory of *karma* and rebirth in relation to *dharma* and salvation. He says:

> The word that each one can reach the state which is in the manner of helping towards salvation through virtuous deeds one has done is conformable to reason and intelligence.[140]

It is through virtuous deeds performed by each man that one can reach salvation. But the relation of *dharma* to salvation gets disturbed and destroyed by the doctrine of *karma* and rebirth. Moreover, de Nobili considers the relation of virtue to salvation to be something acceptable to man's reason and understanding and therefore something valid for, and applicable to, all men.

The first disturbance of this relation comes from the idea that man's social and material condition of high and low castes and poverty and riches are the fruit of actions done in a previous birth,

---

[137] Ibid. pp. 155-156, 157. God in Himself or in His *avatāra* is the form of goodness. *Līlās* destroy His excellent righteous nature.

[138] Ibid. p. 141. God in His *avatāra* should help towards *mokṣa*, and not towards less perfect or sinful deeds which help the body or the life of this world.

[139] Ibid. p. 281. De Nobili refers to Kṛṣṇa *līlās* in paintings. Ibid. Appendix p. ix. Cf ibid. p. 285.

[140] P.J.A. p. 49.

namely, deeds of virtue or of sin.[141] Good results are called *nalvinai*. Thus riches, royal honours, fortunes, etc. are good states and therefore called *nalvinai*. On the contrary, the states of poverty, disease, suffering and other similar states are bad states and therefore called *tīvinai*. It is said that *nalvinai* comes to one for one's enjoyment through one's virtue performed in a previous birth. Thus the virtuous deeds of previous birth are the cause of the present fortunes.[142] So *tīvinai* are one's misfortunes such as poverty, disease, etc. with which one is born. They are punishment for sin committed in a previous birth.[143] That one is in a higher or lower caste is given the same explanation.[144] Thus sin and virtue committed in previous birth are put in an intrinsic relation to the social and material conditions of man in his present life. The latter become the index of man's moral and spiritual states of sin and virtue. We have seen in the second and third chapters that this concept of virtue and sin takes away the real meaning of virtue and sin on the level of personal freedom and knowledge. Such a concept of virtue and sin also makes the understanding of salvation difficult, since salvation is also understood in terms of freedom and knowledge of man who disposes himself for salvation by the practice of *dharma*.

The understanding of sin and virtue according to the theory of *karma* and rebirth shows the concept of salvation according to Hinduism to be different from that of Christianity.[145] Besides this, de Nobili shows that the interpretation of sin and virtue in terms of karmic effect creates difficulties in the understanding of heaven and hell as the last ends.[146] If one accepts the theory of *karma* and rebirth, it is difficult to admit heaven and hell as final ends in the next world as the state either of enjoying the fruit of virtue or that of suf-

---

141 Ibid. pp. 10-12.

142 Ibid. p. 11.

143 Ibid. pp. 12-13. Cf. Also A.N. pp. 316-317.

144 P.J.A. p. 10.

145 The theory of *karma* means that man is caught up in the cycle of births (*saṁśāra*). *Mokṣa* or salvation means one is liberated from this bondage. Cf. *B. Gītā* 4, 9; Salvation means liberation from the cycle of births and reaching God. The expression 'reaching the shore' for salvation comes from conceiving life as ocean. De Nobili adopts this term, e.g. *mōcca karaiyēṛutal*.

146 A.N. pp. 223-224. De Nobili argues from the Christian idea of heaven and hell as the last ends.

fering punishment for sin.[147] If one suffers punishment for the sin of a previous life, one cannot speak of the final hell as a state of punishment for sin.[148] So too if a man enjoys the fruit of virtue done in a previous birth, such as wealth and pleasures in this life, one cannot speak of a state in the world beyond where one could enjoy the fruit of virtue.[149] Salvation and its absence are understood in terms of heaven and hell respectively. The idea of suffering or enjoying the fruit of virtue in a series of births according to the theory of *karma* makes the final end of heaven or hell unnecessary.

Another difficulty that arises from the doctrine of *karma* and rebirth is the determinism implied in it. If, for example one did only righteous deeds in a previous birth, by the inexorable law of *karma* he would do only righteous deeds in a subsequent birth. The law of *karma* being operative, he would always remain a good man. If, on the contrary, one did only sinful deeds in a previous birth, by the same law of *karma* he would only commit sinful deeds in the present life. That would mean he would always remain a sinner.[150] The law of *karma* is deterministic and would thereby destroy the meaning of *dharma* which is to be done in freedom and with knowledge and the meaning of salvation which lies in and through the way of *dharma*.

ii. *Removal of Sin (Pāvanivāraṇam)*

The theory of *karma* and rebirth creates difficulties concerning forgiveness of sin or the removal of sin.[151] It is said that God punishes a man for the sins of his previous birth during the present life. For example, it is said that Cukrivan was born as the son of a paraya and that he had a bad character. That would mean men would not approach him. One would say that he was suffering for the sin of his previous life.[152] He is thus said to atone for the sins he does not know.[153] For the removal of sins and guilt, one must know

---

[147] Ibid. p. 223.

[148] Ibid.

[149] Ibid. pp. 223-224.

[150] Ibid. pp. 270-271.

[151] Cf. Bror, op. cit. De Nobili prefers to use *pāvanivāraṇam* for forgiveness of sin. *Nivāraṇa* in skt. means "keeping off" or "prevention." *Pāvam* is the Tamil form of skt. *pāpa*.

[152] P.J.A. pp. 58-59.

[153] Ibid. p. 62.

them and repent of them. If God ordains punishment for sin in subsequent births such as poverty, diasease, etc. he is said not to give right means for the removal of sin.[154] De Nobili considers that the removal of sin achieved through a series of births cannot imply properly repentance of sins. Only repentance of sins would help salvation.[155] According to the theory of *karma* and rebirth, one suffers for his serious sins for a short time in one birth and one is likely to have no fear of sins. The scheme of a series of births can encourage sin. De Nobili considers that the scheme of births to repair one's sins according to the theory of *karma* is not a perfect means of removal of sin required for salvation. He also observes that since sin is an infinite malice, the difference of social conditions of men and passing sufferings of this life cannot expiate sin.[156]

The same theory in its explanation of reward and punishment for virtue and sin speaks of man being born like plants and animals. This renders the personal meaning of salvation unintelligible.[157] De Nobili criticises in particular the idea of the human soul entering the bodies of animals and plants, since the human soul is expected to reach a good state from its state of existence in the bodies of animals or of plants for which one must perform good works. De Nobili remarks that however they (the Hindus) do not enjoin such deeds for the human soul imprisoned in the bodies of animals and plants. They do not consider how the human soul in the bodies of animals and plants may reach a higher state.[158] In such a concept of human soul, the positing of the free spiritual acts of virtue and sin is not possible. One cannot speak of human soul committing sin and practising virtue in such an existence, so that it may reach a bad or good state.[159] De Nobili sees that such a theory instead of helping the practice of virtue and attainment of salvation, creates obstacles to them. Moreover, the idea that the human soul enters the bodies of animals and plants would only increase sin for men have to cut

---

[154] Ibid. p. 58.

[155] Ibid. pp. 74-75.

[156] Bertrand II, p. 7. Albert Laerzio cites a letter of de Nobili in which de Nobili mentions this reason why the theory of *karma* cannot help towards forgiveness of sins.

[157] P.J.A. pp. 37-39.

[158] Ibid. pp. 37-38.

[159] Ibid. pp. 38-39.

plants and animals for their living which would at the same time be destroying the life, a great sin.[160] Thus de Nobili finds that the way of salvation through a series of births according to the law of *karma* creates more difficulties and hindrances than provide means for salvation.

Pāvanivāraṇam (the removal of sin) is an important element in the concept of salvation and is related to the understanding of *dharma* as righteousness. De Nobili remarks that there is no one who is not without desire for forgiveness of sin [161] because everyone is aware of the evil that comes from sin. It is concerning the means for obtaining forgiveness of sin that difficulties arise. This has to do with different concepts of sin in Hinduism and Christianity.[162] De Nobili explains how sin comes about according to the Christian understanding.[163] One of the wrong concepts of sin is to understand it in material terms. The image of sin is dirt. The dirt must be washed in water, whereas sin is internal dirt, and it affects the soul. De Nobili sees only the material notion of sin present in the practices of the Hindus, such as baths in rivers for the removal of guilt.[164] Faced with this understanding of sin, de Nobili stresses sin as being a human act (*actus humanus*). He mentions definition of sin which could be rendered into English as:

> Giving up of that which is according to reason and adoption of that which is against reason.[165]

---

[160] Ibid. pp. 39-40. Hence *ahiṁsā* is recommended.

[161] *Kāṇṭam* I, p. 9. De Nobili makes this remark on the desire of men for forgiveness of sin as something 'given'. Cf. T.T. p. 399.

[162] In Christianity sin is an offence against God. It is ethically wrong and opposed to the personal will of God. In Hinduism, the theory of karma weakens this aspect of sin, though the idea that sin is an offence against the divinity (Rg veda, 5.8.5, 7.89) is not absent. Here prayers are addressed to Varuna for forgiveness with the knowledge that sin has displeased him. Cf. De Smet, 'Sin and its Removal' in *Religious Hinduism*, ed. Neuner, Allahabad, 1964, pp. 122-123; 129-130. Cf. Bror, op. cit., p. 156. In theistic Hinduism, sin is considered a stumbling-block in the way of union with the deity. Dhavamony, *Love of God, pp. 52-54.*

[163] *Kāṇṭam* I, p. 9. Here de Nobili explains the personal notion of sin.

[164] Ibid.

[165] P.J.A. p. 62. It is a rendering of "Piramānikkap partiyāka, appiramānikkac cuvikāram pāvam." (T.T. p. 400).

De Nobili explains further this point in terms of the act of the will:

> That the will (*manatu*) says 'no' to that which is just according to reason and that it delights in that which is against reason and says 'yes' to it is sin.[166]

De Nobili explains the content of 'that which is according to reason' and 'that which is against reason' as *piramāṇikkam* and as *appiramāṇikkam* respectively.[167] He stresses the role of free will in sin. The will that has consented to sin, until it turns from sin, remains in sin.[168]

De Nobili's critique of the idea of removal of sin in Hinduism is based on the key-idea of repentance. Repentance is required by the nature of sin which is an act of the will. De Nobili finds this aspect absent or unclear in Hinduism,[169] namely, the idea that one should repent of one's sin for having offended God who is all good. Besides, it is Christian doctrine that a sin freely committed puts the soul of man in an internal state of sin which perdures until man repents of it and turns his will from sin.[170] It is repentance which is personal human act that would make a man acceptable to God. Even great sufferings and pains which a man may undergo will not help a man remove his sin without the repentant act of the will turning from sin. Mere sufferings without the repentant act of the will are likely to make one more hardened.[171] De Nobili uses this concept of repentance which stresses the internal and personal character of sin, to criticise its absence in general in the practices prescribed

---

[166] P.J.A. p. 62.

[167] T.T. pp. 400-401. *Piramāṇikkam* is defined in terms of *piramaṇam* which is the way (*neṛi*) taught by God who is the form of justice for the salvation of man because it is the perfect way of virtue. All thoughts and deeds which pertain to the order of *piramāṇam* are defined as *piramāṇikkam* whose opposite is defined as *appiramāṇikkam*. We note here that giving up of *piramāṇikkam* and adoption of *appiramāṇikkam* is sin not only in an ethical sense but also in the religious sense of being against that which God has taught man for his salvation.

[168] P.J.A. p. 62.

[169] A.N. p. 218. De Nobili says that the idea that without repentance there would be no removal of sin is acceptable even to non-Christians.

[170] P.J.A. p. 63.

[171] Ibid. pp. 63-64.

for the removal of sin.[172] It is believed that one marvels at the waters originating from the mountains, and says that it is something divine.[173] One comes to believe that through these waters (*tīrtams*) one can obtain the removal of sin.[174] According to de Nobili forgiveness of sin is one of the six signs of true religion, which sign is absent in Hinduism according to him.[175] Bathing in the sacred rivers like the Kaveri would not help the removal of sin or of guilt. There is no removal of guilt without the will to give up sin. A Sanskrit verse explains this idea of repentance:

> Jalena janita pankam, jalena paricuttiyate, manaca nimittam pavam, paccatapena cuttiyate.[176]

The meaning of this *sloka* is:

> Just as mud formed by water if it falls on the body, is purified by water, so too sin committed by the will is removed by repentance.[177]

Therefore, the right means for forgiveness of sins is repentance, and not baths in rivers. The latter without the personal acts of knowing

---

[172] Ibid. p. 64. De Nobili uses *paccāttāpam* for repentance. A.N. pp. 218-219. Here he uses *anutāpam* in the same sense.

[173] A.N. p. 379. The idea of sacred waters exists in Hinduism. De Nobili refers to *tarmatīrtam* (the holy or sacred waters) in Ramacetu (*Ramesvaram*). He criticises bathing in sacred rivers as a means of removal of sin, since it implies a material notion of sin. De Nobili criticises this idea in his treatise *The Signs of True Religion* (which exists only in a Portuguese translation as the fifth part of *Catecismo*, tr. B. da Costa 1661, Cap. ff. 199-201). In this treatise de Nobili speaks of the observances used by the Hindus with a view to obtaining removal of sin.

[174] Ibid. p. 414, M.V., pp. 98-99.

[175] KP, pp. 67, 71-72. Cf. also da Costa, *Catecismo*, Quinta parte, cap. II, 199-201. It speaks of the true means of removal of sin as one of the signs of true religion. Cf. *Kāṇṭam* I, Introduction, p. 45.

[176] KP, p. 72. Cf. Dubois I, p. 268. He cites a poet called Venianna and translates him as follows: "C'est l'eau qui cause la boue, et c'est elle aussi qui la nettoie. La volonté est la cause du peché, et c'est elle seule qui peut en purifier." The verse quoted in KP corresponds to this poem of Venianna. That would mean KP probably owes this verse to this author. It also shows that the idea of repentance is not absent in Hinduism. Dubois himself cites this author to show that such an idea is present in Hinduism.

[177] K.P. p. 72.

God, loving him, sorrow for sin committed, all of which are included in the concept or repentance will not avail unto the removal of sin. Faith in such means would be against reason.[178]. De Nobili criticises also acts of worship done for the sake of removal of sin, since the gods worshipped here demand many observances that offend against reason and which therefore cannot help removal of sin. But that one worships the true God in the temple, that one has perfect sorrow for one's sins and that one is determined to walk in the way of virtue, all this is like a lake of good water that helps remove dirt.[179]

De Nobili views critically the practices of almsgiving and austerity as means of the removal of sin. Austerity and almsgiving in so far as they involve control of self and asceticism could help remove the causes of sin, and therefore could help towards removal of sin. De Nobili recognises this. Actions like this could also lead towards other things which are good.[180] But the morality of austerity and almsgiving is determined by the intention. It is the intention that helps determine if actions like the practices of austerity and almsgiving are *dharma* or *adharma.*[181] Thus if prayer, austerity, almsgiving are done toward created things like the sun, and not towards the one true God, they are a disorder and sin. Besides austerities however severe they might be, cannot be the cause of removal of guilt without perfect repentance which is an essential requirement on the part of man for the removal of sin.[182]

De Nobili has a sharp criticism of the religious act of uttering the names of deities or of gods in Hinduism for obtaining forgiveness of sin. It is said that if one wore the rosary (*rudrakśa*) or if one were to utter with his mouth the name of Rama or Narayana, however great a sinner one might be, all his sins would fly away like a

---

[178] A.N. p. 414, ibid. pp. 412-414. Here de Nobili explains the natural origins of *tirthas* against the sacral idea of *tīrthas*. He explains away the divine quality attributed to them by the sense of wonder of man.

[179] *Kāṇṭam* I, pp. 49-51. De Nobili says that without the theological knowledge of God, love and repentance of sin, baths in rivers (*tīrthas*) by themselves will not help forgiveness of sin.

[180] T.T. p. 412.

[181] Ibid.

[182] Ibid. p. 404.

bird.[183] De Nobili refers to a verse *Kantapurāṇam* which he explains as follows:

> If one were to pronounce the names that exist for Rudra, Rudra would come running to him like the cow that comes near its calf. Just as a bird on the tree frightened by the stone thrown at it would fly away, so too his sins would be removed and he would reach heaven.[184]

In the same work, another verse speaks of one calling the name of Śiva. De Nobili renders its meaning as follows:

> Before the one who pronounces the name of Śiva, Śiva would dance. Even Yaman [185] would be subject to such a person. On his face Lakṣmi [186] would always dwell. Just as snow disappears before the sun, so too all his sins would disappear. He would not be drowned in the sea of sin. If one who lives on earth at the moment of death were to pronounce the name of Śiva-Śiva, would reach heaven.[187]

In another verse that de Nobili quotes, it is said that by the correct loud utterance of Śiva-Śiva, one's sins would be burnt like a palmyra palm that dies when struck by lightning. Besides, it would lead to the end of a series of births. De Nobili renders the meaning of the verse as follows:

> If one were to hear correctly Śiva-Śiva, all his sins would be burnt just like a palmyra palm that would be blighted and fall through the lightning that struck it. There would be no rebirth for him. Besides this, if anyone would pronounce three times well Śiva-Śiva by the mouth, Śiva would keep him for his correct uttering of Śiva-Śiva. For uttering Śiva-Śiva for the other

---

[183] *Kāṇṭam* II, p. 198-201.

[184] Ibid. p. 198.

[185] Yama is the god of death. His abode is called *Yamalōka*.

[186] Lakṣmi is the goddess of wealth and material prosperity. Cf. Donald Jean and Johnson, *God and Gods in Hinduism*, p. 75. She is Viṣṇu's consort. She is said to be reborn with each of Viṣṇu's incarnations.

[187] In the verse noted, the word for heaven is *cārūppiyam*. De Nobili in his commentary prefers to use the term *mokṣa* instead.

two times, because there is no fruit that God can give, there would be an insoluble debt on him.[188]

De Nobili criticises such utterances of the names of Śiva or those of Narayana and Rama, since they are understood in a mechanical sense for obtaining forgiveness of sin.[189] He does not describe this practice as *nāmajapa* (prayer of the divine name) but only as utterance (*uccaraṇam*) which has a nuance of mechanical repetition according to rules, ritual and grammatical.[190] The chief criterion for the sound doctrine of removal of sin and guilt is repentance for one's sin. De Nobili's judgement on the utterance of the names of gods recommended as means for forgiveness of sin in Śaivism and Vaiṣṇavism is that in the utterance of the divine names, there is no idea of repentance present. Rather it would only encourage sin. Besides, only God can forgive sins which are against Him who is all-good. By praying to created things saying "forgive", one cannot obtain forgiveness of sin.[191]

There is an idea of 'the mixed state' of sin and virtue which de Nobili tries to correct in relation to the personal act of repentance. The idea of 'mixed state' is a difficulty proposed by the Hindus to him. If one is in this 'mixed state', how does one get out of this state?[192] One could see a material notion of sin in the idea of 'mixed state'. Against this idea, de Nobili explains the state of sin and the state of virtue. Thus if after one has done many virtuous deeds, one commits a serious sin, then there is no 'mixed state' of sin and virtue in such a person, but only a state of sin, for that is the nature of sin. Sin affects the state of the will. Sin cannot co-exist with virtue, for

---

[188] *Kāṇṭam* II, pp. 199-200. One important element of *mokṣa* (attainment of *vīṭu* [lit. home]) according to Hinduism is to be free from the cycle of births (*saṁsāra*).

Ibid. The word for *mokṣa* in this verse is 'the home where the Lord dwells (*kartan valpati*).

[189] Ibid. p. 200. Cf. also M.V. pp. 98-99.

[190] *Kāṇṭam* II, p. 213. De Nobili calls it *namōccaraṇam*, e.g. *Civōccaraṇam* (*Civa uccaraṇam*). The idea of *uccaraṇam* seems to stress the aspect of mechanical repetition. De Nobili does not consider the aspect of *bhakti* in the prayer of the name. Cf. Dhavamony, *Love of God*, p. 79. He remarks that in the Tamil Saivite mystics, repentant love emerges.

[191] T.T. pp. 401-402. Cf. also KP. pp. 43-44. It is said that gods themselves perform acts of expiation for themselves. Hence they cannot forgive sins.

[192] A.N. p. 301.

sin unrepented keeps the will in a state of acceptance of sin. Hence one cannot speak of 'mixed state' of sin and virtue.[193]

iii. *The Concept of the Ultimate End and Dharma*

De Nobili examines the concept of the final end as salvation in terms of *svarga* and *mokṣa* in Hinduism. We shall consider the concept of the final end in general, then the intermediate heaven (*svarga*) and its different expressions in different sects, and finally the concept of *mokṣa*.

De Nobili mentions three words for the end of man: *avati, oṭukkam* and *kati*. Of these he uses *avati* and *oṭukkam* more frequently than *kati*.[194] *Oṭukkam* is that goal and end that ultimately comes to the soul of man. Such an end has been ordained for man.[195] That man reaches his final end (*avati*) means that he reaches perfect beatitude beyond which nothing else can be desired. De Nobili uses the three words more or less in the same meaning of final end of the human soul. He uses another triad of words for the end in a more general sense, applicable to things which have been made (*kārya*), namely *antam, avati* and *pirayōcanam*.[196] He makes a further precision of the end of a thing (*avati*) by defining it as follows:

> The state in which a thing can attain in faultlessly perfect measure the good due to come to it, such a state is said to be the end (*avati*) to the thing.[197]

Besides, the end differs according to inanimate substances, irrational living beings and intelligent beings. A house has its end when it fulfils the condition of a house in its structure; a tree is said to reach its end when it has all the characteristics of a tree with leaves and flowers, etc.; animals are said to reach their end when they have all the members required by its nature and by which it has its well-being. The end of such things confined to the nature of things themselves is

---

193 Ibid.

194 Ibid. p. 324.

195 Ibid.

196 N.C.C. p. 7.

197 A.N. p. 325.

called *antarkata avati* (internal end).[198] But praise of God from the creature is extrinsic end.[199] In the same way one could speak of man's end as both that which is according to his nature and that which is above his nature, which comes through the grace of God.

All this de Nobili explains, for morality is bound up with the final end of man.[200] Intelligent beings always act for a purpose. "That such and such a thing is intended by an intelligent cause in its operation (*kāriyattolil*) could be said to be *antam, avati* and *pirayōcanam*".[201] Besides, an operation (*kāriyam*) can have ends of which one would be principal and the other subordinate.[202] For the human soul created by God has its principal end which is the Supreme Being in direct vision of God.[203] De Nobili takes note of the problem of final end present in Hinduism. There is an awareness and preoccupation with the end of man. In the ethical philosophy which is a section in *Cintāmaṇi*, de Nobili says that there is a reference to the famous question of *finis operis* and especially the end (final) of the good and the bad. There is a discussion as to whether natural beatitude of man consists in contemplation alone, or also in action.[204] Again, explaining the meaning of Brahmin, de Nobili points out that the perfection and felicity of the perfect wise man (*sapiens*) consists in contemplation of God primarily and, as it were, essentially, and secondarily by way of preparation (*dispositive*) in the use of speculative sciences, use of practical reason and practice of virtues.[205] Again it refers to the beatitude of man in this life. De Nobili shows that this beatitude refers to wisdom or knowledge (*sapientia*) which is incorruptible good of this life. This meaning is given by the word *śāśvatam* in the verse that de Nobili quotes from

---

[198] Ibid. pp. 325-326.

[199] Ibid. p. 326.

[200] The Thomistic (for that matter Christian) morality is an ethic of the final end. Cf. Gilson, *Saint Thomas Moraliste*, pp. 23-32.

[201] N.C.C. p. 7.

[202] Ibid.

[203] Ibid.

[204] I.C. pp. 23, 56.

[205] Ibid. pp. 9-10. De Nobili finds in Manu (1, 97) the relation of virtue to beatitude (or contemplation of God) as a way of disposing oneself to contemplation, a view which St Thomas too expresses in s. Th. 1,2, q.3, a.5 and 2,2, q.180, a.2. The relation of virtue to beatitude is *ratio dispositiva*.

Manu in support of this.[206] He recognises these ideas present in this section and the valuable understanding of beatitude or the final end of man as consisting in contemplation of God. De Nobili discusses also the nature of perfect beatitude. He says that there should be three marks for the perfect beatitude of man, i.e., his final end;[207] but in the work he explains only two marks: i. that it fulfils the perfect desire of man and ii. that it is not mixed with any kind of evil.[208] This means that anything in the world such as riches, pleasure and honours which are the cause of happiness in the world cannot be the final end, since they do not perfectly satisfy the desire of man.[209] Such things are the final end for *lōkayatas*, for they hold that all human life comes to an end with death.[210] For them the final end of man is in this world itself.[211] Such an end does not have the characteristics of true and perfect beatitude. De Nobili would apply these marks of beatitude to the Hindu concepts of *svarga* and *mokṣa*.

iv. *Svarga*

De Nobili gives the meaning of *svarga* explaining it as it occurs in the epics (*kāvyas*).[212] *Svarga* is that part which is "about the descriptions of physical beatitude as they (the Hindus) conceive it, and also of whatever kind of beatitude one can hope for after this life." [213] But this is still a general term as de Nobili explains it here.

---

[206] I.C. pp. 55-56. De Nobili renders Manu (2, 146) as follows: "Inter duos patres, id est secundum naturam, et secundum sapientiam pater secundum sapientiam maior est, quia ex nativitate secundum sapientiam quae a Brahmane profiscitur incorruptibile bonum huius vitae..." Here de Nobili considers only the idea of the Hindus that beatitude of man already in this life consists in contemplation of God. Here he doesn't enter into discussion if the Hindus believe that beatitude after death consists also in contemplation of God. This idea is implicit in the text of Manu he quotes. Cf. A.N. pp. 405-406. Here de Nobili refers to a view which says that heaven or beatitude consists in a direct vision of God. I.C. p. 31. Cf. the quotation from *Taitt. Aranyaka*, 10, 10, 3a where *amrtatvam* is used. De Nobili translates it as beatitude. *Amrtatvam* is a concept of final salvation. Cf. De Smet, art. cit., p. 367. Cf. Mahadevan, op. cit., p. 66 on the relation of *dharma* to *mokṣa*.

[207] A.N. p. 327.

[208] Ibid. pp. 331-368.

[209] Ibid. pp. 329-331.

[210] Ibid. p. 401.

[211] Ibid., also p. 389. Cf. *Kāṇṭam* I, p. 5.

[212] I.C. pp. 17-18.

[213] Ibid. p. 18. Cf. *Narratio*, p. 142. *Svarga* "in altera vita locus voluptatis", "explens omnem cupiditatem."

In *Āttuma Nirṇayam*, he discusses what the term has come to mean.[214] De Nobili explains the meaning of *svarga* as follows: *Cuvarkam* (the Tamil for skt. *svarga*) is divided into *cu* and *kam*. *Cu* refers to the pleasure aspect and *kam* means 'attaining.' This is how de Nobili explains the meaning of *svarga* etymologically.[215] The pleasure aspect is given its content in the *purāṇas*. De Nobili finds that they refer to pleasures of a sensual nature.[216] It is the place where the individual soul comes to enjoy sensual pleasures as the fruit of virtue performed on earth. The chief criticism against this idea of *svarga* is that pleasures of a sensual order cannot be that fruit of virtue practised on earth.[217] *Svarga* is compared to a beautiful garden adorned with palaces. A man who practices control of the body, sacrifices his riches in order to walk in the way of virtue, receives only the perishable joys of *svarga* as reward.[218]

It is also said that the individual souls when they go to *svarga* through death, leave their physical bodies behind and assume divine or celestial (*tivya*) bodies.[229] Such bodies are resplendent with light.[210] But *svarga* itself is described in terms of material pleasures and sensual enjoyments.[221] In *svarga* there are gods who are said to enjoy such pleasures. That gods who have resplendent divine bodies and they enjoy such pleasures goes against the nature of divine bodies. It is a disorder.[222] It is also an error to say that gods who are in *svarga* with such glorious heavenly bodies are also punished and are subject to maledicition.[223] It means that *svarga* is not unmixed happiness. Moreover, *svarga* is within the scheme of the cycle of births according to the theory of *karma*.[224] This intermediate end for man's virtue, de Nobili rejects. Besides this, de Nobili points out

---

214 A.N. p. 370.

215 Ibid. *Svarga* (*svar ga*) literally means 'going' or 'leading to heaven'. Cf. Monier-Williams, p. 1281.

216 A.N. p. 370.

217 Ibid. pp. 374-375. This would also be the same criticism of the different heavens according to the sects. Cf. ibid. pp. 390-394.

218 Ibid. p. 371.

219 Ibid. p. 371.

220 Ibid. p. 381.

221 Ibid. pp. 371-372.

222 Ibid. pp. 381-382.

223 Ibid. pp. 377-378.

224 Ibid. p. 402.

that the moral contradictions present in the idea of *svarga* being the reward of good actions. He quotes a vedic saying: "Let him who desires *svarga* offer sacrifice" [225] which implies a moral contradiction. Here one is asked to sacrifice for the attainment of *svarga*. *Svarga* with its morally unacceptable pleasures is proposed as reward of sacrifice. The contradiction present in the saying is that *svarga* with its sensual and morally objectionable pleasure is considered the reward of sacrifice (*yajña*) and virtuous deeds.[226] It is also said that gods like Devendra in *svarga* create obstacles to virtuous practice like austerity, whereas austerity and other such virtuous practices are acceptable to God who is all good. If so, it would be wrong to say that gods are virtuous.[227] The idea that people in *svarga* reject *dharma* involves many contradictions. *Svarga* which is the reward of virtue becomes the cause of evil. Moreover, the nature and state of *svarga* should be higher than that of the earth. But it is said that the sages on the earth curse gods who are in *svarga* [228] or that those who are in *svarga* receive good through ascetics on earth. This takes away the idea of *svarga* as end and reward for virtue.[229] This relation between earth and *svarga* upsets the right relationship between virtue and its reward as its end. Virtue is performed in order to reach the end. Those who have not yet reached the end cannot be in a higher state than those who have reached. Those who are Brahmins perform sacrifices and other good deeds to attain to the higher things of *svarga*. But the sage Visvamitra is said to have performed austerities, so that he might attain the status of Brahmin or Brahminhood. Thus Visvamitra desires a lesser good.[230]

v. *Heaven According to Different Sects*

Different sects speak of their own heavens as *vaikuṇṭam*, *kailācam* and *piramalōkam*.[231] *Vaikuṇṭam* is said to be the place

[225] Ibid. p. 375. *Svarga kamo yajeta* occurs in: a) *Tandya mahbrahmana* (= *Pancavimsa Brahmaṇa*) 16.15.5. b) *Taittiriya Saṁhita*, 2.5.5.4, and is very often quoted in Pūrvamīmāmsā literature.

[226] A.N. pp. 375-377.

[227] Ibid. pp. 385-386.

[228] Ibid. p. 386.

[229] Ibid. p. 384.

[230] Ibid. p. 385.

[231] Ibid. p. 390.

where the individual soul will enjoy perfect bliss according to the followers of Vaiṣṇavism.[232] Those of Śaivism hold *kailācam* to be the place where the soul will enjoy its final end of perfect bliss.[233] The different groups do not consider the contradictory things spoken of in the *purāṇas*, though they consider them acceptable.[233] They say that the individual soul reaches its end in the world of Brahma or in *vaikuṇṭam* or in *kailācam* and in their own way. But if one considers the description concerning them, one finds them contrary to reason and understanding.[235] *Vaikuṇṭam*, says de Nobili, derives its name from the name of the woman called *Vaikuṇṭa* which is the name applied to her son. He is called *Vaikuṇṭan. Vaikuṇṭan* is *Viṣṇu* who lives with Lakṣmi. The place where they live is called *vaikuṇṭam*. Similarly, it is said that Rudra lives with Pārvati. The place where they live is called *kailācam*. These places are considered the final end for the soul in the respective sects.[236] De Nobili criticises these ideas of heavens as being the final end for man, for in them God is understood to be imperfect. It is said in the *purāṇas* that Viṣṇu and Rudra receive happiness through Lakṣmi and Pārvati respectively. If so, it means that Rudra and Viṣṇu are not perfectly blissful. They cannot, therefore, grant perfect bliss as the form of the final end to men, for no one gives what one does not have.[237] According to the *purāṇas*, moreover, *kailācam* and *vaikuṇṭam* are said to be places on earth.[238] If one carefully examines the nature of these places, they are not found to be *mokṣa* where the souls can enjoy perfect bliss.[239] The concept of *vaikuṇṭam* means that one who reaches *vaikuṇṭam* will not be born again like any other being. This meaning is pointed out

---

[232] Ibid.

[233] Ibid.

[234] Ibid. The basis of these beliefs is in the *purāṇas* which contain contradictory things. De Nobili does not merely refer to the weak points of puranic Hinduism but points out also that they accept the *purāṇas* as religiously valid. This would lead to wrong understanding of God and *dharma* and *mokṣa*.

[235] Ibid.

[236] Ibid. p. 391.

[237] Ibid. pp. 391-392.

[238] Ibid. p. 393. It is said that in *vaikuṇṭam* rivers flow such as the *viracā*. It also said that Ravana went to root out the sacred mount of *kailācam*, which is said to have frightened Parvati.

[239] Ibid. pp. 393-394.

by the name given to Viṣṇu Cēnārtan which means "to cut all births."[240] *Vaikuṇṭam* is the cause that no other birth comes to the soul that exists in *vaikuṇṭam* and that the soul exists without return to another birth for good. Thus it is said that one reaches the good which is the form of the final end in it. This is the concept of *mokṣa*. But de Nobili is critical of the concept, since it is said that Viṣṇu carries his wife on his breast and that he enjoys in *vaikuṇṭam* morally unapprovable pleasures show that he is not perfect.[241] Though they say that "*vaikuṇṭam* is the place where one is saved",[242] that which is enjoined for the attainment of it is unacceptable, since it includes sin. On the contrary, one must conquer anger, lust and greed for obtaining *vaikuṇṭam*, if it is indeed *mokṣa.*[243] As for *kailācam*, it is said that Śiva who is in *kailācam* is imperfect, since he is said to carry Pārvati with him.[244]

De Nobili is not completely unaware of the possible symbolic interpretation of the puranic description of God and *mokṣa*. He says that one could say that many of the sensual pleasures spoken of in God and *mokṣa* of *vaikuṇṭam* and *kailācam* could be understood in a figurative way. One could describe heaven in symbolic language (*upōtkāta alankāram*).[245] De Nobili recognises this type of language as valid. What he objects to is that morally unacceptable things can be used figuratively to describe the perfections of God and of heaven, for they go against the perfect bliss of heaven (which is unmixed with evil and sin) and the nature of God. De Nobili says that the word *svarga* cannot be used for *mokṣa*, since it will raise in the minds of those who hear it ideas of sensual pleasures of *svarga.*[246] Hence de Nobili argues that the word *svarga* can never be used for the bliss of heaven on account of what it has come to mean in the *purāṇas*. Here de Nobili refers to a controversy concerning the use of the term in the Christian religion.[247]

---

[240] Ibid. p. 403.

[241] Ibid. pp. 403-404.

[242] T.T. p. 80.

[243] Ibid.

[244] A.N. p. 404.

[245] Ibid. p. 398.

[246] Ibid.

[247] Ibid. pp. 395-397. De Nobili says that his Christian adversaries do not seem to accept his argument against the use of the term *svarga* for heaven. Cf. ibid. p. 396. "Though the

vi. *The Final End (avati) for Sin (Naraka)*

In connection with our discussion on *svarga*, we may refer to the concept of *naraka* (hell) in Hinduism, for it is understood to be within the cycle of births.[248] Just as a man who practises virtue on earth goes to *svarga* which is a place of enjoyment of the reward of virtue and acquires a body of splendour, so does one (here human soul) through sin comes to exist in hell (*naraka*) and acquires a special body. Such a body is called *yatana carīram* meant for suffering.[249] Then it is said that the soul with the body of punishment after suffering for a while in hell, is born again on earth as a stone, a tree, a reptile, or as birds or animals or as man.[250] De Nobili refutes the idea of special body of splendour in *svarga* and the special body of punishment in hell with the idea that the soul does not need a body for its spiritual activities, such as freedom of choice to say yes or no.[251] Furthermore, the arguments for the refutation of the theory of *karma* and rebirth hold good here, since hell is considered within the cycle of births. For de Nobili the revealed religion is the rule and

---

name of *svarga* is the name which the pagans (the Hindus) have given to the state of Devendra, we who follow the revealed religion have given the term the meaning of true bliss, we consider we can use without being wrong the term *svarga* to mean the bliss of heaven." De Nobili argues that since the word is associated with sensual pleasures of unacceptable nature as held by the Hindus (majority of them), a few Christian communities cannot make it mean heaven by convention (or agreement). Henry Henriques in the translation of *Doctrina Christiana*, namely, *Kiriccittiani Vaṇakkam* (in *Vaṇakkam* ed. S. Rajamanickam, Tuticorin, 1963) uses *corkam* (*svarga*) for heaven (pp. 8, 17, 31, 34, 53) but he also uses *mokkicam* (*mokṣa*) in the sense of bliss or beatitude. He uses *corkavāsi* (*svarga vāsi* = dwellers in *svarga*) in the sense of those in heaven, and *mōkkicapērkaḷ* for the blessed of the beatitudes. Cf. *Tampirān Vaṇakkam*, in *Vaṇakkam*, pp. 10-11. Cf. Bror, op. cit., pp. 172-173. De Nobili has changed these words into *moccam* (*mokṣa*). Cf. Pr. Ap. pp. 148-149. De Nobili refers to the work called *Capitolo* (Cf. Pr. Ap. p. 150, A.N. pp. 396-397) which was composed by a Hindu on the instruction of a Christian. Despite the instruction, says de Nobili, the poet in the verses of *Capitolo* put the Hindu notion of *svarga* rather than that of heaven in the Christian sense. The verses were accepted without question on the Fishery Coast. De Nobili sedulously avoids the use of *svarga* even for the garden of the first parents. Others like G. Fernandes named it *pūtala cuvarkam* (*svarga*). De Nobili rejects this use *Kāṇṭam* II, p. 112.

248 A.N. pp. 565-566, 575-577.

249 Ibid. p. 565. *Yatana* means torment or punishment, especially tortures of hell. Cf. Macdonell, *A Practical Sanskrit Dictionary*, p. 244. *Yatana śarira* means body for punishment.

250 A.N. pp. 565-566.

251 Ibid. p. 566.

criterion according to which he rejects the Hindu idea of hell.[252] In this connection it must be recalled that de Nobili considers that there is the idea of *apokatastasis* present in Hinduism. The Hindus hold that all will finally reach *mokṣa* after the destruction of all the worlds and after the great deluge and after the destruction of hell.[253]

vii. *Heaven* (*mokṣa*)

We shall now consider the concept of *mokṣa* proper to Hinduism. It is more than the relative and intermediate end of *svarga* which is still within the cycle of births. De Nobili says that some assert that the final end of the soul can be attained (or realised) through *mōccam.*[254] One realises the final end through (attainment of) *mokṣa*. This is a correct statement by itself. But de Nobili finds many deficiencies in what they come to describe as the nature of *mokṣa*, or in what *mokṣa* consists. Yet it is agreed upon the idea that it is God who gives heaven to all.[255] Then de Nobili goes on to discuss the different descriptions of *mokṣa* and the definition given thereof. If the soul is in the presence (*cānnittiyam*) of God, by the glory of such a presence heaven will be realised in the soul.[256] ii. Nearness (*cāmippiyam*) of God is the perfect cause of the soul's enjoyment and experience of heaven.[257] iii. Another description says that absorption in God (*cāyucciyam*) makes the soul attain to

---

[252] Ibid.

[253] Ibid. pp. 575-576. Here there is a reference to *pralaya* (deluge). This is an allusion to the four *yugas* (periods), namely, *krta*, *treta, dvapara* and *kali*. At the end of all the *yugas* there is *pralaya* with return to formlessness. Cf. ibid. p. 593. De Nobili in his apologetic for the Christian doctrine of hell rejects them. Cf. p. 576. De Nobili, however, mentions that the Hindus even when they accept that hell could be eternal for some sinners, they do so only superficially and as a manner of speech.

[254] Ibid. p. 404. Heaven is explained in terms of the relation of the soul to God.

[255] Ibid. p. 405.

[256] Ibid. p. 405. De Nobili does not present the different states of *mokṣa* as gradual steps in the attainment of *mokṣa* within the same sect. He presents them as different ways of understanding *mokṣa*. The usual four steps or stages in the attainment of *mokṣa* are: *salōkya* (residence in the realm of God), *sāmīpya* (getting to be in the vicinity of God), *sārupya* (gaining the form of God) and *sāyujya* (absorption in God) as in Śaivism. Cf Mahadevan, op. cit. p. 201. De Nobili gives *cānnittiyam* as one more state of *mokṣa* distinct from that of *cāmīppiyam* (*sāmīpya*).

[257] A.N. p. 405.

heaven.[258] iv. The fourth way of defining heaven is this: If the soul does not disappear or dissolve (*layamāka pōtal*) in God, it cannot reach heaven.[259] The name for such a disappearance of the soul in God is *cārūppiyam*.[260] Then de Nobili refers to another way of understanding of *mokṣa*. v. It is said that if the soul sees God, in such a vision the experience of the soul will be realised in the soul.[261] De Nobili says that if such a view is to be stated accurately, those who hold it must say that the vision spoken of here must be described as direct vision because one could say that the soul sees God on earth through inferential knowledge (*anumāna*) and testimony (*śabda*).[262] That the soul sees God by which it attains to *mokṣa* must be described correctly as direct vision (*pirattiyaccam*). Such a vision is called by them *cālōkkiyam* (*sālōkya*).[263] De Nobili says that this understanding of heaven as the direct vision of God is correct and true in this point alone. But they do not express adequately how perfect bliss comes to the soul through direct vision.[264] De Nobili recognises that their saying is true, that the beatitude of heaven consists in direct vision of God.[265] In his further critique of different ideas of *mokṣa*, he leaves out this way of understanding of *mokṣa* and examines others.

The idea of *mokṣa* that comes from the soul being in the presence of God is not very different from *cāmīppiyam*. *Cānnittiyam* has to do with 'being in the nearness' of God or 'presence' of God.[266] It is said that if the soul is in the presence of God, that alone should be the perfect cause of the experience of *mokṣa* that comes to the soul. *Cānnittiyam* is explained by de Nobili as meaning 'to be before' (here before God).[267] This is distinct from *cāmīppiyam* and *cālōk-*

---

[258] Ibid.

[259] Ibid.

[260] Ibid.

[261] Ibid.

[262] Ibid.

[263] Ibid. pp. 405-406.

[264] Ibid. p. 406.

[265] De Nobili evaluates this concept of *mokṣa* as better than the other views, since it comes closest to the Christian concept of *mokṣa*.

[266] Ibid. p. 406.

[267] Ibid.

kiyam.[268] Those who hold the view say that just as the lotus flower opens in the presence of the sun, so too will the soul enjoy the perfect bliss of *mokṣa* in the presence of God.[269] This alone is the direct cause of the attainment and experience of heaven.

De Nobili examines the concept of *cāmīppiyam* as a state of heaven. The word *cāmīppiyam* means 'to be near' [270] "They say that simply because the soul is near God, it attains the perfect bliss of heaven."[271] Those who hold the above two views of *mokṣa,* namely, *cānnittiyam* and *cāmīppiyam* do not consider the nature of God and His presence everywhere. God who is bliss and the form of knowledge is present everywhere and knows all things perfectly. Hence one could say all things are in His presence [272]. So too God 'touches' all things by His power. If so, all things are near Him [273]. If we follow the meaning of the two words, *cānnittiyam* and *cāmīppiyam,* we may affirm that all irrational beings, all men of earth, all those who are in hell, even devils are in the presence of God and in the vicinity of God. But we know that these do not have the experience of heaven. For these reasons de Nobili finds these two concepts of *mokṣa* inadequate.[274]

viii. *Cārūppiyam (skt sārūpya)*

We shall now consider the concept of *cārūppiyam* as examined by de Nobili. Those who explain the state of *cārūppiyam* give this name "to the soul becoming one form with God."[275]. The image used to explain this concept of heaven is this:

> Just as wood disappears in fire, so too does the soul in God disappear[276].

---

[268] Ibid. pp. 406-407.

[269] Ibid. p. 407.

[270] Ibid.

[271] Ibid.

[272] Ibid.

[273] Ibid.

[274] Ibid. pp. 407-408.

[275] Ibid. p. 410.

[276] Ibid. pp. 410-411. The word used for 'to disappear' is *layamāy potal*. De Nobili takes it to mean 'to disappear' or 'to be dissolved or absorbed'.

De Nobili then gives the reason why this concept cannot be accepted. We know from experience that if a thing gets absorbed in another thing, then the thing that absorbs it receives growth and suffers change [277]. De Nobili argues further from the image of food absorbed into the human body through digestion, which leads to change and growth in the body [278]. So too oil in the burning lamp gets absorbed so that the lamp burns anew continually [279]. De Nobili explains the same phenomenon of changes of physical elements with some more examples.[280] All this shows the fact of disappearance that takes place in things. Now when we say that the individual human soul undergoes absorption in God, it would mean that God suffers growth and change. If one accepts absorption of the soul in God, it would mean accepting in God a quality which is against man, for it makes the soul disappear. In God who is the form of all goodness and who is merciful towards human beings, there is infinite power to create man and save him. There is no quality in Him that will ruin human beings. That which is good by its very nature produces only good and never simple destruction [281]. In the destruction or absorption of the human soul, God cannot produce any good [282], either for Himself or for man. To say that by such absorption, man has the experience of heaven does not make sense, since the individual soul disappears. This conception of heaven in which there is absorption of the soul in God is unacceptable [283]. It could only be said to be simple destruction [284]. That the soul has the experience of heaven means that it exists. If heaven is supreme bliss, it must exist or inhere in a thing, else it cannot be said to exist. One cannot speak of the non-existence of a thing, just as one cannot speak of a man yet to exist, for both are alike in this that they have non-being. The individual soul that undergoes absorption and the individual yet to exist share non-existence. If so, that which suffers absorption cannot

[277] Ibid. p. 411.

[278] Ibid. pp. 411-412.

[279] Ibid. pp. 412-413.

[280] Ibid. pp. 415-416.

[281] Ibid. p. 417.

[282] Ibid. pp. 417-418.

[283] Ibid. p. 419.

[284] Ibid.

have the experience of heaven [285]. The perfection of God that He is the form of supreme bliss and that He is the perfect beatitude cannot be attributed to the individual soul that has undergone absorption or has disappeared[286]. If heaven consisted in the absorption or disappearance of the individual soul, it would mean that it desires this disappearance and strives after it. It would also mean that the ascetics and holy men who strive after heaven by performing austerity, prayer, meditation and such virtuous deeds, do them for their own destruction. This is what is implied in the concept of *cārūppiyam* [287]. It will destroy the intelligibility of the finality of virtue which good men do. Such a concept will create difficulties for the understanding of *dharma.*.

ix. *Cāyūcciyam (skt sāyujya)*

The word *cāyūcciyam* means either 'to be with' or 'to be mixed with' (Tamil. *kalantirukkiṛatu*).[288] De Nobili says that of these two meanings, one must accept the second, for if we accept the first, there will be no difference between *cāmīppiyam* and *cāyūcciyam.*[289] He goes on to show that *cāyūcciyam* cannot be a correct concept of heaven [290]. According to the meaning of this state of heaven, the individual soul becomes one (mixed and united) with God just like two waters that mix among themselves. Such a 'mixing' of the soul with God is said to be the direct cause of the experience of heaven for the soul.[291] This means that things which are the place of the mixing (Tam. *kalappukku āspatamāyirukkiṛa*) must have parts, whereas God is without parts (*akaṇṭam*), i.e., simple.[292] The idea of

---

[285] Ibid. p. 420.

[286] Ibid. p. 421.

[287] Ibid. pp. 422-423.

[288] Ibid. p. 408.

[289] Ibid.

[290] Cf. Bror, op. cit., p. 173. He says that de Nobili does not hesitate to use the term *cāyūcciyam* for heaven. It is not correct. Bror refers to *Upatēcam*, ed. Rajamanickam, Tuticorin, 1965 (a work compiled from de Nobili's works with some changes and from the works of another missionary). Here the use of *cāyūcciyam* for heaven is rejected.

[291] A.N. pp. 408-409.

[292] Ibid. p. 409.

mixing like water mixing with water would mean that something more would come into existence. Such a mixing cannot be accepted with regard to the union of the human soul with God. These types of merging or mixing with God are not true of the union of the soul with God.[293]

The notions of *cāyūcciyam* and *cārūppiyam* do not consider the two distinct realities of God and man, and they remove the possibility of experience of the supreme bliss of heaven which is born of direct vision of God and of love.[294]

c. *Veda as Religion and as Sacred Scripture in Relation to Dharma*

After having examined de Nobili's understanding of the different concepts of religious Hinduism in relation to *dharma* and salvation, we shall consider how de Nobili evaluates *Veda* as religion and scripture in relation to the same. He perceives that one could understand *veda* (in Tamil *vētam*) in a narrow sense as the *māyāvādins* did. It is said according to the *veda* itself that one who does not know the law (*legem*) is not Brahmin.[295] De Nōbili explains what the word *veda* means.[296] The word *veda* does not mean only the law (in the sense of religion) but any science the handling of which belongs to Brahmins. The word *veda* comes from the root *vid* which means understanding. *Vidāti* means 'to know'. De Nobili point out the general meaning of *veda* as knowledge from its application to different things.[297] Thus, for example, *Ayur veda* means the science of medicine; *Gandharva veda* means the science of music. Similarly,

---

[293] Ibid. pp. 409-410. These are arguments de Nobili gives to show that *cāyūcciyam* destroys the nature of God. He explains three kinds of mixtures which lead to three results: i. increase, ii. a new thing and iii. birth of one and destruction of another. The last would be present in *cāyūcciyam*.

[294] Ibid. pp. 507-508. Cf. also *Kāṇṭam* III, pp. 575-576, 581. We present here de Nobili's understanding of *cāyūppiyam* and *cāyūcciyam*.

[295] *Narratio*, pp. 142, 144.

[296] Ibid. p. 144. "Voce illa *Veda* non significari Legem tantum sed quamcumque scientiam, cuius tractationem ad Brachmanes spectare ultro concedimus; vox enim *Veda* desumitur a radice Vid, quae dicitur in intellectione: unde *Vidāti*, id est scire. *Aiur Veda*, id est, scientia medicinae; *Gandar Veda* id est, scientia canendi. *Vedānta* id est, finis scientiae, quo nomine suam theologiam Branchmanes nuncupant."

[297] Ibid. p. 144.

Vedānta means 'the end of knowledge' which word is used by Brahmins for their theology. De Nobili uses the same word for religion in general and for the Christian religion in particular.[298] *Veda* also refers to the written scriptures which are an authoritative source for religion. It is in this double signification that the word *veda* is to be understood. De Nobili is aware of this double sense and uses it in both.

i. *Veda as Scriptures*

Concerning the *vedas,* de Nobili mentions the four *vedas* of the Hindus: *Yajur veda* (Tam. *Ecuru*), *Rg veda* (Tam. *Ruku*), *Sāma veda* and *Atharva veda.*[299] He says that *Atharva veda* does not exist in the region where he lived. Only a few sentences are known here. According to him most of the things written in *Atharva veda* belong to the *śudra* usage of magic.[300] He makes a comment on the *veda* in so far as it is a concept of revelation. The word *veda* is used for different scriptures like *Tattva veda, Gandharva veda, Ayur veda.*[301] Thus de Nobili points out that these are called *śruti, nigama, āgama* and *veda.*[302] They belong to the category of the revealed word. The claim that a *probandha* or *āgama purāṇa* has been revealed by God is not a sufficient criterion of its being truly revealed scripture.[303] One speaks of the *āgamas* as utterances of God (*īcura pirokkitankaḷ*).[304]

---

[298] N.C.C. p. 2. Cf. Bror, pp. 66-67.

[299] T.T. p. 362. This is the order in which de Nobili gives the four *vedas*. He had read the *Yajur veda*. What he had read, he gives in the first place. Cf. I.C. p. 29. Cf. Caland, p. 51. Cf. Gispert-Sauch, op. cit., pp. 9-10, f.n. 20 on *Taitt. Up*. It belongs to the *Yajur veda* as known in S. India.

[300] T.T. pp. 362-363. The *veda* called *cukla* (white *Yajur*) existed in the country of Orya (Orissa).

[301] Ibid. p. 363.

[302] *Śruti* is properly the word for revelation. Here de Nobili mentions *śruti, nigama, āgama* and *veda* as having the same meaning. All these have the same authority of the *vedas*, though *veda* is applied usually to the four *vedas, Rg, Sama, Yajur* and *Atharva*. We note here that de Nobili adopts the term *vētam* in the meaning of revealed word. Cf. T.T. p. 364.

[303] *Kāṇṭam* II, pp. 210-211.

[304] *Āgamas* is the name generally given to Saivite scriptures. Cf. Zaehner, *Hinduism*, pp. 83, 130. One uses this name also for Vaisnavite scriptures. Cf. Dhavamony, *Love of God*, p. 117. It is said that there were twenty eight *saivāgamas* or *siddhāntas* revealed by Śiva himself.

or as their being the form of God or as their having been uttered by sages or seers enlightened by God.[305]

Each *matam* (sect) regards certain books as the *veda*. Śaivites call their *āgamas* utterances of God, namely, the *vedas.*[306] Then de Nobili says that Vaiṣṇavites and other wise men consider the four thousand *prabandhas* to be the *veda* in so far as they have been uttered by God (i.e. *Tiruvāy Moli* which means the word of the divine mouth) who took *avatāra.*[307] This *veda* owes itself to God in *avatāra.* When Vaiṣṇavites accept *Yajur veda* for example, they speak of principal utterances and secondary utterances in it; but they reject the secondary sentences, since they consider them to be wrong.[308] Some others say that the original epic *Rāmāyana* is the *veda* for *śudras.*

It is said in *Yajur veda* that Brahma, Viṣṇu and Rudra, the sun, the moon, the air are gods. De Nobili says that in such books Rama, Kṛṣṇa are not mentioned. The scriptures which mention the latter gods cannot be old, but late in origin.[309] These are difficulties concerning the nature and number of the four *vedas.* De Nobili says that if one asserts that there are only four *vedas,* all that has been said about what different sects consider their *vedas*, as mentioned above, shows that there are more than four *vedas.* Besides, it is also said that *vedas* in the world are infinite.[310] They are given the name *veda* in so far as they have been spoken by God. "Words uttered by God are said to be the *veda".*[311] But to say that one who does not follow one of the four *vedas* must be called 'protestant' *(patitan)* or a man of low condition cannot be accepted, since different sects having different *vedas* do exist.[312]. But though the word *veda* is used by differ-

[305] *Kāṇṭam* II, p. 212. Zaehner, *Hinduism*, p. 9. The corpus of the sacred literature of the Hindus are of two kinds in general. According to the authority, *śruti* is the *veda* of the supreme authority, existing eternally, heard by *ṛṣis* (seers). *Śruti* means 'that which has been heard.'

[306] T.T. p. 363.

[307] Ibid.

[308] Ibid. pp. 363, 365.

[309] *Kāṇṭam* II, pp. 202-203. Different scriptures were written at different periods, since men of different sects wanted to establish their sects with their own scriptures.

[310] T.T. p. 364. Cf. I.C. p. 32. Cf. also Mahadevan, p. 39 on the phrase *ananta vedah.*

[311] T.T. p. 364. The same meaning of *veda* de Nobili adopts for the Christian religion. For this cf. the phrase *tēvōkkitta vētam*.

[312] Ibid. p. 364. This is a narrow view. In Hinduism all accept the authority of the *vedas*, namely, the four *vedas*, the Brahmanas or sacrificial texts, *Araṇyakas* (forest treatises), which

ent sects for their own scriptures, there are contradictions between them.[313]

ii. *Veda as Religion*

De Nobili understands *veda* in the sense of religion. Religion is that which reveals the nature of God and the virtuous conduct *(tarmacarittiram)* for salvation. That is the purpose of true religion. It means religion is known by its content on the two points of God's nature and determination of *dharma.*

> Religion must reveal God's nature and the due virtuous conduct perfectly together as a unity for salvation that is life.[314].

Therefore, it is not enough to say that God revealed religion. What is more important is how and what has been revealed by God. That a religion has been revealed by God is considered to give authority to belief and a criterion for acceptance of it. This idea is present in it. But it is still a relative and extrinsic criterion, with the possibility of error. The intrinsic criterion demands that the nature of the content of the revealed religion does not contain anything which is against reason and right understanding. If it does so, then it could not have been revealed by God.[315] Any observance or a practice that is contrary to right reason is sinful observance. De Nobili says that in Hinduism, there are some observances of this nature.[316] As such they have been taught. In the matter of definition of virtue, de Nobili points out that what is not virtue has been presented as virtue. He asserts that the following of virtue is the way to heaven. This is

---

culminate in the *Upanisāds*. Cf. Zaehner, *Hinduism*, p. 9. The sects de Nobili refers to (Śaivism and Vaiṣṇavism) accept the authority of the *vedas*, but also they have their proper *vedas* outside the classical works of the *vedas*.

[313] T.T. pp. 365-366. Between Vaiṣṇavites and Śaivites, there is conflict. Vaisnavites accept the Yajur Veda, especially those passages and utterances that speak of Narayana as God and reject others. So too Saivites accept only those texts that speak of Rudra as God in the *Yajur Veda*.

[314] *Kāṇṭam* II, p. 212.

[315] Ibid. p. 212. De Nobili points out the want of normative thinking on the nature of religion in Hinduism. Cf. ibid. pp. 210-211.

[316] T.T. pp. 76-77, 83.

how the relation of virtue to salvation is expressed. If so, de Nobili says that one who does not know for certain the nature of virtue and sin will have difficulty in attaining salvation.[317] He gives examples of observances which show that determination of what virtue and sin is wanting, or that it is imperfectly done. The worship of created realities, practice of *sati,* polyandry, polygamy are being approved, which confirms the defective determination of the virtue and sin.[318] De Nobili refers to another wrong idea concerning the conquest of passions. To conquer the feelings of lust and enmity one gives his wife to another and witnesses to her being violated. Through this means one conquers the passions.[319] Another error de Nobili finds concerning the prescription of the kinds of food one should eat and other observances concerning cleanliness and ablutions. These are made the object of religious teaching. De Nobili's criticism against it is that such observances concern the external behaviour of cleanliness or social manners, which will differ from place to place, whereas that which concerns salvation applies to all men *qua* men, and is therefore universal. The observances concerning food, etc. cannot be universal.[320]

Another important function of religion is that it reveals correctly the determination of the nature of God. Now in Hinduism, de Nobili finds that many created things are being worshipped as if they were God.[321]. Thus the sun, and men long dead, are considered to have attained divine nature.[322]. De Nobili says that though some had the knowledge that there was one God, they failed to know His nature. The very efforts of establishing God's nature led to the origin of different religions.[323] De Nobili finds that the *purāṇaprabandhas* do not help towards the correct determination of the form of God's nature.[324] and that the Hindu sects failed in this is shown in the dif-

[317] *Kāṇṭam* II, p. 219.

[318] Ibid. p. 233. Cf. also T.T. pp. 80-81. We have pointed out the doctrine of *karma* and rebirth does not help the determination of *dharma*. All the Hindu sects agree on the doctrine of rebirth and *karma*. Cf. P.J.A. p. 7.

[319] T.T. p. 80; cf. also Appendix, p. i. ibid. p. 82. De Nobili refers to *Śaktipuja*. Cf. Dubois, T. pp. 401-404. Cf. also *Kāṇṭam* II, p. 89.

[320] T.T. p. 48.

[321] *Kāṇṭam* II, p. 227.

[322] Ibid. pp. 226-227.

[323] Ibid. p. 186.

[324] Ibid. pp. 190-192.

ferent ways it has been done.[325] We shall see how in another way the determination of the form of God's nature has been made difficult.

In Hinduism, which is a group of sects[326], de Nobili is faced with contradictory views concerning their religious beliefs, especially about God. Hence a religion with contradiction cannot be accepted. De Nobili's opinion is that want of knowledge of the form of God's nature is the cause of different sects (which he calls *vētamatams*) and *purāṇaprabandhas.*[327] Since in such religions there are mutual contradictions and since they contain things which go against reason, one cannot say that God who is the form of truth revealed them all.[328] De Nobili affirms that all religions which owe their origin to man say contradictory things.[329] The contradiction creates difficulties for the understanding of salvation, the different religions are expected to serve. They speak of mutually contradictory things concerning God, and also of morally unacceptable things. If so, to hold that in every religion *(neṛi)*, God is present does not make sense.[330] That God would be present (in Tam. *mun nirpārenuṛu*) in each one's religion is a reference to the salvific meaning of religion. De Nobili does not seem to accept this meaning. It is true that in such religions *(vētamatams)* there have been taught some utterances of *dharma* and righteous conduct.[331] Even about the law of *māyāvādins,* de Nobili remarks that they say many things compatible with true religion, which could, therefore, be accepted by Christians. He asks if good men among Brahmins should reject the pearls in them because other evil men collect wrong things in them.[332] De Nobili is ready to ac-

---

[325] T.T. p. 398.

[326] I.C. p. 24. De Nobili observes that owing to the variety of sects, there is diversity in theology (*adhyātmika*), the science of God. Ibid. p. 26. He says that on account of this variety, there is no one lawbook for all Brahmins.

[327] *Kāṇṭam* II, p. 201.

[327] Ibid. De Nobili uses *akkiyāna mārkkam* for non- Christian religions which stresses the ignorance of God's nature and *dharma* present in them.

[329] T.T. pp. 258-259. Here de Nobili refers to the non-Hindu religions like Islam, Jainism and Buddhism which hold different views of the use of statues (*vikrakam*) for worship.

[330] Ibid. p. 262.

[331] Ibid. pp. 77-79. *Kāṇṭam* II, p. 216. De Nobili speaks of the few *dharmavākyas* in Hinduism.

[332] I.C. pp. 36-37.

cept these good utterances *(dharmavākyas)* but because they are also mixed with errors concerning God and *dharma,* one may not consider that they could be helps to salvation.[333] The errors affect religion as a whole, especially as a way of salvation.[334] Therefore the question is not the presence of individual good utterances of *dharma,*[335] but religion as a whole which is a sum total of all utterances which are considered to be the source and rule of the life of man in relation to salvation. De Nobili compares the few *dharmavākyas* to stars on a dark night, and the true religion to the sun. The reason is that the few *dharmavākyas* are found mixed with erroneous conceptions of God and of the matter of teaching against sin. Hence these religions which utter *dharmavākyas* along with such errors cannot help towards salvation.[336]

d. *Caste and Religion*

Another important point that de Nobili criticises is the relation between caste and religion. De Nobili distinguishes caste (skt *jāti*) from religion. The former owes its existence to the order of the world *(lōkakrama)* and convention and agreement of men which concern principally social *(laukīka)* goals.[337] Religion must not be understood as a characteristic of a particular caste. De Nobili also shows that such a distinction between castes which are a social reality and religion is present in Hinduism itself. Thus one does not say that because Brahmins and those of the royal caste *(Kṣatryas)* who belong to Śaivism and Vaiṣṇavism have changed castes. *Kṣatryas* and Brahmins do not abandon caste observances proper to their castes when they join, say, Śaivism and Vaiṣṇavism.[338] Similarly, different castes wear the same religious symbols, which shows castes are not a

---

333 T.T. p. 77.

334 K.N. p. 118.

335 T.T. p. 77, *Kāṇṭam* II, pp. 216-218. In K.N. p. 118 they are called *maturavacanakaḷ* (sweet utterances). In I.C. p. 37 they are called 'pearls' (*margaritae*).

336 T.T. pp. 77-78. *Kāṇṭam* II, pp. 215-216.

337 M.V. p. 86, T.T. pp. 18-19. Here cf. M. Weber, *The Religion of India*, London 1967, p. 27. He considers the ritualistic duties to be the *dharma* of caste. Cf. P. Dahmen, *Robert de Nobili S.J.*, Munster 1924, p. 25, f.n. 2. In this connection cf. the origin of castes in a functional sense.

338 M.V. pp. 86-87.

religious reality.[339] If one sees a man of a low caste wearing *linga*[340], one cannot say that his religion is that of a low caste. Rather *linga* is the symbol of Śiva and not that of the man who wears it.[341]. That a person of a low caste worships Śiva is not an offence to Śiva, and his worship of Śiva cannot prevent a Brahmin from worshipping Śiva. Here de Nobili explains the meaning of religious symbols. The purpose of wearing religious symbols is that one wants to show that which he believes in his heart must correspond to what he says or does externally, that his religion is good, that he wants to express what he wears is its symbol, and that he belongs to the particular religion he believes in. Thus Brahmins, *Śudras* and *Caṇḍālas* follow Śaivism. This does not mean that this religion is that of Brahmins or that of *Caṇḍālas.* De Nobili says that to consider and to say that it does mean that it is a religion of Brahmins or of *Caṇḍālas* cannot be *dharma.*[342] De Nobili perceives a clear distinction between social status and reality of caste and the religious status and reality of a sect *(matam).* Therefore whatever be one's religion, one can also observe caste observances independently of one's sect.[343] We could also say that whatever be one's caste, one can follow the sect or religion one desires. De Nobili has observed that people of different castes follow the same religion of Vaiṣṇavism.[344] He takes pains to explain the distinction between caste membership and religious affiliation. This is one of the importnt and constant points of his catechetical teachings. De Nobili rejects the caste notion of religion.[345] He argues as follows for his rejection of the caste notion of religion. If a religion is identified with a particular caste, it would mean that the particular religion has to prescribe or enjoin social observances. But the purpose of true religion is to teach and enjoin all that is virtue and forbid all that is sin with a view to the salvation of man.[346] Virtue is a matter that concerns all men regarding salvation, and sin is evil for

---

[339] Ibid. p. 87.

[340] *Linga* is the phallic symbol under which Śiva is woshipped, and it is also worn as a symbol of Śiva.

[341] T.T. p. 24-25.

[342] M.V. pp. 41-42.

[343] T.T. pp. 25-26, 41.

[344] Ibid. pp. 26-27.

[345] Ibid. p. 35.

[346] Ibid.

all men and its avoidance by all men is necessary for salvation which is the goal of all men. Caste observances cannot be the content of revelation, but only knowledge of virtue and sin with a view to salvation. They alone apply to all men, and religion *(vētam)* must teach only this. Caste observances are relative to particular castes and therefore they cannot be the object of universal teaching and prescription.[347] This means that *varṇadharma* cannot be said to have a direct relation to man's spiritual status and salvation.[348] De Nobili rejects this conception of *varṇadharma.* He also refers to anther idea of religious affiliation of Brahmins in which their social reality is identifield with the following of religion. It is said that only he who follows one of the four *vedas* could be said to be a Brahmin and a noble. If one does not follow one of the four *vedas,* one is called a man of low caste.[349] It is said in the same way that only if one follows one of the religions which exist among the learned men of India, one could be called *Brahmin*, *Kṣatrya* and *Vaiśya.*[350] De Nobili rejects this idea of *Brahmin*, *Kṣatrya* and *Vaiśya.* His contention is that the fact one is *Brahmin* or *Kṣatrya* or *Vaiśya* is not immediately relevant to salvation,[351] but only that one walks in the path of virtue.[352] At the same time that men of different castes follow one religion does not make them one caste or one clan *(kulam).* In other words, de Nobili keeps the distinction of religion and caste, rejecting any direct theological significance as present in the idea of *var-*

---

[347] Ibid. pp. 35-36. Virtue is a moral demand for all men. It is *māṇavadharma*. It is *māṇavadharma* in so far as it concerns actions of right virtuous behaviour. It can be the object of religion, since religion by its definition concerns the knowledge of the way of salvation for all men.

[348] G.H. Mees, op. cit., pp. 50-51. Mees aptly remarks that when people praise the caste system, they mean the theoretical system of *varṇa*. The theoretical and ideal *varṇa* (*chaturvarṇya)* which comes to be the expression of the spiritual progress of man is distinct from caste (*jāti*) which has come to exist in the concrete historical conditions.

[349] T.T. pp. 359-360. Cf. also *Narratio*, pp. 142-143. Here de Nobili says that this is an opinion current only among the sect of *māyāvādins*. He rejects this exclusive definition of Brahmin.

[350] Ibid. p. 360. It is identification of religion with caste. It means Brahmin, *Kṣatrya*, *Vaiśya* are considered religious terms rather than social terms. De Nobili considers this concept invalid on moral and theological grounds of *dharma* and universality of salvation.

[351] Ibid. De Nobili quotes a popular saying concerning man's last end: "At the gate of heaven (*svarga*), scavenger and king are equal."

[352] Ibid. p. 513.

ṇadharma. That one is in a particular caste belongs to the dimension of civil society, and not to the religious dimension of man.

e. *The Hindu Sects as Different Ways of Salvation*

God who is the form of truth cannot reveal different kinds of religions.[353] If one accepts that God can reveal different religions or sects as one sees here, one does not have a criterion of good and bad religion. De Nobili regards the multiplicity of religions as being taught by man.[354] Such religions taught by man won't help towards salvation. In this context, de Nobili rejects the idea that all religions are ways to salvation.[355] He quotes the arguments of the Hindus:

> They say that just as there are many ways to go to a city, and just as many rivers end in the ocean, so too it is possible to determine (the nature of) God and reach heaven.[356]

De Nobili would admit that different religions lead to salvation only if they look to the same truth.[357] He rejects the idea that different religions which do not have regard for truth can lead to salvation. For him truth concerns the determination of *dharma* (virtue or righteousness) and the nature of God in their relation to salvation. De Nobili's view is that many false religions come into existence through ignorance and man's free will.[358]

f. *Salvation of Non-Christians*

De Nobili considers the salvation of a good non-Christian as belonging to one of the non-Christian religions. The good non-Christian rejects the erroneous ideas of God in his religion and considers God to be the principal and original cause of the world. He performs virtuous acts for the sake of this one God and does not

353 Ibid. p. 91.
354 *Kāṇṭam* II, p. 186.
355 T.T. p. 469.
356 N.C.C. p. 34.
357 Ibid.
358 Ibid. pp. 40-41.

consent to sinful deeds. He does not know the true religion of God through no fault of his.[359] De Nobili says that all the theologians are agreed that the merciful God will not condemn such a man.[360] At the same time, de Nobili observes, heaven which is the direct vision of God is above the power of the intellect of man. Man reaches the beatitude of heaven through faith in God which is above the nature of the intellect of man and through love of God which is above the nature of the will of man.[361] De Nobili goes on to say that the faith and love of God of the good non-Christian spoken of above are proportionate to his nature. The knowledge of God that he has comes to him through the help of reason which is a quality of created intellect. Such knowledge cannot be said to be above the nature of the created intellect of man. Hence the love of God that is born of this knowledge is proportionate to the nature of the will of man.[362]

Thus de Nobili goes on to speak of the relation of such knowledge and love of God to the salvation of the good non-Christian in question. Such knowledge and love of God he has and other virtuous acts he does help to prevent him from falling into serious sin. They cannot be said to be the direct cause of sanctifying grace. Nor can it be said to be meritorious (*mōccacātakam*) unto salvation.[363] Yet condemnation of such a man cannot be in keeping with the mercy of God.[364]

After this, de Nobili speaks of the ways in which God's saving grace comes to such a person as understood by theologians. First, God who rules everything with right order will not allow disorder to exist in the matter of salvation. He will send an earthly teacher or

---

[359] T.T. pp. 413-414.

[360] Ibid. p. 414.

[361] Ibid.

[362] Ibid. p. 415. It does not mean that knowledge and love of God which the good non-Christian has is purely natural. These acts of faith and love of God need the help (actual grace) of God. What de Nobili means by 'natural' knowledge or 'natural love of God' is that it does not yet include the theological virtues of faith and of charity which man receives with the grace of justification. The good deeds a non-Christian does, his knowledge and love of God before justification are to be understood as ways of preparing himself for the grace of justification. It is the doctrine of St. Thomas. Cf. S. Th. I, 2, q. 109, a. 6.

[363] 'Meritorious unto salvation' (*mōccacātakam*) means that one is already in the state of sanctifying grace.

[364] Ibid. p. 415.

one from heaven to teach such a man the truths needed for salvation. If such a man hears the teaching of the truths and does not accept them, he will not be saved. If he accepts the supreme truths of faith revealed by God, then in such an acceptance he receives faith that is above the created nature of man. With such a faith if he has love of God with the grace of God, then such acts are directed towards God, and are above the nature of man. They will lead to salvation.[365]

If there is no teaching of the truths of faith given to such a man of virtuous life who has not committed serious sins, the virtuous deeds done by him for the sake of one true God, though they are not the direct cause of forgiveness of sin, they amount to having removed the obstacles to sin.[366] Similarly, if such a man has rejected cruelty towards others for the sake of God, he has removed the obstacle to God's manifestation of His mercy. It is accepted that God cannot but grant His grace to a man for his salvation if he does all that he can.[367]

> If he has done virtuous deeds according to his ability, then can it be assumed that God has granted him the grace to know the divine mysteries needed for salvation through a teacher.[368]

This means that God who is the form of mercy has deigned that such a man obtains the sanctifying grace for the forgiveness of sin and the theological virtue of charity for the attainment of the perfect beatitude of heaven.[369] Here de Nobili remarks that though the virtuous deeds performed for the sake of one true God by such a person are not the direct cause of forgiveness of sin and of sanctifying grace, yet because obstacles of sin to the grace of God were removed through such virtuous acts, they were beneficial, and they could not be said to be fruitless.[370]

---

[365] Ibid. p. 416.

[366] Ibid. p. 417.

[367] Ibid. pp. 416-417.

[368] Ibid. p. 417.

[369] Ibid. p. 416.

[370] Ibid. pp. 417-418. Since all the good deeds of the non-Christian are understood as preparation for the grace of justification, they belong to the beginning of conversion under the impulse of grace.

Then de Nobili discusses the salvation of another type of non-Christian. There is a non-Christian who has not heard the Gospel through no fault of his. Following the non-Christian religions, he had committed many sins. He then finds through reason that sins are wrong conduct and rejects them. He begins to live like the good non-Christian spoken of above. He recognises God to be the one true God, repents of his past sins and desires ardently to know the way of salvation. For God's sake he practises virtue and seeks after the way of salvation.[371] The opinion that God will save one who strives hard to the extent he can after salvation is in keeping with His infinite mercy. That God will grant without fail the help which is the saving divine grace to such a repentant good non-Christian is an opinion acceptable to all theologians.[372] That the Lord will grant the grace of hearing the Gospel (or the spiritual teaching) to the repentant non-Christian who does all he can in the name of the Lord is also in keeping with the infinite love of God.[373] De Nobili says that of the two opinions, one cannot decide which one is more certain doctrine. He says that he has explained what is in keeping with the gift of divine grace and justice.[374]

---

371 Ibid. p. 418.
372 Ibid. p. 419.
373 Ibid. pp. 419-420.
374 Ibid. p. 420.

PART TWO

DHARMA IN CHRISTIANITY

CHAPTER FIVE

THE CONCEPT OF RELIGION (*VĒTAM*)

a. *The use of ñānam*

In our study of de Nobili's concept of religion (*vētam*) we must examine how he uses the expression *ñānam* (knowledge) and its relation to the definition of religion.

De Nobili defines *ñānam* as follows:

> To determine (the nature of) the Supreme Being who is the form of knowledge and the virtuous actions for the attainment of heaven.[1]

The end (*pirāyōcanam*) of such knowledge is heaven (*mōccam*) which is "life eternal."[2] *Ñānam* in this context is not knowledge of the things of this world, but knowledge of God and of the virtuous conduct needed for salvation. In another place de Nobili, rendering "veritatem meditabitur guttur meum" into Tamil translates *veritatem* as *paramañānam*.[3] He defines paramañānam "knowledge of the highest being such as God."[4] *Ñānam* is, therefore, spiritual knowledge of God, of virtue and of salvation (or heaven) as its goal. De Nobili uses *ñanōpatēcam* (spiritual teaching) as the title of his five-volume work of catechetical instruction of the Christian religion.[5] In the first volume (*Kāṇṭam* I) de Nobili explains what the spiritual teaching (*ñānōpatēcam*) is about.[6] It does not concern itself with the

[1] N.C.C. p. 1. The word used for 'to determine' is *nirṇayam* which means complete ascertainment or determination. Cf. Bror, op. cit. p. 63 on the use of *ñānam*.

[2] Ibid. De Nobili uses *mōccam* (skt. *mokṣa*) to mean now as heaven, now as salvation, now as life eternal, now as reaching God.

[3] T.T. p. 3. The Latin text is from the Book of Proverbs, VIII:7.

[4] Ibid.

[5] Cf. the bibliography for the different works with the title *Ñānōpatēcam*.

[6] *Kāṇṭam*, p. 5.

affairs or conduct proper to the world (*lōkaviyāpāram*), nor with futile fables, but with the knowledge of God and the ascertainment of the means (*upāyam*) of renunciation of sin. Besides this, *ñānōpatēcam* concerns what one must do to receive the grace of God, to walk in the way of righteousness (*tarma vali*) until death. If one knows these things one may be said to have received *ñānōpatēcam.*[7] De Nobili's expression 'to receive the spiritual teaching' (*ñānōpatēcam*) refers to the gift aspect of faith. It is given to one who desires salvation.

The Christian teacher (*carkuru*) who imparts spiritual doctrine is spoken of as 'a spiritual merchant' trading in *ñānam.*[8] True knowledge of God means knowledge of God's nature. Such knowledge is present in the religion revealed by God. This is more than the knowledge that God is the one Lord who is the original cause (*ātikāraṇam*).[9] It is *ñānam* which comes from the revealed religion of God.

De Nobili explains the spiritual knowledge of faith as enlightenment. He says that the teaching of Christ brings enlightenment (*nānateḷivu*) to man and helps his conversion.[10] The aspect of enlightenment of *ñānam* is expressed through such phrases as "light of knowledge" (*ñānappirakācam*),[11] 'clarity of knowledge' (*nāna teḷivu*) and 'the form of light' (*pirakācacurūpam*).[12]

Ñānam when received and assimilated by man develops a spiritual form (*ñānavaṭivu*) within and 'organs' which are the virtues (*tarman*) of faith, hope, love of God, patience and other such virtues.[13] The spiritual teaching (*ñānōpatēcam*) is said to be ambrosia and food for the soul.[14] One who receives the spiritual teaching not only acquires spiritual form (*ñāna vaṭivu*) but also is born in a

---

[7] Ibid.

[8] T.T. p. 494. *ñāna vartakan.*

[9] *Kāṇṭam* II, p. 186.

[10] C.C. (Cf. Bibliography) pp. 34-35. *Teḷivu* in Tamil could mean knowledge. Cf. Burrow and M.B. Emeneau: *A Dravidian Etymological Dictionary*, Oxford, 1961, n. 2825, p. 225.

[11] T.T. p. 22; T.C. (Cf. Bibliography) p. 5.

[12] N.C.C. p. 1.

[13] *Kāṇṭam* III, p. 469.

[14] N.C.C. p. 1.

spiritual way *(ñāna cenmam)* through baptism *(ñānasnānam).*[15] Baptism is a spiritual birth. This spiritual birth takes place through the reception of the spiritual teaching. Besides these uses, we have evidence from his letter that de Nobili called the Christian religion "Spiritual Law" (*ñāna vētam*)[16] though he does not use it in his catechetical or apologetic writings. He was aware of its use in Hinduism too. De Nobili uses *añāna matams* to signify non-Christian religions.[17] Those who follow the *ñānavētam* are called *ñānis. Ñānis* are the followers of the Christian religion. They bear the title through faith.[18] The followers of non-Christian religions are called *añānis.*[19]

De Nobili also uses *Pirāmaṇar* (Brahmins) for the Scribes in the Bible. They are called *Pirāmaṇa cāstri.*[20] Here we may recall de Nobili's interpretation of the office of Brahmins as knowledge in the first chapter.

Knowledge of God: We shall note here some observations of de Nobili on our knowledge of God. It is to be understood always in its salvific significance. God who is the ocean of goodness cannot be known exhaustively. De Nobili affirms that every man can know God to the extent that is required for his salvation.[21] Besides, to have the required saving knowledge of God, God himself must help man. This help of God comes to man as religious knowledge (*vētavisayaka ñānam*) which God deigns to reveal in His *vētam.*[22] This help is also needed because of the fact that man's attempt to determine the nature of God leads to aberrations.[23] Then de Nobili refers to the source (*piramāṇam*) of knowledge of God. Man knows God

---

[15] *Kāṇṭam* III, p. 469.

[16] Bertrand, II, p. 21. De Nobili in a letter to his provincial Alberto Laerzio (according to Bertrand dated 24 Dec. 1608), writes that the Hindus of Madurai considered him a teacher (*Guru*) of the Spiritual Law. I.C. p. 93. He says that the expression *jñāna vēdam* exists among the Hindus.

[17] T.T. p. 505.

[18] Ibid. p. 375. "Vicuvācamuḷḷa ñānikaḷ enkiṟa nāmatārikaḷ" cf. also ibid. pp. 362, 382.

[19] Ibid. p. 382.

[20] C.C. p. 40; cf. 28 Serm. pp. 107-108. The Levites to whom Zachary belongs are called *Pirāmaṇar* which could stress the cultic aspect of priests.

[21] *Kāṇṭam* I, pp. 5-6.

[22] *Kāṇṭam* II, p. 195.

[23] Ibid. De Nobili refers to the aberrations present in puranic Hinduism

here below through *anumānataricanam* [24] and *catta taricanam.*[25] *Catta taricanam* (knowledge through testimony) applies to religion. *Vētam* is a source of knowledge of God. *Anumānataricanam* refers to knowledge through reason with the help of thinking according to cause and effect. That God is a spirit is unknowable through the senses. He can be known only through reason (here called *anumānataricanam*) and the *vētam* (which is *catta taricanam*).

b. *Determination of the Attributes of God (Kaṭavuḷ Nirṇayam)*

We shall now examine one of the principal points of *ñānam* and *ñānōpatēcam*, namely, determination of the attributes of God. This examination is important for the understanding of the concept of *vētam* in its double meaning of religion and scripture and of *tarmam* and *atarmam* made known by the *vētam*. That the *vētam* is the source (*piramāṇam*) and rule (*cūttiram*) of saving knowledge (*ñānam*) and of *tarmam* and of *atarmam* is to be founded in God's nature. This is what de Nobili tries to do in his works under study.

De Nobili lays great stress on the determination (*nirṇayam*) of the nature of God rather than on the existence of God, since he is faced with the Hindus who believe in one way or another in one Supreme Reality. For the problem is not, therefore, whether or not God exists, but what this Supreme Being is like. When he speaks of *ñānam* of God, he refers to it as knowledge of God unto salvation, (*mōccacātakam*).[26] It is not, therefore, merely knowledge that God exists and that He is one.[27] The *dharma* of salvation requires a knowledge of what He is like. Therefore ignorance is blameworthy not so much because it is ignorance of God's existence or of His oneness, but because it is the ignorance of His nature.[28] It is only

---

[24] N.C.C. p. 15. In skt. *anumāna darśana*; De Nobili finds in *Nyāya śāstram* four ways of knowing our sources of knowledge (*Pramāṇa*) of which he makes use of three: *Pratyakṣa* (direct perception), *anumāna* (inference, knowledge through signs), and *Śabda* (testimony). Cf. N.C.C. pp. 14-15,21. Cf. Banerjee, op. cit., pp. 57-59.

[25] N.C.C. p. 25. *Catta taricanam* is the Tamil form of skt. *śabda darśana*.

[26] *Kāṇṭam* I, p. 24.

[27] Ibid. p. 23, cf. also 26, Serm. p. 1. The reason why de Nobili speaks of the knowledge of the existence of one God as distinct from that of the nature of God is that the Hindus recognise the existence of one supreme reality, while they speak of God's attributes in a contradictory manner among themselves.

[28] *Kāṇṭam* I, p. 23.

through knowledge of God's nature and His attributes (*cupāvarūpam* and *laccaṇam*) that one can distinguish the true understanding from a false understanding of God. Besides, one needs to know if one worships the true God, if he would grant *mokṣa*, forgive sins and if he is the true creator (*kartā*).[29] Thus knowing God truly is needed for *mokṣa* since false knowledge of God will lead to sin, and it will not help one fulfil God's will.[30] Such a knowledge of God, not merely that of God's existence and His unicity, is the foundation of right living (moral behaviour) and right religion of worship, conducive to salvation. Thus such a knowledge is connected with righteousness. God's nature has a relation to *dharma*. God's nature is described as *tarmacupāvam.*[31] Nothing could be attributed to God which destroys His righteous nature (*tarmacupāvam*). He can act only according to the all-perfect manner of righteousness (*cakala tarmamērai*), justice (*nīti*) and truth (*cattiyam*).[32] Because he is the form of righteousness (*tarmacurūpam*), he alone can be the source of the form or righteousness to men.[33] De Nobili uses the expression *puṇṇiyavān* (the virtuous One) for God.[34] This expression again is a reference to the righteous nature of the deity. Another expression equivalent to that of *tarmacurūpam* is *nīticurūpam* (the form of justice or righteousness). God's righteous nature bears a relation to man's righteous behaviour. Thus God who is *nīticurūpam* can enable man to attain salvation only through virtuous conduct (*puṇṇiya naṭakkai*).[35] God is *tarma māttirai*, the measure of righteousness or of man's virtuous conduct.[36]

For de Nobili, it is important to establish correctly the righteous nature of God for only then, religion (*vētam*) which is utterance (*vākkiyam*) of God making known *tarmam* and *atarmam* [37] can be reliable. *Dharma* in the order of salvation has a close relation of God's nature. De Nobili deliberately stresses the moral righteousness

---

29 K.N. p. 106.

30 *Kāṇṭam* II, p. 29.

31 T.T. p. 157.

32 Ibid.

33 Ibid. p. 118.

34 *Kāṇṭam* I, p. 46.

35 A.N. p. 552.

36 KP p. 24. In Skt. *dharma mātra*.

37 N.C.C. p. 3.

of God and thus proposes a moral concept of God in contrast to the Hindu concept, in which moral righteousness is weak, at least as de Nobili had known it from his own limited knowledge of Hinduism.

God's nature can be known only through attributes, (*laccaṇam*). He expresses it as follows:

> Being in itself, without beginning, incorporeal form of all goodness, omnipresent, the first cause of all, such a being I worship.[38]

In the verse, he expresses the determination of God's attributes (*kaṭavuḷ nirṇayam*) and then explains each of the attributes. This he does for the reason that the *dharma* of salvation requires knowledge of what sort of God one worships. De Nobili felt the need to present *kaṭavuḷ nirṇayam* in the context of contradictory concepts of God in different sects, and the ambiguity of the righteous nature of God in puranic literature. Only the Being as expressed in the verse cited above is worthy of being worshipped as God. Only the true knowledge of the righteous nature of God as expressed in the *lakṣaṇas* in the verse is a guarantee that man's worship, prayer, etc. are addressed to the true God. Such religious acts of worship, prayer, etc. become *dharma* only if they are directed to God who is known to be such as expressed in *kaṭavuḷ nirṇayam*. The religious duties of the worship of God, prayer, etc. imply a value judgement.

Of all the attributes of God, we shall briefly comment on God being *camastra cupa curūpiya,*[39] for in this attribute all moral perfections of God are conceptually understood. He is goodness without limit. The argument (*niyāyam*) of this attribute (*laccaṇam*) is as follows: "Therefore, infinite knowledge, infinite strength, faultless justice (*nīti*), infinite happiness, infinite mercy must necessarily be present in him without the least defect, along with perfectly indefectible goodness."[40] That God is the form of righteousness (*tarmacurūpam*) belongs to this attribute of God's goodness. Knowing God therefore

---

[38] K.N. p. 108. The skt. verse written in Tamil characters runs as follows: "Cuyampu anāti acarīrī camastha cupa curūpiya: carva viyāpi carvēcam nitānta (written as nitānam) namāmi akam."

[39] Ibid. p. 109.

[40] Ibid.

means knowing God's goodness and His righteousness. Our knowledge of God is not, therefore, a contentless knowledge that He exists or that His being is one, but knowledge of His nature which matters very much for our notion of religion and *dharma*.[41] De Nobili continually stresses the perfections of God's nature, that is, His being the form of goodness (*nanamaicurūpam*) for the same reason. This is the constant theme of God language in His writings.[42] That God is *camastacurūpi* means that all perfections are present in Him. That God is the form of mercy or graciousness is the expression of His infinite goodness.[43] So too, His being the form of truth (*cattiyacurūpi*).[44] He is the form of truth by His very nature.[45] Because He is the form of truth, He is *āptan* (trustworthy). While explaining these moral perfections, de Nobili uses the term *curūpam* as suffix with the words expressing perfections. Some examples are *tarmacurūpam, tayaicurūpam, nīticurūpam.*[46] This deliberate use of *curūpam* with perfections, especially applying to God is meant to stress that these perfections are present in God by his very nature. There are not qualities either secondary or indifferent to His nature. They go to define itself (*cupavarūpam*). Sometimes there is identification of God's perfection with His being. Thus de Nobili says "the being of God (*carvēcuran*) is goodness (*nanmai*)." [47] Similarly, he says "the being of God is knowledge." [48] He uses another inverse order of the same expression, namely, "knowledge (*ñānam*) which is God." [49] Also, expressions like "God is the form of knowledge,[50] he

---

[41] It is to be noted that in the Judaeo-Christian notion of God that God is righteous is stressed. Without this note, holiness of God cannot be correctly understood.

[42] 26 Serm. p. 9.

[43] T.T. p. 419.

[44] N.C.C. p. 10.

[45] Ibid. p. 11.

[46] In God being and good are interconvertible. Cf. A.N. p. 552. One can understand, in the same way the expression like 'God is *paramānanta curūpi*'. He is *ananta parmānantacurūpi*. Here cf. the late formulation of God concept as "Sat Cit Ananda." Cf. Gispert-Sauch, op. cit., p. 1 on the phrase *saccidananda*. It occurs in late *upaniṣads* like *Nrsimhottaratapaniyōpaniṣad* 1-7; *Ramapurvatapaniyōpaniṣad*, 9.2. This formula is not found in the classical *upaniṣads*. Cf. *Kāṇṭam* III, p. 578.

[47] *Kāṇṭam* I, p. 32.

[48] Ibid.

[49] Ibid. Tamil text: *ñānamenkiṟa carvēcuran.*

[50] N.C.C. p. 1, *ñānacurūpi*.

is *curuva kiyāni* (in Skt. *sarva jñāni*) all knowledge.[51] Only if moral perfections are attributes of the divine nature, could one see the intrinsic connection between His nature and His teaching of *dharma*. This also becomes a criterion by which one can distinguish a true concept of God from a false one. Knowledge of God includes also knowledge that He rewards the good and punishes the wicked.

God being the creator of man, He is the source of all goodness for man. *Nirṇayam* of God's nature and His attributes is always to be understood in relation to man and creatures. In the relation of the Creator to man, He can impart the teaching of righteousness (*tarma upatēcam*) only if He is the form or righteousness (*tarmacurūpam*). In the same way if He is *ñānam* He can give man *ññapirakācam* (the light of wisdom) and in the same way He is *paramakiyānacurūpi* (the form of all knowledge).[52]

That God is the source of all good means that He is the cause (*kāraṇam*) of all good as effects (*kāryam*). But he is not the univocal cause (*anurūpa kāraṇam*)of the good as effects (*kāryam*). If He were the univocal cause, that would introduce division (*pinna pētam*) in His nature[53] and would destroy His perfection of being all good. That God is not the univocal cause of effects implies chiefly that He is not man-woman in His nature. There is no male and female in Him in the sense of His being univocal cause (*anurūpakāraṇam*).[54] He is indeed the perfect cause (*uttamakāraṇam*) of all beings but not their univocal cause (*anurūpakāraṇam*).[55] Such an evaluation of God being the cause of all beings is implied in the phrase, "*Nitānam namāmi akam*."

That God is the first cause of all created beings is an important aspect of the concept of God. In the verse on the *nirṇayam* of God, *carvēcam* refers to His being the first cause of all.[56] De Nobili argues from cause to effect of the things of the universe to the existence of

---

[51] *Kāṇṭam*·III, p. 154.

[52] KP 28.

[53] *Kāṇṭam* I, p. 38.

[54] Ibid. pp. 39-40.

[55] 26 Serm., p. 11. That he is *ananurūpakāraṇam*.

[56] N.C.C. pp. 107 and 110. *Carvēca* (Skt. *sarvesam*) means literally 'Lord of all'. De Nobili takes it to mean 'the first cause of all'.

[56] KP., p. 12, *Kāṇṭam* I, pp. 14-16.

the unlimited first cause.[57] He refers to a verse from *Civañāna Cittiyār* which says, "The world consists of three classes of masculine, feminine and neutral beings which are born in certain order, preserved and destroyed. Therefore, there must be one cause of all these beings, who is the beginning and end, a being by Himself remaining in Himself, eternal, blissful, form of knowledge. This is my firm convinction." [58] Similarly, that God is one is supported by a verse from *Tirukkuṛaḷ* "'A' (*akaram*) is first in the alphabet of letters; the first for the world is God." [59] It is also said that the leaves and fruits of branches of trees are the effect of the seed. So too for the world there is one being (which is the cause). Only through ignorance (without *teḷivu*) one may not know this.[60] We observe here that the knowledge in question is religious knowledge of God for salvation, and that it includes knowing Him as Creator of the world and the way of His creation.[61]

Nirṇayam of God through attributes is proposed by de Nobili in this form, so that it serves as a criterion to know who the true God is and thus come to worship him.[62] *Dharma* of worship of God requires knowledge not only of God's perfect holiness but also of Him as the Supreme Being. No one else can be worshipped as God. This is 'ethical monotheism'. The concept of one God and that He is the form of all goodness is the foundation of religious ethics. Here 'religious' is understood as including belief in God who is totally distinct from all that is created. The *dharma* of the act of religion, namely, worship is based on the knowledge of the true God. The last phrase of the Sanskrit couplet defining the attributes of God makes the verse a prayer of adoration.[63] Mere *ñānam* that God exists is not enough for salvation. *Nirṇayam* of God's nature is im-

---

[58] I.C. p. 30. Cf. *Kāṇṭam* I, p. 18, gives only the 2nd line. Cf. Dhavamony: *Love of God*, pp. 224-225, Aruḷnanti is the author of *Civañāna Cittiyār*. The verse occurs in the 2nd section called Cupakkam. The idea of causality is *satkāryavāda* according to which the effect is in the cause. Nothing can come out of nothing. But this verse does not speak directly of *satkāryavāda*. It is said that God is the only being that gives (*tarupavan oruvan vēṇṭum*).

[59] KP p. 13.

[60] Ibid. No authorship is given for this poem. We note here the use of '*teḷivu*' for *ñāna*.

[61] 26 Serm., p. 1.

[62] K.N. pp. 106-107.

[63] Ibid. p. 107. The meaning of the skt phrase as given by de Nobili runs as follows: "Only the Being with such attributes do I worship."

portant.[64] Knowledge of what God is is intimately connected with righteous behaviour of man for the attainment of salvation. To walk in a way pleasing to God or to know God's will correctly is rooted in the knowledge of His nature (*cupāvarūpam*) and His attributes (*laccaṇam*).[65] His righteous nature (*tarmacupāvam*) is the unchanging foundation of all virtue. "Knowing the nature of God rightly without denying His infinite perfections, without attributing to Him 'sports' (*līlās*) which are morally wrong in nature and which therefore should not be attributed to Him and to have known through true faith that He is such is said to be the foundation of all virtuous actions (*cakala puṇṇiya viruttis*)." [66]

c. *Names of God*

The right knowledge of God goes with the use of correct names for God. De Nobili therefore uses different words for God. It is worth examining how he uses them. Thus when he adopts *carvēcuran*, he explains it like this: "The meaning (*artam*) of the word *carvēcuran* is: *caruva* (skt. *sarva*) means 'all'; Icuran (*Iśvara*) means Lord (*Karta*). Therefore the meaning of the term *carvēcuran* (*sarveśvara*) is Lord of all." [67] This word is adequate to express God's unicity. De Nobili examines then the use of the word *tēvan*. This term could be used out of courtesy for an angel sent by God. Hence de Nobili says that this word should not be used for angels even if it be permissible, and that its use should be confined to God alone.[68] In this way one avoids any danger of making angels God. De Nobili says that the names *parāparavastu* and *carvēcuran* on account of their conventional acceptance (*rūttiyārtam*) could be used only of God and never of angels, even by way of courtesy.[69] In the third *Kāṇṭam* of *Ñānōpatēcam* de Nobili gives names for God expressing his perfec-

---

[64] *Kāṇṭam* II, p. 141.

[65] KP p. 14.

[66] *Kāṇṭam* II, p. 220.

[67] *Kāṇṭam* I, p. 19. Cf. Bror p. 91. Cf. Here K.N. p. 107 in the Skt. verse *carvēcam* which means "Lord of all." Cf. Monier-Williams, p. 1188. It is also a name of Śiva.

[68] *Kāṇṭam* II, pp. 9-11; cf. *Kāṇṭam* III, p. 3. Thus he uses, *tēvan arulicceyta vētam* (religion revealed by God).

[69] *Kāṇṭam* II, p. 11.

tions.[70] They are: *parāparavastu, carvēcuran*, *cuvāmi*, *kartan*, *carvattukkum vallavar* (Omnipotent), *ātiyum antamum illātavar* (one without beginning and end), *tānāy irukkiṟavar* (one who is by himself), *cakala nanmai curūpi* (the form of all good), one who knows all and who rules with unfailing order (*kiramam*). These words are not synonymous.[71]

Another name for the Supreme Being, the Lord of the universe is *Viśveśvara* which is a name of a form of Śiva. De Nobili would consider it adequate by its etymological meaning (*yogārtha*) to signify God as the Lord of the universe. But he doesn't use this term in this form, but this name of God is present in the word *vicuvēcuravāti* (skt. *viśveśvaravādins*) which means theologians.[72]

De Nobili uses *pirumavāti* for theologians.[73] This expression is rooted in the word Brahma with the final short vowel which means according to de Nobili God in general.[74] This means that in de Nobili's opinion Brahma is an acceptable expression for God. But he does not adopt it for regular use for God for the reason that it would be misunderstood as Brahma of *trimūrti*. Another expression de Nobili uses for God is that He is *kēvala āptan* (one who is absolutely reliable) with regard to religion because He is the form of truth (*cattiya curūpi*).[75] God is also *tātā* (one who gives).[76]

In the discussion of the names and expressions for God, de Nobili stresses the accuracy of the God-language. This is understandable in the face of differing concepts of God in Hinduism. Correct God-language reflects also correct understanding of who God is.

---

[70] *Kāṇṭam* III, p. 14.

[71] Ibid. p. 14. One could add here *cuyampu* (in Skt. *svayambhu*) as in K.N. p. 107. Cf. Macdonell: *A Practical Sanskrit Dictionary*, p. 371. *Svayambhu* means Brahman. Literally it means self-existent. We may mention here also *kaṭavuḷ* as in the name of the work *Kaṭavuḷ* Nir*ṇayam*. N.C.C. p. 63. Burrow, op. cit. p. 79, gives the meaning of *kaṭavuḷ* as one who transcends speech and mind.

[72] *Kāṇṭam* II, p. 49. Cf. Monier-Williams, p. 994, on *Viśveśvara*. Cf. also *Kāṇṭam* III, pp. 7-8 on the Hindu names of God.

[73] *Kāṇṭam* II, p. 22.

[74] I.C. p. 9. T.T. p. 72. Here de Nobili accepts the use of *parapiramam* (*parabrahma*) in the sense of the Absolute.

[75] N.C.C. p. 3.

[76] Tātā expresses the aspect of giving in God, cf. *Kāṇṭam* I, p. 73. In T.T. p. 482, God is called *vētiyan*. It means one who instructs in *vētam* (religion).

Knowledge of God's nature (*cupavarūpam*) is important for right love (*patti*) towards Him and worship of Him,[77] as it is the root cause (*mūlakāraṇam*) of the whole of *dharma*. If one does not have true knowledge (*cattiyañānam*) of God, one cannot be a truly righteous man (*tarmapārakar*).[78] Thus living in *dharma* is rooted in one's knowledge of God, especially His nature. The very name of God is the form of righteousness (*tarmacurūpam*).[79]

We mention here de Nobili's use of the concept of Guru for God. We are here interested in its religious meaning.[80] Guru understood in the sense of teacher is applied to God. De Nobili understands God to be the *kuru* of all men. God who is the form of knowledge (*ñānacurūpi*) is the principal cause of all knowledge (*ñānam*) and understanding of all men. Hence, He is the *kuru* of all men.[81] That God is *kuru* of all men places all men in the condition of disciples (*cīsar*). All men are in a situation of *sisyas* (*cīsarūpam*) *vis-à-vis* God. God who is the invisible *kuru* becomes the visible *kuru* in Christ.[82] Here we speak only of God as *kuru* (not the incarnate Christ as *kuru*) because of its connection with the concept of *vētam* which we shall presently examine. God is the teacher of the way of *tarmam* for salvation which is the content of *vētam*.

d. *Veda as Religion*

We have, in the previous chapter, referred to the etymological and wider meaning of *vētam* [83] which is knowledge. Our interest here is its religious use in the sense of religion and sacred scripture.[84] *Vētam* in the above two senses has the common element of knowledge (*ñānam*) concerning God and the way of salvation. We shall first examine this double use.

---

[77] N.C.C. p. 4.

[78] Ibid. p. 58.

[79] *Kāṇṭam* III, p. 92.

[80] Pr. Ap. p. 59. The general non-religious definition of a *guru* is 'one who makes clarity by explanation'. It means teacher. Bertrand, II, p. 21. Hindus came to the new *guru* (de Nobili) and accepted him as their *guru* to receive instruction (probably *dīkṣā*) from him. Bertrand mentions *bikchi* which is probably *dīkṣā*. For *dīkṣā* as *upatēcam* see T.T. p. 41.

[81] N.C.C. p. 5.

[82] T.T. p. 118. We shall examine Christ as *Guru* in the next Chapter.

[83] Cf. Ch. IV on the *Veda* as Religion and as Sacred Scripture in relation to *Dharma*.

[84] Cf. Bror p. 66.

Here is a statement of de Nobili in which he says that he explained "the manner through which ignorance (*akkiyānam*) came into existence and that such religious sects (*vētamatams*) are not the way to salvation and that only the religion graciously revealed by God (*carvēcuranāl aruḷicceyta vētam*) is the way to salvation..." [85] Here de Nobili uses *vētam* and *vētamatam* in the sense of religion. The disciples of Christ said that "*vētam* preached by them was revealed by God" [86] as the way to salvation. Whenever de Nobili uses *vētam* as the way to salvation (*vaḻi* = Way) he uses it in the sense of religion.[87] *Vētam* is also used for the Gospel (*cuvicēṣam*). The risen Christ tells his disciples to preach the Gospel that is religion (*vētamākiṛa cuvicēṣm*).[88] Here too *vētam* is used in the sense of religion. De Nobili avoids in general the use *mārkkam* for religion since he perceived an association of its meaning with caste (*jāti*).[89] But the use of *mārkkam* for religion is not entirely absent. He designates non-Christian religion as *akkiyāna mārkkam.*[90] The Christian religion is called the 'Royal Way' (*irāca mārkkam*).[91]

Following the *vētam* means walking according to the *vētam*. It is called *vētanucāram.*[92] Following of a *matam* is *matanucāram.*[93] Besides this use of *vētam*, de Nobili calls *vētam cittāntam*. He says "the *vētam* which is *cittāntam*" (*vētamākiṛa cittāntam*).[94] This use is sig-

---

[85] 26 Serm. p. 57. Here we refer to other words: *camayam* and *matam*. Cf. *Kāṇṭam* I, p. 7, where de Nobili speaks of *vētam*, *camayam* and *matams*.

[86] Ibid. p. 135.

[87] KP, pp. 6, 74. Here *vaḻi* (way) for the *vētam*, 26 Serm. p. 56. God's *vētam* is said to be royal righteousness (*rāca nīti*) to walk in the way of virtue. Cf. C.C. p. 5. God wanted His *vētam* to spread throughout the world. Cf. ibid. p. 62. Pilate tells the Jews to judge Christ according to their own *vētam*, in the sense of religious law.

[88] 26 Serm. p. 132.

[89] T.T. p. 513-514, cf. the phrase *mārkkam pūrukiṛatu* (to enter *mārkkam*), means entering into the way of caste, 'entering *Paravar mārkkam*.' Cf. also pp. 515-516.

[90] KP pp. 72, 74. We can understand the difficulty of de Nobili concerning his Christians whom he did not like to be called *parankis* and Christianity to be named *Paranki Mārkkam*. Prangui is rather the Arabic form of Franks (Latin, Francus).

[91] T.T. p. 461.

[92] Ibid. pp. 12, 367; 369: Here *vētam* and *vētanucāram* are used in the sense of religion.

[93] Ibid. p. 294.

[94] Ibid. p. 470. Cf. Dhavamony: *Love of God*, pp. 4 and 6. In T.T. the phrase is "Kartar aruḷicceyta vētamākiṛa cittāntam..."

nificant, for it is the term used for the Saivite religion though the term *siddhānta* by itself means established doctrine in which sense also de Nobili uses the expression.[95] As for the use of the term *matam* for the Christian religion, he avoids it as a rule. However, he says that the Christian religion cannot be accepted " as one *matam* among the *matams* taught by men." [96] So he understands *matam* as religious doctrine taught by men alone, if Christianity were to be a *matam* in this sense, it would be only a religious doctrine, a creation of man, and would not be the *vētam* of God.

e. *Veda as scripture*

De Nobili uses *vētam* in the sense of Sacred Scripture in the Christian context.[97] He speaks of Mary as having read the *vētam* regularly and meditated on it and as having understood the meaning of *vētavākkiyas.*[98] There is also the use of *vētappiramāṇam* in the sense of religious Scripture. It is said in the treatise *Āttuma Nirṇayam* that truths concerning the nature of the human soul will be explained with the help of *vētappiramāṇam*.[99] *Vētappiramāṇam* here is used in the plural and therefore refers to religious scriptures. We have seen here the double sense of *vētappiramāṇam*, namely, scriptures and religion. We shall now examine the use of *vētam* in the sense of religion. At the same time, we recognise the intimate connection between the two meanings of *vētam*.

f. *Religion (vētam) as divine utterance*

De Nobili uses frequently the phrase, *Carvēcuran aruḻicceyta vētam*, meaning 'religion graciously revealed by God." [100] That means *vētam* has to do with God. God is the source of religion. De Nobili uses this phrase to point out the revealed character of religion. The

---

95 *Kāṇṭam* II, p. 285.

96 T.T. p. 344.

97 For the Hindu use of the *Veda* for Scripture cf. Ch. IV of this thesis.

98 T.C. p. 5 cf. 28 Serm. p. 114. The Jewish elders are said to have known *vētam* (scripture). Cf. also A.N. p. 482, N.C.C. p. 112, the Ten Commandments are called *vētakarpanai*.

99 A.N. p. 17 *vētappiramāṇam* (in skt. *Veda pramāṇa*). Cf. also ibid. p. 523.

100 Ibid. p. 18.

meaning of the Tamil phrase *aruḷicceyta* is not just equivalent of 're-vealed.' It refers to the compassionate will of God in revealing His *vētam*. The divine act of revealing His *vētam* for the salvation of man is, at the same time, the expression of divine grace (*aruḷ*) for man. Hence, the phrase *aruḷicceyta* for 'revealed' is significant. Here we refer to another expression for revealed scripture, *tēvōkittavētam.*[101] De Nobili uses the phrase in Tamil in its Sanskrit meaning. It means 'religion uttered by God'. This phrase stresses the revealed character of religion. In contrast, the Tamil phrase *carvecuran aruḷicceyta vētam* brings out the gracious will of God in revealing his *vētam* which is absent in the Sanskrit phrase *tēvōkkitta*. De Nobili uses the two phrases to stress the revealed character of the Christian religion.

Vētam is also defined with reference to its truth character. Truths uttered by God are *vētam.*[102] "True words (*cattiya vāk-kiyankaḷ*) spoken by God are called *vētavākkiyam.*"[103] De Nobili uses expressions like this: "*vētam* of God,"[104] *Cattiya vētam*,[105] to stress the only true religion. Besides, God is called *vētiyan*, that is, one who writes the lesson of faith on the palm leaf which is the heart of man.[106]

g. *Veda as the Way*

The religion of God is also understood as the Way. The words used are *neṛi*[107] or *vaḻi*. These two words signifying 'way' are the Tamil equivalent of Skt. marga. In *Tūṣaṇa Tikkāram*, de Nobili says "nirmala puṇṇiya neṛiyākiṛa vētam" (religion that is the faultless way of virtue).[108] De Nobili uses a variant of this phrase, *cakala nirmala puṇṇiya neṛi.*[109] It means 'the all perfect way of virtue' which is the *vētam*. Here religion is equated with *puṇṇiyaneṛi* (the way of virtue).

---

[101] T.T. p. 3.

[102] N.C.C. p. 3.

[103] N.C.C. p. 2, cf. T.T. p. 364. This refers to the sacred scriptures which become the source of religion.

[104] Ibid. p. 2.

[105] T.T. p. 189.

[106] Ibid. p. 482.

[107] Bror, p. 57. It is a common Śaivite word. T.T. 54, de Nobili uses "kaṛtar karpitta neṛi" (the way taught by the Lord meaning religion).

[108] T.T. p. 12.

[109] Ibid.

De Nobili uses the term *nirmala* to show the nature of the Christian religion in contrast to other religious sects (*matams*) which are mixed with error. Religion as the Way is always the way of salvation. "The religion of God is the way for salvation." [110] In *Ñanōpatecā Kuṛip-piṭam*, the following phrase is used: *vētamākiṛa vaḻi.* [111] That is, 'the way that is religion.' The concept of the way is not only essential to the understanding of religion but is itself used for religion. This concept of the *veda* as the way is important for our understanding of its meaning.

It is said that the Way of salvation taught by God is *vētam.* [112] If so, the concept of the way remains to be explained. It is explained by the simile of what a king does who wills that his subjects live according to right order. The king sends a letter to all his subjects by means of which he expresses his will to reward the well-behaving ones and to punish the erring ones. Seeing the letter signed by the king, the subjects would accept it as the king's letter. So too God who is the form of justice revealed a *vētam* like the king's letter to the world. In this *vētam*, He makes known to all what *dharma* is and what sin is and the reward for the one and the punishment for the other. Man needs to recognise the signs of the true *vētam* which is God's letter to man.[113] Since God wills to save men, the will expressed in the *veda* must somehow exist in the world.[114] God is like the father of a family who if He in *ñānapitā* (a religiously wise father), will lead the family in the way of righteousness (*nītineṛi*) through his counsel and advice. God who created the world is the Father (*pitā*) of men. He as the Father rules the family of men by revealing what virtue (*puṇṇiyam*) and sin (*pāpam*) are.

h. *One Religion and Different Ways of Salvation*

According to de Nobili 'ways of salvation' cannot mean 'religions of salvation', since in his view the Hindu religious sects he knew

---

[110] Ibid. p. 35, 26 Serm. p. 56, cf. also N.C.C. p. 35: 'To reach one must walk in the way of the *vētam*.

[111] KP p. 6.

[112] *Kāṇṭam* I, p. 7.

[113] Ibid. pp. 7-8.

[114] N.C.C. p. 5.

held contradictory doctrines on God. But if the same truths concerning God are held, as is the case with the Christian religion (*catya vētam*), then he says that the different states (*āciramam*) such as *camucāratarma āciramam* (married state) *canniyāca tarma āciramam* (the state of *sannyāsins*), different penances and such other ways of *tarmam* can be acceptable ways of salvation.[115] Only in this sense can 'different ways of salvation', i.e., different ways within one '*vētam*' (religion) be accepted in so far as they are oriented towards the same supreme truth of God.[116] Different ways of *dharma* must, therefore, go with the same truth concerning God or the ultimate reality. De Nobili holds that the Christian religion is the one religion that has the same truth on God in which different ways of *dharma* exist as acceptable ways to salvation or to heaven (*mokṣa*). For him there is no problem with different ways of living of *dharma*, provided the same truth is held concerning God. He cannot accept different *matams* (religious sects) which hold different definitions of God contradictory to each other as equally legitimate ways of salvation. Only if one walks in the way of *vētam* (religion) that speaks of the highest truth, i.e., God correctly, one will find it a help unto salvation.[117] In this sense de Nobili rejects the idea that each one can be saved in his own *matam*. What concerns moral living, there is one morality and virtuous living for rich and poor alike.[118]

i. *The Truth Aspect of Veda*

We shall now examine the character of *veda* as *satyavākya*. In *Nittiya Cīvana Callāpam* the disciple asks the teacher how one attains the spiritual fruit of salvation (*ñānapirayōcanam* which is *mōccam*).[119] The answer is that one attains it by the following of the *vētam*. *Vētam* is then defined as follows: "true utterances spoken by God in many and different ways are the *vētavākkiyas*." [120] De Nobili further explains *vētam:* "Likewise to holy men (*makāttumākkaḻ*), God re-

[115] Ibid. p. 34.
[116] Ibid.
[117] Ibid. p. 35, T.T. p. 469.
[118] T.T. pp. 468-469, M.V. pp. 89-91.
[119] T.T. p. 2.
[120] Ibid.

vealed many and different truths for the salvation of the world. With their mouths as *stilus*, God wrote the *vētam*; it is not the case that the holy men taught the *vētam* through their own righteous understanding." [121] Thus *vētam* originates principally from God, and not from right-mindedness (*tarmaputti*) of holy men. In this definition of *vētam*, the quality of truth is stressed. To define *vētam* as truth-utterances (*cattiya vākkiyankaḷ*) is to introduce normative thinking in the concept of religion, especially as the unfailing source of knowledge that leads to right knowledge of God and that of the way of salvation. This meaning is brought out by the use of words like *vētappiramāṇam*. It is said that *vētam* is *piramāṇam* and *cūttiram* for the way of virtue in relation to heaven.

The truth of *vētam* is to be clarified and determined under two aspects: the truth content of *vētam* and the truthfulness of the Revealer. Now the truths of *vētam* manifest the truthfulness of God. *Vētam* as truth-utterance becomes intelligible only if the revealer is reliable. That is why *vētam* is not only *cattiya vākkiyam* but also *āptavākkiyam*. *Vētavākkiyam* is to be reliably true. "That *āptavākkiyam* is the same as that which is spoken by God for *āptan* is the one who utters the good truly." [122] The *āptavākkiyam* of *vētam* concerns the good. When the good is truly spoken, then there is *āptavākkiyam*. God speaks the good for man truly. The content of *vēta vākkiyam* is that which is good. De Nobili then explains how God is *āptan*. "God is by nature the form of truth (*cattiyacurūpi*) and the form of all good (*cakala nanmai curūpi*). He is the only one who can be called *āptan*. No created reality is the form of truth (by nature). Hence the created things can through ignorance and free will fall into falsehood... Only God can be called absolutely reliable (*kēvala āptan*)." [123] The reliability of *vētam* is rooted in God's nature.[124] Because God is good by nature, He can reveal the good truly. He can reveal Himself only as good because that is what He is by nature. Now *vētavākkiyam* as utterance of God must reflect the two qualities of God which are truth and the quality of *āptam* (reliability) concern-

---

[121] Ibid. 'righteous understanding' is expressed as *tarmaputti*.

[122] N.C.C. p. 3. also p. 10. Cf. Banerjee, op. cit., pp. 74-79 on *āptavacana* and *āpta*.

[123] Ibid.

[124] This is the meaning and purpose of *nirṇayam* of God in the treatise *Kaṭavuḷ Nirṇayam*.

ing the good. They are essential to the right knowledge for salvation. *Vētam* in order that it may be the source and rule (*piramāṇam* and *cūttiram*) of the whole faultless way of virtue (*cakala nirmala puṇṇiyaneṟi*) must be known to speak the truth in a reliable way. For salvation one must know only those *vētavākkiyankaḷ* that speak of truth and righteousness (*tarmam*).[125] That is to say, *vētam* must reveal faultlessly the *nirṇayam* of God and *tarmam*. Thus in de Nobili's presentation of Christianity, one sees a constant preoccupation with the truth feature of religion and its quality of reliability (*āptam*). Hence the definition of *vētam* as *vākkiyam* uttered by God is not sufficient to be a criterion of the truth and reliability of *vētam* to be the source and the rule of the faultless way of virtue. It need to be further defined in relation to its content as truth and its quality of reliability.

j. *The Meaning and Object of Religion* (*vētam*)

We shall examine here the meaning and object (*artam*) of religion. In the *N.C.C.* the disciple asks what the meaning (*artam*) of religion is.[126] The teacher answers by saying: "The meaning of the term *vētam* is that which makes known (reveals) *tarmātarmam*. That is to say, *vētam* makes known that which is *tarmam* and that which is *atarmam.* This is the object and meaning of religion revealed by God. The teacher explains it further: "The name *vētam* came to exist because the word uttered by God makes known and teaches that such and such a thing is *tarmam*, and because it shows that such and such a thing is sin and forbids it." [127] In the passage, there is an additional note added to the meaning of *vētam*. Religion does not merely reveal what *tarmam* and *atarmam* are but also prescribes that *tarmam* be followed and forbids *atarmam*. Thus it becomes a norm of right and wrong moral behaviour and moral obligation. Hence *vētam* is said to be for everyone *cūttiram* (rule) and *piramāṇam* (source) of virtuous conduct (*puṇṇiyanaṭakkai*).[128] De Nobili says in *Kāṇṭam* II that only in the religion revealed by God, virtue (*puṇ-*

---

[125] T.T. p. 78.

[126] N.C.C. p. 3.

[127] Ibid. p. 3; cf. also KP p. 55.

[128] N.C.C. p. 3.

ṇiyam) has been faultlessly taught. He believes that only the *vētam* revealed by God is the way to become a virtuous person (*puṇṇiyavān*) and to attain salvation.[129] That *vētam* must reveal *tarmam* and *puṇṇiyacarittiram* is a constant element in the definition of *vētam* in de Nobili.[130] One could recall phrases like *vētam* being "the way of perfect virtue" (*paḷutaṟṟa puṇṇiyattin vaḻi*) [131] or 'the wholly faultless way of virtue (*cakala nirmala puṇṇiyaneṟi*').[132]

Thus *vētam* which not only makes known *tarmam* and *atarmam* but which commands *tarmam* to be followed and forbids *atarmam* has an aspect of obligation and a normative character. Therefore, to know God's religion and to follow it is, according to de Nobili, an obligation for all.[133] If religion is to be the rule and the source of virtuous life, there cannot be even the least support or approval of sin in it. In religion thus understood, all that is sin should be forbidden and all that is virtue must be prescribed.[134] This does not mean that all virtues are exhaustively taught or that all sins are exhaustively and explicitly mentioned as forbidden. Rather it means that only that which is virtue is approved and prescribed, and whatever is sin stands forbidden by religion. Therefore that religion enjoins virtue and that it forbids sin must be understood not in a quantitative sense but in a qualitative sense. The way (*neṟi*) taught by God is called *niyāyaneṟi* (the way in conformity with right reason).[135] The content of this *niyāyaneṟi* is this:[136] "Since God is the first cause (*ātikāraṇam*), man must know Him, must offer sacrifices (*pūcaikaḷ*)

---

[129] *Kāṇṭam* II, p. 221.

[130] T.T. p. 78. "Religion must reveal those utterances which speak fautlessly of the determination of the nature and attributes of God and of the righteous deeds for living together."

[131] M.V. p. 165.

[132] T.T. p. 12. *Kāṇṭam* I, p. 58.

[133] T.T. p. 19. Cf. I.C. p. 93. De Nobili says that the word *vedam* is usually employed to signify law (*lex*). He recalls expressions such as *satya vedam* (true law), *asatya veda* (false law), *jñāna vedam* (spiritual law), *ajñāna vedam* (bad law), in use among the Hindus. Then he says that *vedam* which is a common word for doctrine is applied to doctrine for living (*ad doctrinam vivendi*) just as the Hebrew *torah* meaning doctrine (or instruction) is used for law (*lex*). *Vētam* means therefore, both law and doctrine for living, and thus a norm for living. This meaning enters the definition of religion.

[134] T.T. pp. 19, 35, 36.

[135] Ibid. p. 150.

[136] Ibid.

and other such acts of adoration, devote some time to such actions, respect parents, and others of such nature, love one's neighbour as oneself and regard others as one's own brothers, since all men were created by the same God. Man must not do unjust harm (*aniyāya imcai*) to any one in mind, speech and body (*manō vākku kāyattināl*) and must do to another what he believes to be good for himself.' This is the *niyāyaneṛi* taught by God for man's salvation.[137]

The religious meaning of *dharma* is explained in relation to salvation as follows: 'Like a king who makes his subjects turn to *tarmam* through his reward and forbids sinful actions through punishments, God who is to save all peoples, must make known what is virtue and make men desire virtue through His reward. So too He must reveal what sin is and forbid it through His punishment, and thus make men hate sin. Since among virtues (*tarmankaḷ*) to have love (*patti*) of God is the most perfect virtue (*uttama tarmam*), he must teach his *tarmam* and insist also that to say there is another God besides him and worship him is a serious sin.[138] 'Thus God as *kuru* must teach the virtues of righteousness (*nīti tarmankaḷ*) [139] in different ways (*taricanankaḷ*) to peoples who are in the form of disciples (*cīṣarūpam*). God created man for heaven (*mōccam*) and he must help him and give him strength to reach this end (*avati*)'. It also means knowing the truths which otherwise man would not know.

De Nobili in another place says that "the name *vētam* is applicable only to that which is the true way to the attainment of the shore of heaven." [140] When it is said that such a way is the all perfect way of virtue (*cakala nirmala puṇṇiya neṛi*) it means that it has been revealed by God, that it shows all that is virtuous behaviour (*puṇṇiya ācāram*) which helps one reach the shore of heaven, and that it forbids all sin that leads to hell. The body of such utterances deserves the name of *vētam*.[141] Thus he says that "the gracious Lord

---

[137] This is the doctrine of the *vētam* for living (*doctrina vivendi*).

[138] N.C.C. pp. 3-5. Here one wonders if de Nobili understands *tarmam* taught by God purely in a legalistic sense of God's authority alone for its justification. But he explains *tarmam* also as expression of, and as in conformity with *recta ratio*.

[139] Here *nīti tarmankaḷ* (plural form in Tamil of *nīti tarmam*) is to be understood as 'virtues of righteousness' rather than that of virtue of justice in the narrow sense.

[140] T.T. p. 188.

[141] Ibid.

(*tayāparakartar*), willing that His *vētam* should spread everywhere has established only the virtues of righteousness (*tarmamkuṇankaḷ*) and virtuous actions (*puṇṇiya viruttis*) in the *vētam* of His Gospel which helps all men reach salvation and has forbidden only the desire for sin and behaviour of unrighteousness as an obstacle to it (salvation).[142] Man *vis-à-vis* the teachings of *tarmam* is in a state of obligation to follow them. "To all men, there is an obligation (debt) to know God and worship him, to walk according to *tarmacarittiram* (deeds of righteousness) in the religion revealed by God..."' [143]

k. *The Relation of the Ethical to the Religious*

De Nobili expresses the relation between the religious and ethical in his vocabulary as follows. The terms used for religion (*vētam*) such as *neṛi, cakalanirmala puṇṇiyaneṛi, tarmaneṛi* or *vaḻi* express this relation. *Tarmam* in the moral sense enters the definition of the way of salvation and *vētam*. *Vētam* is the source of *tarmam* because *vētam* is said to reveal all *tarmam* and *atarmam*. We see an identification of right ethical behaviour with right revealed behaviour in the definition of *piramāṇikkam* and *appiramāṇikkam*.[144] *Piramāṇam* is defined "the manner of right reason and order of righteousness." [145] This is the definition of *piramāṇam* in an ethical sense. Then de Nobili explains *piramāṇam* as also the *neṛi* taught and revealed by God for salvation of men. "That is, because the way (*neṛi*) taught by God who is the infinitely perfect form of justice (*nīticurūpam*), for salvation of men is the faultless path of virtue (*puṇṇiya vaḻi*), this *neṛi* could be said to be *piramāṇam* in this context." [146] When taught by God as the way of virtue for salvation, *piramāṇam* becomes a means of revelation. Therefore *piramāṇikkam* which are actions, thoughts and words in conformity with *piramāṇam* come to be the content of the revealed *vētam*. Therefore we could say *piramāṇikkam* are actions, thoughts and words in conformity with the *vētam*. De Nobili does not leave

---

[142] Ibid. p. 49.

[143] Ibid. p. 65.

[144] Ibid. p. 400.

[145] Ibid.

[146] Ibid. cf. above in this chapter our discussion of the use of *pirmāṇam* under the headings: the veda as religion and the *veda* as scripture.

the concept of *vētam* in this context open to any arbitrary notion with regard to *piramāṇikkam*. When *piramāṇam* (therefore also *piramāṇikkam*) passes on into the religious context, it retains its original ethical sense, though it has the added note of its being revealed by God as the way to salvation. Besides, de Nobili adds that *vētam* itself has been revealed to *niyāyamuḷḷa putti* (moral understanding) [147] of man. That means that through *niyaya putti* man recognises the perfectly right *piramāṇikkam*.

Why is the way taught by God who is the form of righteousness, for the salvation of man *piramāṇam*? Because it has itself been defined as "the manner of right reason and the order of justice" and because it is the "perfect way of virtue."[148] Hence the way taught by God alone cannot be sufficiently clear to be known as *piramāṇam*. The content or 'what' of the way needs to be recognised as the way of virtue. That it is the way of virtue is also accessible to reason. In this sense *piramāṇam* alludes to the normative aspect of the way of salvation insofar as it is virtuous. But it is also the way revealed for salvation and is so taught by God in His *vētam*. *Piramāṇam* understood only in an ethical sense cannot by itself be the way of salvation. Only through the revelation and the saving will of God, it becomes a way for salvation, but it is the way congruent with His nature of righteousness. That is why de Nobili continually refers to the righteous nature of God [149] in contexts where he speaks of *tarmam* in an ethical sense in relation to God and salvation.

The relation of the ethical to the religious is seen in the way de Nobili defines sin: "Sin is said to be contradiction of reason (*aniyāyam*) because it is against reason (*niyāyamuḷḷa putti*) which God gave man and against the *vētam* which enjoins all virtues unmixed with sin." [150] Thus what is morally wrong (*aniyāyam*) is sin (*pāvam*) insofar as it is against the revealed religion that prescribes virtue unalloyed with sin. Based on the close relation of unity of the ethically good and bad with the religiously good and bad, de Nobili uses terms and expressions which bring out this unity. These expressions and terms used by de Nobili create the language

---

147 Ibid. p. 400.
148 Ibid.
149 Ibid.
150 Ibid. p. 401.

of religious ethics in which one may see also the distinction of the ethical from the religious. Thus speaking of repentance,[151] de Nobili says that sin consists in giving up the way of righteousness (*nītiyuḷḷa neṛi*) and in the acceptance of the unrighteous (*appirmāṉikka cuvikāram*). So too for true repentance one must renounce the unrighteous and accept the righteous (*piramāṇikkam cuvikāram*). *Piramāịkkam* is that which the revealed religion enjoins and, at the same time, that which is in conformity with right reason. Sin is defined as "the absence of righteousness." [152] Righteousness (*niyāya nīti*) here is not purely moral righteousness. It is also righteousness revealed by God. Man needs God's help to live in this righteousness. Without it man is likely to fall into sin. Sin which is an obstacle to salvation and which is the opposite of the way of righteousness (*nītineṛi*) is explained as *aniyāyam* (unrighteousness). Sinful observances (*pāva ācārams*) are said to be incompatible with *niyāyam* and *nīti.*[153] *Niyāyam* and *nīti* are primarily ethical terms. That which is against *nīti* and *niyāyam*, God forbids in His religion. Hence, they refer to righteousness revealed in His religion. Sinful *ācārams* are not only incompatible with right reason but also because they are obstacle to man's salvation and contradict the righteousness revealed in God's religion required for man's salvation. "Such observances are called sin because they become an obstacle to man's reaching the shore (salvation) and because through them he falls into the abyss." [154] The reason for their being sin is not just the ethical insofar as they are incompatible with right reason, but because they are also incompatible with the righteousness necessary for the salvation of man. Though one could understand this as the ethic of the final end on the level of reason, it is to be understood here as the revealed religious ethic of salvation. What does not help the final end of man or his salvation can only be sin. That is how de Nobili argues. Since sinful observances are incompatible with right reason, these God has forbidden in His religion.[155] They are forbidden by God also because they lead to the fall of man from the way of salva-

---

151 Ibid. pp. 404-405.

152 *Kāṇṭam* III, p. 65.

153 T.T. p. 45.

154 Ibid.

155 Ibid. The sinful observances here referred to sum up the 10 Commandments in terms of those forbidden by them.

tion. Here we see both the distinction and the relation of the ethical and the religious in the explanation of sin. In the same way the distinction and relation between the two is seen in de Nobili's explanation of virtue.

Concerning the relation between the ethical and the religious in our author, we note the two ways in which the ethical is related to the religious and in which the religious is related to the ethical. The first way to relate the ethical to the religious is by way of accepting the ethical as the content of religious *dharma*. Thus murder, desiring the wife of another, stealing, bearing false witness are against the right reason (*nītyniyāyam*). They become actions forbidden by the *vētam* also.[156] The second way concerns the relation of the religious to the ethical. It is done by showing that which is taught by religion is in conformity with right reason. Thus one could see these two ways in the case of the 10 Commandments. The 10 Commandments are said to be *vētakrpanai* (religious commandments).[157] They are conformable to reason, and their content ethical. At the same time, *dharma* in a revealed sense as necessary for salvation is more than *dharma* purely in an ethical sense.

1. *Religius Use of Dharma*

In our analysis of the religio-ethical meaning of *dharma* we must point out the specifically religious use of *dharma*.[158] While explaining certain observances of Israel,[159] de Nobili says they would be signs of the mysteries of divine righteousness (*tarmarakacyam*) and help keep the knowledge of these mysteries in their hearts.[160] Here *tarmarakacyam* is to be understood as referring to mysteries of God's saving actions. De Nobili uses here *tarmam* for the thought of salvation or for things that pertain to salvation. This religious use is an adoption of the Hindu use of *tarmam* in relation to salvation.

---

[156] Ibid. p. 45.

[157] K.P. p. 68.

[158] Paul Haecker: 'Dharma in Hinduismus' in *Zeitschrift für Missionswissenschaft und Religionswissenschaft* 49(1965) p. 96. "Der Dharma ist religios nicht nur, weil das spezifisch religiose Brauchtum dazu gehort, sondern vor allem deswegen, weil er eine Beziehung zum Heil hat. Auch dies gehort zur Definition des Dharma."

[159] For example, circumcision, holocaust offerings.

[160] T.T. pp. 48-49.

De Nobili uses '*tarmavaḻi*' for the Christian religion.[161] He says that those who have accepted the *tarmavaḻi* must give up certain observances (such as polygamy) which will contradict the *tarmavaḻi*. It is said that the holy men suffer for the religion which is the way of righteousness [162] and it is sometimes called *cakala nirmala puṇṇiyan-eṛi* (the faultlessly perfect way of virtue).[163] Sometimes, the term *ñānōpatēcam* is itself used in the religious meaning of the way of salvation. "*Tarmavaḷi* which is *ñānōpatēcam*" refers to the Christian religion itself.[164] If *ñānōpatēcam* is *tarmavaḷi, upatēcam* (teaching) given by Christ for salvation is called *tarma upatēcam*.[165] These expressions show the religious meaning of *tarmam*, that is, in the sense of having to do with salvation.

Besides this use, *dharma* is used in a personal way with the same religious meaning. Thus the followers of the Christian religion are called *tarmapārakar*.[166] They have heard the *tarma upatēcam* of Christ and have accepted it. The assembly of such *tarmapārakar* is called *tarmapārakar capai.*[167] Sometimes, de Nobili uses *puṇṇiypārakar* in the same meaning of *tarmapārakar*.[168] *Tarmapārakar* have to continually wage war against the devil and other enemies in order to reach the beatitude of heaven (*mōcca paramānantam*). De Nobili uses *tarmapārakar* in another meaning of theologians.[169] Those who are learned in the *vētam* are *tarmapārakar*. *Tarmam* is also used in general for anything that has to do with salvation and religion. The meritorious state for attaining heaven is called *tarma antastu.*[170] This expression is used when de Nobili says that "to say that mere man could attain *tarma antastu* (the state of righteousness) more than the *tarma antastu* reached by the Lord who is the form of

---

[161] Ibid. p. 445.
[162] Ibid. p. 313.
[163] Ibid. p. 345.
[164] Ibid. p. 463. *Ñānōpatēcam* is the spiritual law as de Nobili calls the Christian religion whose content reveals the way of salvation as the way of righteousness.
[165] *Kāṇṭam* III, p. 293, the phrase is *tarmattin upatēcam*.
[166] T.T. p. 172.
[167] Ibid. pp. 171, 172.
[168] Ibid. p. 183.
[169] Ibid. p. 487.
[170] Ibid. p. 180.

infinite goodness in His assumed human nature" would be wrong. There is another interesting use of *tarmam* for miracle. De Nobili calls a miracle *tarmam*. The is *tarmamākiṟa putumai* (miracle that is *tarmam*).[171] The reason for calling a miracle *tarmam* lies in its being in conformity with the will of God. Only so it can be called *tarmam*. Since it is according to the will of God, a miracle cannot be performed according to the sinful will of man.[172] De Nobili uses *tarmam* in the general sense again of having to do with true religion as the way of salvation. Speaking of the obligations of parents towards their children, he says that they must teach all that pertains to "*tarmaviṣayam*" which concerns the salvation of their souls.[173] They must "teach all that pertains to *tarmaviṣayam* for their salvation..." *Tarmavīsayam* here refers to matters of the soul and salvation, though it refers also to virtuous behaviour.

It is to be noted that our examination of the religious use of *tarmam* as *vētam* and as the way to salvation [174] shows that *tarmam* has at the same time an ethical sense. The religious meaning of *tarmam* resolves itself as religio-ethical. *Tarmam* in this double sense expresses both the nature of religion and the relation of *tarmam* to salvation. *Vētam* not only teaches the virtuous way (*tarmaneṟi* or *puṇṇiyaneṟi*) but is itself *tarmaneṟi* or *puṇṇiyaneṟi* or *tarmavaḻi*. The ethical sense inherent in the religious use of *tarmam* is a guarantee against any distortion or aberration of the religious meaning of *tarmam*. It has to do with the truth quality of religion. This does not imply that the religious meaning of *tarmam* is reduced to the ethical. Religion is *tarmaneṟi* not only because it is the way of virtue but also because it is the way to the *summum bonum* of man, heaven revealed by God.

Forgiveness of sin (*pāvanivāraṇam*) revealed in the religion of God is in consonance with right reason. One of the marks of the *vētam* is that it promises forgiveness of sins. In it there is means (*upāyam*) for perfect forgiveness of sins (*cakala pāvanivāraṇam*), but in it is also all sin forbidden and there is no approval even of the

---

171 Ibid. p. 340.

172 Ibid. p. 340.

173 Ibid. p. 389.

174 For de Nobili, *tarmam* in its religious sense means the revealed way of righteousness unto salvation.

least sin given in it.[175] This is one of the signs of true religion.[176] For forgiveness of sin, one must give up the following of unrighteous deeds and accept to follow righteous ones.[177] The religion of God reveals this and demands it as a condition for forgiveness. This is true repentance for forgiveness, which true religion must teach. That God forgives sin is a truth known from revelation but this forgiveness is conditioned by man's ethical response to turn from unrighteous things and to embrace the way of righteous deeds. For true forgiveness, it is required that man turns away freely from sin, and it is a condition that is intelligible to human reason and ethically meaningful. It is also religiously meaningful. The true way of forgiveness revealed in *vētam* is also in consonance with right reason.

Here we would like to point out that if *dharma* in the religious sense is normative of *dharma* in the ethical sense, it is also vice versa, that is, *dharma* in the ethical sense is regulative of the religious. This latter aspect de Nobili seems to stress more, since he had to present Christianity to the Hindus. He profits by the *humanum* of the natural law which is common to all men. But that does not mean that he ignores certain valid religious elements present in Hinduism.[178] On the religious level, however, it is difficult for de Nobili to find a common element which could be normative in some way of the true religion. This was due to his belief that Christianity alone is the only true religion of salvation. For the credibility of religion one has to appeal to reason. This is what de Nobili does. The non-Christian religious sects (*vētamatams*) have features which are not in conformity with right reason.[179] The stress of the ethical in religion is seen not so much in the definition of religion itself as in de Nobili's continual use of ethical epithet for things to do with religion, such as *kiramam*, and *niyāyam.*[180] For that reason religion cannot be less ethical. Hence for de Nobili *tarmam* in the ethical sense is normative of the truth character and reliability (*āptam*) of religion, though not the only

[175] T.T. pp. 92-93.

[176] *Kāṇṭam* I, cf. Introduction, p. 45. Where the summary of the Vth *Kāṇṭam* of *Ñānōpatēcam* is given. It deals with the signs (*laccaṇankaḷ*) of religion. The right doctrine on the nature of sin and its forgiveness is one of its signs, cf. 26 Serm., p. 55, cf. also K.P. p. 67.

[177] T.T. p. 404.

[178] Cf. on the *tarmavākkiyankaḷ* present in Hinduism, e.g. T.T. p. 77.

[179] *Kāṇṭam* II, p. 209.

[180] *Kāṇṭam* I, p. 58.

norm. Hence the relation between the *tarmam* of religion and the ethical *tarmam* must be understood in this way. Moreover, the language of righteousness or of justice is close to and not incompatible with the language and message of righteousness in the Bible.[181] The biblical word for righteousness is *dikaisune*. De Nobili translates it usually as *nīti.*[182] Christ is said to have taught *nīti*. What Christ taught is *nītineṛi*. When one walks in it, one will suffer for it. *Nītineṛi* comes to express the Christian religion itself. It is called *nīticurūpavaḻi.*[183]

One could remark that de Nobili ignores the central meaning of love in the Christian religion. This would not be entirely correct, for he does say that "the whole of religion (*vēṭam*) revealed by God consists in the only thing which is love" (*cinēkam*).[184] Moreover, he presents love (as *patti* towards God and *cinēkam* towards one's neighbour) as the highest virtue (*uttama tarmam*).[185] We shall speak more about the *dharma* of *bhakti* in the next chapter. However, we must observe here that de Nobili does not attempt to name the Christian religion as the way of love (e. g. as *patti neṛi*).

m. The Christian Religion is Common to All Races, Castes and Countries

De Nobili found that the use of Paranki [186] to signify Christians, the use of Parnaki *mārkkam* or Paravar [187] *mārkkam* to signify the Cristian religion[188] and the expression 'entering *mārkkam*, or 'entering *kulam*' to signify baptism [189] created a confusion concerning the universal nature of the Christian religion in the minds of the new converts from Hinduism. Paranki was used as synonymous with

[181] Bror, pp. 149-150; here cf. his comment on *nīti*.

[182] T.T. pp. 495-496, cf. C.C. p. 234. Here righteousness (*dikaisune*) is translated as *nītiniyāyam*. Cf. also 26 Serm. p. 87 (in beatitudes) *nītiniyāyam* is used.

[183] T.T. p. 213. Cf. C.C. p. 28, "That Christ should be baptised to fulfil all justice." Here justice is translated as *nīti*.

[184] M.V. p. 170.

[185] N.C.C. p. 4.

[186] Pr. Ap. p. 158.

[187] Paravar are the fishermen, here the caste of fishermen in the state of the Tamils (the State of Madras in S. India).

[188] T.T. p. 514.

[189] Ibid. Cf. Pr. Ap. p. 165.

Christian by Gonçcalo Fernandes.[190] De Nobili found from his own experience that the word Paranki was not an adequate term to designate Christians. In Madurai, according to de Nobili, the Hindus used the term Paranki for the Portuguese.[191] The term came to signify also Europeans who were recognised to be different in their way of life, especially in food and dress. It became a term of contempt.[192] De Nobili found therefore that this term in its restricted meaning was unsuited to signify Christians. In his opinion, the word Paranki did not formally evoke the meaning of Christian in the minds of the Hindus in Madurai. On the contrary, it suggested that Parankis belonged to a race of low extraction.[193] De Nobili's opinion is that Paranki meant formally race or caste which was recognised by the dress they wore.[194]

If Paranki had the meaning of a particular race or the people of a particular nation, one could not use the expression Paranki *mārkkam* to signify the Christian religion, for that would mean that Christianity was a religion of Parankis, and therefore that it was not meant for other races.[195] De Nobili gives the same reason for rejecting the expressions Paravar *mārkkam*.[196] or *Tampirān mārkkam* [197] to signify the Christian religion. This latter expression was used by Muslims to signify their own religion.[198] De Nobili rejected the expression "to enter the *kulam* of Parankis" for baptism.[199] This was

---

[190] Pr. Ap. pp. 158, 164. T.T. p. 514.

[191] Pr. Ap. p. 159.

[192] Ibid. pp. 163-164.

[193] Ibid. pp. 159. On p. 161, de Nobili says that in Tamil it refers to a disease which he calls in Latin Gallicus (*morbus*). In T.T. pp. 514-515, de Nobili says that *Tampirān mārkkam* used by Muslims to mean Islam has besides the connotation of joining caste, as in Islam. If Christians were to use this term, Hindu converts would think that it means that to become Christian is to join the caste of Christians and be thus repelled from Hinduism.

[194] Pr. Ap. p. 164. Our interest here is only to show de Nobili's criticism of the word Paranki to signify Christian as inadequate. Christianity was a religion of all races, castes and nations.

[195] T.T. 514; Pr. Ap. pp. 165-166. Here one could question de Nobili's statement "marcam non legem significat." (p. 165). He restricts the term to mean the manner of life of castes. For this reason he avoids in general its use to signify religion, though not completely.

[196] Ibid. p. 514.

[197] T.T. pp. 514-515.

[198] Ibid. p. 515.

[199] Pr. Ap. p. 165; T.T. 514.

inadequate to express the Christian meaning of baptism. Rather it evoked the idea that baptism was a ceremony of initiation into a particular caste as the word *kulam* indicated.

De Nobili works out a distinction between what is social and what is ethico-religious in this context. Thus for him, Paranki is social in meaning and it is not synonymous with Christian. His reasons for the distinction are important from what he understands religion to be. Religion (or *cattiya vētam*) *qua* religion concerns salvation of man and the way to attain it. In this sense, religion concerns every man. Therefore caste, race, nation which are particular and relative [200] cannot be the object of religion. To hear and accept the truths of *ñānōpatēcam* does not make all those who do so belong to one caste and to one condition of life.[201] That the Christian religion is a religion for one caste and that those who follow it become low (*nīcar*) [202] or Parankis is wrong. The object of religion is to reveal *tarmātarmam* and *cattiyācattiyam* for salvation.[203] Its object is not to reveal the particular and changing social customs and observances of castes.[204] These matters pertain to the conduct of life in civil society of men, and they are different according to different castes and groups of men, whereas the object (*artam*) of religion concerns righteousness to be done and sin to be avoided for the attainment of salvation. If, on the contrary, religion were to be identified with a caste and Christian religion were to be called Paranki *vētam*, it would imply that the social observances (*laukīka ācārams*) prescribed by religion, be they noble or low in dignity, should be the meaning and object of religion to be prescribed by it and to be followed by all men. De Nobili points out these consequences of the use of the phrase Paranki *vētam* for the Christian religion. Thus when he says that Christianity is not confined to one race and that all races can live in it, he wants to show that caste is not religion.[205] In giving a sum-

---

[200] T.T. p. 27.

[201] Ibid. Here the concrete problem that the admission of castes would introduce division in the Church, is to be distinguished from making castes a religious reality. It is against the latter de Nobili fought.

[202] Ibid.

[203] N.C.C. p. 6.

[204] T.T. p. 23.

[205] Pr. Ap. p. 88. "... Christi legem non esse determinatam ad unam particularem stirpem, sed omnibus licere, in ea vivere sine propriae amissione stirpis, seu dignitatis."

mary of what he taught, de Nobili says that in the holy religion, men of whatever race or caste can live and that both nobles and men of lower social groups can be saved.[206] De Nobili's rejection of Paranki *mārkkam* is not only to avoid the identification of religion with one particular social cultural group, but also to point out that the use of it would mean missing the meaning of religion which is the way of salvation for all men.

The purpose of *Veda* is accepted to be that "God who is the merciful One (*tayāparan*) revealed the religion for the salvation of all men and that he prescribed only virtue that helps all reach salvation and forbade only sin which is an obstacle to salvation for all; therefore God is not present in His religion to forbid social *ācārams* proper to different castes and what is improper (*nicitta*) behaviour in social conduct of life" [207] (*laukīkanaṭakkai*). Therefore, understanding baptism as a ceremony of entering a caste community is incorrect.[208] It is for this reason that de Nobili rejects the use of *mārkkam pukiṛatu* for baptism.[209] His term for baptism (*ñānasñānam*) stressed the spiritual character of the sacrament. *Ñānasñānam* is not an observance for one caste. It is an observance that Parankis, Paravar, Brahmins, Rajas and men of all races can receive for forgiveness of sins.[210] That to enter the religion of God is to enter (*kulam pukiṛatu*) is to be rejected, for it would mean entering a caste.[211] Following the Faultless Way of Virtue (*nirmala puṇṇiyaneṛi*) has nothing to do with caste. *Nirmala neṛi* as the religion of God is the way of life for all men to reach the shore of salvation. The way of caste (*cāti*) concerns observances of civil society. Therefore, the expressions which mix the way of religion with the way of castes are not compatible with the concept of religion, as defined by de Nobili.[212] The words one uses in connection with religion must express

---

206 Ibid. p. 76.

207 T.T. p. 36.

208 Ibid. p. 41. In Śaivism, people belonging to different castes receive *dīkṣā*. So too baptism is received by men belonging to different castes.

209 Ibid. p. 514.

210 Ibid.

211 Ibid. Cf. Pr. Ap. p. 165. "Parangui culam puguda venumo" = "visne fieri christianus?"

212 T.T. p. 515. De Nobili says that this is a mixing up of what he calls *mata aṭaivu* (the way of religion) and what he terms as *cātikkaṭutta mērai* (the way of caste).

the object or meaning of religion. Therefore, he sounds a note of warning against the idea of considering entering the Church to be a change of caste.[213] One does not change one's caste when one joins the Church. The only thing forbidden for all *jātis* is sin and the only universal obligation for all men is the practice of virtue. Therefore all men without giving up *laukṛka ācārams* can join the Church.[214] The criticism here directed against attribution of religious meaning to social observances and those of castes is in order in a discussion of the definition and understanding of religion. This criticism is important in the context of the mission of the apostles (*paramkurus*), for their mission is not to make men give up their social *ācārams* and language which have nothing morally wrong in them, but to make them follow the way of salvation — the way of heaven.[215] In the definition of *vētam*, as worked out by de Nobili, there is a distinction between the social and the religious. The concept of *vētam*, as presented by de Nobili, is inseparably ethico-religious.

n. *Observances (Ācārams) in the O.T.*

It is interesting to note how de Nobili explains many observances which are apparently cultural and not clearly religious prescribed in the O.T. for the people of Israel. In consonance with his definition of the meaning of religion which is the *dharma* and truths for the salvation of man and which therefore cannot have social *ācārams* as its meaning and object, de Nobili gives an explanation that is significant. "When it is said that in ancient times God prescribed certain observances for those of one group (*cāti*), He enjoined on them some observances as signs of those *tarmarakcyams* (mysteries of god's saving righteousness) so that knowledge (*ñānam*) of these mysteries might remain in their minds just as he taught some *tarmarakacyams* through words..." [216] From this it is clear that some *ācārams* (which do not seem to concern strictly virtue or salva-

[213] M.V. p. 86.

[214] Ibid. p. 92. Cf. Pr. Ap. p. 166. "God is God of all races and the holy Gospel is the law of all (religion) in which Parankis, Christians of St Thomas, Japanese, Chinese and other nations can remain and attain their eternal salvation."

[215] M.V. p. 87.

[216] T.T. p. 36.

tion, were enjoined on Israel as signs of God's saving mysteries. For them they were not social observances (*laukīka ācārams*).[217] They were signs of the great deeds (*tiviya arputankaḷ*) God would do for them later. There was no obligation to observe them for other groups of men even in the ancient times of theirs. These observances have ceased to be binding on Christian believers of today, since the things of which they were signs have been realised.

The distinction between the social and the religious observances and matters of the way of salvation is stated clearly. "If one considers the way of heaven, it is all a matter of virtue and of nothing else."[218] This de Nobili says against some of the missionaries imposing their own social customs on the new converts from Hinduism. Therefore he continues "this being the case, since it is shown that there is no connection between what kind of food a *kuru* eats and the nature of virtue (*puṇṇiyam*), it appears there is no reason for the Lord's teaching that the *caṟkuru* (the Christian teacher) who teaches them (the gentiles) the Faultless Way of Virtue must eat the food they eat." [219] This was the argument of those who did not want to adapt themselves to the conditions of the people to whom they were preaching the Christian religion. What is of interest to us in this passage is the distinction of what is social (*laukīkam*) and what is a matter of the virtuous Way for salvation. Here one could recall the Council of Jerusalem imposing on the gentile Christians that they should not eat meat mixed with blood.[220] The observance was imposed on them not because it was morally good or an intrinsic demand of the Christian faith, but because the Jews might not suffer too big a scandal and that unity might be preserved between Jewish Christians and gentile Christians and that the Jews might not be hindered from hearing the Gospel.[221] In this context, de Nobili refers only to the observances that are not strictly moral and religious. He leaves out the reference to the pollution of idols and fornication. The

---

[217] Ibid.

[218] Ibid. p. 499.

[219] Ibid.

[220] Acts, 15:20. "But that we write unto them, that they abstain from pollutions of idols, and from fornication, and from things streangled, and from blood."

[221] T.T. pp. 501-502. Cf. E. Hamel, "L'Ecriture, ame de la theologie morale?" in:: *Gregorianum*, 54(1973) pp. 17-25.

motive of the concrete observance made upon the gentile Christians is the unity and charity in the Christian community and concern for salvation.

o. *Equality of Redemption*

De Nobili avoids a caste or a nationalist notion of religion. This he does because the Christian religion is a religion for all. The theological basis for this notion of religion is the universal salvific will of God. "That the Creator's holy will to save all men (to cause all men reach the shore) is the purpose of creation." [222] De Nobili constantly and clearly enunciates the universal salvific will.[223] He refers to the word of Scripture that "God wills to save all men,"[224] while refuting the caste notion of religion. "God who is merciful wills that His religion spreads everywhere so that all men may reach the shore of salvation."[225] All men are sinners and, therefore, need salvation [226] and desire forgiveness.[227] It is from this basic truth of faith that the universality of the Christian religion derives itself. Therefore the religion of God is the way for all men to reach *mokṣa.*[228] Its object (*artha*) is not to reveal matters that belong to the secular (*laukilika*) life of man, but to reveal the way of salvation.

---

[222] *Kāṇṭam* II, p. 294; A.N. p. 553. God deigns to grant *mōccam* to all men.

[223] N.C.C. p. 4, A.N. pp. 484-485.

[224] P.J.A. pp. 91-92.

[225] T.T. p. 49. We have discussed in ch. IV the salvation of non-Christians.

[226] M.V. p. 51.

[227] *Kāṇṭam* I, p. 9.

[228] Ibid. pp. 27, 43, T.T. pp. 511, 513.

CHAPTER SIX

DHARMA AND SALVATION IN CHRISTIANITY

a. *Avatāra in Christianity*

i. *Nature of Avatāra*

De Nobili adopts the term *avatāra* to signify the incarnation of the Son of God but he qualifies the term as *manusaṣa avatāram,*[1] because if he were to use *avatāra* without qualifying it as *manuṣa* (human), it could be understood as *avatāra* in any other non-human form, as it is understood in Hinduism.[2] De Nobili uses *manuṣa avatāra* (human incarnation) to signify assumption of human nature which is constituted by body and soul and to exclude pure assumption (*parikirakam* - skt. *parigraha*) of the human body alone.[3] De Nobili argues that if *manuṣa avatāra* were to be understood purely as the assumption of human body without the soul, it would be *jaṭa avatāram* (*avatāra* in an inanimate body).[4] Human incarnation of Christ means that the Son of God assumed human nature which is soul and body (*āttuma carīramākiṛa manuṣa cupāvam*).[5] If on the contrary, human incarnation were to mean that God assumed human body, it would mean according to de Nobili that divine nature be-

---

[1] T.T. pp. 142 ff. Synonymus for manuṣa avatāra, ibid. p. 28. *narāvatāra* (*nara avatāra*). Ibid. pp. 105, 130, *tēva avatāram. Kāṇṭam* II, p. 307, *tēva parikirakam* for *avatāra.* In Tamil, *avatāram.*

In our discussion we use *avatāra* habitually instead of 'Incarnation'.

[2] Cf. Ch. IV of the thesis. Since many *avatāras* are attributed to Viṣṇu, it is necessary to specify *avatāra* in Hindu context.

[3] T.T. pp. 158-159, *Kāṇṭam* III, p. 288. De Nobili explains here the wrong way *manuṣa avatāra* could be understood according to the Hindu concept.

[4] T.T. Here de Nobili doesn't show a correct knowledge of the Hindu notion of body. *Jaḍa* (inanimate matter) as opposed to *Cētana* (sentient being). Cf. Monier-Williams, p. 409.

[5] T.T. p. 158.

came the form of the human body as the human soul is the form of human body. This would bring limitation to the all-perfect God.[6] Therefore, human incarnation cannot mean assumption of the human body alone (*carīrōpāti*).[7] Human incarnation is assumption of human nature. The assumption of human nature by the Son of God is also called *mānkiṣa ayikkiyam* (in Skt. *māṃsa aikiam*), i.e., 'union of flesh.'[8] Here de Nobili has clearly the biblical meaning of the "the Word was made flesh" in mind.[9] In explaining further the nature of the union of human and divine natures, he says that "the divine person of the Son who has his nature without division has the human nature in the manner of a united (bound) instrument..." [10] Jesus who is God and man has human nature as instrumental cause (*nimittakāraṇam*) and as supporting base (*āciriya ātāram*) of the human actions of Jesus, but the subject or the agent to whom the actions of God-man are attributed is called *nāmatāram.*[11] The divine person is the agent of attribution. The mystery of 'union of flesh' is a great marvel,[12] and a great mystery, and it is the way for man to reach the last end of the one triune God (*trittuva ēkattuvam*) through faith and the beatific vision.[13]

In *Cēcunātar Carittiram*, the author says that God in his incarnation (*manuṣa avatāra*) gave Himself to man and united him to Himself in a bond that is closest and irrevocable and willed that God be man and that man be God.[14] Incarnation is here understood not merely as union of human nature with the divine person of the Son, but also as a gift of God's self to man so that man comes to be God in the sense of His call to live in closest union with Him and share in some way God's goodness.

---

[6] Ibid. pp. 158-159.

[7] Ibid. p. 159.

[8] *Kāṇṭam* III, pp. 48, 49.

[9] Jo. I, 14.

[10] M.V. p. 69.

[11] Ibid. p. 69. De Nobili uses *nimittam* in the sense of 'instrument' here. Cf. ibid. pp. 69-71. That the divine person of the Son is *nāmatāram* of the human actions in incarnation is significant for understanding of the infinite merit of Christ for the salvation of men.

[12] *Kāṇṭam* III, p. 48; T.T. p. 128.

[13] *Kāṇṭam* III, pp. 48-49.

[14] C.C. p. 1.

ii. *One Avatāra*

The assumption of human nature by God which is incarnation, God did only once. One incarnation is perfect enough to show forth God's mercy and justice. If one were to admit that God did the greatest marvel many times, it would mean limitation in the perfection of the miracle of incarnation.[15] That incarnation took place only once is understandable, if one considers what de Nobili says on 'the union of flesh' (*māṃsa aikiam*). It is the closest and irrevocable union and it excludes many different *māṃsa aikiam* or many *avatāras*. Plurality of incarnations is excluded, which could come about through the other persons of the Bl. Trinity, since the Christian truth is that only the Son became incarnate. Neither the father nor the Holy Spirit became man. While explaining the symbolic character of the dove form in which the Spirit of God descended on Jesus during his baptism in the Jordan, de Nobili cautions that this appearance has nothing to do with *avatāra.*[16] Appearance of the Spirit of God in the form of a dove is not an *avatāra* like the human *avatāra* of the Son, in the sense that the Spirit assumed in a bond of union the form of a dove.[17]

Another misconception of the incarnation of Christ from the Hindu meaning of incarnation would be to think that it could be brought about through the power of *māyā*[18] or *līlā* (divine sport). This would make the real and irrevocable union of human nature with divine nature a mere appearance. Christ's birth or his appearance in flesh through Mary is no *līlā* nor is it through *māyā.*[19]

---

[15] T.T. pp. 128-129.

[16] *Kāṇṭam*, III, p. 240. In explaining *avatāra* de Nobili is constantly aware of the Hindu and Christian concepts of *avatāra*. There are not many *avatāras* in Christianity as in Hinduism nor in differenr forms as in Hinduism.

[17] De Nobili takes for granted that the Spirit of God appearing in the form of a dove is the third Person of the Bl. Trinity which may not be acceptable to modern exegesis.

[18] I.C. p. 25 on *Māyā*. Cf. Monier-Williams, p. 881. *Māyā* is "illusion (identified in the *Samkhya* with *Prakrti* or *Pradhana* and in that system, as well as in the *Vedānta*, regarded as the source of the visible universe)". Here it refers to M*āyā being one of the nine energies (or śaktis)* of Viṣṇu.

[19] *Kāṇṭam* III, p. 72.

iii. *Purpose (nimittam) of Avatāra*

'The union of flesh', the irrevocable bond of God with human nature is for man's sake, that is, for his salvation. We shall examine here the purpose of incarnation, as de Nobili explains it. The purpose (*nimittam*) and the goal (*pirayōcanam*) of *avatāra* is that the Lord wills to save man. To save man means showing the way to heaven (*mōccam*). "Therefore, it could be said that to show the way that leads to heaven (*mōccam*) could be the purpose (*nimitta*) and the fruit or goal (*pirayōcanam*) of the Lord becoming incarnate" (*manuṣa avatarā*).[20] This alone could be the principal reason of incarnation. Showing the way to *mokṣa* is saving man (in Tam. *racittal*).[21] Incarnation is the excellent way of saving man. Its purpose does not concern man's attainment of worldly goods but his attainment of the indestructible and indefectible beatitude which is heaven.[22]

Dharma is the purpose of *avatāra.* This is expressed in the language of *dharma* de Nobili uses. While describing the virgin birth of Christ, this is what he says:

> That men may inhale the fragrance of righteousness (*tarma vācanai*) and diffuse from themselves such a fragrance of righteousness, the Lord who has taken on human nature with all its fragrance of meritorious virtue (*tarma puṇṇiya parimaḷam*) may come forth from the flower which is the virgin without the opening of (the flower)..."[23]

The human nature assumed by Jesus brings righteousness to men because it is filled with the perfume of *dharma.*

Jesus is born of the Virgin Mary like the perfume coming out of a flower. For de Nobili, the *avatāra* of Christ is itself the perfume of *dharma* that proceeds out of the flower which the Virgin Mary is. So too *dharma* explains the death of Christ. When the incarnate God dies, it is for the righteous cause of showing the way of salvation.[24].

---

[20] T.T. pp. 142-143.

[21] Ibid. p. 143.

[22] Ibid. p. 144.

[23] Ibid. p. 136.

[24] Ibid. p. 176.

Antonio Vico in his letter to Fr. General Vitelleschi speaks of the objections raised by a *jñāni* against the Christian idea of incarnate God. The jñāni admits one God who is spiritual, invisible and infinite. He also admits all His infinite perfections. But he considers a God who became man, who suffered, who was poor and who died for the salvation of men a fable. Such a God cannot be God.[25] De Nobili refers to this objection. The objection of the Hindus is expressed like this.[26] If God is powerful to save man without His dying in His human *avatāra*, why should He die? De Nobili says that whatever God does, one can ask why God does not do it (incarnation) in another way. He has willed to do it in a particular way. In that He has manifested His knowledge, power and grace.

Showing the way of salvation is a righteous purpose (*tarma nimittam*). In the explanation of the purpose of incarnation, de Nobili mentions the forgiveness of sin. It is for the removal of sin of man (*nara pāva nivāraṇārtam*) that there is incarnation (*nara avatārā*)[27] That God-man made reparation for our sin through suffering is distinctly a Christian idea. Such an idea is not present in the Hindu understanding of *avatāra.*[28]

The life of the Incarnate Son of God becomes also source of the knowledge of *dharma* that leads to *mokṣa.* In it one comes to know his thoughts and his behaviour. They are in the form of perfect virtue. They can help one reach *mokṣa*. His thoughts and actions can only be *dharma*[29].

If showing the way of salvation is the meaning of incarnation, it is important to know the incarnate God does it. The nature and way of salvation concerns always righteousness and virtue (*dharma*). The way of *mokṣa* revealed by him is the virtuous way and the royal way of *dharma* (*tarma irāca vīti*),[30] or *irācamārkkam* (*rājamārga*).[31]He taught all those virtuous ways (*puṇṇiya mēraikaḷ*) which are to be

---

[25] Bertrand II, p. 212. Vico's letter to Fr Vitelleschi (Nov. 1622).

[26] T.T. pp. 163-164.

[27] Ibid. p. 28. Cf. also N.C.C. p. 31. Cf. also *Kāntam* III, p. 32.

[28] Dhavamony, "Hindu Incarnations", p. 168.

[29] T.T. pp. 185-186.

[30] *Kāṇṭam* III, p. 147.

[31] Ibid. p. 144. Here de Nobili uses *mārkkam* in a religious sense which he rejects in the use of *parankimārkkam.*

observed by all men [32] and the way of observing righteous conduct (*tarmacarattiram*) in the right order.[33] In the human nature of the incarnate God, He cannot commit the least sin. All His desires and actions (*vicāram* and *carittiram*) have the form of perfect virtue and they are *dharma* helpful unto salvation.[34] The way of heaven (*mokṣa*) is the virtuous way (*cukirtavaḻi*). Showing man the way of virtue (*cukirtam*) for reaching the "shore of heaven" is one of the reasons of incarnation. This was also the work of the Apostles Jesus sent.[35]

The way to salvation (in Tamil *karaieṛutal*) taught by the incarnate Christ is the faultless way of virtue (*palutaṟṟa puṇṇiya vaḻi*).[36] The reason for incarnation is understood as God saving man by manifesting His perfect justice and mercy.[37]

Another expression of the purpose of incarnation concerns the relation brought about between man and Christ and between man and God. By the union of human nature with divine nature in the Son, men were made brothers (in Tamil, *tampikaḷ* meaning literally younger brothers) and were entitled through Christ who prayed to the Father (*pitā*) to call God Father (*pitā*) in their prayer.[38]

The purpose of *avatāra* is, therefore, expressed in God's gift of Himself to man, in union of man with God and in showing man the way to salvation, and that as the way of *dharma.* It includes also the repairing of the sin of man and the uniting of man to God by freeing him from sin.

iv. *The use of Guru for God Incarnate*

De Nobili uses the term *kuru* (Skt. guru) not only for Christian teachers or missionaries but also for God and especially for God-man, i.e., Christ in particular.[39] In this first *Defensio*, de Nobili gives

---

[32] Ibid. p. 150.

[33] Ibid. p. 232.

[34] T.T. p. 181.

[35] *Kāntam* III, p. 281.

[36] Ibid. p. 443.

[37] 26 Serm. p. 60.

[38] M.V. p. 12.

[39] BRACHMANN, in *Roberto Nobili*, refers only to this use. We note here that de Nobili uses for the Holy Orders *kuruppaṭṭam* (title of *guru*). Cf. *Kāṇṭam* II, pp. 478-479. This name puts accent on the teaching function (giving of *upatēcam*) of the priest. Ibid. p. 479, it is said that the

a definition from a *smṛti* text. *Guru* is defined as "one who illuminates with explanation which may concern philosophy or religion or other matters and disciplines."[40] It is also applied to God in Śaivism.[41] According to de Nobili, God who is the invisible *kuru* (Teacher) becomes a visible *kuru*, i.e. Christ.[42] "That (God) the invisible *kuru* in his divine nature, should become the perfect and the visible *kuru* for the salvation (*iraccikka*) of the world through the human soul and the body He has assumed is to be accepted." De Nobili uses continually *kuru* in place of Jesus Christ, and that with reference to the Incarnate God. The purpose of God becoming incarnate is to be the visible *guru*. The plan of God to save man means not only assuming human nature, but through it becoming the visible divine Teacher (*kāṇappaṭṭa tivya kuruvānavarāka*) in the world.[43] *Kuru* has to do the work of teaching or of showing the way of salvation and of helping man to reach it through His reparation of sin.[44] When de Nobili uses the expression 'the visible *kuru*' to signify the incarnate God, it is always with reference to the work of teaching the way of salvation. This is constantly present in his theological writings.

There is also a tendency in de Nobili to refer to the One to

---

special work of *guru* is to give *upatēcam* and to give good counsel to those who have heard *upatēcam* and thus save them.

Yesudas: "Indigenization or Adaptation?" *Bangalore Theological Forum*, no. 2 (1967), pp. 39-52. He does not consider this idea at all.

[40] Pr. Ap. p. 58. The work is commentary work called *Amarasingha*, part called *Brahma*. Cf. DAHMEN, *Roberto de Nobili*, p. 26.

[41] H.W. SCHOMERUS: *Der Caiva-Siddhānta*, Leipzig, 1912, pp. 290-317. He explains the role of *Satguru* in *Śāiva Siddhānta*, especially the appearance of Śiva to the soul to grant in the knowledge that leads to liberation. Cf. *Tiruvācagam*, (ed) G.U. Pope, Oxford, 1900, on the role of Guru in the life of Māṇikkavācakar, pp. xxi-xxv; cf. also pp. xliv-xlvi, on the doctrine of Guru in the Śaiva system according to Umaphathi's *Tiruvarutpayan* (The Fruit of Divine Grace), ch. 5. Cf. also DHAVAMONY, *Love of God*, pp. 281-282. Cf. SCHOMERUS: *Indische Erlösungslehren*, Leipzig, 1919, p. 199. He points out that Jesus should be presented as Guru though mindful of the difference of Jesus as Guru from that of *Śaiva Siddhānta*.

[42] T.T. p. 118. The invisible *kuru* becoming the visible *kuru* recalls the Śaivaite concept of God working his grace in the form of a visible *kuru* or teacher. Cf. DHAVAMONY, ibid. p. 282, also p. 178. We note here that de Nobili doesn't use 'messiah' in his works. 'Christ' less frequently. Cf. Bror, p. 107. Guru though not an *avatāra* concept takes the place of *avatāra* in Śaivism. If the appearance of God in flesh is *manuṣa avatāra*, His function is that of a *kuru*.

[43] *Kāṇṭam* II, p. 272.

[44] Ibid.

come (messiah) as *tēvakuru* (divine Teacher).[45] The incarnate God as visible *kuru* is also referred to as *caṟkuru.*[46] Speaking of the expectation of the Messiah to come by Israel, de Nobili uses *teyva kuru* for the one expected. The Jews with faultless faith always expected the event that a divine *guru* would come to man.[47] 'The divine *kuru* to save mankind' is what the meaning of the messiah is. Such a saviour is termed *teyva kuru*. Again speaking of the salvation of those men before the coming of Christ, de Nobili says that God granted grace to them "in view of the divine *kuru* to come."[48] The incarnate God in His divine and human nature is designated as *tivya kuru* (the divine Teacher), i.e., "*tivya kuru* who is true God and man at the same time" (*meyyāna carvēcuranum manuṣanum onṟāyiṟukiṟa tivya kuruvānavar*).[49]

The function of the Messiah is again designated in two other significant contexts. In *Tēvamāta Carittiram*,[50] it is said that Jesus "after forty days of his fast, went out as *caṟkuru*" to give his divine teaching. When Jesus begins his public life, he begins it in the function of *caṟkuru*. In the *26 Sermons* de Nobili, while speaking of the baptism of Christ and the apocalyptic vision and the voice of the Father that said He was well pleased with him, says that the meaning of this vision is also to show that "Jesus was the *caṟkuru* who came to teach the faultless truth to the whole world."[51] The use of *kuru* in this context which expresses the function of the Messiah is again significant. Therefore, we could say that de Nobili uses *kuru* in a way in the place of Christ.

---

45 Ibid.

46 De Nobili uses *kuru* for God and Christ like the Śaivaite use of *kuru*. Cf. f.n.2, cf. T.T. 211, *parama kuru* applied to God and to Christ, M.V. p. 9.

47 *Kāṇṭam* II, p. 275.

48 T.C. p. 120, *26 Serm.* p. 82. Cf. also T.T. pp. 3-4. *Caṟkuru* is used of a prophet, a Catholic missionary or priest. The action proper to a *caṟkuru* is to teach the supreme truths in right order and without any fault or mistake for the salvation of man.

49 Kāṇṭam II p. 301, cf. also *Kāṇṭam* III, p. 139: the One to come. *28 Serm.* p. 113: "He was the divine *kuru* to come for renouncing riches and pride." Cf. CC. p. 2. Mary is said to be the mother of "the perfect kuru".

50 T.C. p. 20. DHAVAMONY, *Love of God*, p. 178. According to Tiruvuntiār, one of the 14 *Śaiva Siddhānta Śastras*, *Śiva* appears in the form of guru and instructs the self in knowledge and love which is known as *tīccai.*

51 26 Serm. p. 82. Here de Nobili uses only Ecunatar and not Jesus Christ.

In the catechetical and apologetic works in Tamil, de Nobili uses habitually *kuru* for Jesus Christ, while explaining the words and deeds of Jesus in his public life. Of course, we must note here that he does not use *kuru* exclusively for Christ. But the predominant use of *kuru* for Christ reflects his attempt to use it in place of Christ.[52] Thus he says that "Lord came into the world as *tevākuru...*"[53] or he uses the phrase that "God became human *kuru* (*manita kuruvai*) and imparted teaching (*upatēcam*).[54] It is also said that while the Son of God born of the Virgin Mary "went about as *tevakuru*" (divine teacher), he taught his disciples (*cīsar*) the Lord's prayer.[55] The statue (*curūpam*) of Child Jesus is also referred to as *curūpam* (good form) of the divine *kuru.*[56] There is also another clear use of 'divine kuru' for God in His state of incarnation when it is said that God "himself came as divine *kuru* as having taken human form" (*manuṣa curūpam*).[57] The divine *kuru* as God-man came to enable men to walk in the royal road leading to salvation. The way to salvation is the all perfect and pure way of virtue (*cakala nirmala puṇṇiya vaḻi*) he himself walked and in this manner he taught the path of *dharma* for salvation in which all men can walk. The divine *kuru* taught the supreme truths for salvation and thus he gave his *paramacattya upatēcam* as the gift or grace (*piracātam*).[58]

v. *Dharma and Avatāra*

De Nobili explains the purpose and nature of *avatāra* in terms of *dharma* of salvation. All the words, deeds and life of the divine *kuru* are directed to this most excellent *dharma* and are expressions of his perfect righteousness. He is, therefore, the *kuru* par excellence.[59] Christ has the primacy over all *kurus*. The function of *kuru*

---

[52] Nowhere does de Nobili mention clearly how he came to use *kuru* for God or for the incarnate God lest it should draw probably strictures from his critics.

[53] *Kāṇṭam* III, p. 138.

[54] KP p. 68, cf. C.C. p. 29: "Jesus was the *caṟkuru* who came to teach perfectly truth to the whole world." T.T. p. 232. He is "the divine *kuru* seen (*kāṇappaṭṭa tēvakuru*).

[55] M.V. p. 6.

[56] T.T. p. 208.

[57] Ibid.

[58] A.N. p. 298.

[59] *Kāṇṭam* III, p. 232.

is teaching (*upatēcam*) but this teaching is done by means of the virtuous deeds of the divine *kuru.*[60]. The teaching of the divine *kuru* to the disciple on the way to heaven is compared to the teaching of dance by the teacher of dance. The virtuous conduct helpful unto salvation is described as dance (*naṭanam*). Man must have good practice in this dance. *Paramakuru* became man to teach the dance of virtue (*puṇṇiya naṭanam*) by his own dance of virtue.[61]

De Nobili stresses the newness of *dharma* taught by the divine *kuru*. God taught during the period of the Old Testament (which de Nobili calls the old *vētam*) His commandments according to the spiritual maturity of those people.[62] To those to whom he gave the new alliance (new *vētam*), he taught the perfect conduct of *dharma*, since they were spiritually mature.[63]

De Nobili is careful to add that the difference between the old and new *vētams* (the two testaments) is the same as the difference between the condition of a child and that of a grown-up man, and that both the testaments (*vētams*) were uttered by the only one God. Therefore there is no contradiction between the two.[64] The newness of *dharma* taught by the divine *kuru* is understood with reference to the 10 Commandments. De Nobili says that the right reason of man in its right understanding always revealed the Ten Commandments in a general way.[65] However, God who is the Supreme Being taught always all those in the holy assembly (*capai*), of those who walked according to His will. This was the case, says de Nobili, until the time of Moses. With the liberation of Israel from Egypt, the Ten Commandments were given again. Finally, the Son of God who assumed human nature and who lived on earth as the divine *kuru* re-established them anew.[66] These commandments which God taught in ancient times, Jesus, the divine *kuru* taught again and some mat-

[60] Ibid. p. 146.

[61] T.T. pp. 211-212. This evokes allusion to the dance of Śiva (*Naṭarāja*) which is symbolic of his cosmic functions of creation or destruction, cf. ZAEHNER, *Hinduism*, p. 85.

[62] N.C.C. p. 31.

[63] Ibid. pp. 31-32.

[64] Ibid. De Nobili here alludes to the Marcionite heresy which rejected the OT and the God of the OT as having nothing to do with the God of the N.T. Cf. *Oxford Dictionary of the Christian Church*, London, 1974, p. 870.

[65] M.V. pp. 108-109.

[66] Ibid. p. 109.

ters in them he revealed anew.[67] For example, he mentions the love of enemies and praying for those who caluminate and returning good to those who do disservice. The divine *kuru* gave a new commandment.[68] "I give a new commandment which is mine. That is to say, just as I have loved you, love one another. The world will know through this love that you are my disciples..."[69] Then de Nobili explains why this is the special commandment of the divine *kuru.*[70] If the love-commandment is perfectly fulfilled, all commandments are fulfilled. It is the first of all the commandments, the 'root' of all other commandments, from which they come to exist as trunk and branches.[71] This is how de Nobili explains the primacy of charity. It is the meaning of charity as the form of all virtues.[72] The love that is commanded here is not merely human love but it is a love that imitates the love of the divine Teacher for his disciples. The love of the divine *kuru* for his disciples concerns their righteous life and their attainment of *mokṣa.* In the same way the disciples must show their love for one another in their desire for salvation of others and their readiness even to lay down their lives for this purpose. It is this kind of love the divine *kuru* revealed as his new commandment to the world.

The divine *kuru* taught the nature of all virtue (in Tam. *Cupāvarūpam* of *cukirtam*) and showed the way of acquiring different virtues.[73] He taught *patti* (love) as the highest virtue, its nature, in what it consists and the fruit that comes from it through the grace of God.[74] All that Jesus in his *avatāra* said, thought and did were perfect *tarmam* and pure merit (*puṇṇyam*) for he himself did all that he did according to the divine command.[75] The sacrifice of the divine *kuru* and his suffering for not giving up of the way of virtue (*puṇṇyaneṛi*) showed forth the virtuous fortitude (*tarmatairiyam*).[76] In the

[67] *Kāṇṭam* III, pp. 283-284.
[68] Ibid. p. 326.
[69] Ibid..
[70] Ibid. pp. 327-328.
[71] Ibid. p. 327.
[72] Cf. S.Th. 1,2, q. 62, a. 4; 2,2, q. 23, a. 7,8.
[73] *Kāṇṭam* III, p. 288.
[4] Ibid. pp. 288-289.
[75] M.V. p. 77.
[76] T.T. p. 225. It is virtuous fortitude because of its saving purpose.

assumed nature of the incarnate Lord, even the least sin cannot come about, since He is infinitely holy.[77]

The teaching of Jesus is the teaching of *dharma* which provokes opposition.[78] His teaching is ambrosia (*amirtam*).[79] The spiritual teaching (*ñānōpatēcam*) taught by divine *kuru* excels wordly sciences, and it could have been taught only by the divine *kuru*.[80] The spiritual teaching is the higher *jñāna*. "The Lord whether outside the manifestation of *avatāra* or whether he dwells in human nature of body-soul in the manner of dwelling in a house which is ineffable, the Lord who is light by Himself (*cuyancōti*) cannot but live in the manner of all *tarmam* His knowledge (*ñānam*), justice (*nīti*) and truth" (*cattya*).[81]

Such a Lord can assume human nature, be born of a woman and live and die, all of which has nothing against right reason. "Therefore God who is the form of righteousness (*nītiniyāyam*) may consent to such things that they may come to pass for different righteous reasons".[82]*Avatāra* in itself has nothing morally wrong. Rather there are many reasons of *dharma* for which God becomes man.

The divine *kuru* teaches by his own actions. Thus he renounces riches and honours to teach that they are not the way to salvation.[83] He revealed and taught two ways through which man might not fall a victim to the three desires which lead to sin, namely, desire for wordly honour, desire of lust and desire for riches.[84] The two ways he taught were the ways of complete renunciation and the way of married life according to right order.[85] The divine *kuru* taught the true beatitude that comes to those who are poor in spirit, to those

---

[77] Ibid. p. 105.

[78] *Kāṇṭam* III, p. 293.

[79] T.C. p. 21.

[80] 28 Serm. p. 122.

[81] T.T. p. 157. The expression of 'dwelling in house' is weak to express the intimate union of human and divine natures in incarnation.

[82] T.T. p. 109. "Righteous reasons", *tarma kāraṇankaḷ*. De Nobili meets objections against incarnation of God from the point of *Dharma* and not those objections that can come from the infinite perfections of God.

[83] Ibid..pp. 125, 146.

[84] *Kāṇṭam* III, p. 285.

[85] Ibid. pp. 286-288.

who are without anger and who are humble, to those who weep for their sins, to those who have hunger and thirst in the matter of righteousness (*nītiniyāyam*), to the merciful, to the pure, to those persecuted for the sake of righteousness (*nītiniyāyam*). All of them will reach the shore of heaven. The divine *kuru* revealed that to these the name of 'the blessed' would rightly apply.[86] We shall later in the chapter examine more in detail the content of Christian *dharma*. De Nobili has adopted both *avatāra* (Vaiṣṇavite in origin) and *kuru* (Saivite in origin) to explain the Incarnation of the Son of God, His life and mission.

b. *Suffering and Dying Saviour*

The idea of a suffering God-saviour is an unacceptable idea to the Hindus. It is an offensive idea (*tūṣaṇam*)[87]. De Nobili tries to answer this *tūṣaṇam* in his *Tūṣaṇa Tikkāram*(which is a refutation of calumnies). He says that if showing the way of salvation is the purpose of incarnation and proper reason (*yōkkiya nimittam*), then the sufferings and the hard exertions that come from it are in harmony with reason, and show the excellence of God and manifest His grace to men. If so, through them there cannot result any blasphemy (*tūṣaṇam*) from them.[88] De Nobili wants to show in particular that there is no calumny or stigma attached to God consenting to die in the assumed human nature. He explains the death of Christ in terms of *dharma*. "If death comes for the reason of righteousness (*tarmanimittamāka*), such a death can only bring honour and glory, and there will be no place for any fault or calumny for the reason of such a thing."[89]

[86] Ibid. p. 289.

[87] Radhakrishnan says: "A suffering God, the deity with a crown of thorns, cannot satisfy the religious soul." Cf. Philosophy of Rabindranath Tagore, London, 1918, p. 15, quoted in the article "Hindu Incarnations" by DHAVAMONY, in *Studia Missionalia*, vol. XXI, 1972, p. 168. Ibid. Fr. Dhavamony remarks on Kṛṣṇa *avatāra*: "However divine and merciful be Kṛṣṇa presented in the Hindu Scriptures and in the theologies which commented on them, he is never a 'redeemer' in the sense of personally taking on himself the responsibility of human race and saving it from the consequences of sin." Cf. Bertrand II, pp. 211-212.

Cf. SCHOMERUS: *Indische Erlösungslehren*, pp. 200, 203.

[88] T.T. p. 160.

[89] Ibid.

According to de Nobili showing the way of salvation is the perfect virtue (*uttama tarmam*). It is for this reason that the Lord allows death to come about in his assumed human nature. It is not a *tūṣaṇam.*[90]

De Nobili then explains the righteous nature of Christ's death in different ways. In the world, if man protects a city from its enemies and dies for this reason, he is considered great and honourable. If so, the Lord dying in his assumed human nature for the purpose of saving all humankind can only be infinitely honourable and praiseworthy.[91] Again, one would praise one if one were to die for his friends who might be a hundred thousand. This love for friends too is considered honourable and praiseworthy. But the Lord died for men who were sinners — men who committed a great offence and who were only slaves (*tācar*). Such a death shows the limitless grace of God and brings him infinite praise.[92] Again, if a man dies so that he could bring happiness to a town for a short period, his death too is considered praiseworthy whereas when the Lord died so that all men might reach heaven and enjoy the perfect bliss and joy, his death was infinitely glorious and there was no least fault or stigma (*tūṣaṇam*) in it.[93] Only those who do not see the power and mercy of God do not accept it and instead calumniate against it.[94] The Lord by accepting death in his assumed human nature wanted to show the way of salvation which consisted in man's readiness to lose all for the sake of his last end, God.[95] In the following of the way of the Lord, one could be killed by wicked men. As lovers of God would not hesitate to die for such a reason, Christ was ready to die at the hands of sinners.[96] Such a death was meant to show "the precious *tarmam* of dying for the Lord".[97] It is a death that makes known the way to the serious *dharma* of 'dying for the Lord'.

---

[90] Ibid. p. 14.

[91] Ibid. p. 161.

[92] Ibid. p. 162.

[93] Ibid. pp. 162-163.

[94] Ibid. p. 163. Here is an allusion to the Hindus who find it difficult to accept a suffering and dying Saviour.

[95] Ibid. p. 164.

[96] Ibid. pp. 164-166.

[97] Ibid. pp. 166-167. It is martyrdom.

Such a death is infinitely meritorious and praiseworthy.[98] An intelligent man resting content in *dharma* can only praise a *carkuru* who makes known *tarmacarittiram* for which he comes to be hated. The Lord who is *carkuru* knew the hatred of the jews to kill him. Yet he continued his preaching, for he could not cease from the *dharma* of saving men. It was for this reason he was killed. Therefore, a man of *dharma* cannot but praise the Lord who died for the perfect *dharma* of saving men.[99] De Nobili's argument to show that there is no offence (*tūṣaṇam*) attached to the death of the divine *kuru* shows the different aspects of *dharma* involved in it. He is interested in the reasons that are meaningful and relevant to the understanding of *avatāra*. If *avatāra* concerns showing the way of salvation which is a serious *dharma*, suffering and death of Jesus the divine *kuru* becomes a revelation of the context of *dharma* of showing the way of salvation, for by death the Lord showed his mercy to man,[100] his unconditional love in dying for slaves (*tācar*) and his faithfulness to righteousness.[101] It is to be noted that de Nobili is trying to answer the difficulty of the Hindus in accepting a crucified God. This is seen in all the above-mentioned explanations, for he ends each explanation with the remark that such and such a death for such a noble purpose is honourable, praiseworthy and that there is no calumny attached to it.[102] De Nobili says that the Hindus say that the Lord could have saved man without dying in his assumed human nature. De Nobili sees in this objection a basic fallacy: One could say that the Lord could have saved man in another way. If one grants this, one could put the same objection against whatever way the Lord could have chosen, that is, one could ask about any way chosen: Why not in another way? Rather one must acknowledge the will of God, His knowledge, His grace to save man in this special way and praise Him. Here we can recall the explanation of reparation of man's sin through Christ's suffering and death.[103]

---

[98] Ibid. p. 167.

[99] Ibid. pp. 167-168.

[100] Ibid. pp. 168-169.

[101] Ibid. pp. 162, 175.

[102] Ibid. pp. 163, 168.

[103] *Kāṇṭam* II, pp. 297-298. Man committed the infinite evil of sin and deserves infinite punishment, which he can never completely serve. The incarnate Lord repaired the infinite debt of man through his death and paid the debt of the sinful man to God.

That de Nobili presents the Christian doctrine of *avatāra* and of the death on the cross of the divine *kuru* in terms of *dharma* is meant to make it acceptable and meaningful to the Hindus for *dharma* is that which one understands as something one must live and die for.

In the third *Kāṇṭam*, de Nobili gives twelve reasons for the passion of Christ most of which concern Christ's teaching of different *dharmas*, the meaning of sin and the defeat of the lordship of the devil over men.[104] These reasons are given in an apologetic framework of justifying the passion. Explaining the death of Christ on the cross, de Nobili says that it is to be noted that the cross is the symbol of Christ and not the symbol of the one who wears it. That is to say, the cross is not a caste symbol but the flag of Christ's victory over sin, the devil and the world.[105] This de Nobili mentions because of the mistaken idea of some taking it for a symbol of Europeans (Parankis).

c. *Virtuous conduct in Christianity*

In the previous chapter we pointed out the religious use and meaning of *dharma*. Here we shall try to show how de Nobili explains virtuous conduct and virtues in Christian life.[106]

i. *Holiness*

We shall first examine what it means to lead a holy life.

De Nobili expresses the idea of holines in terms of *dharma*. Simeon who received the child Jesus in the temple is said to have

---

[104] *Kāṇṭam* III, pp. 418-419.

[105] Ibid. p. 412.

[106] De Nobili uses *tarmam* or *cukirtam* (skt. *sukrita*) for virtue Kāṇṭam III p. 288. Ibid. p. 65, *nalvinai* a Tamil word for *cukirtam*, the opposite of which *tīvinai*, though these two words could refer to non-moral good action or evil. The opposite of *dharma* is *adharma* and *akritya*. *Adharma* is used along with *pāvam* (*papa*) to mean sin as in A.N. p. 81: *atarman* of *pāvam*. In A.N. pp. 466-467, *ācārikappuṇṇiyam* is used for virtues to be observed or virtuous duties. This expression occurs only once. In *Kāṇṭam* III, p. 316. *Anunayavirtutti* is used for virtuous actions. Thus *tapacepam* are *anunayavirtutti*. This is also a rare use. The common word *puṇṇiyam* is used for virtue or merit resulting from virtue.

walked in the way of *dharma*: "He walked for a long time in the way of *tarmam* (righteousness) faultlessly, advanced in years and was adorned with all virtues."[107] Anna together with her spouse Zacharias is said to have "walked in the way of *tarmam* with great love."[108] In the benedictus of Zachary, in the verse 8, de Nobili use "*arc. tanam* and with such *cakalatarmam*."[109] Here holines (*arc. tanam*) is called all righteousness. In another place, *tarmam* is used in the meaning of holiness. God who created us for the beatitude gives desire of righteousness (*tarmavicāram*) so that we could "scale the tower of holiness" (*tarmakōpuram*).[110] The way to *mokṣa* is the way of holiness, and it is the way of righteousness. It is *tarmavaḻi.* It is the way in the form of righteousness (*tarmarūpavaḻi*).[111]

Here we shall briefly examine words of righteousness and holiness used of persons. De Nobili uses *tarmakuṇa campannan* (skt. *dharmaguṇa sampanna*) in the sense 'one who is full of virtues' (*tarmakuṇam*). The *kuru* who preaches the Gospel must be a *tarmakuṇa campannan.*[112] Another word frequently used by de Nobili is *tarmapārakan* (skt. *dharmapāraka*) which means 'one who follows the true *vētam*'. It is used of believers who make up the Church since they follow and live according to *dharma.*[113] *Tarmapārakan* is also the one who struggles in the way of *dharma*,[114] or *puṇṇiyapārakar* (pl. of *puṇṇiyapārakan*) in the same meaning of *tarmapārakar.*[115] *Tarmapārakar* is used also in the sense of theologians insofar as they explain the right sense of religious belief and practices.[116] *Makāttu-*

---

107 *Kāṇṭam* III, p. 179.

108 28 Serm. p. 107.

109 *Kāṇṭam* III, p. 102. "Holiness and righteousness" is rendered as *arc. tanam* which is *tarmam.* Ibid. p. 92; The Lord's holy name is *tarmacurūpam* cf. A.N. p. 598, Beschi refers to de Nobili's definition of sanctus as *arc. ciyaciṣta. Arcciyam* means 'veneratio'. *Ciṣta* means "bonus quasi ita bonus ut omnium veneratione dignus sit." Here we can note that the biblical '*dikaisune*' is translated as *nītiniyāyam*, cf. 28 Serm. p. 119: Christ asks John the Baptist to baptise him in order "to do all *tarmankaḷ* (*dharma*). Here *dikaisune* is rendered as *tarmam.*

110 *Kāṇṭam* I, p. 58.

111 A.N. p. 547.

112 T.T. p. 485.

113 Ibid. p. 172. *Pāraka* has the meaning of "crossing over to the other bank". Therefore it means 'advanced', here advanced in *dharma*.

114 Ibid. p.. 349.

115 Ibid. p. 183.

116 Ibid. p. 487.

ma (skt. mahātma = great soul) is used of holy men too.[117] St. Paul is called *makāttuma.*[118] The blessed in heaven are *makāttuma.*[119]

ii. *Dharma of showing the way of salvation*

De Nobili mentions the virtue of showing the way of salvation as the most excellent *dharma* of all *dharmas*. "(If we consider) all righteous conduct (*tarmacarittiram*), showing the right way for men to be saved is the most perfect righteousness (*tarmam*)."[120] That is why whatever is obstacle to man's salvation is sin, not only because it is against right reason.[121] Whatever has to do with salvation of man has the nature of *dharma*, for it is the final end of man.[122] In the Benedictus of Zachary, that 'the Lord remembers his covenant' is translated as "the Lord remembering his holy word (*tarmavacanam*)[123] of the covenant." The covenant of God has to do with the manifestation of His grace. The Lord wills that in the world men defeat the enemy of sin and cause the victory of righteousness (*tarmaceyam*) to come into existence in the world.[124]

iii. *Dharma as theological*

In the explanation of Christian life de Nobili uses *tēvaviṣayaka* in the sense of 'theological' (i.e. as having God directly for object).[125] This phrase he uses in two ways. First in the sense of 'having God for object' in a general way and then in the sense of God-

---

[117] Ibid.

[118] Ibid. p. 496.

[119] Ibid. p. 289. St. Francis Xavier is *makāttuma* and *yati cūran* (the great sage). Cf. also p. 98.

[120] *Kāṇṭam* III, p. 232. If to tend to the last end is proper to man, then whatever helps the last end is righteous. Thus helping one reach one's *avati* is *dharma* par excellence, cf. T.T. p. 56, it is called *uttama tarmam*; ibid. p. 176, it is to be the perfect *tarmam.*

[121] T.T. p. 45.

[122] Tähtinen, p. 44. He refers to a statement of Sabara which says "that which leads man to the highest good (*nihsreyasa*)" is *dharma*', From Sabara's *Bhāsya on Mīmāṁsā Sūtra* I, 1.2.

[123] *Kāṇṭam* III, p. 102.

[124] A.N. p. 300. *Tarmaceyam* (skt. *dharmajaya*).

[125] K. HORMAN: *Lexikon der Christlichen Moral*, Innsbruck, 1976, Tugend. cols., 1610-1611, "ordained immediately to God i.e. to have God for material and formal object" (S.Th. 1,2, q. 62, a. 1).

given theological virtues of faith, hope and love. Thus the theological virtue of love (*tēvaviṣayaka patti*) is both a gift and a God-oriented virtue. The whole life of man can acquire this orientation. Thus man in the darkness of faith "strives after the conduct without sin which is in the way of all perfect virtue which he does with great effort. Such a work is called *tēvaviṣayaka cēvaka tarmam*" (*dharma* of service [or worship] having God for its object.) [126] The righteous life of a believer is a service of God — a worship, i.e., an act of religion. Faith is theological (*tēvaviṣayaka*) and righteous deed (*tarmacaritiram*).[127] *Tēvaviṣayaka* is used along with 'mysteries' for 'divine mysteries' (*tēvaviṣayaka parama rakaciyam*).[128] Another use of *tēvaviṣayaka* in the phrase *tēvaviṣayaka varumam* (hatred of God) of those in hell. The hatred of the damned has God for its object and it is the opposite of the theological love (*tēvaviṣayaka patti*).[129] *Bhakti* having God for its object is a gift of God. *Tēvaviṣayaka patti* is the theological virtue of love or charity. Thus the use of *tēvaviṣayaka* is limited to such cases. It is not used for all virtues nor is it used habitually for virtuous life in general, though virtuous life of a believer is directed towards God. We mention here the case of its use for Mary's meditation and love of God (*tēvaviṣayaka tiyāna patti*).[130]

When God the possessor of religion (*vētam*) writes the word (*vācakam*) of faith which concerns truth, he does so on the palm leaf of the heart. Since the intellect (*putti*) and will (*manacu*) are the supporting subject of faith and *bhakti*, they are the living palm leaf. With the help of the stilus which is *kuru*, the writer (God) writes the word (*vācakam*) of knowledge (*ñānam*), faith (*vicuvācam*) and love (*patti*).[131] Just as *bhakti* is a gift of God, faith is a gift too. God writes it as the word of knowledge (*ñāna vācakam*) of faith in man. The theological virtue of faith is often used with *patti* (love).[132]

---

[126] A.N. p. 480. It expresses *ordo ad Deum.*

[127] Ibid. p. 466.

[128] *Kāṇṭam* II, p. 186.

[129] A.N. p. 559.

[130] *Kāṇṭam* III, p. 68.

[131] T.T. p. 482.

[132] *Kāṇṭam* III, p. 554 "tēvaviṣayaka vicuvāca patti mutalāna cukirta kuṇankaḷ" (theological faith, love and virtues beginning with such). Cf. A.N. fi. 251. The word for faith used by de Nobili is *vicuvācam*. He doesn't use *śraddha* for faith anywhere.

iv. *Dharma of Bhakti (theological)*

De Nobili uses *patti* for the human response to the grace of God.[133] There is another word *cinēkam* (skt. *sneha*) used instead of *bhakti*. De Nobili uses it occasionally for love of God for men.[134]

Cinēkam as love existing in God is used by de Nobili while explaining the Bl. Trinity. The Holy Spirit is the undivided love (*cinēkam*) of the Father and the Son.[135] The verb *cinēkittāl* is used for love of God for Himself. But de Nobili tends to use generally *patti* for man's love of God, and *cinēkam* for of love of man for man as in the case of fraternal love and *paccam* for love things.[136] Love for natural good is *paccam*. *Paccam* is natural love (*cupāvapaccam*) like love of one's life.[137] One should have love (*patti*) for God above one's love (*paccam*) of one's life. So too love of riches and honours is also *paccam*.[138] In the fraternal command the word for love is *cinēkam*.[139] Love of Jesus for his disciples is *cinēkam*.[140] God gives *mokṣa* to his children who are loving (*cinēkitarāy* or *cinēkitta piḷḷaikaḷ*).[141] Here we note the use of pattan (skt. *bhakta*) lover of God.[142]

Bhakti is a significant term to be used in Christian theology, just as it is an important term in the Hindu theistic literature. De Nobili

---

[133] *Kāṇṭam* II, p. 187, Bror, p. 206. Cf. DHAVAMONY, *Love of God*, pp. 13-22 for its etymology and its religious meaning, love of God (from man to God) and love of God for man. Bror, p. 206 discusses the problem of using *bhakti* for God's love for man since Christianity is a religion of grace. This use is absent in de Nobili.

[134] T.T. p. 327: *tēvacinēkam* as *dharmaguṇa*, cf. Bror, pp. 205-208. God's love of man is expressed as grace. Cf. later in the chapter our analysis of terminology of grace.

[135] 26 Serm. pp. 57-58.

[136] M.V. p. 168 "cakalattin pēril vaikkappaṭṭa paccam" (love had for all things) but to God *bhakti*. For loving another as oneself, the word 'to love' is *cinēkittaḷ*. Cf. also ibid. p. 170.

[137] T.T. p. 482.

[138] A.N. p. 466.

[139] *Kāṇṭam* III, p. 327.

[140] Ibid. The Gk. word 'agape' is both for love of God for man and love of man for God. T.T. p. 232, de Nobili uses *paccam* in combination with *bhakti*. "*uttama pacca pattiyākiṟa*".

[141] *Kāṇṭam* I, p. 24.

[142] *Kāṇṭam* III, p. 326. T.T. p. 357. *tēvapattan*, ibid., p. 317, *canu* is used as "the acceptable one". Cf. also A.N. pp. 302-303. Cf. Bertrand, II, p. 17: In a letter to the Provincial written on 24 Dec. 1608, de Nobili says that one of his converts by name Calista received the name Jesoupattan, meaning lover of Jesus. Cf. ibid. p. 322. Da Costa mentions the name of one of the catechists as Yesou Adien (servant of Jesus). Cf. PR.Ap. pp. 155-156 on the use of *aṭiār* (*aṛiār*). In this work Dahmen in f.n. 114 renders *ariar* as *uliyar* which means servants. *Atiār* (Tamil word for *bhakta* in general) is a rendering of *sancti Dei* (*carvēcuranuṭaya aṭiar* = servi Dei).

tries to restrict the term only to its religious use, though it could be used in secular meaning.[143] He uses it more particularly for man's loving response to God, though it is used for one's love of saints such as Mary.[143] When it is used for love of God, it is qualified as theological (*tēvaviṣayaka*) virtue of God.[145] *Bhakti* is considered the most perfect virtue. It is said "to have patti in God is the most excellent virtue (*uttama tarmam*).[146] It is also said that "among all virtues (*cukirtakuṇankaḷ*) the theological virtue of love (*tēvaviṣayaka patti*) is the highest virtue (*cukirtam*)."[147] *Bhakti* is described as *cukirtakuṇam* or *tarmam*.

Bhakti is often expressed together with faith in the phrase "*tēvavisayaka vicuvāca patti.*"[148] Both are theological virtues. Again, *patti* is used as *tarmavicāram*.[149] *Patti* is used also for the response of angels to God's love.[150] Here we are interested in man's relation to God. *Bhakti* is the adequate response of man to the divine *guru*. Thus the followers of Jesus had faith and love (*patti*) in him as the Saviour of the world.[151] The Risen Jesus asks Peter: "Do you have greater love (*patti*) for me than the love (*patti*) these others have?"[152] The faithful love of the disciples and that of Peter is called *patti* towards Jesus. In this solemn context of Peter's triple avowal of love, the use of *bhakti* is most adequate. *Bhakti* is the loving response of Peter to Christ.

De Nobili considers that *bhakti* has been taught by God himself for the salvation of man. God teaches this highest *dharma*.[153] Jesus,

---

[143] DHAVAMONY, *Love od God*, pp. 14-17. In M.V. p. 145, de Nobili does use *bhakti* for love of children for parents.

[144] T.C. p. 41. The object of *bhakti* is God. Cf. Dhavamony, p. 22.

[145] *Kāṇṭam* III, p. 289.

[146] N.C.C. p. 4. Cf. BROR, op. cit., p. 44. He says that *dharma* has no place in *jñānamārga* or *bhaktimārga* because it is more or less legalistic. De Nobili uses it for the supreme virtue of charity. It is an example of ethico-religious meaning of *dharma*.

[147] *Kāṇṭam* III, p. 289.

[148] Ibid. p.. 554, A.N. p. 251. Sometimes the virtue of *Bhakti* is expressed as *tēvapatti*, i.e. *bhakti* having God for object, cf. A.N. p. 215. Cf. DHAVAMONY, op. cit. pp. 80-81. Sometimes *vicuvācappatti*, not *vicuvāca patti* is used meaning that faith that is as in M.V. p. 124, Dhavamony, p. 22: There is difference between faith as belief and love (*bhakti*) as loving surrender).

[149] *Kāṇṭam* II, p. 8. For angels *patti* exists only as desire (*vicarām*) since they are spirits.

[150] Ibid. p. 6.

[151] C.C. p. 42.

[152] *Kāṇṭam* III, pp. 462.463.

[153] N.C.C. p. 4.

the divine *guru*, "revealed what the theological virtue of love (*tēvaviṣayaka patti*) is like, in what it consists and the fruit that accrues to it through divine grace." [154] The divine *Guru*, Jesus taught this excellent *tarmam* through his own death on the cross.[155] *Patti* is necessary for the attainment of salvation.[156] "Virtuous conduct (*puṇṇiyacarittiram*) taught by the Lord as the way of reaching the shore (of *mōccam*) which virtuous conduct results from the grace of God and freedom of man is to have *bhakti* in God above all according to right order. This is the virtuous conduct (*puṇṇiyacarittiram*) and the way taught (by God) for salvation." [157] Here *bhakti* is considered by de Nobili to be the way of salvation which is *bhaktimarga* in its double sense of being the virtuous conduct and the way of salvation.[158] The theological virtue of *bhakti* which is needed for salvation is based on the knowledge of God. "Since the God-oriented *patti* which is of necessity required for man to reach the shore of heaven, such *patti* he will not have if man does not know God faultlessly at least in a vague manner." [159]

De Nobili speaks of natural *bhakti* towards God which a man has apart from supernatural faith, while he speaks of the salvation of man of 'good faith' and apart from God's grace.[160] The supernatural virtue of *bhakti* one cannot have by one's own natural power, since it transcends human nature. Only the supernatural *bhakti* can be the way of salvation.[161] In this context, de Nobili uses *tēvaviṣayaka patti* in the general sense of *bhakti* having God for its object, and not in the sense of supernatural virtue of charity.[162] The supernatural virtue of *bhakti* comes to exist in man through knowledge (*ñānam*) that comes from the divine word and the divine grace.[163] Thus *bhakti* is

---

[154] *Kāṇṭam* III, p. 289.

[155] T.T. pp. 232-233.

[156] KP p. 9, N.C.C. pp. 8-9.

[157] T.T. p. 148.

[158] Dhavamony, Love of God, p. 170.

[159] *Kāṇṭam* II, p. 187.

[160] T.T. p. 415. It is a distinction intellectually made. It is questionable if in the existential order man could have only natural *bhakti* of God. De Nobili uses the distinction to bring out the gift aspect of saving *bhakti*. Cf. OHM, *Liebe zu Gott*, pp. 46-47: The Church has rebuked opinions of those who rejected as false and futile natural love of God, cf. Denz. 1034, 1036, 1038, 1239.

[161] T.T. p. 414-415.

[162] Ibid. p. 415.

[163] Ibid. p. 416.

not only God-oriented but also revealed and taught by God as necessary for salvation.[164] Insofar as *bhakti* is God-oriented, it is possible for man to have *bhakti* for God only, if he knows him rightly. If one does not know God's nature (*cupāvacurūpam*) rightly, one cannot have *bhakti* nor can one worship him.[165]

Bhakti towards God which is necessary for salvation is essentially love of God above all things and above all loves. "It is to be said that the virtuous one has greater love (*patti*) towards God above all loves (*paccam*) for all other things."[166] Love of God above all things is verified in the matter of believing and worshipping one God.[167] The Christian idea of the love of God has this content that it is to be preferred to all other loves. What this *bhakti* for God above all things means de Nobili explains also in his *Mantira Viyākkiyānam.*[168] Since God who is the supreme being, the form of all good, the first cause, the last end, the One who gives all good principally (as the principal cause), all men must have true *bhakti* towards the true God above the love (*paccam*) people have for themselves. Love of God above all things means that one is ready to suffer and even to lose one's life.

Another expression of the ultimate character of *bhakti* for God is to love God properly as the last end. In the rendering of the articles of faith according to the Apostles' creed, "I believe in God the Father the Almighty", "I believe in the Son...", I believe in the Holy Spirit", de Nobili puts this way, "I believe in God the Father the Almighty with love as befitting the last end"(*anta yōkkiya pattiyāka*) (in Skt. *antayōga bhakti*).[169] One believes in God with *bhakti* due to God as the last end.[170] Thus faith of the Creed is not mere belief in God but also love of God who is the last end (*avati*). Faith in God in its full sense is both belief and love (*bhakti*). Similarly, one believes in the Son and in the Holy Spirit with *bhakti* as due to their being one's last end. '*Anta yōkkiya pattiyāka*' is used for faith in all

---

164 STELZENBERGER, *Moraltheologie*, Paderborn, 1965, pp. 153-156. *Caritas* is needed 'necessitate medii et praecepti'. T.T. pp. 122-124.

165 N.C.C. p. 4.

166 P.J.A. p. 108. Here one is reminded of the Thomistic distinction of 3 kinds of love, *amor complacentiae*, *amor benevolentiae* and *amor concupiscentiae*, cf. Stelzenberger, p. 181. For '*bhakti* for God above all' cf. T.T. 148, 185.

167 N.C.C. p. 4.

168 M.V. pp. 123-128.

169 Ibid. p. 59. A.N. p. 597.

170 M.V. p. 65.

the three persons of the Bl. Trinity, whereas for other articles of faith just "I believe" is used.[171] Faith is not merely belief (*fides quae*) but also personal act of love-*bhakti* (*fides qua*). Hence to faith is added *anta yōkkiyapatti* which is de Nobili's commentary on the nature of faith in the three persons of the Bl. Trinity of the Apostles' creed. Loving God above all things means also loving him as the last end. In this explanation of faith, there is a relation between knowledge and love (*ñāna* and *bhakti*) in Christian meaning of belief. Since God is all good, all powerful, and Creator, he is worthy to be believed and loved.

Speaking of the command given by God to the first parents, de Nobili mentions the three theological virtues. God had forbidden the first parents to eat the fruit of the tree of knowledge, so that they might have the virtue of faith (*vicuvācam*), hope (*nampikkai*) and love (*patti*) and thus be saved.[172] Here the theological virtues are mentioned as necessary for salvation. But the theological virtue of *bhakti* is necessary for all to be saved including a non-Christian who believes in one God and who leads a righteous life, though he has not known the Christian religion.[173] Similarly, there is no forgiveness of sin without *patti.*[174] De Nobili speaks rarely of the virtue of hope but he often speaks of faith and love (*patti*).[175]

Bhakti is shown especially in doing the will of God. We note the expression "faultless *bhakti* in the matter of walking according to the will of God..."[176] Men are devotees (*pattar*) of God who walk according to the will of God.[177]. We may refer to another Tamil word, namely, *aṭiyār.* De Nobili mentions this word in his *Defensio* of 1610 as having been used in the Credo in the article on the communion of saints.[178] It means servants of God. It is the Tamil equivalent of *bhakta*.[179] Walking according to the will of God is con-

---

171 Ibid. p. 59.

172 KP p. 50.

173 T.T. p. 416.

174 A.N. pp. 414, 589. *Kāṇṭam* III, p. 476.

175 T.T. p. 216. (Cf. the expression *vicuvācappatti* on p. 229).

176 Ibid.

177 *Kāṇṭam* I, p. 24.

178 Pr.Ap. pp. 155-156. This word is rarely used in Tamil works, since de Nobili prefers to use *pattan.* P.J.A. p. 62.

179 DHAVAMONY, *Love of God*, p. 29. The significance of the word is that one can reach the feet of the Lord by loyal service.

cretisation of *bhakti*. De Nobili uses *pattiyōkam* (*bhaktiyōga*) once while speaking of Mary's pious reading of Scripture. Her reading of Scripture is done as *pattiyōkam*, i.e., as discipline or exercise of *bhakti* towards God.[180] De Nobili answering the objection that God could have made a world without sinful violence, says that if God had done so how would one know what love of God above all things means and in what it consists.[181] Suffering insults, persecution can also be the occasion for man to show his *bhakti* and give up sin.

Bhakti enters all virtues, whether one gives alms rich in merit (*tapōtānam*) or one does any other virtuous action. That one does all these with fautless *bhakti* towards the Lord is the order or the right way for all virtues to be practised.[182] If the commandment of love is perfectly fulfilled, all commandments are fulfilled. Hence it is the principal (*piratāna*) commandment and it is the root (*mūlam*) from which all other commandments arise as branches. It is the idea also of the School that charity is the form of virtues.[183] It is *bhakti* towards the Lord above all things that makes one's virtues the means of increase of sanctifying grace and the beatitude of heaven (*mōccānantam*). It is the direct cause of this. [784] Meditation (*tiyānam*), prayer (*cepam*) and such actions (*virtuttis*) become pleasing as incense when they are done with the fire of God-oriented *bhakti* (*tēvaviṣayaka patti*).[185]

v. *Bhakti of the Blessed*

Heaven (*mōccam*) is the supreme bliss (*paramānantam*).[186] The bliss of heaven results from the direct vision of God , from love (*pat-*

---

[180] T.C. p. 5. Cf. DHAVAMONY, op. cit. p. 14. *Bhakti yōga* = discipline of loving devotion. Cf. ZAEHNER, *The Bhagavad-Gītā*, p. 146. He translates *bhakti-yōga* as "discipline of love and devotion."

[181] A.N. pp. 122-215.

[182] T.T. p. 42.

[183] *Kāṇṭam* III, p. 327, cf. G. GILLEMAN, *Le primat de la charité en Theologie Morale*, pp. 41-55, also St. Thomas, "Caritas forma virtutum," S.th. 2, 2, q. 23, a. 8.

[184] T.T. p. 421.

[185] A.N. p. 536.

[186] T.T. p. 421. *mōccānantam* is also used. Cf. KP p. 33; *mōccapākkiyam* (skt. *mokṣa bhāgya*), Tātihnen, op. cit. p. 85. In *Brhadāranyaha upaniṣad* IV.iii.32, *mokṣa* is described 'as supreme happiness' (*paramānanda*).

ti) and union with God through love.[187] We note here that not only direct vision of God is the cause of the bliss of heaven but also love (*patti*). The praises the blessed give to God are expressions of love (*patti*). They are free from the pain and effort which is the lot of people in the world. The love in heaven is gift and fruit (of virtuous life on earth) and hence it is the cause of perfect happiness and joy of contentment.[188] The joy of heaven is also called *paramacukam* (skt. *parama sukha*).[189] The beatitude of heaven is described as 'beatitude of salvation' (*karayerṟattinuṭaya pākkiyam*) [190] which God alone can give. *Paramānantam* comes as fruit of the battle of righteous life. Hence it is called 'victory of supreme bliss' (*paramānanta ceyam*).[191] God who sees himself is *paramānantacurūpi* (the form of supreme bliss).[192] That the blessed become fellow participants of God's nature means that they become also fellow participants (*tuṇai*) of the infinite bliss (*ananta paramānantam*) of God.[193] The object of the supreme bliss is God himself[194] in whom *paramānantam* exists by nature.[195] The bliss of God is given to the blessed according to their capacity. "The Lord Himself with girdle around his waist serves them." [196]

On the earth man knows God only through faith (*tēvaviṣayaka vicuvāca taricanam*). In this state the perfect beatitude is not given to

---

[187] A.N. pp. 515-517. T.T. p. 122, "*mōccānantam* (bliss of heaven) is pure goodness" (*kevala nanmai*).

[188] A.N. p. 521.

[189] Ibid. p. 515.

[190] Ibid. p. 545. *Cukam* means happiness with a nuance of comfort, easiness but *ānanda* which also means happiness is one of the three attributes of Atman or Brahman in the *Vedānta* philosophy. cf. GISPERT-SAUCH, op. cit., p. 1. Cf. MONIER-WILLIAMS, pp. 1220-1221 for *sukha* and p. 139 for *ānanda.* Cf. BROR, p. 180, for *paramānanda sukham* for *mokṣa.*

[191] K.N. p. 106.

[192] T.T. p. 231. De Nobili is aware that in Hinduism too God is conceived as *ānantam.* Cf. *Kāṇṭam* II, p. 187. Cf. Tähtinen, p. 85.

[193] *Kāṇṭam* III, p. 578. "To share in the *paramānantam* of God (*paramānantatil kūṭutal*). De Nobili explains this participation (communion) of the blessed with God with regard to all divine perfections. Ibid. pp. 576-579. Also A.N. pp. 510-513. Here de Nobili explains what is meant by 'becoming united (*tuṇai* or diff. reading *iṇai*) with God and become participant (fellow) of his divine nature. Here cf. DHAVAMONY, *Love of God*, p. 81, for *bhajati* the root word of *bhakti* having the meaning of participation.

[194] A.N. p. 536.

[195] Ibid. p. 537.

[196] Ibid. p. 536.

man. So too man, insofar as he is a wayfarer, can turn away from *bhakti* towards God. But in heaven the soul elevated by the divine light in the direct vision of God's glory will not turn away from its love towards God.[197]

The transformation of the blessed (*mōccavāci*) is spoken of in Scripture in different ways. "The blessed in heaven become fellows (*tuṇai*) and members (*ankiṣam*) to the divine nature." [198] They "are like God since they see God." [199] God will be all in all to everyone of the blessed.[200] De Nobili refers to another text: "They in the light become the form of the light." [201] His rendering of *lumen gloriae* is probably influenced by this idea. What is to be noted here is that the One Supreme Being is the cause of beatitude of the blessed in heaven. God is all in all to them.[202]

The union of the blessed with God in heaven is explained with the simile of iron in the fire. De Nobili mentions the properties of iron: colour (blackness), coldness, hardness. In fire iron is not destroyed. The properties of fire are found in the iron and some of the properties of the iron are not perceived. In the same way, the soul loses the blackness of ignorance (*añānam*), the coldness of want of love (*patti*), the dirt of sin, the hardness of not being submissive to the will of God and the heaviness of desire for the thing of the world.[203] The one who sees God (*tēvatiṣtan*) has knowledge, love and obedience to the will of God. Through love (*patti*) the soul desires only that which God wills. It will always be adorned with sanctifying grace with its will fixed on good. It does not rest content in anything else any more except in God.[204] Thus the blessed adorned with beatific vision, *bhakti* and special graces will be filled with happiness. Hence it is the faultless beatitude (*paramānantam*) which is heaven, and the final end (*avati*) of the soul (*cīvan*).[205]

---

[197] Ibid. pp. 508-509.

[198] Ibid. p. 510. The Greek text says *koinonoi* in 2 Pet. 1.4. Hence the rendering *tuṇaiyāi* in Tamil expresses this more accurately than *ankiṣam* (which means 'part').

Cf. also *Kāṇṭam* II, p. 100. The idea of being sharers in the divine nature is expressed here.

[199] Ibid. cf. I Jn. 3.2.

[200] Ibid. cf. I Cor. 15.28.

[201] Ibid. cf. Ps 35,9. "In the light they see the light." The same text in *Kāṇṭam* III, p. 576.

[202] Ibid. pp. 510-511, also pp. 515-517.

[203] *Kāṇṭam* III, pp. 513-514.

[204] A.N. p. 514.

[205] Ibid. p. 515.

Speaking of love of the blessed, de Nobili mentions two types of love: *cinēka paccam* which is perfect, since it desires only the good of the friend. Love of another for the good of oneself is *cuvāpēcca paccam* (natural love). *Bhakti* of the blessed is *cinēka pacca patti* (which is love of a friend).[206] In the beatific vision of God's infinite goodness, the soul sees God as infinite goodness worthy of being loved limitlessly.[207] Love (*patti*) itself becomes the cause of perfect happiness, unlike the love of those still in the world, which exists with pain and difficulty. The blessed are said to praise God. Their act of praise is to be understood in terms of love (*patti*).[208]

vi. *Fraternal Love*

Bhakti towards God flows into, and is connected with, fraternal love. De Nobili stresses the foundation of universal charity. This foundation lies in the truth of creation that God is the Creator of all men. Since the Supreme Being (*Parāparavastu*) is the first cause (*ātikāraṇam*) of all beings, He is the original parent (*ātipitā*).[209] In a similar manner, the first man created in the image of God is the first parent, after God, of all men. That God created the first man and woman is the means (*upāyam*) given by God that there must be unceasing and perfect love (*cinēkam*) among men without any enmity. That men are born of the first couple means that they must love each other in the manner of younger and elder brothers (of the same family).[210] Thus through the creation of the first parents by God, God becomes the first father (*ātipitā*) of all men. The golden rule of love of neighbour is that one loves one's neighbour as oneself and that one should not do in body, mind, word any unjust harm to one's neighbour and that one does that which is true good for oneself to another.[211] This universal fraternal love based on creation is necessary for salvation. To violate this love will be an obstacle to salvation.[212] It is the righteous way (*ñāya neṛi*) for salvation taught by

---

206 Ibid. p. 518.

207 Ibid.

208 *Kāṇṭam* III, p. 521.

209 *Kāṇṭam* II, p. 38, *Ciṛisti nimittam ātipitā* = the first father on account of creation.

210 Ibid. pp. 38-39, T.T. p. 150.

211 T.T. p. 150.

212 *Kāṇṭam* II, p. 39.

God. This love must be present in one's prayer. When one prays for the blessings of God, one mustn't have any enmity against any one and must love one's neighbour as oneself. When one prays to God, one must consider all men his younger and elder brothers. It is to show this mutual love which ought to be present among men that in the Our Father we call God as 'our Father', not 'my father.' [213]

The fraternal commandment is the second of the two commandments in which all the Ten Commandments are summed up. That is, love of God (*patti*) above all love (*paccam*) and love of neighbour as one loves oneself. The second commandment of love of neighbour means that one does that which is pleasing to oneself to another, avoids doing the evils which are evils to oneself.[214] The love of neighbour as love of oneself is to be correctly understood with regard to the petition for forgiveness. This petition is an expression of the love of neighbour as the love of oneself. Asking for forgiveness is not done "in consideration of God" (*kartanai uttēcittu*) or for God's sake, for the divine guru has taught in the Our Father "forgive us our debts as we forgive our debtors." [215] This means that praying for forgiveness to God alone in view of God alone is evasion of the commandment of the love of neighbour. Without forgiveness of one's neighbour, one cannot fulfill this commandment, nor can one be saved.[216] Our prayer to God has reference to our neighbour.

Another aspect of the commandment of love of neighbour is that one must love one's enemies. The divine guru taught his disciples that they "must pray to God that good may come to the enemies and they must do favours to the enemies." [217] If on the contrary, the disciple desires to pray that the Lord should punish the enemies, then he shows himself not to be the disciple of Jesus. It means rejecting the teaching of the divine guru, and it brings condemnation.[218] Love of enemies is also the positive righteous observance (*tarma ācāram*) of the commandment "Do not commit murder." One can fulfil this commandment perfectly only if one has love

---

[213] M.V. p. 13. Cf. Y.M.-J. CONGAR, *The Catholic Church and the Race Question*, (UNESCO) Paris, 1953, pp. 15-16.

[214] Ibid. pp. 168, 170.

[215] Ibid. p. 23.

[216] M.V. p. 23.

[217] T.T. p. 334, also p. 317.

[218] Ibid. This also means rejecting the teaching that the virtuous will suffer persecution.

for one's enemies, prays for those who calumniate, and does good to those who do evil.[219] De Nobili says "the whole of the religion (*vēt-am*) revealed by God is said to consist in the one thing which is love" (*cinēkam*).[220] Here we point out only the idea that the religion of God consists in love. Later in the chapter, we shall see how de Nobili explains this with reference to the Ten Commandments.

vii. *Other virtuous acts and virtues in Christian life*

De Nobili calls acts of religion and religious observances *tar-mam.* Thus religious acts of worship, prayer, meditation are *dharma*. Worship of the divine guru is *tarmakiryai.* The wise men who came to see the Messiah desired the *tarmakiryai* (the righteous act) of worshipping him.[221] The religious exercises of penance, *cepam* (prayer), *tiyānam* (meditation) are actions of righteousness (*tarmaviruttis*), since they are performed with devotion towards or for of the sake of the one true God.[222] Prayer, meditation, worship (*pūcai*) are acceptable to God as strong perfume in the presence of the Lord better than incense.[223] So too prayer, abstinence and fast done in the religious context of even for the dead are virtuous acts (*tar-makiryai*).[224] Jesus himself practised 'prayer meditation' (*cepat-tiyānam*, i.e., *tiyānam* that is prayer) on the mountain.[225] Prayer and meditation are righteous acts (*tarmakiryiai*) which help us walk in the way of righteousness (*tarmam*) and overcome the obstacles of everyday on the way of *tarmam.*[226] Mary is said to have lived with the virtuous action (*cukirtavirutti*) of God-oriented meditation (*tēvaviṣayakatiyānam*).[227] Miracles wrought by the Lord are called

---

[219] C.C. p. 33.

[220] M.V. p. 170.

[221] *Kāṇṭam* III, p. 171.

[222] Ibid. p. 187. Cf. *Dizionario Enciclopedico di Teologia Morale*, diretto da Leandro Rossi et alii, Roma, 1974, under the title *Religione* pp. 882-884. They all express *ordinem ad Deum.* "Religio proprie importat ordinem ad Deum" (S.Th. 2, 2, q. 81, a. 1).

[22] T.T. p. 305.

[224] 26 Serm. p. 125.

[225] C.C. p. 31, in Tamil, *Ceppatiyānam* means *dhyāna* which is *japa* according to grammar, a case of two words explaining one concept.

[226] K.P. p. 5.

[227] *Kāṇṭam* III, p. 68.

tarmam insofar as they are desired by man who is a slave (*tācan*) that they be wrought according to the will of God.[228] Austerity is virtuous action (*cukirta carittiram*). Anna the pious woman is said to be full of such virtuous action as austerity.[229] Fast and abstinence are said to be "*tavacu tāna tarmankaḷ.*" They could be understood as *tapō-dāna dharma* meaning virtuous actions (*dharma*) which are rich in merit (*tapō-dānam*).[230] Anna, the pious woman spent her life doing meritorious and virtuous actions such as prayer (*tapōcepa anunayavirutti*).[231] *Tapō-* is used here in the sense of 'meritorious'. Thus de Nobili speaks of the one "who strives after divine worship (*tēva pūcai*), prayer (*cepam*) and in such 'meritorious actions (*tapō-tarmam*)..." [232]*Tapō-tarma* here means virtuous action that is meritorious. *Dharma* is itself used in the sense of merit. It is said that Christ taught the right manner of meritorious almsgiving (*tarmatānam*).[233] *Dharma* is used also in the sense of almsgiving which one may do for souls in purgatory.[234]

The temples (*tēvālayam*) are principally built that worship (*pūcai*) and offerings (*naivēttiyam*) which are virtuous acts (*tarmacarittiram*) could be offered to God there.[235] Gurus who have authority to teach (*ācāriya pītakuru*) and who have to do the virtuous action (*tarma ācāram*) of showing the way of salvation to others must be adorned, especially with three virtues (*tarmakuṇam*). Only through the virtues of humility, incessant prayer and serious penance a guru becomes approved for teaching.[236]

---

228 T.T. pp. 340, 341.

229 *Kāṇṭam* III, p. 186.

230 Ibid. p. 401 f, cf. MONIER MONIER-WILLIAMS, p. 437, *Tapō-dāna* giving of religious merit. T.T. p. 422-423, here de Nobili uses *tapō-tānam* which could mean 'merit-giving actions'. '*Tapo tānankaḷ* which are *puṇṇiyakiriyai* (meritorious actions).

231 *Kāṇṭam* II, p. 316.

232 A.N. p. 231.

233 C.C. p. 33, Jesus taught *tarmatānam* (meritorious almsgiving).

234 *Kāṇṭam* II, p. 401.

235 T.T. p. 72. *Naivētya*, its original meaning is offering of eatables presented to a deity. Cf. MONIER-WILLIAMS, p. 570.

236 *Kāṇṭam* III, p. 232. Cf. DUBOIS, op. cit., t. I, pp. 164-166 on the qualities of a guru taken from *vedānta-sara*.

Humility

Humility a is specifically Judaeo-Christian virtue which demands a special attitude of man towards God.[237] This *dharma* de Nobili calls as *cakalanīti* (meaning all righteousness) to fulfil which Jesus accepts to be baptised by John the Baptist.[238] De Nobili understands 'all righteousness' to mean that one who is perfectly humble will obey God who is all justice perfectly. That is "One who walks in this way (with humility) will no doubt observe all virtuous observances (*tarma ācāram*) which is justice (*nīti*)."[239] That is, all righteous observance is justice (*nīti*, in gk. *dikaisune*). Humility enables one to fulfill all justice (righteousness). Jesus the divine guru himself taught this virtue in his baptism.[240] This virtue is necessary for salvation.[241] The words used for humility mean by themselves 'being low'.[242] Thus a *Caṇḍāla* is said to be in a lower position of caste. Being low in this sense is not the moral virtue of humility. When the words like *tālcci* used for the moral virtue of humility they must mean something different.[243] This is the content of humble behaviour of a believer. Men endowed with understanding, adorned with faith and *bhakti* accept God, as the principal cause of all that is good. Man having faith and *bhakti* knows himself to be created by God and acknowledges all the good he has received from the One who is the form of all good. Considering all the good actions of virtue the humble man will praise God who has granted all out of His mercy, instead of praising himself. He would desire that all do the same. The humble man would believe that but for the grace of God, sin which is absence of righteousness (*ñāyanīti*) would result. He would consider himself unworthy of even the least good he receives and regards all good as grace of God. He also knows that the virtue which would merit heaven, he would not get without the grace of God. He would rely only on God's grace and for this he would pray

---

237 HORMANN K., *Lexikon der Christlicher Moral*, Demut pp. 242-246. Cf. HARING, *La Loi du Christ*, Tournai, 1955, pp. 330-342.

238 *Kāṇṭam* III, p. 233, cf. Mt. 3,15, *pasan dikaisunen*.

239 Ibid. p. 233.

240 Ibid. p. 232.

241 Ibid. p. 142.

242 *Tālcci*, a Tamil word means the virtue of being humble or lowly in heart. Ibid. p. 64, de Nobili uses words *taṇimai*, *nayicciyam*.

243 Ibid. p. 64.

incessantly.[244] The virtue of humility is the foundation of all virtues. This *dharma* shone forth brightly in the Blessed Virgin Mary.[245] Humility is praised as being more precious than a blue precious stone.[246] In the last Judgement humility of the saints will be revealed.[247]

Poverty

Poverty as a virtue is necessary for salvation and is needed as a remedy for man.[248] The love of God above all things demands that for its sake one is required to give up riches and honours. The divine guru himself showed this in his renunciation of riches.[249] In the beatitudes, the poor in spirit for the sake of God deserve heaven. The basic attitude towards the Gospel (*ñānōpatēcam*) is that of poverty. *Ñānōpatēca Kurippiṭam* quotes the poet Nālaṭiyār to point out the transient nature of riches.[250] *Bhakti* towards God requires this. Poverty thus understood is a *dharmaguṇa.*

Other Virtues

We mention here obedience (*ciravaṇam* skt. *śravaṇa*) along with poverty, which too is a *dharmaguṇa.*[251] Man is called to imitate the virtues of truth, justice and mercy which are found in God.[252] The virtuous must be adorned with the perfect *dharma* of patience in the midst of those who persecute them. This is the lot of those who walk in the way of faultless virtue.[253] They are enjoined by the divine guru to have simplicity (*ārccavakuṇam* skt. *ārjava guṇa*) of heart

---

[244] Ibid. pp. 64-65.

[245] Ibid. pp. 66-67.

[246] T.T. p. 305.

[247] 26 Serm. p. 141.

[248] *Kāṇṭam* III, p. 142. Humility along with poverty, suffering is salutary for a sinner.

[249] T.T. pp. 164-166, 218: Those who lose riches in the way of virtue will find the loss a spiritual profit.

[250] K.P. pp. 8-9.

[251] T.T. p. 305. Poverty and obedience refer here to the religious vows of poverty and obedience along with chastity (*paricutta viratattuvam*).

[252] Ibid. p. 140.

[253] Ibid. pp. 213-214.

without guile.[254] It is a *dharmaguṇa* that adorns the disciples of the divine guru.[255] *Ārccavakuṇam* is understood as the manner of being without anger (state of non-anger), a quality that must be present in the disciples. This is the meaning of the divine guru asking the disciples to have the qualities of the serpent and of the dove.[256] De Nobili calls knowledge (in Tamil *aṛikkai*) and power (*palam* skt. *bala*) which are given to the virtuous people as reward and as *dharmaguṇas*. Here the *dharmaguṇas* of knowledge and power are to be understood as meritorious qualities of the virtuous when they become their possessors.[257]

Suffering and Dharma

Showing the way of salvation which is said to be the highest *dharma* goes also with another act of *dharma*, namely, that of 'preventing sin.' Preventing sin is perfect *dharma*. For the sake of this perfect righteousness (*uttamaa tarma nimittam*) John the Baptist died. Through his words of *dharma* and counsel of *dharma* (*tarmavacanam* and *tarma putti*) he wanted to prevent the sin of Herod. For this he was killed.[258] In this connection, we must refer to the *dharma* meaning of suffering. De Nobili explains the meaning of suffering in terms of *dharma*. Against the idea that suffering is punishment for the sins a of previous life (*pūrvajanma*), de Nobili explains the meaning of suffering as being the occasion of virtue. Through suffering and sickness one can live the virtue of patience and grow in *bhakti* towards God and give up sin. Such could be the will of God in sending suffering to man and not for his sins as a punishment.[259] That man may attain such virtues as *bhakti* for God, patience and other virtues, God ordains suffering (*nirpākkiyam*) for man. God wills that man through suffering be prevented from sin and be persuaded to walk in the way of virtue. That men may have understand-

---

[254] Ibid. p. 214. Cf. MONIER-WILLIAMS, p. 151. He gives the following meanings of *ārjava*: rectitude, sincerity, honesty, frankness, propriety of act or of observance.

[255] T.T. p. 221.

[256] Ibid. p. 222.

[257] *Kāṇṭam* III, p. 541.

[258] Ibid. pp. 277-279.

[259] A.N. pp. 215-216.

ing of the way of virtue for heaven (*tarmaputti*), God sends suffering.[260] Suffering is thus educative, not punitive. They have the righteous goal of salvation. For a sinner, suffering could bring the good of the counsel of virtue.[261] For the virtuous, suffering could be means of growth in virtue and grace and through it they can learn detachment from the world.[262] Besides, the virtuous undergoing suffering for the sake of the Lord without giving up the perfect way of virtue (as in the case of martyrs) would persuade other men to suffer for the sake of heaven.[263] Suffering for the sake of God is virtue (*tarmam*).[264]

De Nobili doesn't speak of suffering as participation in Christ's suffering but speaks of suffering for the sake of the Lord, for the sake of *dharma*. Those who follow Christ will meet with suffering, persecution and calumny. The martyrs who lay down their lives manifest their serious desire not to lose grace, and that by their death others may find the way to salvation.[265] To die for the Lord is the precious *tarmam* of martyrdom which the Lord himself showed by his own death.[266] The sufferings of the virtuous that come through sinners increase their joy. The disciples who love the divine guru will be hated by sinners. Sinners will consider it a virtue (*puṇṇiyam*) acceptable to God to kill the disciples of Christ.[267] They cannot bear the virtuous who faultlessly walk in the way of virtue in words, in deeds, and thought. As the divine guru has said, they will kill the virtuous and consider it a virtue in accordance with righteousness (*nītiniyāyam*).[268] Those who have heard and accepted the teaching (*upatēcam*) of the divine guru are called *tarmapārakar* and their number is small in comparison with those who do not accept it.[269] Sinners who are bigger in number will persecute the *tarmapārakar*. *Tarmapārakar* are sent like lambs among wolves and they will die

[260] Ibid. pp. 317-320, 322.
[261] Ibid. p. 320.
[262] T.T. p. 318.
[263] Ibid. p. 324.
[264] A.N. p. 122.
[265] T.T. p. 325.
[266] Ibid. pp. 166-172.
[267] *Kaṇṭam* III, pp. 328-329.
[268] Ibid. p. 331.
[269] T.T. p. 171.

fearlessly for the sake of following the truth (*cattya anucāranimittam*).[270] The following truth (*cattiya anucāram*) concerns the highest truth (*parama cattiyam*) of God and His religion for salvation.[271]

The divine guru himself is the example for the *tarmapārakar* who will undergo suffering. In his life of teaching, the poor heard *his teaching whereas the Scribes (pirāmaṇa tivyapārakar*) and priests (*kurukkaḷ*) desirous of more riches and pleasures plotted to kill him. But the divine *guru* through his death made the way to heaven possible.[272] The virtuous learnt the righteousness of the divine guru in his death so that they might not lose grace and heaven.[273] That the virtuous unwilling to give up justice (*nīti*) of walking in the way of faultless virtue (*nirmala puṇṇiyaneṛi*) suffer pain and persecution is helpful unto salvation (*mōccacātakam*).[274] This they do desire, contemplating the sufferings of Christ himself for the salvation of men. This is also what one should meditate upon, when one looks at the figure of the crucified Christ.[275]

While speaking of the meaning of suffering, de Nobili presents Christian life as a spiritual warfare. Men must defeat the enemies of sin and cause the victory of righteousness (*tarmaceyam* in Skt. *dharmajaya*) to exist in the world. The victory of *dharma* is the order of justice (*nītikiramam*) which is to be in the world. This is the will of God.[276] The virtuous (*tarmapārakar*) fight against Satan and other spiritual enemies. This fight consists in bearing insults, other similar sufferings from wicked men in their efforts to walk in the perfect way of virtue (*nirmala puṇṇiya neṛi*).[277] But the warfare of the virtuous is different from that of the world. In the world's warfare one destroys or kills one's enemies physically. That is victory in the world's warfare, but in the spiritual warfare one must endure with patience all sufferings. One must be ready to suffer and die for the

---

[270] Ibid. pp. 172-173.
[271] Ibid. p. 229.
[272] Ibid. pp. 174-175.
[273] Ibid. pp. 225-226.
[274] Ibid. p. 228.
[275] Ibid. pp. 228-229.
[276] A.N. p. 300.
[277] T.T. p. 349.

sake of not giving up justice (*Nīti*) and truth. For the virtuous who fight this warfare, heaven becomes the victory of supreme bliss (*paramānantaceyam*, in Skt. *paramānandajaya*) itself.[278] For the virtuous the world is a place of spiritual battle (*raṇa stalam*).[279]

d. *The Ten Commandments and Dharma*

As for the Ten Commandments, the divine guru did not abolish the law and the prophets but he re-established them in a new way with clear priority of values and demands of radical purity.[280] Hence the disciples of the divine guru continued to proclaim the Ten Commandments. Those in the Holy Church then try to live according to the Ten Commandments.[281] Concerning the knowledge of the commandments, it must be observed that the rightly judging rational knowledge (*natu ñāyamākiya aṛikkai*) of man had made known these commandments in general.[282] They are taught by reason and are compatible with reason.[283] The right reason of man (*ñāya putti*) which is the vicar (*piratāni*) of God (as voice of conscience is) forbids man to live in sin.[284] The teaching of reason also has to be compatible with it. Commenting on the command given by God to the first parents, de Nobili says that the command not to eat the fruit of the tree of knowledge was given precisely because commandments taught by natural law and conscience which is the vicar of God could not be unambiguously and solely a command of the Lord. De Nobili says that the first man had to obey the command solely because it was command of the Lord.[285]

---

278 Ibid. p. 231.

279 A.N. p. 120.

280 M.V. p. 109. The Tridentine catechism made the Ten Commandments thus understood and it became the moral teaching of the Church too. Cf. *Catechismus Concilii Tridentini*, (MDLXXIIII). Romae, pp. 359-365.

281 M.V. p. 109.

282 Ibid. p. 108.

283 *Kāṇṭam* II, p. 118. Cf. HAMEL: *Les dix paroles*, Paris 1969, pp. 29-30. Except the first which does not yet affirm monotheism but only forbids the worship of gods besides Yahweh and the third which speaks of the sanctification of the Sabbath, they are of natural law and available to human conscience outside of Revelation.

284 *Kāṇṭam* II, p. 119.

285 Ibid. pp. 117-119.

The Ten Commandments were taught by God and given to the members of the Church which is the Church from the beginning of creation.[286] The holy men continually taught them until the day of Moses. With the liberation of Israel, God gave the Ten Commandments to Moses. They were re-established by the divine guru, Jesus and given to the Church, so that those of the Church may walk according to the will of God.[287] The excellent guru (*carkuru*) taught the Ten Commandments perfectly, so that man might live perfectly according to the will of God.[288] The Commandments which are accessible to reason come to be expressed as the will of God in the Church. Hence the Commandments could be said to have existed always.[289] They are the commandments of religion revealed by God.[290] The way of the commandments is the way of righteousness (*tarmavaḻi*). God has promised heaven to those who walk in the way of the commandments.[291] In *Tūṣaṇa Tikkāram*, de Nobili gives a summary of the Ten Commandments and remarks that these form the righteous conduct (*tarmacarittiram*) taught by the religon given by God and the conduct pleasing to him.[292]

De Nobili distinguishes two kinds of the formulation of the Ten Commandments, namely, the negatively formulated commandments (*vināpūta*, in Skt. *vinābhūta*) and those which are positively formulated (*avināpūta*, in Skt. *a-vinābhūta*).[293] This is the division of the divine commandments. Thus, "do not worship creatures as God, do not murder, do not desire another man's wife,' and other such commandments are *vināpūta*. One has obligation always to walk according to them. At no moment can anyone violate them. That which is forbidden ought not to be done at any time.[294] The positive commandments (*avināpūta karpanai*) such as 'worship of God, hon-

---

[286] The idea is that from the beginning of creation, there were men faithful to God whose continuity is supposedly seen in Israel.

[287] M.V. p. 108. In contrast, *dharma* is never the personal will of God in Hinduism. Haecker, art. cit., p. 100.

[288] 26 Serm. p. 86.

[289] M.V. pp. 107-108.

[290] Ibid. p. 91: *Vētakarpanai*.

[291] 28 Serm. p. 150.

[292] 26 Serm. p. 55.

[293] T.T. pp. 83-84.

[294] *Kāṇṭam* II, pp. 228-229.

our parents, love one another' and other such virtuous acts (*tarmakiryai*) are enjoined on man to observe. Performing acts of such virtue is an obligation only on certain occasions, not an obligation to be obeyed every moment. They are obligation for all but not for all moments.[295] After this explanation de Nobili continues with another point, that is, certain matters are forbidden since they are by their nature evil. They are always forbidden, even if there is no positive prohibition from God. Such things God will never approve nor will he permit that man can consent to them.[296] Besides this, there are matters which are evil insofar as they are forbidden. An example is forbidding of certain foods.[297] That which is enjoined by the Commandments, positive or negative is called *tarma ācāram* and *tarmamērai.*[298] That which has been taught as *tarmam* in the Ten Commandments one must fulfil positively and hate the sins forbidden.[299] The Ten Commandments are explained to be in conformity with right reason (*nītinīyayam*) and with the will of God. Sin is against reason (*aniyāyam*) and betrayal of God (*cuvāmiturōkam*).

e. *Āśrama dharma*

i. *Saṃsāradharma*

Jesus taught the double *dharma* of renunciation (*canniyāca*) and of married state (*vivāka tarmam*).[300] We shall examine how de Nobili explains the married state (which he calls *Camcāratarmam,*[301] meaning a state in the world in opposition to that of complete renunciation (*canniyācam*). Life in the world, which is *camcāratarmam*

---

[295] Ibid. pp. 229-230.

[296] Ibid. p. 230.

[297] Ibid. pp. 230-231.

[298] C.C. p. 33.

[299] M.V. p. 170.

[300] T.T. pp. 127-128. They are *āśramadharma.* Cf. also p. 124. The pursuit of wealth (*artha*) and pleasure (*kāma*) which are the two of the four objects of life according to Hinduism (*artha, kāma, dharma* and *mokṣa*) has to be conducted according to right order. Cf. MAHADEVAN, p. 66 on the four objects of life in Hinduism. *Vivāka dharma* corresponds to *grahastha.* N.C.C. p. 34. De Nobili mentions here *brahmacārya aśrama* in the Christian religion. Cf. also T.T. p. 124: De Nobili refers to it as the "just state before marriage."

[301] T.T. p. 389; *Kāṇṭam* II, p. 87. De Nobili uses *dharma* for the two states of renunciation and of marriage. In the phrases *canniyācatarmam* and *camcāratarmam* (or *vivākatarmam*) *tarmam* refers to that which has been established,' i.e.the regulated or ordered states.

does not directly speak of the righteous nature of the married state. It refers only to the established state of mariage. *Camcāratarmam* is also designated as *vivākatarmam* insofar as the married couple are expected to bring forth children for the growth of mankind according to the will of God.[302] That is the end (*finis*) of marriage. In the *dharma* of marriage, monogamy is the right order. That is how God created it in the beginning.[303] It was so at the beginning of creation and it was taught so by the divine guru. One must live in union with one woman until death. It was revealed in this way by God.[304] Since *vivākatarmam* is to last until death, marriage that is not to perdure until the end (*ācīvitāntam* in skt. *ā-jīvitāntam*) is an obstacle to love (*cinēkam*) between husband and wife, and it is disorderly.[305] If *dharma* of marriage is to be marriage of righteousness (*tarmavivākam*), which binds husband and wife into one body, then going with another woman (*parasthri kamanam*) or going with another man (*parapuruṣa kamanam*) will go against the righteous observance of marriage (*tarmavivāka ācāram*), for God's will is that they be one.[306]

The end (*pirayōcanam*) of marriage is bearing of children (*putracantānam*), their education, especially in the way of salvation.[307] Marital union is justified only for this purpose. Hence *ācīvitānta vivākam* is wrong, since such purpose (*pirayōcanam*) cannot be fulfilled,[308] besides its being an obstacle to true mutual love. It is wrong observance (*tur ācāram*) and disorder in the observance of marriage which is (*tarmam*).[309] De Nobili stresses the education of children in the way of salvation as being part of the end (*pirayōcanam*) of marriage (*vivākatarmam*).[310] Parents must give their children teaching in *dharma* (*tarma upatēcam*) and in righteous conduct (*tarmacarittiram*). Fulfilling this end of marriage would be ruined by polygamy. Fulfill-

---

[302] *Kāṇṭam* II, p. 39.

[303] Ibid. pp. 39-40, 71. *Kāṇṭam* III, p. 284. "One woman to one man, one man to one woman. That is the bond of *tarmavivākam* taught and enjoined by God, cf. KP, pp. 48-49.

[304] *Kāṇṭam* II, p. 43.

[305] Ibid. p. 52.

[306] *Kāṇṭam* II, p. 86.

[307] Ibid. p. 50.

[308] Ibid. p. 55.

[309] Ibid. p. 57.

[310] Ibid. pp. 58, 65-67.

ing this end on the contrary, would make marriage (*tarmavivākam*).[311] For de Nobili, the righteousness (*tarmam*) of *tarmavivākam* is judged solely by the end (*pirayōcanam*) of marriage which is procreation of children (*puttiracantāna lāpam*) and their education in *dharma*. This alone is the reason for husband and wife to come together and live as one. Love in this understanding seems to be the means of fulfilling the end of marriage.[312] It is according to this nature and purpose of marriage de Nobili explains sins against *tarmavivākam* such as adultery, polygamy, etc.[313] The commandment given to men at the beginning of creation to increase and multiply is of the type of *avināpūta karpanai* to observe which there is no obligation at all moments and to all people. It is a general obligation for mankind and not a commandment for every one to fulfil.[314]

ii. *Sannyāsa dharma (Tamil - Canniyāca tarmam)*

Of the two ways of the states of *dharma* taught by the divine *guru*, the second is *canniyāca tarmam.*[315] *Canniyāca tarmam* insofar as it is complete renunciation of all desire for wealth, honour and pleasure, it is total renunciation (*carvaparittiyākam*) embraced by the *kurus* who preach the religion of God. This total renunciation is that of three desires, desire of land (*maṇṇācai*), desire of woman (*peṇṇacai*) and desire of gold (*ponnācai*).[316] The desires concern honour, pleasures and riches. The total renunciation of the good guru is that he has burnt all the trash with desire (*pācam* which means 'bond') that surrounds his body and dedicates his life to the matter of salvation (*mutti*-Tamil form of Skt. *mukti*).[317] Total renunciation is the more perfect manner of living in the way of *tarmam* which is *canniyāca tarmam. Canniyācis* are the followers of *canniyācam.* The Lord

---

[311] Ibid. pp. 74-75.

[312] Ibid. p. 86. Cf. also T.T. p. 389.

[313] *Kāṇṭam* II, pp. 81-82, 86.

[314] Ibid. pp. 231-232.

[315] *Kāṇṭam* III, p. 149, T.T. p. 124.

[316] KP, p. 69. The word for desire is *ācai*. Another word in Tamil *paṟṟutal* which has the meaning of 'grasping'. De Nobili uses this word. *Kāṇṭam* III, p. 149.

[317] KP p. 69. Cf. the verse.

who taught man that he should give up all desire or that he should have desire according to right order with a view to salvation, chose among the two kinds of *tarmam*, the first one of *canniyāca tarmam.*[318] He lived it himself before he taught men to observe it. He practised total renunciation and thus the divine guru taught it by his own example.[319] Faithful to the doctrine of the Council of Trent,[320] de Nobili explains that the state of renunciation (*canniyācam*) with vows to the Lord is the most excellent virtue (*uttama puṇṇiyam*) and the highest counsel of virtue (*tarma putti*).[321]

The virtuous one would consider the virtuous acts (*tarma viruttis*) of the celibates (*virattars*) by vow the way of higher *puṇṇiyam* for men and women to walk. It is a counsel that the divine guru can give to some. There is no fault on the part of *carkuru* (the Christian preacher) in preaching this counsel to men.[322]

Canniyācam is the way of righteousness (*tarmavaḻi*).[323] Unlike in Hinduism, one can embrace *canniyācam* even when young. There is no age limit set to the state of *canniyācam*. De Nobili says that he cannot be said to hold that *canniyāca tarmam* done by an old man is not *tarmam.*[324] He also says that the guru who preaches this *tarmam* in no way does wrong (even though some may fall through unfaithfulness). Rather he does a meritorious action.[325] De Nobili here refers to the Calvinist doctrine that one should not embrace celibacy.[326] Renunciation (*canniyācam*) goes with austerity (*tapacu*). That is why they are known as *tapacis.* The virtues of humility, virginity and poverty of spirit are also the virtues shown by the divine guru.[327] Thus there are two states of life (*āśramas*), *samśāra āśramadharma* (per-

---

318 T.T. pp. 127-128.

319 *Kāṇṭam* III, pp. 149-150.

320 Trent S. XXIV can. 10 (Denz. 1810).

321 *Kāṇṭam* II, pp. 233-234.

322 Ibid. pp. 234-235.

323 Ibid. p. 236.

324 Ibid. p. 233. Cf. BERTRAND II, p. 51. De Nobili in his letter to his provincial in 1609 speaks in great admiration of Alexis, a young man who pronounced his vows as *sannyāsi* against the customs and ideas of the country. Here de Nobili hints at the objection of the Hindus against embracing *sannyasa* in youth.

325 *Kāṇṭam* II. pp. 240, 243.

326 Ibid. p. 243.

327 C.C. p. 33.

taining to the married) and *sannyāsa āśrama dharma* (pertaining to those who have renounced the world) in which states men strive after salvation. De Nobili tells two of his disciples that they should not consider the perfection of Christian life like that of statues or that of block of marbles but that of weak men of flesh as God has created them. Despite their weakness and misery, they should not destroy their passions but sanctify them by changing their object. They will arrive at it through knowledge and love of true God. He demands nothing which is impossible, because His grace makes possible and even easy that which He demands.[328]

f. *Freedom and Dharma*

The preaching of *dharma* by the divine guru supposes that men are free to listen to the Gospel. When God gave the means for salvation, he gave it in accordance with man's nature, i.e., man can choose one or the other as long as he lives as wayfarer in this world. He can hate the sin he committed and turn his will to the good of virtue.[329] Men are unlike angels whom the divine guru did not come to save. He came to save men who could turn away from sin to virtue. Speaking of the 'higher' nature and 'lower nature' in man, de Nobili says that lower nature (*cupāvamanacu*) spontaneously recoils before pain, death, etc. It pertains to 'lower nature' in a non-moral sense. It is a quality of the lower nature. Through this quality neither sin nor virtue results.[330] The other 'nature' is rational will (*ñaāyamuḷḷa manatu*) which is of the higher nature through which sin or virtue comes to be committed.[331] Man who has a rational will can either sin or do virtue. Man's freedom implied in the saying of St. Augustine "God who created you without your help won't save you without your help."[332]

An objection raised is: Why God can't make man do virtue always. De Nobili tries to answer this objection. Those who hold

---

[328] Bertrand II, p. 214. Vico mentions this in his letter written to Fr. General, Vitelleschi (Nov. 1622).

[329] *Kāṇṭam* II, pp. 283-284.

[330] *Kāṇṭam* III, pp. 340.

[331] Ibid.

[332] A.N. p. 542.

that God should give freedom to man so that he may practise always *dharma* must also hold that rewards should be given before work. That would mean reward without responsibility. It would mean the inconsistent position that what is given to those who have reached the end (*avati*) should be given to those who are still on the way to the end.[333] It is in freedom man practises virtue, so that he may reach salvation. Without freedom, man cannot do meritorious acts of virtue for salvation (*mōcca cātakatarmam*).[334] The will of God is that man fulfills virtues with free will.

In the catechetical writings de Nobili uses the language of responsibility. The farmer who cultivates crops, finally enjoys the fruit at the harvest. Likewise man through the work of virtuous actions will reach the home which is heaven.[336] The life of man in the world as wayfarer is the period of sowing. The world is the field of sowing. As one sows, so one reaps. Sowing is the way to the final end of man which is heaven.[337] It is the biblical language of responsibility. It assumes that man is free to choose between good deed and bad deed.[338] Man has obligation to cultivate the land, i.e., to live a righteous life.[339] That God has ordained that life of man in the world is to be the period of sowing and that the heaven is to be the fruit of sowing. We know it from the scriptures (*vētapiramāṇam*).[340] For the fruit of virtue which is meritorious (*puṇṇiyam*), the soil that is needed is free will. If this earth has *tarmakiryai* both as seed and rain, it cannot but yield fruit, i.e., merit. If the merit (*puṇṇiyam*) is not generated, the cause is personal freedom which doesn't respond to divine grace[341] Here de Nobili uses the language of the parable of the sower of the Gospel of Matthew, Ch. 13 which brings out the different responses men give in their freedom to the word of God.[342] The biblical expression that man is wayfarer in this world,

---

[333] Ibid. p. 88.

[334] Ibid. p. 92.

[335] *Kāṇṭam* III, p. 432.

[336] KP, pp. 33-34.

[337] A.N. pp. 580-581.

[338] Ibid. p. 546. Cf. the use of the Tamil words *nalvinai* (good deed) and *tīvinai* (bad deed).

[339] Ibid. p. 606. Cf. Mt. 13.

[340] Ibid. p. 606. Cf. Mt. 13.

[341] T.T. p. 439.

[342] Ibid. pp. 441-446.

and that his home is *mokṣa*, also brings out the responsibility of man *vis-à-vis* the grace of God.[343]

Dharma is also to be interior. One who has received *upatēcam* (teaching) in baptism develops virtues (*tarmakuṇankaḷ*) as inner organs. "He who bears the teaching obtains the virtues of faith in the truths to be believed, hope and love for God (*tevapatti*) necessary for salvation, patience and other such virtues, it is a matter to be accepted that he has received a spiritual form (*ñānavaṭivu*) with its faultless members (or organs)".[344] 'Spiritual teaching' (*ñānōpatēcam*) is the spiritual form with its members which are the *dharmaguṇas* of faith, hope and love along with patience and other such virtues. Therefore *dharmaguṇas* become inner principle. The divine guru taught the inner virtue which is sinlessness.[345] That is purity of the soul. He taught that if only one had the inner purity of the soul, the external observances could be pure. Man must strive after this purity.

g. *Dharma and Grace*

In presenting the theology of grace, de Nobili does it in close connection with *dharma.* First a word on the terminology of grace de Nobili uses.[346] If grace is God's help for man's salvation, then terms used for grace are terms to describe God's initiative towards man's salvation. One expression of grace is *iṣtam* (like). It is said that the angels when they were created, enjoyed the *iṣtam* of God. Such 'divine like' (*tēva istam*) is called *varappiracātam.* The bad angels (*turmanacu*) are said to have lost the 'divine like' (*tēva iṣtam*).[347] St. John the Baptist is said to be filled with 'divine like' (*tēva iṣtam*) in his mother's womb.[348] *Varappiracātam* is used as a general word for grace. Thus the 'divine like' (*tēva iṣtam*) that filled the Baptist is

---

343 *Kāṇṭam* II, p. 283.

344 *Kāṇṭam* III, p. 469.

345 M.V. p. 88.

346 BROR, op. cit. In this work, he examines the terms used for grace by De Nobili. Cf. pp. 181-215. Here we mention all the terms, even those not touched by Bror.

347 *Kāṇṭam* II, p. 27. *Varappiracātam* stresses the gift aspect in a double sense for *vara* and *piracātam* (*prasāda*) meaning gift. God's love for man is grace, divine like, favour.

348 *Kāṇṭam* III, p. 88.

'*varappiracātam*'. The word *piracātam* (skt. *prasāsa*)which means gift is the word that is used in combination. We could say that *piracātam* and *varappiracātam* are the words used for grace in a general sense.

Another word used for God's love is *piriyam*. It has the same meaning as *iṣṭam*. In the prayer 'the Hail Mary' de Nobili uses *piryatattam*.[349] *Piriam* is described as the grace of the divine like (*tēvaiṣṭappiracātam*). *Tattam* means 'all good given by God' (gifts of God to men). These words stand essentially for the gift of favour and like or good pleasure of God. Grace, according to these terms, is the gift of divine pleasure.

Besides the words mentioned above, there are other words of God's graciousness. *Kirupai* expresses God's compassion. Through God's *kirupai* Mary is preserved from original sin.[350] *Kirupai* is the grace given to man that he may do virtuous acts which merit heaven which he cannot merit otherwise.[351] Another word for grace is *anukkirakam* (skt. *anugraha*).[352] The Apostles after the resurrection of Christ preached the Gospel "doing countless miracles through the grace (*anukkirakam*) of God."[353] Mary prays for the grace (*anukkirakam*) that she may be able to show to the world the Son of God.[354] Mary is comforted by the angel that the child to be born of her will be born through the grace (*anukkirakam*) of God.[355] God gives desires (*vicāram*) which are above the nature of man by which virtuous actions leading to salvation are done. These are graces (*anukkirakankaḷ*) granted by God.[356] *Anukkirakam* is used in its verbal form (*anukkirakittal — tarmavicārankaḷai anukkirakittu aruḷunkinṛa*).[357] One could mention another word *tayai* (skt. *dayā*) meaning mercy which is used quite often. Mercy shown to man by

[349] M.V. p. 42.

[350] *Kāṇṭam* II, p. 308-309, cf. BROR, op. cit. p. 85, M.V. p. 19. Cf. also *kirupa katāccam*. 'look of mercy'.

[351] A.N. p. 472.

[352] BROR, p. 184, *Kāṇṭam* III, p. 66. *Piracātam* which is *kirupai*.

[353] 26 Serm. p. 135, cf. also p. 63, the Lord promises to do *anukkirakam* to Mary to preserve her virginity. Cf. T.C. p. 7. The same word in the same context. Probably 26 Serm. quotes from this work.

[354] C.C. p. 9.

[355] 28 Serm. p. 109.

[356] *Kāṇṭam* III, p. 433.

[357] T.T. p. 74.

God is grace. The poor receive the Gospel. God's mercy (*tayai*) comes to them as rain from the clouds. The poor are more open to the grace (*tayai*) of God than the proud.[358] *Tayai* of God could be external like the spoken word, sufferings, and other such things. Internal grace (*tayai*) could be like that of salutary fear and hatred of sin.[359]

We shall now examine the relation between *dharma* and grace. De Nobili uses words for grace in general and words for grace with particular meaning. *Kirupai, piracātam, varappiracātam, anukkirakam* are used for the grace of God in a general way. *Iṣtapiracātam* and *tēva iṣtapiracātam* are used in the sense of 'sanctifying grace'. When the bad angels are said to have lost *tēva iṣtam*, it is sanctifying grace that is meant.[360] Thus *piracātam* of *teva iṣtam* is the life of man, i.e. his life of grace. It is called life of the soul (*cīvanuṭaya piḷaippu*).[361] This restricted sense of *iṣta* and *tēva iṣta-piracātam* is fairly constant in de Nobili.

Grace is virtue-producing and merit-bringing (*cukirtam* and *puṇṇiyam*). Grace of God, i.e. sanctifying grace (*tēvaiṣtam*) is a virtue (*cukirtakuṇam*).[362] *Tēva iṣtapiracātam* is one of the virtues (*tarmakuṇam*).[363] It is a *tarmakuṇam* that adorns the soul.[364] The Blessed Virgin is to be adorned with the *tarmakuṇam* of divine grace (*tēva iṣtapiracātam*).[365] That grace comes from God means that it comes from His very being. Hence God is said to be the form of grace (*kirupaicurūpam*).[366] Grace of God is said to be the form of all justice (*ananta nīticurūpam*).[367] This demands that man walks in the fear of God, rejecting sin. Grace of God is given according to right order (*kiramam*). The divine grace because it is at the same time infinite justice (*ananta nīti*) will be done to man in a way that it does

---

358 Ibid. pp. 434-435.

359 Ibid. pp. 435-436.

360 *Kāṇṭam* II, p. 27. Thus *tēvaiṣtam* is *kripa*. Cf. *Kāṇṭam* III, p. 404.

361 M.V. pp. 19-20. BROR, p. 183. He refers to the use of *tēvaiṣtapiracātam* as in T.T. p. 415 but does not observe that it is a word for the special concept of 'sanctifying grace.'

362 *Kāṇṭam* III, pp. 404, 405 and 433.

363 T.T. p. 326.

364 *Kāṇṭam* III, p. 469.

365 T.T. p. 203.

366 Ibid. p. 74.

367 *Kāṇṭam* III, p. 93.

not detract from his infinite justice.[368] *Kripa* which is compassion, is not unjust. Thus, though God who is triune can forgive all sin, yet His grace of forgiveness is done according to right order. Man, on his part, through repentance must turn away from sin to the way of virtue. Then the grace of God (*kirupai*) of forgiveness comes into existence in right order.[369] The right order of grace is seen in another way. One who lives on earth continually strives after walking in the way of virtue. God will not fail to grant His grace (*kirupai*) at the moment of his death. One who has continually spent his life in wilful sin wrongly hopes to be saved at the moment of death.[370] There is a right hope for the grace of God and there is a wrong hope. "Sinners doing many different serious sins hoping to reject sin at the moment of death and thus to be saved can be said that they desire sin, and it cannot be said to be right and good hope."[371]

Grace of God is, on the one hand, a free gift which is unmerited and which is above the nature of man.[372] And, on the other, it demands righteous behaviour on the part of man. Mere virtuous actions (*tarmakiryai*) will not be salutary (*mōcca cātakam*). It is through sanctifying grace (*ṯeva iṣtam*), virtuous deeds of men become meritorious and helpful unto salvation. Salvation is above the nature of man. So too the meritorious deeds of virtue (*mōccacātaka puṇṇiyam*)[373] The virtuous man knows that he cannot do even the least meritorious virtue by his own power.[374]Beatific vision which is *mōccam* is above the powers of the human soul. The supernatural help which is 'special grace of God' which enables man perform meritorious acts for salvation is different from what God does according to nature. The latter is help in the order of nature.[375] Of meritorious acts of virtue for salvation done by created man, man is not the principal cause but instrumental cause. One who is in the state of

---

[368] A.N. p. 594, cf. *Kāṇṭam* II, p. 308.

[369] Ibid. p. 440.

[370] *Kāṇṭam* III, p. 587-588.

[371] Ibid. p. 588.

[372] *Kāṇṭam* III, p. 598. De Nobili uses *ciravaṇika satti* (*śravaṇa śakti*) meaning 'obediential potency' *vis-à-vis* God's actions on man which are above the power of human nature. Here de Nobili doesn't use it in relation to grace but in relation to the eternal pains of the damned.

[373] Ibid. p. 433.

[374] Ibid. pp. 65-66.

[375] Ibid. p. 471.

sanctifying grace when he does acts of virtue, has for object things which are above the power of human nature.[376]

Grace which is supernatural is given to man, on the occasion of *dharma* yet freely given by God. Since it is God's will to save all men, for its fulfilment he ordained virtuous conduct (*puṇṇiyacarit-tiram*) to be the way.[377] God has promised heaven to man who walks in the way of virtue. But even all the virtuous actions done by man cannot be the cause of the salvific will of God but solely God's own will to show His grace to man, though for its orderly fulfilment he has ordained that man walk faultlessly in the way of virtue. For the fulfilment of the divine salvific will, *tarmakiryas* are necessary.[378] Virtuous life is at once man's striving and God's grace in freedom.[379] Without man's walking in the way of virtue, God will not save him.[380] But walking in the way of *dharma* requires God's help.[381]

The grace of God comes to man for performance of *dharma* in the form of desires of *dharma* (*tarmavicāram*).[382] De Nobili uses always this word for God-given impulses or desires as grace, which when accepted become real meritorious virtue. The 'incipient grace' of God comes to man as *tarmavicāram.* Angels are said to be instrumental in arousing desires for *tarmam.*[383] God who created man for heaven grants different *tarmavicāram* to man, so that he may scale the tower of virtue (*cakala tarma kōpuram*).[384] These desires of *dharma* may come through listening to the words of holy men. God's religion is another grace. Man must accept these graces freely. The saving grace is a serious gift. In granting this gift God didn't will to destroy the free will of man. "That man with his free-will consent to the desires of virtue (*puṇṇiyavicāram*) and thus fulfil the due virtues is the

---

[376] Ibid. pp. 471-472.

[377] *Kāṇṭam* II, p. 294, P.J.A. p. 85.

[378] *Kāṇṭam* II, pp. 294-295.

[379] A.N. p. 542.

[380] Ibid. p. 543.

[381] *Kāṇṭam* I, p. 11.

[382] Cf. S.Th. 1,2, q. 109, a. 6. The initial help of God comes to man which interiorly moves the soul or which inspires a good desire. "Auxilium gratuitum Dei interius animam moventis sive inspirantis bonum propositum."

[383] *Kāṇṭam* II, p. 7.

[384] *Kāṇṭam* I, p. 58.

unfailing and orderly divine will that came to be...' [385] God gives to all desires of virtue which is His grace, for salvation (life). Man must freely consent to them or if he doesn't, he is not saved.[386] This is the meaning of granting 'sufficient grace' for salvation of each and every one. It is for this reason God gives desires of virtue, so that man may avoid sin and do *tarmam.*[387] God has given freewill to man so that he may strive after *dharma* by accepting *tarmavicāram.*[388] At the same time, Chiristian teaching on grace is aware of man's weakness. In the performance of virtue (*cukirtam*), man must rely entirely upon God's help (which is *kirupai piracātam*) for which he must ceaselessly pray to God.[389] When we honour saints, we remember the grace (*kirupai*) God granted to such saints.[390] Freedom of man to love God personally and walk in the way of virtue responsibly goes with reliance on God's grace. God who gives desires of *dharma* and strength to fulfil them is the principal cause of virtue. If man does not consent to them, the fault lies with man.[391] God helps man with His 'stimulating' grace (*eḻuppukiṟa piracātam* = *gratia excotans*) in the heart of man. This is His inner grace.[392] Man's freedom stands in continual need of God's graces (*tarmavicāram*). It is the unfailing cause for man not to sin and it does not hurt the freedom of man in any way. It is rightly called 'efficacious grace' (*cittikiṟa piracātam*). It is a *piracātam* that gives life to the soul.[393] It is efficacious grace in so far as it gives strength to man not to sin and strength to fulfil what is virtuous and meritorious.[394]

For the believer, the life of grace begins with baptism. In baptism man receives sanctifying grace (*tēva iṣtapiracātam*) which is a *tarmakuṇam.*[395] The cause of the birth of sanctifying grace (*tēva iṣtapiracātam*) which is life of the soul is the desire of virtue (*puṇ-*

---

[385] *Kāṇṭam* III, p. 432.
[386] Ibid. p. 437.
[387] A.N. p. 92.
[388] Ibid. pp. 98-99.
[389] *Kāṇṭam* III, p. 66.
[390] T.T. p. 72.
[391] Ibid. pp. 437-438; A.N. p. 472.
[392] T.T. p. 437; A.N. p. 467.
[393] M.V. p. 20.
[394] Ibid. p. 22.
[395] *Kāṇṭam* III, p. 469.

ṇiyavicāram) which God gives for the life of the soul of man. If, for example, fear of death (eternal) and love for heaven (*mōccam*) which is the perfect beatitude, daring to walk according to the will of God and such things as desires of *dharma* are given to man, they produce aversion to sin and are thus a help unto man that he may not sin. They do not destroy the freedom of man.[396] God gives *tarmavicāram* to all men with a view to saving them.[397]

The way to heaven is founded on sanctifying grace. Spiritual poverty, patience without anger, sorrow for sin, desire for justice, mercy towards the poor, purity of heart with aversion to lust, peaceful mind to walk in perfect harmony with the will of God are the beatitude. They are different ways of living sanctifying grace.[398] Sanctifying grace is the foundation of all virtuous and meritorious actions for salvation. In the theology of grace and Christian living of virtue the very virtues are gifts of God. God who is the Father of men gives his children desires of virtue (*tarmavicāram*) with a view to salvation. He gives man the riches of virtues (*tarmakuṇam*) such as knowledge (*jñāna*), virginity, faultless way of married life, and the like.[399] Sacraments have been established by Christ as signs of sanctifying grace (*tēvaiṣtam*) and are visible signs of invisible grace.[400] The growth in sanctifying grace is through *bhakti* for God. All virtuous deeds done with *bhakti* help the growth in sanctifying grace.[401]

h. *Forgiveness of Sin and Dharma*

In our consideration of Christian *dharma* we cannot omit to examine how de Nobili presents the doctrine of forgiveness and repentance. The teaching of spiritual doctrine (*ñanōpatēcam*) includes teaching on what sin is, what the cause of sin is and what the way to reject sin is.[402] We have already referred in the previous chapter to

---

36 M.V. p. 20.
397 T.T. p. 74.
398 Ibid. p. 332.
399 Ibid. pp. 305-306.
400 *Kāṇṭam* III, p. 467.
401 T.T. p. 421.
402 26 Serm. pp. 1-2.

the definition of sin.[403] The way of *atarmam* is the way of sin.[404] Giving up what is according to right reason and what God has ordained for salvation and adopting that which is against right reason and what God has forbidden for salvation is sin.[405] Sin thus defined is what is concretely against right reason (*niyāyaputti*) and what is not compatible with the revealed religion of God.[406] In another place de Nobili says that sinful conduct (*pāvācāram*) is that which is against the Ten Commandments of God taught in his religion (*vētam*).[407] Consenting to sin means that man who sins is the one who consents to this that God doesn't exist for him. The same man wills the enjoyment of sin to be his 'end' (*avati*) in place of God.[408] Sin is also called 'betrayal of the Lord' (*cuvāmiturōkam*).[409] If this is sin, there is no other way to remove sin except repentance for sin and turning one's will from sin. De Nobili calls forgiveness of sin or removal of sin *pāvanivāranam*[410] He always uses this noun form.[411] In *Cecunātar Cartitiram*, in the words of consecration of the cup the word for forgiveness used is *pāvanivāraṇam.*[412] For the true forgiveness (*pāvanivāraṇam*) repentance (*manastāpam*) or (*paccatāpam*) is needed. De Nobili presents this as a doctrine acceptable to other religions, too.[413] Man by his worship of the true God and true repentance (*uttama paccatāpam*) must walk in the way of virtue for forgiveness of sin.[414] Sin is *cuvamitrōkam* (treason against God) insofar it is an of-

---

403 Ch. IV on definition of sin.

404 M.V. p. 20.

405 T.T. p. 74.

406 Ibid. p. 332.

407 M.V. p. 89. Sin is always according to 3 divisions of thoughts, words and deeds just as one practises *dharma* in the 3 ways.

408 P.J.A. p. 64. Ibid., Appendix pp. 1,4. Fr. Leitao writing to Fr. Provincial Laerzio in 1609 mentions de Nobili's doctrine on sin, "an act by which one despises God and embraces evil or as we put it: "avertere se a Deo et convertere se ad creaturas."

409 Ibid. p. 65.

410 *Kāṇṭam* I, p. 50.

411 *Pāva Nivāraṇam.* A.N. p. 218. De Nobili uses the Tamil word *poṟu* for 'to forgive'. He uses the noun form of this *pāvap poṟuttal* as in M.V. pp. 59, 94. The Tamil meaning of *poṟu* is also 'to bear', 'to forbear'. This nuance is present in *poṟu.* In M.V. p. 97 sin is called *kuṟṟam*.

412 C.C. p. 50.

413 A.N. p. 218. *Anutāpam* is used here, meaning repentance for sin. *Paccātāpam* appears to be de Nobili's coinage. The doctrine of repentance taught only by the religion of God is acceptable to other religions.

414 P.J.A. pp. 63-65.

fence against the person of God. Man must repent of it to obtain forgiveness. De Nobili gives a verse: "Sin committed by word, eyes, hand and will (*manacu*) must be removed through word, hand and will." [415] This is the first part of a verse supposedly uttered by wise men. The author of *Ñānōpatēcak Kuṟippiṭam* gives another couplet in Sanskrit meaning rendered as follows: "just as the mire formed by water when it falls on the body is removed by water, so too sin done with the consent of the will cannot be removed except by repentance and weeping in sorrow and determination."[416]

In the Old Testament too, there was no exception to this requirement of repentance. In view of Christ's merit, God graciously granted forgiveness (*pāvanivāraṇam*).[417] The sacrifices (*ōmam* in Skt. *homa*, *pali* in Skt. *bali*) offered in the manner of prayer were done by good men that there might be repentance on the part of sinners.[418] Through the death of Christ and its merit, the Triune God will forgive all sins of men but this forgiveness of sin comes to men in right order (*kiramam*). That is, men must do their part for the grace of forgiveness. It means that one accepts the principal truths of faith, through sorrow turns one's will from sin and walk in the way of virtue. That is how the merit of Christ comes to man.[419]

De Nobili explains three kinds of contrition. The first is the kind of sorrow for sin motivated purely by benefit for body and wordly goods in which sin (which is *piramāṇikkapparitiyāka*, and *appiramāṇikkaccuvikāram*) will not disappear. Hence it will not help towards forgiveness (*pāvanivāraṇam*).[420] The second kind of sorrow is based on man's fear of the loss of eternal heaven and punishment with the eternal fire of hell. This sorrow is based, therefore, solely on the desire for the good of one's own soul (*āttuma pirayōcanam*). Such is the sorrow of a slave (*tācika tukkam*). This is imperfect contrition and

---

[415] KP pp. 6-7. The editor remarks that it is probably composed by the author. Ibid. cf. p. 7f, n. 1. Cf. also A.N. 219. How sin comes about, so sin should be removed, by turning from sin. T.T. p. 411, *nivartakuṇam* (state of turning). Cf. ch. 4 under 'Removal of Sin' on the skt. couplet.

[416] K.P. p. 72. Cf. DUBOIS, t. I, p. 268.

[417] *Kāṇṭam* III, p. 404.

[418] *Kāṇṭam* II, p. 228.

[419] *Kāṇṭam* III, p. 440.

[420] T.T. pp. 404-405. In repentance, at least things known through faith can be the cause of forgiveness as mentioned in *Kāṇṭam* III, p. 475, e.g. hell or heaven.

it cannot by itself help sin to be forgiven.[421] It is contrition of a slave or attrition (*tācika manastāpam*). When one through faith accepts all that is good and all that is in God and loves God above all things, i.e., with *bhakti* towards Him above all things, then repentance (*paccātāpam*) born of such *bhakti* which is God-oriented is filial repentance (*kaumārika manastāpam*) and the cause of forgiveness.[422] Such *bhakti* required for forgiveness of sin is possible only if one has true faith in the truths required for the salvation of man. De Nobili gives the name *paccātāpam* to the sacrament of Penance. Repentance being the important element, the sacrament is known by that element, though another name *pāvacankīrtanam* (indication of sin) is also used.[423] *Paccātāpam* is born of perfect *bhakti* based on the knowledge of God. In true repentance there is firm decision to walk in the way of the Lord which is *appiramāṇika paritiyāka* and *piramāṇikaccuvikāram* (giving up of unrighteous things and adoption of that which is righteous). Austerity and such other things, if done without contrition for sin born of *bhakti* for God, will not help remove sin.[424] The language of de Nobili could have been more accurate for his saying that repentance of sin and turning from sin is the cause of forgiveness should not be understood as forgiveness of sin being within man's own power. It is God who forgives when man repents.[425] God does not forgive without man's turning away from sin. It is also to be noted that like theological virtues of faith and love, contrition helpful unto forgiveness is a divine action and, therefore, above the powers of man.[426] To man who is a wayfarer in this world, God has promised forgiveness if man repents of his sin. Thus the grace of God comes to man according to this right order.[427]

---

[421] T.T. p. 405. Cf. *Kāṇṭam* III, pp. 474-476. He explains 3 kinds of contrition, perfect or imperfect, such contrition should go either with baptism (adult) or with the sacrament of penance.

[422] T.T. pp. 406-407. Here de Nobili explains the Tridentine doctrine on penance and that of the Tridentine catechism. Cf. also *Kāṇṭam* pp. 475-476.

[423] *Kāṇṭam* III, p. 472.

[424] T.T. p. 411. It is *pāvaviṣayaka paccātāpam.* Here de Nobili is apologetic and fails to see that performance of *tapam* (penance or austerity) could be an expression of sorrow for sin.

[425] A.N. pp. 219-220.

[426] Ibid. p. 474.

[427] Ibid. p. 594.

i. *Mokṣa and Dharma*

We shall examine here how de Nobili explains the concept of *mokṣa* in relation to *dharma*. First, a word about the use of *mōccam* for heaven. In Henriques' catechism, *Kiriccittiyāni Vaṇakkam* the word used for heaven is *corkam* (*svarga*).[428] De Nobili rejects this use since, *svarga* is open to misunderstanding on account of some of the puranic descriptions of *svarga* as being a place of sensual pleasures. In the *Defensio*, he says that he uses *moquixam* (*mokṣa*) to remove the ambiguity of *vaṇankaḷil* (in the skies) which could mean either 'air' (*aerem*) or heaven (*caelum*).[429] *Mokṣa* is a *grantha* (sanskrit) word "which formally means glory or place of glory." [430] Then de Nobili gives a definition taken from a work called *sanniāxi darmam* which stressed the aspect of liberation. Here is his rendering of the skt. verse: "id est ex omni parte perfecta faelicitas *privans* hominem tristitia, et dolore." [431] That is 'in every way, bliss liberating man from all sorrow and pain.' De Nobili's adoption of the expression *mōccam* for heaven is definitely an improvement. It is a word that stressed the meaning of freedom of heaven acceptable to Christian theology.[432] The Tamil word for *mokṣa* is *vīṭu* which comes from the verb *viṭutal* meaning 'to let free'. It has the same root meaning of *muc*, the root of *mokṣa*. *Vītu* is used for *mokṣa* in Tamil religious literature. The author of *Ñānōpatēca Kuṛippiṭam* uses this expression *moccapākkiyam* which means the beatitude of heaven which is *vitu.*[433] *Vīṭu* means in common parlance 'home'. *Mokṣa* is called also *parakati* (skt. *paragati*) meaning the goal beyond or the supreme goal.[434] All men desire heaven (*mōccam*) which is the goal

---

428 M.V. p. 8.

429 Pr.Ap. p. 154. Cf. M.V. pp. 9,13. Here the word used is *paramaṇṭalam*.

430 *Mokṣa* formally means state of liberation.

431 Pr.Ap. pp. 154-155. Caland reconstructs the definition: "Duhkladhvam sam karotiti moksah." in f.n. III, on p. 154. Underlining of *privans* is mine. I want to draw attention to 'liberating' present in the definition.

432 De Nobili uses *mokṣa* for it has a meaning that could express the Christian concept of heaven, though *mokṣa* as liberation has reference to liberation from the cycle of births (*saṃsāra*).

433 KP p. 33, p. 46 in a saivite poem quoted *vīṭu* for *mokṣa* occurs. Bror doesn't mention this expression.

434 T.C. p. 40, 26 Serm. p. 22. De Nobili uses *parakati* but not *paramakati*.

beyond (*parakati*). *Mōccam* is the goal or refuge (*kati*) for man in the next world (*paralōkam*).[435]

We note here the phrase *mōccacātaka* which means 'helpful unto salvation or heaven' or 'meritorious for heaven.[436] The word *mōccam* is used in the phrase *mōccakarai* (the shore of) meaning the struggle that precedes reaching the shore and the final goal of safety and refuge.[437] We note here the term *karaiyēṟṟam* (reaching the shore), used as synonymous with salvation.[438] Instead of *mōccakaraiyēṟṟam*, simply *karaiyēṟṟam* is used. A related word to *mokṣa* is *vimōcanam* which means 'liberation.' [439] Another word mentioned by de Nobili for heaven is *param* in the Our Father where he translates 'in heaven' as *paramaṇṭalankaḷil.*[440].

Mokṣa is the end (*kati*) for which man has been created. "God created us intelligent beings in the world that we might attain to the good (*pirayōcanam*) of heaven which is the supreme goal (*parakati*)..." [441] That man might obtain and experience the faultless beatitude of *mokṣa* is the purpose of the creation of man.[442] God wills graciously to grant the perfect beatitude of heaven to all men.[443] Heaven is the life of the immortal soul.[444] Beatitude for man is to reach the final end which is heaven.[445] The state of heaven which the soul attains is also known as *cīva mutti* (in skt. *mukti*). It is the state of liberation of man.[446] Heaven which is man's beatitude and kingdom is God himself. "To reach God who caused us to be born is alone heaven (*mōccam*) and beatitude, and there is no other

---

[435] 26 Serm. p. 32.

[436] *Kāṇṭam* III, p. 65; A.N. p. 12: *mōcca cātaka cukirtavirutti.*

[437] *Kāṇṭam* II, p. 214. N.C.C. p. 31. Cf. Tähtinen, p. 85. *Mokṣa* includes two aspects, cessation from pain and presence of bliss.

[438] A.N. p. 298, *karaiyēṟṟamākira cīvanamānatu* (eternal life which is reaching the shore).

[439] Ibid. p. 213. This word is used as "freedom (*vimōcanam*) from the prison of the body, 28 Serm. p. 144 for 'freedom from sin.'

[440] M.V. p. 13.

[441] 26 Serm. p. 22, *Kāṇṭam* III, p. 442. 26 Serm. p. 32, *mōccakati.* Cf. the *Bhagavad-Gītā* for *gati* in 6.45, 9.32, 8.21, 8.15.

[442] P.J.A. p. 77.

[443] A.N. p. 553.

[444] KP p. 5; T.T. p. 78. "Life (*piḻaippu*) which is salvation (*karaiyēṟṟam*) or life which is heaven (*mōccam*).

[445] K.P. p. 33.

[446] Ibid. p. 69. In the poem that describes the true *guru*.

beatitude or good." [447] Heaven (*mōccam*) is more than 'happiness in the yonder world' but it consists in man reaching God. "Man reaching God is his stability, his support and life."[448] Hence *Ñānōpatēca Kuṛippiṭam* quotes *Tirukkuṛaḷ*: "Unless one reaches the feet of the One without compare, one cannot remove one's sorrow of heart." [449] The author after quoting *Kuṛaḷ* says that the wise men (*ñāni*) say this. He also quotes another poet *Paṭṭinattār.* The teaching given to the heart (*nencam*) is this: "Seek always the feet of the excellent Teacher (*caṛkuru*). Consider the body to be the dance of a puppet. Consider relatives to be like the market-place. Consider life to be like water from a pot upturned. This is the teaching (*upatēcam*) to you, the heart." [450] The author quotes from *Paṭṭinatar* two more poems but with different readings. One of them speaks of the transitoriness of what man has when he dies. What will accompany man beyond his death are two things, i.e., virtue and sin.[451] The other poem speaks of the transitoriness of the things of the world and man's dispossession.[452] They too show that man's goal is reaching God and that the wordly good is not the beatitude of man.

Heaven is reward to the virtuous. That is the promise of God.[453] That man walks according to the will of God is needed for reaching heaven which means that man knows what is compatible with His will and what is not.[454] That the soul reaches the beatific vision of God and union with Him is the reward for virtuous conduct (*puṇṇiya carittiram*) such as faith.[455] *Mokṣa* being the last end of man is a serious affair, and it demands, therefore, serious moral effort to strive after it by austerity (*tapacu*), suffering, control of desire and anger.[456] As the author of *Ñānōpatēca Kuṛippiṭam* says, *mōccam*, at the same time, is not something due to one's own sacrifices,

---

447 Ibid. p. 2, T.T. pp. 176-177. God himself is the end (*avatirūpam*) of man and his perfect beatitude.

448 KP p. 2.

449 Ibid. The couplet quoted is from the 1st chap. n. 7.

450 Ibid.

451 Ibid.

452 Ibid. p. 3.

453 P.J.A. p. 85.

454 *Kāṇṭam* II, pp. 23-24. T.T. p. 320, ibid. 321, God has not promised to sinners that He will give *mokṣa* to them.

455 A.N. p. 436.

456 P.J.A. pp. 75-76. T.T. p. 147.

fasts, giving up marriage and embracing the state of renunciation (*canniyācam*). The great diamond of *mōccam* can be given to man only as gift or as favour (*upakāram*).[457] According to the same work, all are not required to retire to the forest to do penance and embrace *canniyācam* without marrying. What is proper is to enjoy the goods of this world according to right reason and to observe the Ten Commandments for reaching heaven.[458] The Apostles after the death of Christ's resurrection preached the *mōccavaḻi* (the way of heaven).[459] The way of heaven concerns virtuous life, and not the non-moral things, such as the types of food people should eat.[460]

The beatitude of heaven is described as *tarmapākkiyam.*[461] God gives the righteous bliss of heaven to those who walk according to His will. In heaven which is unmixed with the least evil, all that is form of virtue (*puṇṇiyacurūpam*) and the good fruit of supreme happiness (*paramacukam*) exist.[462] In heaven *tarmam* and happiness are present together whereas in hell both are absent.[463] To renounce the wordly goods for the sake of heaven is called a counsel of *tarmam*.[464] The blessed who have attained the beatitude of heaven are established in goodness. Their will is established in *tarmam* in an irreversible manner. This is what happens to the virtuous one (*tarmapārakan*).[465] The freedom of the blessed in so far as they are established in good and in so far as they cannot fall into sin, is called "absolutely perfect freedom" (*kēvalankuṟaiyaṟṟa cuvātantiriyam*) and "freedom having solely *tarmam* as its object" (*tarma māttiram viṣayaka cuvātantiriyam*). The contrary is the case with that of the damned.[466]

The blessed are rich in merit through their righteous deeds (*tarmacarittirankaḷ nimittamāka puṇṇiyāttumākkaḷ*) and thus shine

---

457 KP p. 34. A.N. pp. 465, 553: *Mōccatānam* means that God gives *mokṣa* as a gift.

458 KP p. 34.

459 26 Serm. pp. 134-135. 'The way of heaven' is the object of their preaching.

460 T.T. p. 499.

461 Ibid. p. 320.

462 A.N. p. 545.

463 Ibid.

464 T.T. p. 328.

465 A.N. p. 251.

466 Ibid. p. 543.

brighter than diamonds.[467] When they reign with God who is the King of kings, they are adorned with all holy virtues (*cakala paricutta tarmankaḷ*).[468] The blessed who praise the Lord with their *bhakti* will have spiritual joy if they had done such meritorious deeds as having written books to teach the rule of virtue (*tarmaviti*) which is of benefit to those in the world.[469] The blessed have also a better understanding of the righteous (*tarma*) meaning of divine providence with regard to disease and suffering and the divine patience with regard to sinners for their conversion.[470] In the Christian understanding of heaven there is continuity between life of *dharma* on earth and *dharma* in heaven though in heaven it exists in its perfect faultlessness, richness and as fruit and in perfect freedom oriented solely towards *dharma*.[471]

j. *Terminology of Dharma*

So far we examined Christian understanding of virtuous living in relation to salvation according to de Nobili. There is a pervasive use of *tarmam* in his explanation of virtuous living. Here we add a brief note on the way de Nobili uses the word *tarmam* in different combinations. What we say below is not an exhaustive listing of the

---

467 Ibid. p. 535. Cf. Tähtinen op. cit. pp. 71-72, for comment on the close relation between *dharma* and *mokṣa* in Hinduism, p. 72: "*Dharma* in terms of the ultimate result is the means to *Mokṣa*." Cf. also T.T. p. 127.

468 A.N. p. 535.

469 Ibid. p. 525.

470 Ibid. pp. 527-529.

471 Ibid. pp. 55-56. The state of *mokṣa* is *dharma* in nature but in a perfect way. There is no *liberum arbitrium* to choose good and evil. Thus it could be said to have transcended or to have been freed from this restless choice. Freedom of heaven is thus different. The concept of freedom present in the meaning of the expression *mokṣa* could be a seminal concept for the Christian understanding of salvation. It is the freedom to know God, to love God and to rest in God irrevocably — a freedom that comes as fruit of the struggle between virtue and sin with imperfect freedom of the earth. The state of heaven could be said to be 'meta-ethical' in so far as the ethical action born of a choice between good and evil with *liberum arbitrium* doesn't exist there. The Hindu concept of *mukta* is that *mukta* is above good and evil. One who sows *dharma* reaps the fruit of *dharma* as the state of the will (*manacu*) fixed irrevocably in *tarmam* and love. A.N. pp. 56, 58. It is freedom from the state of being a wayfarer who still struggles between sin and *dharma*.

use of *tarmam.* Its purpose is to show how de Nobili uses this significant term of religion and morality.

Dharma manifests itself in the three faculties of mind, speech and actions. Desires of *dharma* given by God as impulses of grace are termed as *tarmavicāram.*[472] It creates desire of *dharma*. To desire the salvation of others is called *tarma manatu.*[473] Good thoughts of virtuous men are *tarma karuttukkaḷ.*[474] *Dharma* manifests itself in words as *tarma vārttai*,[475] as *tarma vacanam* (utterance of *dharma*) used for the word of the covenant,[476] as *tarma upatēcam* (teaching of or on *dharma*) given by the divine *guru,*[477] as counsel or advice of *dharma* (*tarmaputti*).[478] Passages of Scripture exhorting men to the practice of *dharma* are termed *tarma vākkiyankaḷ.*[479]

Dharma to be done or as done are expressed in the phrases like the following: *tarmakiriyai* (skt. *dharmakrya* = actions of dharma),[480] *tarmakarīyam* (skt. *dharmakārya*) which means *dharma* that is in the state of effect such as *bhakti*,[481] *tarmacarittiram,*[482] *tarmācāram* (skt. *dharmācāra* — observances of *dharma* or righteous duties).[483] From the living of *dharma* flows the health of *dharma*, termed as *tarma ārōkkiyam.*[484] Those who follow and who are advanced in virtue are called either *tarmakuṇa campannar* (*dharmaguṇa sampanna*, meaning 'filled with virtues')[485] or *tarmapārakar (dharmapāraka)*[486] or *puṇṇiyapārakar.*[487] To live according to righteousness (*tarmanīti*) along with acceptance of truth amounts to 'going-up' (towards heaven).[488]

---

[472] T.T. p. 119; M.V. p. 20 as *puṇṇiyavicāram.*
[473] T.T. p. 56.
[474] *Kāṇṭam* III, p. 331.
[475] T.T. p. 144.
[476] *Kāṇṭam* III, p. 93.
[477] Ibid. p. 171.
[478] A.N. p. 81.
[479] Ibid.
[480] *Kāṇṭam* II, p. 29.
[481] *Kāṇṭam* III, p. 171.
[482] T.T. p. 171; cf. also N.C.C. p. 31 (*tarma naṭakkai* (walking in *dharma*).
[483] C.C. p. 33.
[484] T.T. p. 209.
[485] Ibid. p. 485.
[486] Ibid. pp. 487, 172.
[487] Ibid. p. 183.
[488] N.C.C. p. 35.

Whatever helps *dharma* unto salvation or virtue is termed *tarmakāraṇankaḷ* (lit. causes of *dharma*, here reasons of *dharma*).[489] John the Baptist says he is unworthy to untie the belt of Christ's holy feet (*tarmapātam*).[490] Here *dharma* is used in the sense of holiness. When Christ assumes human nature, he comes in the fragrance of *dharma* (*tarmaparimaḷam* - perfume of holiness) and he is born as the perfume of *dharma* (*tarmaparimaḷamāy*).[491] Benefit unto salvation is called *tarma - pirayōcanam* (skt. *dharmaprayōjana*). Before the fall of man, the whole of creation served him in the manner of the *dharma* of service.[492]

One who shows the way of *dharma* to others gains the fruit of *dharma* (merit), i.e., *tarma lāpam* (in Skt. *dharma lābha*).[493] The beatitude of *mokṣa* is *tarmapākkiyam*,[494] since it is holy and unmixed with sin. *Tarmaviṣayam* concerns virtue and salvation. Parents have a duty to instruct children in the matter of *dharma* (*tarmaviṣayam*).[495] Sometimes, *dharma* is used of qualities which are not moral in the strict sense but in the sense of holy or blessed. The blessed after the Last Judgement will be adorned with *tarmakuṇam,* such as knowledge (Tamil-*aṟikkai*) and power or strength (*pelam*-skt. *bala*).[496] De Nobili's use of *dharma* is ethico-religious. It is eminently suited to explain religious ethic and religious morality.

---

489 T.T. p. 109.

490 *Kāṇṭam* III, p. 276.

491 T.T. p. 136.

492 *Kāṇṭam* II, p. 102: *Cēvātu tarma mēraiyāka.* Cf. BROR, op. cit., p. 50. In *Tirukkaliṭṛupadiār*, 16, the word *sivatarmam* is used to express service rendered to Śiva.

493 T.T. p. 56.

494 Ibid. p. 56.

495 Ibid. p. 389.

496 *Kāṇṭam* III, p. 541. Cf. MONIER-WILLIAMS, p. 510 gives as one of the meanings of *dharma* as quality, property.

PART THREE

CHAPTER SEVEN

A SYNTHETIC SUMMARY

SECTION I

Dharma in Hinduism

A. DHARMA AND SOCIETY

The concept of *dharma* is a complex one, with different meanings.[1] Yet it could be considered under three aspects: social, ethical and religious. *Dharma* in its polyvalent meaning was known to de Nobili.[2] We have investigated de Nobili's understanding and use of *dharma* in its different meanings. These different meanings we group under the three aspects mentioned above. First we shall consider *dharma* in its social dimension in Hinduism, i.e., in so far as it relates to the order and life of human society.

De Nobili explains the *dharma* of society as it aplies to Hindu society, and as it could apply to any society.[3] He describes it as it exists and then gives reasons for its legitimacy and acceptability which apply to any human society, and which he finds in Hinduism itself. The *dharma* of society is known as *varṇāśrama-dharma.* De Nobili mentions the phrase *varṇadharma* once but not the phrase *varṇāśramadharma.*[4] De Nobili discusses in detail the *dharma* of the

---

[1] MEES, *Dharma and Society*, pp. 8-16. He gives 16 meanings. On p. 3 he says that different meanings of *dharma* indicate only indeterminateness, and not vagueness. Cf. MONIER MONIER-WILLIAMS, p. 510 on different meanings of *dharma.*

[2] Rajamanickam, Informatio of Roberto de Nobili. *AHSI* 39 (1970) p. 254. Also Rajamanickam, *Roberto de Nobili on Adaptation*, p. 201.

[3] I.C. p. 2.

[4] Ibid. p. 57. De Nobili quotes this phrase from Manu. S.K. MAITRA, *The Ethics of the Hindus*, p. 1. He calls *varṇāśramadharma* social ethics. But de Nobili explains that it is a combination of positive laws, conventions of society and moral duties and virtues.

varṇas (varṇadharma).[5] He speaks of the duties of the four *varṇas*,[6] but he uses 'the duty of the stages of life' (*āśramadharma*) only sparsely.[7] Of the four stages of life, *brahmacārya, gṛhastha, vānaprastha* and *sannyāsa*, he does not speak of the third.[8] He speaks of the stage of studentship (*brahmacārya*), the stage of the householder (for which de Nobili uses '*camcāra-āciramatarmam* or *vivākatarmam*, not *gṛhastha*) and the stage of renunciation (*sannyāsa*).

In our investigation we first analysed *varṇāsramadharma* in its social and ethical dimensions in a descriptive way (as ethos), since the *dharma* of the *varṇas* (*varṇadharma*) and *dharma* of the stage of life (*āśramadharma*) include both of these dimensions. We noted that customs and rules which may not be ethical in the strict sense are also called *dharma*.

a. *Dharma of Society (Samājadharma)*

De Nobili views *dharma* of society as consisting not only in the *dharma* of the four *varṇas* (*Brahmaṇa, Kṣatriya, Vaiśya* and *Śudra*),[9] but also customs, traditions, and conventions of society. He accepts *dharma* under its social aspect in a critical way, since *dharma* in the social sphere includes both ethical duties and virtues along with non-ethical duties and observances. If they are ethical, they are justified according to right reason. If they are non-ethical, they are legitimated on the grounds that they serve a good human end, and that they do not contain anything against right reason and true religion.

---

[5] I.C. pp. 3-4.

[6] Ibid. p. 7. Instead of the usual word *dharma* for duty, *tapaḥ* is used in the text of Manu quoted by de Nobili.

[7] N.C.C., pp. 34-35; T.T. p. 124.

[8] The third of the four stages of life, that of the forest-dweller, does not seem relevant to Christian life, in which the life of renunciation and meditation (*sannyāsa*) seems sufficient. It would be interesting to know how much this stage of life was followed in practice in de Nobili's time.

[9] I.C. p. 2. "The office of *Brahmaṇa* is wisdom, that of *Kṣatriya* is protection, that of *Vaisyas* trade and that of *Śudras* service".

b. *Scripture as Source (pramāṇa) of Social Dharma*

De Nobili explains the *dharma* of society largely with reference to the *Manu Smṛti.*[10] *Dharmaśāstras* which are collections of many works are the source of knowledge of the *dharma* of society. De Nobili accepts the idea that scriptures can be a legitimate source of morality. He mentions in particular the *dharmaśāstras* (also called *nītisāstras*) which contain laws and customs prescribed in the country. They have the force of law. All are expected to observe them.[11] *Dharma* of the four *varṇas* is chiefly contained in them. Though the *śruti* (the *vedas*) are the ultimate source of *dharma*,[12] for all practical purposes *dharmaśāstras* are the source of knowledge of *dharma*. That which has been prescribed by scriptures has the force of law. That it is obligatory is made clear by the sanctions which follow its violation.[13]

c. *Dharma and Order of Society (Lōkakrama)*

The criterion of injunction through scriptures alone is insufficient to ground the *dharma* of the four classes as socially legitimate and morally obligatory. The social *dharma* must be justified by the very nature of society. De Nobili's justification of social *dharma* is theological. Unless one knows the end (*finis*), of an action or of acts, one cannot judge if they are right or wrong.[14] De Nobili finds a purpose in the division of society into four classes as it existed in India and was taught by the law-books, especially Manu. He finds the purpose of *dharma* of the four classes in the very nature of society, its goal and order. This he comes to call the order of the world (*lōkakrama*). The myth of creation according to which Brahmins are said to have arisen from the head or face of God (Brahman), kings from the arms, the merchants from the thigh and the servants from the feet, is a symbolic expression of the order of the world

---

[10] Most of the references to *varṇadharma* are from the *Manu smṛti*.

[11] I.C. p. 26.

[12] THAKUR, *Christian and Hindu Ethics*, p. 130.

[13] Ibid. pp. 5-6.

[14] Pr.Ap. p. 91.

(*lōkakrama*) which consists in the division of labour and harmony of functions.[15] De Nobili explains further the purpose and nature of society according to the image of microcosm and macrocosm. The order and division of functions of members of the human body and the harmony with which different members function for the good of the whole body, is reflected in the macrocosm of society. This is called *lōkakiramam.*[16] The *dharma* of society is founded on the nature, goal and order of society.

d. *Consensus and Social Dharma*

The order of a particular society depends on the convention of men based on their agreement (*lōkacankētam*). Here we note that de Nobili accepts the *dharma* of society not merely as it exists; he also understands and explains its legitimacy. The *humanum* of society is explained by the myth of creation and the image of microcosm and macrocosm.[17] Therefore if the law-books enforce duties of classes (*varṇas*) and if the duties of the different classes have the force of law, they are valid obligations insofar as they are rooted in the nature, goal and order of human society. The human good of society is thus guaranteed. Only if the nature, goal and order of society are accepted, can the *dharma* of society be justified. The nature of human society is such that men who make up society are different in their gifts and talents and temperaments.[18] If society is to go on, the different members must perform their several functions in mutual

---

[15] I.C. pp. 56-59. Mahadevan, pp. 69-70. BANERJEE, *The Spirit of Indian Philosophy*, p. 282. The goal of social division is 'maintenance of stability' (*lōkasthiti*) and 'fulfilment' of the demand for social good (*lōkasiddhi*).

[16] A.N. pp. 287-289. Order of society is part of *dharma*. It was also called *dharma*. Cf. N. KLAES, *Conscience and Consciousness*, Bangalore, 1975, pp. 17 and 35, f.n. 4. Etymological meaning of *dharma* which means 'to support' evokes its predecessor word in the *vedas . rta* meaning 'order of the universe'.

[17] Mahadevan, p. 69. The purpose of division of society into four classes is the same as that of Plato's division of the state into three classes (Republic, Bk. IV). The system of classes was evolved to keep society in a harmonius unity.

[18] Ibid. pp. 71-72. That men are different in qualities is accepted in Hinduism.

dependance and for the good of the whole. This is the order of human society in general. The *dharma* of society (here *varṇadharma*) is based on this order of human society. But this latter takes different forms of division of classes and functions in different countries. This is *lōkacankētam* (agreement by consensus) which points to the relative nature of the particular form a community of men takes.[19] *Dharma* of society is accepted by de Nobili as legitimate and valid insofar as it is based on the nature, goal and order of society. That which upholds society is *dharma*.[20] It is according to this criterion of *humanum* on the social level that de Nobili accepts the social laws of Indian society just as one accepts the laws of the nations (*jus gentium*).[21]

e. *Áśramadharma*

De Nobili's approach to the *dharma* of the stages of life (*āśramadharma*) is different from his approach to the *dharma* of the classes (*varṇadharma*). He accepts the three *āśramas* of the student, the householder and of renunciation. He calls them *piramacāri vivākatarmam* and *canniyāci āciramam*. He does not accept the scheme of the four stages of life of Hinduism.[22] De Nobili speaks mostly of the two *āśramas* of the married men and that of the renouncers (*sannyāsins*) as applying to the Indian Christians, since he presents the two *āśramas* as two states of life. He is critical of the violations against these two *āśramas*. Though he rejects the idea that renunciation (*sannyāsa*) should come at the end of the four stages of life, he

---

[19] Cf. Ch. II, discussion on social *dharma*.

[20] Tähtinen, *Philosophy of Value*, p. 70. "*Dharma* is that which upholds society."

[21] I.C. p. 107. MIDGLEY, *Natural Law Tradition and Theory of International Relations*, pp. 84-85. "*Jus gentium* is from the *consensus* of all nations and peoples. It has the force of an agreement and force of law, a system of law common to all nations... constituted through the usage of those nations."

[22] Mahadevan, p. 78. Following the 4 stages of life is not strict in Hinduism. In some special cases, some of the stages can be omitted. De Nobili was against the idea that young men could not become renouncers (*sannyāsins*) since the stage of renunciation came only at the end of the stages of life.

values renunciation highly,[23] since it removes causes of sin and is conducive to right living and helpful unto salvation.

f. *Dharma and Customs*

Concerning the different social customs of food, clothing and cleanliness, de Nobili tries to justify their legitimacy and value through the purposes they intend. If they express a good civil purpose, such as the thread distinguishing one class from another,[24] then the customs are legitimate. *Dharma* embraces social practices and conventions. De Nobili accepts the customs of a country (*dēśācāram*) and customs of a clan (*kuladharma*) as legitimate.[25] The only negative criterion is that they do not contain anything contrary to right reason and true religion. Otherwise one must observe them.

g. *Moral Meaning of Social Dharma*

Concerning *varṇadharma* of the four classes and the *dharma* of the social customs and conventions, one may ask if they are moral in nature. First, one must be aware of the different meanings of *dharma*. *Dharma* includes social (in a non-moral sense), ethical and religious aspects in its meaning. Social *dharma* includes non-moral customs and conventions, ethical qualities and duties, and religious duties and observances patterned according to social classes. De Nobili speaks, for example, of the qualities of a Brahmin according to *Parāśara-smṛti*, which are presented in the scheme of *varṇadharma*:

> Studious work, continence, piety, liberality, truthfulness, virtue, discipline, facility; knowledge, wisdom, his competence to

---

[23] Pr.Ap. p. 59. The ascetic (*sannyāsin*) renounces the desire for gold, the desire for land and the desire for woman.

[24] If the thread is a religious symbol or not is a moot point. De Nobili argues that its primary meaning is social. Our point here is that a mark of civil distinction is legitimate. Cf. I.C. p. 106.

[25] I.C. p. 113. De Nobili accepts the principle that one should adopt the customs (*deśācāra*) of another country as *dharma* of one's class (*kuladharma*). Besides the saying "desacaram kuladharmam" means that every country has its own customs and division of people into classes which one must respect. A foreigner must adapt himself to the *dharma* of the corresponding class in the guest country. Thus it is an element of international law.

embrace what others say truly, — all these go to define a Brahmin. [26]

A Brahmin is expected to have these qualities according to *varṇadharma.* They include both moral and non-moral qualities. Hence de Nobili distinguishes the ethical from the non-ethical in his explanation of *dharma* in Hinduism. But the *dharma* of the classes was binding whether it was ethical in nature or not.[27] Non-ethical duties and observances are binding, too, though they are relative to a particular country and to a particular class of men. In the Hindu understanding of duties, they too are *dharma*.[28]

One may ask still if the *dharma* of the four classes is *dharma* in an ethical sense. The *dharma* of the four classes is based on the legitimate purpose of division of work and harmonious function of civil society. Such is the case with all human society. But the question remains as to whether de Nobili interprets the *dharma* of the four classes to be ethical.[29] His grounding of the *dharma* of society in the nature, goal and order of society which defines the common good, make it ethical in nature.[30] The *dharma* of society is basically ethical in nature, though in its concrete expression it may comprise elements that are not strictly ethical, but which are elements of social manners and etiquette.

When de Nobili explains the duties and virtues of the ideal Brahmin, he does it in such a way to show that they are not qualities

---

[26] Ibid. pp. 8-9.

[27] Here is a difficulty with regard to the ethical nature of *varṇadharma. Varạdharma* is treated as a part of ethics by the Hindu writers on Hinduism. For example, T. P. Mahadevan, Ch. 5. SUSIL KUMAR MAITRA, *The Ethics of the Hindus.* Cf. Introduction and Part I. Mahadevan in his work p. 70 says "And as the system of caste is a purely social adjustment, there is nothing that can stand in the way of its revision and readjustment..." If the system of castes is purely social adjustment, how is it that Mahadevan treats of it under the heading "Ethics" without showing how it is ethical?

[28] Again Hindu writers present *dharma* as ethics without paying attention to the polyvalent meaning of *dharma*. Mahadevan in his *Outlines of Hinduism* treats of it under the heading "Ethics" without attending to its polyvalent meaning.

[29] Cf. MAITRA, *The Ethics of the Hindus*, p. 1. He says that the social ethics of the Hindus is represented in a scheme of *varṇāśramadharma.*

[30] Mess, p. 12. He refers to the definition of Mr. Venkateswara, which would correspond to the ethical definition of *dharma.* He defines it as "the discharge of one's duty as rationally conceived as an aspect of social ethics."

of the rigidly fixed caste of Brahmins, but that they are of wise men everywhere.[31] The *dharma* of *varṇas* which de Nobili considers acceptable is justified by the nature of society.[32] If so, it would correspond to what Mees calls the 'natural hierarchy', which is based on righteousness, and not on birth.[33] In natural hierarchy, the greater the position in the division of classes, the greater the obligation.[34] One could see in de Nobili's treatment of *varṇadharma* the aspects of natural hierarchy and the artificial social hierarchy that came to exist in the actual historical conditions. De Nobili's praise of the qualities of the perfect Brahmin is praise of wise men everywhere.[35] When de Nobili criticises certain standards of behaviour, such as those based on injunction through scriptures and tradition, he shows them to be extrinsic norms which were due to the artificial and socially rigid hierarchy that came to exist.[36] Sanctions for the violations of the injunctions and traditions reinforced the extrinsic character of these rules and rigidity.[37] If the obligations come from external laws (from law-books), tradition, they are extrinsic, and they need to be justified by intrinsic reasons. This is done through the purpose (or *finis*) for which they were enjoined. One must determine whether the purpose is legitimate, that is, if the purpose concerns a human good which has nothing directly against right reason and true religion.

---

[31] Cf. Ch. I. On the *dharma* of Brahmins. In the Hindu understanding of *dharma, varṇāśramadharma* is relative to particular classes and stages of life. Hence it is not applicable to all men. That which is enjoined on all men is called *sādhāraṇadharma.* This classification is helpful. Cf. Maitra, p. 7, on Manu's classification of duties. But it is difficult to say if it is followed strictly. The moral qualities of the perfect Brahmin like "hard work, self control, kindness, almsgiving, truthfulness, righteousness (or virtue)" can be called *sādhāraṇadharma.* Cf. Mahadevan, p. 79.

[32] Mees, pp. 50-51. If *varṇa* is "the idea and theoretical class system as pictured by the eminent sages", it came to be rigid through actual historical circumstances.

[33] Ibid. p. 142. The commentator on 8th verse of 189th *adyāya* of *Sānti-parvan* of the *Mahābhārata* says, "righteousness and not birth, is the cause of the division into *varṇas.*" (quoted from J. Muir, Original Sanskrit Texts, vol. I, p. 142).

[34] Ibid. p. 149.

[35] I.C. pp. 12-13. Brahmins are considered noble because they have the knowledge of truth which is the highest good of man as praised by Gregory Nazianzen.

[36] Mees, pp. 59-60. "The norms of the idea *varṇa* are autonomous, when the Brahmins posited them and they were sanctioned to some extent by the rulers, the norms became heteronomous norms of class or norms of convention and common law."

[37] I.C. p. 5-6.

Mere extrinsic criteria are not sufficient. De Nobili mentions some of the sanctions against the learning of the *vedas* by non-brahmins. Learning of the scriptures is forbidden to non-brahmins according to *Āpastamba sūtra.*[38] Such rules are laid down by Brahmin authorities for the glorification of their caste and preservation of their privileges.[39] Privileges of this kind are strongly criticized by de Nobili.[40]

h. *Spiritual Meaning of Varṇāśramadharma*

In the Hindu understanding of *dharma, varṇadharma* and *āśramadharma* have also a spiritual meaning. In the theoretical or ideal system of four classes, these latter reflect the spiritual status of different classes. De Nobili does not accept the social classes as the index of spiritual progress.[41] Here two points must be mentioned why de Nobili rejects this view of *varṇadharma.* First, it is based on the theory of *karma* and belief in rebirth. The second reason is that in the actual historical situation of castes, the higher castes attached great importance to the dignity coming from their offices, and began to despise the lower castes.[42] Before God all men are equal. Social condition is due to the order of human society.[43]

B. DHARMA AS MORAL VIRTUES

De Nobili speaks of moral virtues as recommended by Hinduism in different stages of its development. He mentions many positive points concerning virtues though he has critical remarks on certain ideas of virtue as proposed in Hinduism.[44]

---

[38] Pr.Ap. p. 93.

[39] Mees, p. 9. He mentions this meaning of *dharma* as the 12th meaning. He says that sometimes this was the meaning of *dharma*.

[40] Pr.Ap. p. 93.

[41] P.J.A. p. 91.

[42] I.C. p. 5.

[43] Ibid. pp. 113-114. The caste rules are primarily civil customs (mos politicus) and have no regard to faith (*absque ullo intuito fidei*).

[44] In Hinduism, duties and virtues which all men must observe irrespective of different classes (*varṇas*) and stages of life (*āśramas*) fall under *sādhāraṇadharma*. De Nobili doesn't use this qualification. For him all virtues and moral duties are binding on all men.

Speaking of the qualities (*lakṣaṇa*) of the perfect Brahmin, de Nobili quotes a text from *Parāśara smṛti* in which many moral virtues are mentioned.[45] De Nobili comments on these qualities noting their order of importance which help one dispose oneself towards wisdom which consists in the contemplation of God. The practice of self-control and virtue leads to contemplation of God. The goal of the practice of moral virtues is contemplation of the true God. Virtue is the means that disposes the human being towards the contemplation of the true God.[46] Wisdom is, therefore, a matter of the contemplation of God. It is the goal of moral life. To show this, de Nobili quotes another text from Manu in which there is an ordering of moral life to the contemplation of God.[47] Moral life intends the final happiness of man which is wisdom and contemplation of God.[48]

Sannyāsa (renunciation) is a value for him. He adopts this way of life for himself and defends it as a positive value in Hinduism which he accepts as a Christian.[49] Virtuous acts such as almsgiving and penance have a value insofar as they remove causes of sin.[50] One important virtue in Hinduism is non-violence (*ahiṁsa*). De Nobili rejects it by reason of the beliefs that lie behind it. *Ahiṁsa* as non-violence towards all living beings is considered supreme *dharma* (*paramadharma*) and torture of living beings is called *adharma* (unrighteousness).[51] What de Nobili rejects is not so much the virtue of non-violence as the influence of the theory of *karma* and rebirth as a motive for this virtue.[52] In this connection we refer to what Thakur

[45] I.C. pp. 8-9.

[46] Ibid. p. 9. Here de Nobili refers to S.Th. 1,2, q. 3, art. 5 and 2,2, q. 180, art. 2: St. Thomas says: "Dispositive autem virtutes morales pertinent ad vitam contemplativam."

[47] Ibid.

[48] Tähtinen, pp. 43-44. He asks himself if *dharma* is an end in itself or a means to an end in Hinduism. On p. 44 he quotes Hiriyanna. "Judging from the literature, that is now available to us, we may take it (*dharma*) to have been generally regarded then as a means to an end or as an instrumental value, the end being the attainment of some good in this life or in the next." This idea is present in St. Thomas, 1,2, q. 3 and 2,2, q. 180, as mentioned above in the chapter.

[49] Pr.Ap. p. 59, p. 111 on the meaning of the *kāvi* dress worn by *sannyāsins*.

[50] T.T. pp. 417-418. Cf. ibid. p. 281. "All are agreed that austerity (*tapa*) is virtuous". (*puṇṇiyam*).

[51] A.N. p. 264.

[52] Ibid. Cf. P.V. KANE: *History of Dharmaśāstras*, Poona, 1941. Vol. II, part II, p. 776. He remarks that *ahiṁsā* has nothing to do with *karma* and rebirth. This motive was used by Manu and others to stress its importance.

says in his *Christian and Hindu Ethics* on the difference between Christian and Hindu ethics:

> ...no shade of Christian ethics is properly Christian unless the philosophy of love is central to it. Similarly, in tune with the whole tradition of India, including Buddhism and Jainism, no shade of Hindu ethics can be called properly Hindu unless the philosophy of non-violence is fundamental to it.[53]

It must, however, be said that de Nobili does not pay attention to the virtue of non-violence in itself, apart from his criticism of the theory of *karma* and rebirth used for motivation of the practice of *ahiṁsā*.

We have mentioned de Nobili's listing of the Buddhist titles of virtuous men which shows that he properly appreciated the moral virtues and moral values present in this sect.[54] He appreciated them wherever they were found. His explanation of the different titles of moral heroes centres on the moral meaning of the titles. He enumerates the titles with a sense of assurance that they are not mixed with idolatory. One notices that most of the titles stress and praise renunciation, conquest of self or desires.[55]

C. MORAL NORM

We discussed above the ethical and non-ethical meanings of *dharma* and its use. Now we shall see how de Nobili discusses the ethical norm with regard to practices and observances which have to do with morality. What he does is a critique of moral standards used.

a. *Tradition*

Tradition can be a standard of morality but only in a relative sense. One may follow a practice or a custom because it is a tradi-

---

[53] p. 200.

[54] I.C. pp. 27-28.

[55] Ibid., for example the titles, *budhers, munindra, malajit, lokajit,* and *vināyaka*.

tion handed down from generation to generation from time immemorial. A custom or a practice acquires the meaning of duty (*dhárma*).[56] But the problem arises as to whether or not it is considered a standard of morality. Customs cannot by themselves guarantee their righteousness. In the morality of marriage, that a married woman behaves like a wife to other brothers of her husband is considered the normal observance of a country or of a class (*deśācāra* or *kuladharma*).[57] That something is an observance of a country or of a clan cannot be a sufficient criterion to judge its moral rectitude. De Nobili doesn't reject the customs as such, but accepts them and recognises the need on the part of a missionary to adopt them.[58] But the final criterion of the legitimacy of a custom, such as the one mentioned above is not tradition but right reason. Polyandry, polygamy,[59] temple prostitution[60] cannot be considered morally right merely on the ground of tradition. Similarly, the idea that touching a low caste man (*caṇḍāla*) and seeing him at mid day is sin, that killing a cobra is a sin, that the custom of *suttee* is a virtue are based on tradition.[61] Reliance on tradition alone as a criterion to judge the righteousness of these practices is not a help. These are examples to show that tradition (*pāramparíyam*) could present that which is not sin as sin, or that which is sin to be virtue.[62] The definitive criterion for moral righteousness rests on the order of right reason (*niyāyakiramam*).[63] Tradition as a moral criterion can only be extrinsic and relative.

b. *Injunction through Scriptures*

Another moral standard that comes under criticism by de Nobili is the idea that something is to be obeyed because it has been pre-

---

[56] BANERJEE, *The Spirit of Indian Philosophy*, p. 278. The author discusses if custom or tradition can be standard of morality. Cf. also pp. 278-279.

[57] T.T. p. 391.

[58] Pr.Ap. p. 106. Cf. I.C. p. 113 where he quotes Manu (2,18). Note the phrase here: "pāramparya kramagata."

[59] T.T. p. 391.

[60] Ibid.

[61] Ibid. p. 51.

[62] Banerjee, pp. 278-279. He says that tradition finally rests on universal consensus (*lokaprasiddhi*) and points out that even the latter is not an intrinsic criterion but an extrinsic one.

[63] T.T. pp. 390-391.

scribed by the scriptures. Here again de Nobili accepts the relative nature of such a standard. What is prescribed in the scriptures is enjoined with the force of law. *Dharmaśāstras* prescribe the duties of the four classes which serve the good of society. But still the prescription or injunction through scriptures is an extrinsic norm. Scriptures can prescribe obligation which is not ethically justifiable.[64]

c. *Sacredness and Dharma in the Ethical Sense*

When all actions are surrounded with rituals and prayers, one may ask how one knows the moral rightness or wrongness of such acts. De Nobili says that eating with recitation of a prayer or bathing with a ritual attached to it, as the Hindus did, were not to be judged wrong *ipso facto.*[65] He rejects the idea that the gentile customs that go with rituals and prayers are *ipso facto* wrong. He tries to see a legitimate human purpose in them which could be retained. He rejects only those things that express superstition or wrong beliefs incompatible with true religion or morality.

De Nobili discusses the element of sacredness, as used in Hinduism to enforce law.[66] This is the case if rituals are prescribed in the scriptures which are supposed to have God as their author. The divine authorship makes people respect the observances prescribed in them.[67] Here de Nobili discusses sacredness of rules and observances as referring to their divine authorship, but sacredness of law and observances must not contradict right reason.[68] The ethical rightness can be judged from the end the law serves. De Nobili does not reject something merely because it is pagan.

Sometimes an action is commended as meritorious for practice.

[64] I.C. p. 46. *Parāśara smṛti* prescribes washing of oneself for having touched the wood is means for the burning of the human body or for having touched a Paraya or a public priest.

[65] Pr.Ap. pp. 100-104, I.C., p. 102. De Nobili distinguishes between *jñānam* and *karma.* Rituals, if based on *karma*, which concerns knowledge of false gods is to be objected. Cf. Ch. III, on religious rituals and *dharma*.

[66] We shall consider under religious *dharma* the meaning of holiness and moral righteousness.

[67] I.C. p. 36.

[68] Pr.Ap. p. 124. It is particularly difficult to decide on the moral goodness of customs if they are found mixed with other practices whose moral goodness is questionable in the scriptures.

A meritorious practice is said to have a commendable social purpose. Thus giving alms to a Brahmin who is devoted to wisdom is an expression of gratitude and respect for the exalted office of wisdom.[69] De Nobili interprets merit in the sense of commending or encouraging a practice. But as for the ethical righteousness, this could only be an extrinsic norm. Religious injunctions, though they could be above right reason, should not contradict it.

d. *Recta Ratio*

De Nobili accepts that men, irrespective of religion, are led by the light of reason (*lumen naturale*).[70] With *lumen naturale*, the Hindus or any other people can know the morally good works and virtues and the morally bad works. They can know the good works that ought to be performed and the bad works that ought to be avoided. The doctrine of Trent is that men can perform good works (in a moral sense) even before justification.[71] De Nobili finds a saying in Hinduism that expresses right reason.[72] It is a definition of sin. Sin is the giving up of certain actions called *piramāṇikka* and adoption of certain other actions called *appiramāṇikka. Piramāṇikka* expresses *piramāṇam* (*pramāṇa*) which is defined as "the way of reason (*niyāyam*) and the order of justice" (*nītikiramam*).[73] Therefore, it is any action, thought or word uttered by man which is in conformity with right reason. Such actions are called *piramāṇikka*. This is evidence of ethical reflection and definition of moral norms in Hinduism. It is also the criterion of right reason present in Hinduism, which de Nobili uses to criticize many practices of Hinduism or things written about them. The words *nīti* and *niyāya* are used together as *nītiniyāyam* to convey the idea of right reason. De Nobili uses it constantly. Later, we shall see how this definition of *piramāṇikkam* is transferred to the religious meaning of sin.

---

[69] I.C. p. 61.

[70] *Narratio*, pp. 8, 90. *Lumen naturale* stands for natural law which is based on right reason. It is also the doctrine of the Council of Trent. Cf. Ch. III on *recta ratio.* Cf. JOHN MACQUARRIE, *Three Issues in Ethics*, pp. 15-16. He points out the value of the presence of moral striving of mankind for dialogue with all men, be they believers or non-believers.

[71] Pr.Ap. pp. 90-91.

[72] T.T. p. 400. The definition already referred to in ch. 3: *Recta Ratio.*

[73] Ibid.

The two elements of right reason are knowledge (*ñānam*) and freedom (*svātantiriyam*). The human act (*actus humanus*) is an act of the human person that goes with knowledge. The activity of knowledge belongs to man's nature.[74] A free act is that which the knowing person posits concerning and on account of a thing known.[75] At the same time, it posits it without compulsion for in such freedom one can say yes or no to the thing known by its own power.[76] Knowledge and freedom enter and define any moral act, be it virtuous or not. The faculty of freedom is called *manacu* (will). These two elements of human acts are weakened in the theory of *karma* and rebirth, for it limits the freedom of man. It means a sort of determinism. According to the theory, one suffers in the present life the consequences or fruits of one's good and bad acts in a previous life. It is a hypothesis. There is no knowledge or rememberance of a previous life and of the actions done in them. It is to be accepted on faith.[77] De Nobili argues according to the same theory of *karma* that one cannot repair or make amends for one's sins, of which one has no knowledge. One cannot reject or repent of a sin one cannot know. Repenting of one's sins means that one turns one's will away from sin.[78] But, according to the theory of *karma* and rebirth one does not know the sin from which one must turn one's will away. The theory weakens the personal nature of virtue and sin. On the ground of knowledge required of one's sins and virtues, the objection of de Nobili is valid.[79] De Nobili supposes that the theory of *karma* implies fatalism. Such a criticism is not objective. He mixes the popular belief in fate (*viti*) and *lāṭalipi* (i.e. writing on the cranium) with the law of *karma* and argues that the law of *karma* means total determinism.[80] He doesn't admit of partial freedom.[81]

---

[74] A.N. p. 31.

[75] Ibid. p. 52.

[76] Ibid. pp. 65-66.

[77] Thakur, p. 188.

[78] A.N. pp. 308-309. Here we must observe that de Nobili does not face all the arguments concerning the effect of sin. He minimises the knowledge of sin through consequences.

[79] Thakur, p. 188. "The real difficulty with the law of *karma*, it seems, is that it introduces unverifiable phenomena into the whole issue so that responsibility for crimes of a previous life can rest only on an unquestioning belief in the validity of the doctrine...".

[80] Cf. Ch. 2, Determinism, Freedom and the Law of *Karma* and Rebirth.

[81] Mahadevan, p. 60. *Karma* does not determine man completely. One admits certain

The theory of *karma* means a certain amount of diminution of freedom, but de Nobili exaggerates this weakness of the theory of *karma* to imply total determinism.[82]

Another difficulty that de Nobili points out is the problem of the moral agent if one admits a series of births in different forms of animals and birds according to each one's *karma*.[83] Here he is faced with a different concept of the human soul.[84] According to the Christian idea, the human soul is the specific form of the human body forming one being of man, soul and body being two incomplete principles.[85] But if the soul can take on different bodies, such as those of animals, the problem of attribution of moral responsibility is made difficult. If the Advaitic idea that one is ultimately the Self, then it would mean that the imperfect actions would be attributed to the Self. That would make the Self imperfect.[86] The difficulties that arise from the different Hindu conceptions of the soul of man, advaitic or non-advaitic, on the nature of morality, to which the Christian idea of the human soul is opposed, are real. De Nobili recognized these difficulties and the basic differences in the conception of man.

e. *Morality and Order of Reason (Krama)*

De Nobili applies the notion of right order (in Tamil, *kiramam*, in Skt. *krama*) in explaining *dharma*. He employs it as an expression of right reason. Hence he calls it the 'order of right reason (*ñāya kiramam*). That which does not correspond to right order is termed

---

amount of determinism. Mahadevan quotes Radhakrishnan: "The cards in the game of life are given to us. We do not select them. They are traced to our past *karma*, but we can call as we please, lead what suit we will, and as we play, we gain or lose. And there is freedom." (quoted from the *Hindu View of Life*). Thakur, op. cit. pp. 175-176. The Law of *karma* is introduced in morality to explain responsibility. Man is responsible for his actions but the real objection is against the theory of *karma* of the previous birth of which one has no recollection. Cf. ibid. pp. 188-189. Cf. P.S. SIVASAMY: *Evolution of Hindu Moral Ideals*, The Calcutta University, 1935, pp. 139-141.

[82] A.N. pp. 270-271.

[83] Ibid. p. 222.

[84] Cf. Ch. 2, The nature of the soul (*āttuma*) of man. There we have examined the different views of the soul which differ from the Christian view of the soul of man.

[85] A.N. pp. 178-180, also pp. 161-163.

[86] Ibid. pp. 131-132.

akkiramam (moral disorder).[87] *Krama* is only a derivative concept of right reason, since moral order is to be further explained in terms of right reason.

f. *Determinants of Morality*

De Nobili uses the determinants (or *fontes*) of morality in his critique of *dharma*. They are object, end (*finis*) and circumstance. De Nobili does not treat of them in a systematic way, but mentions them and applies them to Hindu customs.

Object determines morality. De Nobili recognizes this when he speaks of the idea of order in the moral sphere. He says that sin or moral disorder is disorder in a grave matter.[88] The grave matter determines the morality of an act. A moral disorder can never be virtue, since its nature (*prakṛiti*) is that of sin.[89] We recognize here that object specifies the morality of human acts. He recognizes that *objectum* that determines morality when he says that there are actions which are by themselves bad.[90]

De Nobili mentions also circumstances which determine the morality of human actions. All the essential circumstances go to modify human actions.[91] They can modify either *objectum* or the agent of action (therefore *finis operantis*).

Intention of the subject qualifies the morality of the human acts. De Nobili refers to the Thomistic notion of an act of the will which modifies the morality of the external act.[92] Thus *dharma* and *adharma* (written together as *dharmādharma*) is judged according to the intention (i.e. act of the will). According to the goodness or malice of the act of the will, the external act will be good or bad. De Nobili uses this norm to judge the morality of human acts.[93]

---

[87] T.T. pp. 411-412.

[88] *Kāṇṭam* II, p. 91. Here objective act is not to be taken in its physical being but within the order of right reason. Cf. *Kāṇṭam* I, p. 58.

[89] T.T. p. 427.

[90] Pr.Ap. p. 94: actions *per se mala*. Object has its own *finis* called *finis operis*, cf. *Kāṇṭam* II, p. 57.

[91] Pr. Ap. p. 91. S.Th. 1,2, q. 18, art. 3.

[92] Cf. Ch. 3. Intention and moral action. T.T. p. 411, Cf. Pr.Ap. p. 90. On the Thomistic position, S.Th. 1,2, q. 20, art. 1.

[93] T.T. p. 412. If a king for the maintenance of justice has a thief punished with death, it is right. If one kills another on account of enmity, then killing is murder. The *dharma* of penance

D. DHARMA AND RELIGION (HINDUISM)

In our summing up of the religious meaning of *dharma* in Hinduism,[94] we shall first mention the positive elements that de Nobili recognizes. Then we shall mention the difficulties present in the religious meaning of *dharma. Dharma*, understood in the perspective of the ethic of salvation is the basic approach of de Nobili with regard to *dharma* in Hinduism and Christianity.

a. *God and Morality*

De Nobili presents the concept of God as the foundation of morality and religion as the *dharma* of salvation.[95] His criticism of the religious meaning of *dharma* in Hinduism supposes the idea of God as creator of all beings, and the idea of His being distinct from created things. Only then all God-directed morality can be meaningfully understood. His interpretation of the idea of one God in Hinduism is not sufficiently critical. He calls the Absolute (Brahman) of the *Vedāntins* God without qualifying it. God could be understood as personal whereas the Absolute in the *Advaita Vedānta* is not only impersonal but also is understood in a monistic sense.[96] Though the *Vedāntins* reject plurality of the ultimate reality and accept one ultimate reality, this ultimate reality cannot be God who is creator of all things and a reality distinct from the created things. De Nobili says that the one God who is unique, immaterial is the one who can be known by the light of reason.[97] Concerning creation, de Nobili understands the idea of God who is one, without beginning and end, self-existent, existing by Himself, eternal, blissful and form of intelligence as found in *Cittiyār* as the one universal cause of the uni-

---

though not direct cause of forgiveness of sin, removes causes of sin or unrighteousness. Hence it must be good.

94 Here we use the words 'religion', 'religious' in the sense of having to do with God and salvation without reference to their revealed or supernatural character.

95 Cf. Ch. 4, Concept of God and *Dharma*.

96 I.C. pp. 24-25,30. De Nobili calls Brahma 'God' without paying attention to the nontheistic notion of Brahma of *Advaitins*.

97 Ibid. p. 9.

verse, though there is no idea of creation 'ex nihilo sui et subjecti' in Hinduism.[98] Instead it holds "ex nihilo nihil fit." [99]

De Nobili finds certain positive points about the nature of God in Hinduism. As we mentioned above, the poem of *Cittiyār* mentions certain attributes of God which de Nobili accepts as valid. Then he says that the school of *Jñānis* admits the divine attributes such as that God is Being by Himself, that He is eternal, that He is incorporeal, that He is by nature good, that He exists everywhere and that He is the cause of all.[100] He quotes another text which says that God is "good by His nature." [101] What he proposes in the treatise on the determination of the concept of God (*Kaṭavuḷ Nirṇayam*) sums up the attributes of God which *Cittiyar* and the school of *Jñānis* have mentioned.[102] He proposes in this treatise six attributes of God as criterion for the knowledge of the true God to anyone desirous of salvation. The same things are said of God in Hinduism, as we pointed out above. God, thus conceived, is alone worthy of being worshipped. The treatise *Kaṭavuḷ Nirṇayam* concludes the verse giving the six attributes of God in a *slōka* in these words: "Such a one (God) I worship." [103] That God is worthy of worship means that He is good and righteous by nature.[104] Such a concept of God worthy of worship is found in Hinduism. God is understood to be the one who rewards the good and punishes the wicked. These are the positive aspects in the concept of God which are important for the idea that God is the foundation of morality. Here we may mention what

---

[98] Ibid. p. 30. In Hinduism there is no idea of creation out of nothing (*ex nihilo sui et subjecti*) because the Hindus believe that "nothing can come out of nothing." This theory of creation is called *satkāryavāda.* Cf. Ibid. p. 25. ZAEHNER, *Hinduism*, p. 28.

[99] I.C. p. 25. *Māyāvādins* argue in this way.

[100] Ibid. p. 25.

[101] Ibid. p. 34. "Rtam tva bhagah." If the text were from Taitt. Up. 1.4.3, there should be *taṁ* instead of *ṛtam.* De Nobili renders *ṛtaṁ* as 'good'.

[102] N.C.C. p. 107.

[103] Ibid. The skt. phrase in Tamil is "nitānam namāmi akam." Probably the first word is to be written as *nitānta* (the Supreme).

[104] E. D'Arcy, "Worthy of Worship": A Catholic Contribution, in *Religion and Morality* ed. Gene Outka and John Reeder, Jr., New York, 1973, pp. 173-203. As D'Arcy remarks on p. 200, "...there are the emotions of religious fear and emotion elicited by some sense of the *mysterium tremendum et fascinans*, and the holy one is worshipped because that may be the way to win his favour and keep him in good humour. But an enormously significant development has occurred when he comes to be recognised as worthy of worship."

de Nobili says on the adumbration of the Holy Trinity found in the Hindu scriptures. Though he rejects the idea of *trimūrti* as being inadequate to express the mystery of the Holy Trinity,[105] he says that he has found a passage in the Hindu scriptures in which one can see an adumbration of the Christian doctrine of Trinity. The passage refers to Taitt. Up.:

> Himself is spirit within His own nature, in Him is the one who is also Himself spirit existing from will, and the one existing from the mouth (i.e. the word) resting on the bosom of Him (i.e. the Son) is Himself at the same time the Lord and cause of all.[106]

b. *Difficulties in the Concept of God*

In his criticism of the idea of *trimūrti* of Brahma, Viṣṇu and Śiva, de Nobili concentrates on the moral nature of the gods. The deeds attributed to them in the *purāṇas* go against the glorious attributes of God and are incompatible with reason and understanding.[107] We note here that de Nobili does exaggerate his criticism because of his apologetic purpose to present Christianity as the pure religion.

The Hindu ideas that there is one Supreme Soul (*paramātma*) in all men and that the individual souls (*jīvātmas*) are many would create difficulties in the attribution of moral responsibility. It would mean that the Supreme Soul would be the principal cause of man's sin. When men pray to the Lord for forgiveness, they would be praying to themselves to forgive themselves. This difficulty de Nobili mentions.[108] Thus the religious acts of prayer and worship would be

---

105 CF. Ch. IV on *trimūrti.*

106 I.C. p. 35. Cf. De Smet, art. cit. p. 368. The passage quoted by de Nobili is from Taitt. Up. 1,6,1. S. Radhakrishnan's translation runs as follows: "This space that is within the heart — therein is the Person consisting of mind, immortal and resplendent. That which hangs down between the palates like a nipple, that is the birth-place of Indra." (Cf. *The Principal Upaniṣads*, p. 533).

107 *Kānṭam* II, pp. 190-191. Cf. Ch. IV on the refutation of the idea of *trimūrti*. Cf. Bertrand II, p. 257. Vico considers that the original truths, i.e., the perfections of God have been corrupted into the idea of *trimūrti*.

108 A.N. p. 132. DHAVAMONY, *Phenomenology of Religion*, p. 265.

rendered meaningless. This would also create difficulties in the understanding that God is the protector of *dharma*. If morally unacceptable deeds are attributed to God, He cannot be understood as the guardian of *dharma*. De Nobili is particularly critical of the gods, as mentioned in the *purāṇas*, whose conduct and deeds are not compatible with righteousness (*dharma*).[109] They are said to approve or command deeds incompatible with *dharma*.[110] De Nobili mentions three reasons why in popular Hinduism gods come to be worshipped. They are wonder (*āccariyam*), benefit (*pirayōcanam*) and fear (*payam*).[111] These sentiments dominant in the subjective attitude of worship of the gods have no reference to moral righteousness in them that makes them worthy of worship.

Sinful deeds in God can in no way be explained away. De Nobili counters the objection that though there are sinful deeds in God, they are said not to affect Him. Sinful deeds cannot affect Him, since by His power He can prevent this. De Nobili answers this objection by saying that the righteous use of the power of God concerns the avoidance of sin itself. If so, if God allows sin to befall Him, God is not powerful but weak.[112] The argument that God cannot allow sin to affect Him is explained by the example of a worm that falls into fire. The word cannot make the fire rot but is burnt by it instead.[113] The concept of power is by itself a non-moral concept which cannot be used as a norm of morality. That God is all-powerful cannot mean that He is powerful enough to be unrighteous. God's power is an infinite perfection of His. By His power, God can do only that which is right. That He is powerful to do that which is sinful is weakness which cannot exist in God who is the form of all good.[114] De Nobili tries to counter a non-moral concept of God which is implied in the simile mentioned above.[115]

[109] *Kāṇṭam* I, pp. 45-49.

[110] Ibid. pp. 48-50.

[111] *Kāṇṭam* II, p. 142, N.C.C. pp. 56, 61-63, 69, 71-75. These three motives present in popular Hinduism may go to define what R. Otto calls the 'numinous'. But the idea of the holy must include also the moral element. Cf. R. OTTO, *The Idea of the Holy*, p. 110.

[112] T.T. pp. 93-94.

[113] *Kāṇṭam* I, pp. 42-43.

[114] Ibid. p. 43.

[115] REEDER, "The Relation of the Moral and the Numinous in Otto's Notion of the Holy" in *Relation and Morality* ed. Outka and Reeder, pp. 255-294. Should the idea of the holy include moral goodness? The holy must include the moral element though it does not exhaust it.

c. *Dharma and Incarnation*

The criticism of the moral nature of God by de Nobili is seen in the examination of the Hindu concept of *avatāra.* The purpose of incarnation, according to the Hindu understanding, is the restoration of *dharma* [116] or the saving of the world.[117] Viṣṇu in his incarnation is said to perform many 'sports' (*līlās*) which are morally objectionable. They cannot be explained away.[118] That they are described in religious scriptures (*purāṇaprabandhas*), which are attributed to great sages (*ṛṣis* and *munis*), does not answer the objection that certain of these divine 'sports' are morally objectionable.[119] If the purpose of incarnation is *dharma*, it is contradicted by such divine sports. Besides, God who is the form of righteousness (*tarmacurūpam*) cannot do things that contradict this nature of his.[120] The *līlās* of God would not create desire for *dharma* in the heart of man.[121]

Moral Life and Salvation

d. *Svarga and Dharma*

Moral life is explained in terms of the theory of *karma* which works like a principle of cause and effect, which means wandering of the soul in different existences. This creates difficulties in the understanding of the last end, especially, the final beatitude of heaven (*mokṣa*).[122] From this viewpoint, de Nobili rejects idea of *svarga* for two principal reasons. First, it is described as a place of pleasures which satisfy every desire of man,[123] and whose sensual nature is

116 Cf. the *Bhagavad-Gītā*, 4,7. It presents the purpose of *avatāra*: "For whenever the law of righteousness withers away and lawlessness arises, then do I generate Myself (on earth)." Ibid. v. 8: "For the protection of the good, for the destruction of the evil-doers, for the setting up of the law of righteousness I come into being age after age..." (Trans. from the *Bhagavad-Gītā*, by Zaehner, p. 184).

117 T.T. p. 117.

118 Ibid. Appendix, p. vii.

119 Ibid. pp. 117, 122.

120 Ibid. p. 118.

121 Ibid. p. 281.

122 A.N. pp. 223-224.

123 *Narratio*, p. 142; I.C. p. 18.

morally objectionable.[124] *Svarga* thus understood cannot be reward for virtue.[125] The other reason why de Nobili rejects it is that it is understood within the scheme of *karma* and rebirth.[126] He also rejects the ideas of the heaven of Viṣṇu (*vaikuṇṭam*), the heaven of Śiva (*kailācam*) and the heaven of Brahma (*piramlōkam*)[127] These notions of the final end of man as heaven (*mōccam*) are explained in the *purāṇas* in a contradictory manner. Hence they are unacceptable expressions of the final end of heaven.[138]

e. *Forgiveness of Sin*

De Nobili critically examines the Hindu idea of removal of sin (*pāvanivāraṇam*). The theory of *karma* and rebirth again create difficulties in the understanding of sin, virtue and repentance. Forgiveness of sin is necessary for salvation but de Nobili argues that according to the theory of *karma* and rebirth, one has no knowledge of sins committed in a previous existence. Then he criticises the idea that one's present condition is due to *karma* that results from actions done in a previous life. He rejects the idea that one's suffering or poverty or misfortune in this life is a way of repairing one's sins done in a previous life.[129] The important element required for the forgiveness of sin is repentance. De Nobili says that suffering, poverty, disease, etc. as a consequence of sin alone is not sufficient for the removal of the guilt of sin. There must be knowledge of one's sins of previous life in this life in which one is considered to repair one's sins of previous life. Only then can one repent of one's sins. But no one has knowledge of one's previous life or of sins committed in previous life in this life.[130] This argument of de Nobili is finally based on his refutation of the theory of *karma* and cycle of births which he considers a hypothesis posited without sufficient proof. Though de Nobili accepts the presence of partial freedom,[131] he

---

[124] A.N. p. 370.

[125] Ibid. pp. 374-375.

[126] Ibid. pp. 401-402.

[127] Ibid. p. 390. It is also called *satyalōka*. Cf. Dubois t. II, p. 423.

[128] A.N. p. 398.

[129] Ibid. p. 210, P.J.A. p. 62.

[130] P.J.A. p. 62.

[131] A.N. pp. 228-229; P.J.A. pp. 13, 46.

argues that everything that man does in this life must be explained in terms of *karma* of one's actions in a previous life if one admits the theory.[132]

Then de Nobili criticises the quasi-material notion of sin. He considers that the personal notion of sin is weak, if not absent.[133] He criticises the custom of taking baths in the sacred rivers for the removal of the guilt of sin.[134] De Nobili's criticism of the idea of forgiveness of sin is incomplete. For the apologetic reason of presenting the Christian doctrine of forgiveness, he sees only a mechanical notion in the prayers for forgiveness, and so too in the practices for forgiveness of sin. It is said that if one wears the Rosary of Rudra or if one utters the name of Rama or Narayaṇa, all sin will fly away like a bird.[135] According to him the utterance of the name of Śiva or of Rama or Narayaṇa does not reflect the repentance required for forgiveness of sin, since it is mechanically performed.[136] De Nobili ignores the aspect of love (*bhakti*) that is implicit in such practices and and prayers. The poem from *Kantapurāṇam* expresses love which de Nobili ignores.[137] The utterance of the name of Śiva goes with *bhakti* which can include repentant love, though it is not explicitly stated. De Nobili thinks that such a prayer does not express repentant love.[138] Besides, such practices are directed towards created things like the sun, which are not God. He considers that the practices of austerities and almsgiving do not express repentance.[139]

---

[132] A.N. pp. 268-269. Cf. P.J.A. p. 72. De Nobili is influenced by the idea of *Pūrva Mīmāṁsā* which says that *karma* alone is sufficient to explain the world.

[133] *Kāṇṭam* I, p. 9, T.T. p. 400. The definition of sin "piramāṇikkap parittiyaka, appiramāṇikkac cuvikāram pāvam" is also explained in terms of right reason, and it is not a material notion of sin. Cf. Thakur, op. cit., pp. 182-184.

[134] A.N. pp. 37, 414. M.V. pp. 98-99. We may refer to the *slōka* in KP p. 72. "Jalena janita pankam, jalena paricuttiyate, manacanimittam papam, paccatapena cuttiyate." Cf. Dubois, I, p. 268, for this poem.

[135] *Kāṇṭam* II, p. 198.

[136] Ibid. pp. 199, 213. Cf. also A.N. p. 379. The gods cursed by the *ṛṣi* Kavala are asked to bathe in the waters of Ramacētu (a *tarmatīrtam*) which is one of the 24 *tīrthas* (waters).

[137] *Kāṇṭam* II, p. 198. "If one utters the names of Rudra, Rudra comes running to such a person just like a cow that comes near its calf. Cf. also p. 199.

[138] Ibid. p. 198.

[139] T.T. p. 404. Here we can see that his knowledge of Hinduism was limited. In Vedic hymns, there are penitent prayers addressed to Varuna which are signs of repentant love. Cf. DHAVAMONY, *Love of God*, pp. 52-54.

f. *The Final End of Man (mokṣa)*

De Nobili adopts the use of *mokṣa* for heaven while he rejects the use of *svarga* because of the things of doubtful values spoken about it.[140] De Nobili refers to the idea that the final end (*oṭukkam*) comes to man through heaven (*mōccam*) which is mentioned by the Hindus.[141] Here de Nobili says that all accept that it is God who bestows heaven (*mōccam*) on man.[142] He also refers to the different states (or stages) of heaven.[143] First, we point out here that de Nobili recognises a true value in the understanding of *mokṣa*:

> Some say that if the soul sees God, then heaven consists in such a vision.[144]

De Nobili immediately adds that they should say that such a vision is to be called 'direct vision' (*pirattiyacca tericanam*). He accepts the fact that in this point their statement on heaven is correct.[145]

De Nobili is particularly negative in his criticism of the ideas *cārūppiyam* and *cāyucciyam* which describe man's union with God in the final state of beatitude and which would weaken the understanding of *dharma*. His criticism of *cāyucciyam* is based on the meaning he gives to the word. It means "to be mixed with." [146] That means in *cāyucciyam* the soul becomes mixed with God. This union takes place with God who is simple without parts (*akanṭam*). Through *cāyucciyam* the soul of man is said to disappear like wood in the fire.

In *cārūppiyam* (having the same form as God's), the soul becomes one with God just like the wood in fire, which disappears, so

---

[140] Cf. the subtitle *svarga and dharma* in this chapter.

[141] A.N. p. 404.

[142] Ibid. p. 405.

[143] De Nobili says that the different stages of *mokṣa* such as *cāmīppiyam*, *cālōkkiyam*, *cārūppiyam* and *cāyucciyam* are different ideas of *mokṣa,* whereas they are different stages of it.

[144] A.N. p. 405.

[145] Ibid. p. 406. "Such attainment of the beatitude of heaven through the vision of God, they must call the direct vision of God." De Nobili understands *cālōkkiyam* in this way.

[146] DHAVAMONY, *Love of God*, p. 364. The Tamil idea of *sāyujya* is "*kalappu*." De Nobili gives another meaning of *cāyucciyam*: 'to be with'. (A.N. p. 408). This meaning he ignores on the ground it comes to mean the same as *cāmīppiyam* (being in the vicinity of God).

that only the form of fire remains. De Nobili interprets *cārūppiyam* to mean the destruction or disappearance (*layam*) of the human soul. *Cārūppiyam* means also change in God.[147] Then it would mean that God instead of saving man destroys him, whereas the experience of heaven (*mōccam*) by the soul of man means that it exists.[148] De Nobili considers that the understanding of heaven as *cārūppiyam* and as *cāyucciyam* would render the practice of *dharma* meaningless, since according to such views of heaven, one would perform *dharmas* like austerities, prayers, meditation for the attainment of heaven in which the human soul disappears.[149] He also remarks that *cārūppiyam* and *cāyucciyam* means that the human soul and God are not different realities. If so, they remove the idea of the experience of the bliss of heaven (*mōcca paramānanta anupavam*) born of direct vision and love of God.

g. *Religion (vētam) and Dharma*

De Nobili interprets religion (*vētam*) in terms of *dharma. Vētam* could either mean the sacred scriptures which are believed to be the inspired source of religion, or it could signify the religion itself. The relation of *vētam* between these two meanings is expressed in its purpose. The purpose of religion is to reveal the nature of God with certitude and righteous conduct (*tarmacarittiram*) for salvation.[150] It must declare it without error. De Nobili mentions the different expressions used for sacred scriptures which convey the meaning that they have been revealed by God. The mere claim that religion has been revealed and that religious scriptures have been uttered by God

---

[147] A.N. pp. 410-411.

[148] Ibid. p. 420.

[149] Ibid. pp. 422-423. De Nobili's understanding of *cārūppiyam* and *cāyucciyam* is not accurate. He considers that these two stages of heaven mean destruction and disappearance of the individual soul whereas this is not the meaning given by the Hindus. Cf. Mahadevan, pp. 171-172. Cf. ZAEHNER, *Hinduism*, p. 90. Here we may refer to what de Nobili says on *cālōkkiyam* (being in the realm of God). This means that the soul attains the experience of heaven through the vision of God which should be more accurately described as direct vision of God. This meaning of *cālōkkiyam*, says de Nobili, is true because it comes close to the Christian meaning of heaven. But de Nobili doesn't consider that according to the Hindus, it is the first of the four stages of release (*mokṣa*).

[150] T.T. pp. 78, 84.

is not sufficient to accept that they are so. That which has been revealed by God shouldn't contain error on the nature of God and *dharma*. Revealed religion must declare *dharma* (righteousness and virtue) truly, since the living of the way of righteousness and virtue is the way to salvation. The nature of virtue and the nature of sin are either wrongly or imperfectly declared in Hinduism.[151] The doctrine of *karma* and rebirth in Hinduism does not help define the nature of virtue and of sin correctly.[152] Sometimes non-moral matters such as customs of food and eating are made rules of religious teaching. De Nobili shows that such rules which concern the non-moral civil customs of society cannot apply to all men for salvation.[153] If *dharma* is the purpose and content of religion, the civil customs and laws cannot be the content of religion.

h. *Religion and Caste*

De Nobili sedulously avoided any mixing up of the fact of belonging to caste with the essential meaning of religion.[154] Because one belongs to Śaivism or to Vaiṣṇavism, one is not a Brahmin or *Kṣatrya*. Being a follower of a religion is distinct from being a member of a caste.[155] The reasoning for this is as follows: If religion is intimately associated with a caste (*jāti*), which is a reality of civil society, then social observances and rules will have to be the object of religious teaching and injunction; whereas religion must deal only with matters of the salvation of man primarily, and must prescribe only those things that lead all men to salvation, regardless of the castes to which they belong.[156] The observance of caste (*jāti ācārams*) cannot be the object of revelation and of religious injunction as universally binding on all men who belong to different clans and different social groups.[157] This is an implicit rejection of the

---

[151] Ibid. pp. 76-77, 83.

[152] Cf. P.J.A. which deals with this problem. Cf. also ch. III on *recta ratio*.

[153] T.T. p. 48.

[154] M.V. p. 86; T.T. pp. 18-19.

[155] Ibid. pp. 86-87. Cf. Ayer, p. 186. Cf. also J. GONDA: *Viṣṇuism and Śaivism*, University of London, 1970, pp. 66-67.

[156] T.T. p. 35.

[157] Ibid. pp. 35-36.

idea of *varṇāśramadharma* as having to do with man's spiritual status and salvation.[158]

i. *Salvation of Non-Christians*

De Nobili considers the salvation of a non-Christian who leads a morally good life. He also belongs to one of the non-Christian religions. De Nobili says that such a person rejects the wrong ideas of God present in his religion and considers God to be the first cause of the world. He performs virtuous acts for the sake of this one true God and does not consent to sinful actions.[159] The good non-Christian does not know the true religion of God (i.e. the Christian religion) through no fault of his. De Nobili says that all the theologians are agreed upon that the merciful God will not condemn such a man.[160] At the same time, he observes that heaven which is the direct vision of God is above the power of the human intellect. Man reaches the beatitude of heaven through the supernatural virtues of faith and charity.[161] De Nobili goes on to say that the faith and charity which the non-Christian has before receiving the grace of justification have a proportionate relation to the nature of man. The knowledge of God that he has comes to him through the help of reason. Such a knowledge cannot be said to be above the nature of

---

[158] The four-*varṇa* system is rejected in so far as it is bound up with the theory of *karma* and rebirth. Cf. ch. 2 on the order of civil society. De Nobili would not have any objection to the original ideal of *varṇas* provided there was no linking of the *varṇas* with belief in *karma* and rebirth. C. Mees, p. 73. He points out that the theory of *karma* and rebirth came to the foreground when 'natural classes' (*varṇas*) became hereditary castes. De Nobili would accept *varṇas* as natural classes which are "based on fundamental laws of society and tendencies of individuals and groups in the social composition." *Varṇas* are not bound up with heredity, and they are open-ended classes. The element of openness is seen with regard to the custom of wearing the thread as discussed by de Nobili. Cf. *Narratio*, pp. 104-106.

[159] T.T. pp. 413-414. De Nobili doesn't enter into a discussion if such a good man does good works and rejects sin through his own power or through the grace (actual) of God. De Nobili discusses the salvation of the good non-Christian with reference to the justifying grace or saving grace of God. It is not necessary that the good non-Christian must have a very clear and exhaustive knowledge of God. Cf. S.Th. 2,2, q. 1, a. 7. OHM, *Die Liebe zu Gott*, pp. 439-440. Yesudas, "Indigenisation or Adaptation," *Bangalore Theological Forum*, ((1967), pp. 39-52. He does not consider this point at all.

[160] T.T. p. 414. Also A.N. p. 80.

[161] T.T. pp. 414-415.

the human intellect. Hence the love of God born of this knowledge has also a proportionate relation to the nature of the will of man.[162]

De Nobili does not view such a knowledge and love of God as being supernatural and therefore meritorious unto salvation. That is the meaning of their being proportionate to the nature of man. The knowledge and love which the good non-Christian has and the virtuous acts he does help to prevent him from falling into serious sin in some way but they cannot be the direct cause of salvation.[163] It does not mean that they are done without the grace of God.[164] The condemnation of the good non-Christian will not be in keeping with the mercy of God.[165] De Nobili speaks of the way in which God's saving grace (grace of justification) comes to a good non-Christian as understood by theologians. He says that God who rules everything with right order will not allow disorder to exist in the matter of salvation of man. The disorder would be the condemnation of a good non-Christian who through no fault of his did not know the Christian religion. The theological opinion is that God will send either an earthly messenger or one from heaven to teach him the truths

---

[162] Ibid. p. 415. It means they are not yet meritorious unto salvation but it does not mean they are done without the help (actual grace) of God. It only means that salvation is God's gift. God has ordained virtuous conduct to be the way to the fulfilment of His salvific will. *Kāṇṭam* II, pp. 294-295.

[163] T.T. p. 415. Salvation exceeds the power of human acts.

[164] Ibid. pp. 435-436. We refer here to de Nobili's explanation of grace in other texts and works of his. He mentions the external and internal graces (actual graces), which God gives to all men e.g. fear of eternal punishment, aversion of will to sin, desire to walk according to the will of God, such desires (Tam. *cankarpankaḷ* for skt. *samkalpas*). Cf. A.N. p. 467. Here, de Nobili explains how virtue comes to exist. God gives good desires to man before man's free consent. With free consent it becomes virtue. The free consent itself is born according to the will of God which is also grace (cf. *gratia adjuvans* and *gratia concomitans*).

[165] T.T. pp. 435-36. In our discussion we refer to what de Nobili says in his other works on grace and on the universal salvific will of God. In Pr.Ap. pp. 90-91, he refers to the Council of Trent which says that not all works which non-Christians do are sin and therefore do not deserve the wrath of God. Cf. Session 6, can. 7 (D. 817): "Si quis dixerit, opera omnia, quae ante iustificationem fiunt, quacumque ratione facta sint, vere esse peccata vel odium Dei mereri, aut quanto vehementius quis nititur se disponere ad gratiam, tanto eum gravius peccare: an.s." De Nobili refers to St Thomas (S.Th. 2,2, q. 10, a. 4, esp. ad. 3). Through *infidelitas*, natural reason is not completely corrupted, and there remains some knowledge of truth with which an infidel can do some good works. De Nobili refers to Soto, the Dominican theologian (at the Council of Trent) and the general opinion of theologians who held that gentiles could posit many works which are morally good.

needed for salvation.[166] If such a man hears the teaching of the truths and does not accept them, he will not be saved. But if he accepts the supreme truths of faith revealed by God, then he has faith which comes through the Word of God. Such a faith is above the nature of man. Love of God born of this God-given knowledge of faith is also supernatural. Such faith and love of God are salvific.[167]

Then de Nobili explains the value of the good deeds done by such a good non-Christian before he received the grace of hearing the Gospel. All his good deeds and his renunciation of sin would amount to having hindered sin,[168] though they are not yet the direct cause of forgiveness of sin. The grace of forgiveness belongs to the grace of justification. It is accepted by theologians that God cannot

---

[166] T.T. p. 416. For the idea of God sending a preacher to such a man cf. M. SECKLER, "Das Heil der Nichtevangelisierten in Thomistischer Sicht," in *Theologische Quartalschrift* 140 (1960) pp. 44. In the 12th century, according to Rolandus Bandinellus, there were theologians who for the hypothetical case of a good man who had no opportunity to hear the gospel, advanced the view that God would send a preacher to him or through an inspiration give him the material of faith required. Cf. T. OHM, *Die Stellung der Heiden zu Natur und Übernatur nach dem Hl. Thomas von Aquin*, Munster, 1927, p. 231 on how the mystery of redemption reached the gentiles, esp. on the idea of St. Thomas Aquinas. In his i.Mt. XXI. 2: Thomas says: "unde accessit ad primum, id est populum gentilem per internam inspirationem vel per manifestationem Angelorum." Cf. also i.II. Cor. 4.2.

Cf. P.J.A., Appendix, p. . According to Leitao, de Nobili used to say that if one commits only venial sins in his life, God our Lord will manifest to him before his death His holy Law. Cf. *Narratio*, p. 8. Here de Nobili speaks of non-Christians who labour under invincible ignorance. They are excused from sin of not listening to the Gospel, since they are not bound to hear any one in the matter of salvation.

[167] T.T., p. 416.

[168] Though de Nobili speaks of man's role in preparing himself for the grace of justification, it is not to be understood that it is man's work since here he is concerned principally with the saving grace for the good non-Christian. He is silent on the way grace of God works at different levels (especially the actual graces). Here we can refer to what St. Thomas says in his S.Th. 1,2, q. 109, a. 6. Man cannot be converted to God if God does not convert him. "Hoc non potest esse nisi Deum ipsum convertente", where he cites the prophet Jeremias, 31, 18. "Converte me, et convertar: quia tu Dominus Deus meus." Ibid. St. Thomas says: "homo non potest praeparare ad lumen gratiae suscipiendum, nisi per auxilium gratuitum Dei interius moventis." Ibid. ad.4: "...hoc facit per liberum arbitrium: sed tamen hoc non facit sine auxilio Dei moventis et ad se attrahentis." Cf. OHM, *Die Stellunf der Heiden*, pp. 256-257. De Nobili says simply that man through good deeds and renunciation of sin has removed the obstacles of sin. He does not consider the help of grace needed for it. Ibid. p. 257. The good non-Christian is incapable of removing all obstacles to grace without the help of grace. Cf. also S.c.G. III.160; i.Heb.XII.3.

but grant His grace (the justifying grace) to a man if he does all that he can.[169] This is what he says:

> If he (the good non-Christian) has done virtuous deeds according to his capacity, then it is to be assumed that God has granted him the grace of knowing the divine mysteries needed for salvation.[170]

He says that God who is the form of mercy has graciously willed that such a man obtains the sanctifying grace for the forgiveness of sin and the theological virtue of charity for the attainment of the perfect beatitude of heaven.[171] De Nobili then remarks that though the virtuous deeds performed for the sake of the one true God by such a man are not the direct cause of the saving grace, because through such deeds obstacles to grace coming from sin are removed, yet they are beneficial (here by way of preparation).[172] This remark of de Nobili shows that he is not opposing the good works done before justification to the grace of God, as if such good works were entirely natural without any relation to grace.[173] De Nobili presents

---

[169] T.T. pp. 416-417. Cf. OHM, *Die Stellung der Heiden*, pp. 259-263. He discusses the axiom of Alexander of Hales, "Facienti quod est in se Deus non denegat gratiam." This doesn't mean the beginning of the process of salvation comes from man. Grace in the axiom refers to the justifying grace (*gratia gratum faciens*). It does not refer to actual grace. To do what is in one's power does not mean that one does it without actual grace. The best meaning of the saying summarised by Ohm is: "Wer mit Hilfe der übernaturlichen Gnade Gottes tut was in seinen Kräften steht, empfängt von Gott genügend Gnade, um zur Rechtfertigung und sein ewiges Ziel gelangen." (p. 262) As Ohm says that "facere in se" which is silent on its complete meaning must be completed with "ex viribus gratiae" (p. 263). Cf. S.Th. 1,2, q. 106, a. 6 ad 2; q. 112; a. 3; also i.Rom.X.3, II Sent. D.28, q. 1, a. 4. Nature is not opposed to supernatural grace but it is oriented towards it.

[170] T.T. p. 417.

[171] Ibid.

[172] Ibid. pp. 417-418.

[173] Cf. A.N. pp. 466-467. God's grace is needed for the birth, growth and existence of man; grace is needed for the practice of ordinary human virtues of protecting one's parents and the poor, of giving one his due. For these virtues God's help comes in the form of good desires and love of virtue. Cf. ibid. p. 468. If man needs God's grace for such things, much more does he require the higher special graces for salvation and for meritorious virtues. OHM, *Die Stellung der Heiden*, p. 241. According to St. Thomas, obediential potency is that according to which a creature can become whatever God wants it to be. (Cf. III. Sent. d. 2, q. I a. 1). Ibid. pp. 242-243. It is nothing else but the capacity of obedience of man's nature to the will of God with

all that the good non-Christian does as a preparation for the grace of justification. At the same time, says de Nobili, God who has willed to save man continually gives His graces as good desires to do *dharma* and avoid sin.[174] De Nobili presents the good deeds and avoidance of sin of a good non-Christian as those which prepare him for the reception of the saving grace. That man may reach heaven God gives numberless graces, including the beginning of conversion.[175]

Then de Nobili speaks of a non-Christian who had not led a good life. Following the non-Christian religions, he had committed many sins. He then rejects them, since they are against right reason and begins to live a good life. He recognises God to be the universal cause of the world and shuns all sin and repents of his past sins. He seeks ardently to know the way of salvation and performs all virtuous deeds for the sake of one true God.[176] De Nobili says that God will save such a man who strives, as far as he can, after the way of salvation. This also is an opinion acceptable to all theologians. It

---

a view to a higher reality. S.Th. 3, q. I, a. 3 ad.3. Ohm explains that grace which is supernatural (actual or sanctifying) is not "contra naturam sed secundum naturam". Human nature possesses an obediential potency which is a potency for grace and beatific vision. Human soul is naturally open to grace. S.Th. I,2, q. 113, a. 10. "Naturaliter anima est gratiae capax: eo ipso quod factus est ad imaginem Dei capax Dei per gratiam, ut Augustinus dicit." Cf. also S.Th. 3, q. 9, a. 2; I,2, q. 109, a. 5, ad.3. Therefore there is no opposition between nature and grace. Human nature is pre-disposed for grace in all its forms. Grace does not destroy nature but elaborates and transfigures it.

174 A.N. pp. 86, 92-93; T.T. pp. 435-436. Cf. S.Th. I,2, q. 112, a. 3, OHM, *Die Stellung der Heiden*, pp. 257, 258: Man prepares himself for the saving grace by good deeds and avoidance of sin. The good deeds before the grace of justification have no relation of proportion to the saving grace but they are related to the grace because they are done with the help of actual graces.

175 A.N. pp. 98-99. God gives sufficient helps to man for his attainment of heaven. Cf. ibid. pp. 110, 127. To all who are sinners, as long as they live on earth, God gives His divine helps that they may turn from sin. Cf. Sickler, art. cit. p. 51. St. Thomas speaks of three conversions in S.Th. I, q. 62, a. 2 ad 3. The third conversion is preparation for the grace of God. It is this de Nobili speaks of in T.T. pp. 417-419: turning from sin and doing virtuous deeds.

176 T.T. p. 418. Cf. OHM, *Die Stellung der Heiden*, pp. 256-257. Unless God converts man, man is not converted. Rejecting sin, leading a life of virtue, repenting of one's sins and seeking ardently the way of salvation, these things are possible only with the help of God's grace. Are they not among the numberless graces God offers to man? Cf. A.N. p. 110, also T.T. pp. 435-436. Unless God first seeks man, man will not be seeking God. Cf. S.Th. I, 2, q. III, a. I ad 3. God's help internally moves the mind before justification to give up sin. That a good non-Christian gives up sins is God's grace. S.Th. I, q. 62, a. 2 ad 3.

means that God will infallibly grant His divine grace to such a man who after giving up sin strives after salvation ardently.[177] In the explanation of the salvation of such a man, de Nobili says that the Lord will grant to the repentant sinner the grace of hearing the Gospel (or the spiritual teaching). It is also in keeping with His infinite mercy and grace.[178] In this discussion the salvation of a non-Christian who through no fault of his has not heard the Gospel is to be understood in relation to the universal salvific will of God.[179] It means that God gives sufficient grace to all men for their salvation.[180]

The salvation of a non-Christian is considered not purely that of an individual apart from any religion, but that of an individual belonging to a non-Christian religion. In his avoidance of errors about the belief in God and His attributes and practice of virtue a Hindu can get help from his own religion, as would be the case with a person belonging to the school of *Jñānis*.[181] Though de Nobili conceives the life of the good non-Christian in question without a clear reference to such a help, he does not exclude the possibility explicitly that such a good man may get help from the good elements present in his religion. The idea that it is God who grants salvation to man is common to the Christian and to the good non-Christian; as considered here it precludes the idea of self-redemption.

---

177 T.T. p. 419.

178 Ibid. p. 420.

179 There is abundant evidence in de Nobili of the universal salvific will of God. Cf. P.J.A. p. 92; T.T. pp. 433, 304-305. God through creation of men is the father of all men. All men are His children. Sinners are His younger children; the virtuous are His elder children. Here de Nobili speaks of all men without reference to the Christian religion, therefore in a context of universal salvific will of God. Cf. also A.N. pp. 124, 553-554. God has created man only for *mokṣa*. Cf. *Kāṇṭam* II, p. 100. Though God could have ordained a natural end for man, He has ordained through His goodness the higher end of *mokṣa* for all men.

180 A.N. pp. 92-93, 98-99, 102, 108-109, 110, 111.

181 I.C. pp. 30-31, also pp. 36-37.

SECTION II

Dharma in Christianity

a. *Dharma and Religion (vētam)*

De Nobili works out the religio-ethical meaning of *dharma* in different ways. In his definition of religion (*vētam*) he expresses the meaning and purpose of religion. Religion has to do with knowledge of God and His nature, and with the virtuous conduct required for the attainment of salvation. Such a knowledge in the religious sense is named *ñānam.*[182] *Ñānam* is knowledge imparted by religion concerning the Supreme Being (*paramañānam*),[183] of virtue (*dharma*) and of heaven. Here *dharma* stands in relation to God and man and salvation. The religious meaning of *dharma* consists in this relation. That which leads to salvation as well as the religious knowledge called *ñānam* go to define the meaning of *dharma*.[184] The teaching of religious knowledge is termed *ñānōpatēcam*;[185] it brings life to the soul.[186] When received well in the heart, it becomes a source of inner strenght to walk in the way of *dharma*; like food which helps the life of the body.[187] Christ Himself is said to have given the spiritual teaching (*ñānōpatēcam*) for the salvation of man.[188] The same spiritual doctrine is given by the Christian preachers who are called *carkurus*.

One important element of this spiritual teaching is the knowledge of God. For de Nobili knowledge of God is knowledge of His nature.[189] Right knowledge of God is needed for salvation. The reason why de Nobili stresses the right knowledge of God's nature is that though there is belief in the existence and oneness of God in Hinduism,[190] there are erroneous ideas of God's nature in it. Man's

---

182 N.C.C. p. 1.
183 T.T. p. 3.
184 Haecker, p. 96.
185 Because of this meaning, he uses this expression for the five part catechetical work.
186 T.T. p. 463; N.C.C. p. 1.
187 T.T. p. 463.
188 Ibid. p. 517, de Nobili calls the Gospel as vētam (*cuvicēṣamāna vētattai*).
189 K.N. p. 106.
190 I.C. p. 30.

relation to God depends on the right knowledge of God. For this the attributes of God are proposed. The virtue of religion — the due worship of God, prayer and virtuous acts of penance, offering of sacrifice, suppose, knowledge of the one true God who is good and righteous.[191] All virtuous acts done in the name of God suppose such a right knowledge of God. Right knowledge of God's nature has to do with the whole of *dharma* in relation to salvation. God Himself is the form of righteousness (*tarmacurūpam*). All *dharma* is rooted in God who is the form of *dharma*.[192]

Vētam in its double meaning of scripture and religion is the source of *dharma* understood in its religious sense. But *vētam* can be a reliable source of the knowledge of *dharma* depends on the fact that it owes its authorship to God. It is to be His revealed word. The Christian religion is 'religion uttered by God'.[193] Religion, as uttered by God, is absolutely reliable (*āptavākkiyam*) because God Himself is absolutely reliable (*kēvala āptam*).[194] But this presupposes the knowledge that God is the form of all goodness.

Religion as the word revealed by God alone is not, however, sufficient as definition. Hence it is defined with reference to its content and meaning. The meaning or purpose of *vētam*, as the expression should mean, is to make known *dharma* and *adharma* (that which is righteous and that which is unrighteous).[195] It not only makes known but also commands *dharma* to be followed and forbids *adharma*. God, the divine Teacher of men teaches men, His disciples, the virtues of righteousness (*nītitarmanakaḷ*).[196] Such is the meaning

---

[191] K.N. pp. 106, 121.

[192] T.T. pp. 118, 139-140. Here we must observe that God's holiness is not merely an expression of His transcendence and of His being totally other. His holiness in Judaeo-Christian religions is understood as moral holiness too, an idea stressed by the theology of the prophets. Schelkle, op. cit., pp. 171-173. The two elements of ethical goodness and the numinous together form the concept of the holy in Judaism and Christianity in an "indissoluble synthesis." Cf. R. OTTO, *The Idea of the Holy*, p. 110.

[193] T.T. p. 3. 26 Serm. p. 55. Here we refer to the phrase *carvēcuran aruḷicceyta vētam* (religion graciously uttered by God). T.T. p. 83: here Christian religion is referred to as *cattiya vētam* (true religion). N.C.C. p. 8. It is the 'divine word' (*tiruvākku*).

[194] N.C.C. p. 3, *Kāṇṭam* I, p. 58. God revealed a religion that makes known all righteousness.

[195] N.C.C. p. 3.

[196] Ibid. p. 5.

and content of religion. Therefore it becomes a rule (*cūttiram*) and measure (*piramāṇam*) of virtuous conduct.[197] Though the meaning of religion consists also in making known truths and untruths, de Nobili tends to put emphasis on the religious meaning of *dharma*. Therefore we can understand why he calls the Christian religion often as the "way of all pure virtue (*cakala puṇṇiyaneṛi*).[198] The Tamil word *neṛi* meaning the 'way' is used here for religion. Another word used in the same meaning is *vaḷi*. The assemblage of utterances graciously spoken by God, teaching all the vituous observance (*puṇṇiya ācāram*) helpful unto salvation and forbidding all sins leading to hell is the true way to salvation. To this the name *vētam* truly applies.[199] This is the meaning of religion when it is named as the 'way of all pure virtue.'

Knowledge (*ñānam*) understood in the religious sense connotes the same meaning of *vētam* as the 'way of all pure virtue'. It is said that the divine Teacher (*tivya kuru*), namely, Christ taught the doctrine of righteousness (*tarma upatēcam*).[200] This teaching of *dharma* becomes the spiritual teaching given by the divine *guru*, namely, *ñānōpatēcam*.[201] The spiritual teaching concerns the way of righteousness, that is to say, the religion of righteousness. Thus we note the phrase 'the way of righteousness' (*tarmavaḻi*) which is the spiritual teaching [202] shows righteousness as its content. Sometimes religion is referred to simply as the 'way'.[203] The Christian religion is referred to simply as the 'way of righteousness' (*nītineṛi*).[204] It is the way of righteousness (*tarmavaḻi*) taught by the divine Teacher (*kuru*).[205] From our discussion it becomes clear that de Nobili would call the Christian religion more often the way of righteousness.[206]

---

197 Ibid.

198 T.T. p. 188.

199 Ibid.

200 T.T. p. 223; *Kāṇṭam* III, p. 293.

201 C.C. p. 31. Cf. 28 Serm. p. 122. It uses *ñānōpatēcam* for the teaching given by Christ.

202 T.T. p. 463.

203 KP p. 6. *Vētamākiṛa vaḻi* (the way that is religion). Cf. Acts 9:2, 16:17, the way of salvation (Gk *odos soterias*), 19:9, 23. The way stands for Christianity.

204 T.T. p. 313.

205 C.C. p. 46.

206 The expression *mārkkam* is not preferred by de Nobili because of its use for the way of castes. Cf. T.T. p. 514. Here it is used by him in a religious sense. Cf. Bror, p. 56. He says that

Speaking of the observances enjoined on Israel in the O.T., de Nobili uses *dharma* in the sense of righteousness. These observances are said to be the signs of the mysteries of righteousness (*tarma rakaciyankaḷ*).[207] *Dharma* means here the saving righteousness of God. The preaching of *dharma* concerns not merely virtue and sin but the way of salvation.[208] Those who heard the teaching of righteousness of Christ are called *tarmapārakar*.[209] It means that they are followers of righteousness. They go to form the assembly of the followers of righteousness (*tarmapārakar capai*) which is the Church.[210]

b. *Religion and the Dharma of Love*

One all-important element in the Christian religion is the love of God (*patti*) [211] and love of neighbour. Love of God is not merely man's effort to love God. Love of God is revealed as a commandment and enters the meaning of religion.[212] Love of God is the supreme virtue taught by religion. De Nobili in his work *Mantira Viyākkiyānam* concludes his commentary on the Ten Commandments with this remark:

> The whole of religion (*vētam*) revealed by God consists in one thing which is love (*cinēkam*).[213]

The highest *dharma* which is love sums up all that is religion. Here love includes both love of God and love of neighbour.

The act of showing the way of salvation is called the great virtue and righteous conduct.[214] The purpose of the incarnation is also this

---

de Nobili accepts the use of *tampirān mārkkam* (the way of God), whereas he rejects this use. Cf. also T.T. p. 514.

[207] T.T. pp. 48-49.

[208] *Kāṇṭam* III, p. 293.

[209] T.T. p. 172.

[210] Ibid. pp. 171-172.

[211] N.C.C. p. 52. Love (*patti*) is man's response to God's grace (*kirupai*) which is His love for men.

[212] Ibid. p. 4, *Kāṇṭam* III, p. 334. God reveals its nature (*cupāvacurūpam*).

[213] *Kāṇṭam* III, p. 289. "Of all the virtuous qualities (*cukirtakuṇankaḷ*) God-oriented love (*tēvaviṣayaka patti*) is the highest virtue.

[214] Ibid. pp. 232, 506. "Preaching the gospel is a virtuous act (*puṇṇiya carittiram*). It is to be done with love (*patti*)."

act of righteousness.[215] Explaining the commandment of fraternal love given by Christ, which says "love one another as I have loved you," de Nobili says that Christ's wish for His disciples was that they should live according to His will, practise all virtues and thus attain salvation.[216] Thus the righteous act of showing the way of salvation comes to be the expression of the love of Christ. The work of the divine Teacher is to lead men to the divine lotus feet of the Lord.[217]

In the explanation of righteous conduct and practice of virtues, de Nobili stresses the primacy of charity.[218] Fulfilment of the commandment of charity leads to the fulfilment of all other commandments. It informs all other commandments and all virtues.[219] It is the principal commandment and the root from which sprout 'the twigs and branches' of all other commandments.[220] St. Thomas calls charity the 'form' of all virtues.[221] According to him the 'form' of an act in moral matters comes principally from its end. In morality that which gives to an act orientation to the end, gives it also its form. St Thomas says that charity ordains all acts of all virtues to their final end. Therefore charity is the 'form' of all virtues.[222] The final end of man according to revelation is man's attainment of the Triune God in the beatitude of heaven.[223] According to de Nobili the act of showing the way of salvation to men is the highest *dharma* and that it is an expression in some way of love. If charity is said to be the 'form' of all virtues, it is also the 'form' of the deed of righteousness (*tarmacarittiram*) of showing the way of salvation to men.[224] Preventing sin is an aspect of showing the way of salvation to another.

---

[215] T.T. p. 176.

[216] *Kāṇṭam* III, pp. 326-328.

[217] KP p. 81. The idea is expressed in a poem.

[218] *Kāṇṭam* III, p. 327. In this context he has in mind fraternal charity but primacy of charity applies together to both love of God and love of neighbour. Cf. also M.V. p. 170.

[219] *Kāṇṭam III, p. 327.*

[220] Ibid.

[221] S.Th. 2, 2, q. 23, a. 8. CF. G. GILLEMAN, *Le Primat de la Charité en Theologie Morale*, p. 41. Cf. B. HÁRING, *La Loi du Christ*, Belgium, 1957, tome II, p. 114.

[222] That charity is the form of virtues should not be understood as the 'formal cause' as opposed to 'material cause', but a superior form that form that informs the 'form' of all virtues. Gilleman, op. cit., pp. 53-54. Häring, op. cit., pp. 53-54. Häring, op. cit., tome I, p. 119.

[223] Cf. Ch. VI on *mokṣa* and *dharma*.

[224] A.N. p. 288; *Kāṇṭam* III, p. 232.

Therefore it is also the highest *dharma* (*uttama tarmam*).[225] Charity is the form of this virtuous deed, too.

The theological virtue of charity is the principal warrant for the obtaining of the beatitude of heaven. It is love of God above all things.[226] Love of God thus understood and produced through faith brings man to ultimate beatitude.[227] This divine charity is shown in the observance of the commandments that the divine Teacher has taught. The divine Teacher has said:

> The following of the divine commandments is the sign of theological charity.[228]

That observing the commandments is the sign of love of God is verified in the divine Teacher Himself. He followed the commandment of the Father to show His perfect love (*patti*).[229] Love is authenticated in the observance of all the commandments. The love of enemies and prayer for them is a necessary requirement of a disciple of the divine Teacher.[230] In the final beatitude of heaven through love the human soul becomes united with God.[231] This union of the human soul with God through *bhakti* is explained as participation and communion with the divine nature and as transformation to become like God.[232]

With the primacy of charity in the Christian religion, could one call the Christian religion a religion of love — *bhaktimarga*? De Nobili nowhere uses this expression. The frequent expression is 'the way of all pure virtue' (*cakalanirmala puṇṇiyavaḻi*) or the "way of righteousness" (*tarma vaḻi* or *tarma neṟi*) as we mentioned earlier in the chapter. But if the highest *dharma* is love (*patti* or *cinēkam*) [233] and if all religion consists in love,[234] could one not call the Christian

225 *Kāṇṭam* III, pp. 277-279.

226 P.J.A. p. 107; T.T. pp. 148, 185; Also M.V. pp. 123-128.

227 N.C.C. pp. 8-9.

228 *Kāṇṭam* III, p. 334.

229 Ibid. p. 334.

230 T.T. p. 334.

231 Ibid. p. 508; *Kāṇṭam* III, p. 576.

232 *Kāṇṭam* III, p. 576.

233 Ibid. p. 289. The theological virtue of charity is mentioned here but the primacy of charity includes love of God and love of neighbour.

234 M.V. p. 170.

religion one of love? De Nobili does not attempt to express the Christian religion in this way. He names the Christian religion as the way of salvation, as the way of righteousness or of justice.

Virtuous conduct which is realised through the grace of God and through the freedom of man is ordained by God to be the road to salvation. De Nobili says that such virtuous conduct is to have love for the Lord above all things:

> It can be said that it is the virtuous conduct and the way of salvation taught by the Lord.[235]

Here love (*patti*) is called virtuous conduct and itself is the way to salvation. If Christianity is a religion of grace, *bhakti* itself comes through the grace of God to man and is taught by Him. The Lord who teaches *bhakti* as the highest *dharma* and as the way unto salvation enables man to love Him through His grace, though man must love in freedom. God's love of man is His grace and it is the cause of man's love of God.[236] The words used for grace such as *kirupai*, *iṣtam* as in the expression *tēvaiṣtam*, *piriyam* express basically God's love for men. In one work, de Nobili refers to love as grace.[237]

c. *The Meaning of Dharma in Incarnation*

The purpose of incarnation and its goal is to teach and show the way to heaven.[238] and to undo the bondage of sin.[239] This is the

---

[235] T.T. p. 148. Cf. OHM, *Die Liebe zu Gott in den nichtchristlichen Religionen*, p. 46. Love of God above all things in fallen nature is not possible. It is the opinion of St. Thomas. S.Th. I,2, q. 109, a. 3 ad I. Also in I Cor. 12.1. Cf. Ohm, p. 464. Christianity offers the means to perfect love of God and of Christ.

[236] Bror, p. 220. He says that there is hesitation on the part of Christians to adopt the term *bhakti*. He also remarks that *bhakti* is not a Key-word in the Christian message. On the part of de Nobili there is no hesitation to use the term as our study has shown (cf. ch. VI on *bhakti*). Concerning the idea that Christianity is a religion of grace (Bror, p. 220) and not a religion of *bhakti*, it must be said that if *bhakti* is understood entirely as man's act of love of God, Christianity is not a religion of *bhakti*. If God teaches *bhakti* and enables man through His grace to practise it, then it is graced-*bhakti* without which there is no salvation. Theological virtue of charity means this. Cf. G. PARRINDER, *Upanishads, Gītā and Bible*, London, 1975, p. 91: "Christianity is essentially a way of devotion (*bhaktimarga*)."

[237] 26 Serm. p. 32. *Cinēhamākiṛa iṣtappiracātam*.

[238] T.T. pp. 142-143.

[239] N.C.C. p. 31.

work of salvation.[240] The purpose (*nimittam*) thus understood is a purpose of righteousness (*tarmanimittam*), since showing the way of salvation is the faultless virtue (*tarmam*).[241] De Nobili says that this purpose of righteousness is manifested in the very birth of Christ.[242] The fragrance of righteousness (*tarmam*) present in the human nature of the divine Teacher is ordained to be spread among men. The Supreme Teacher (*paramakuru*) became man and taught men the 'dance of virtue' (*puṇṇiya naṭanam*).[243] The life of the incarnate Teacher was meant to show the royal road to righteousness (*tarma irāca vīti*) for salvation.[244]

De Nobili explains the different virtues of the divine Teacher as realisation of the purpose of the incarnation which is to show the way of salvation and to make men walk on this royal road. His humility, poverty, renunciation of the pleasures of the body and honours and riches come to define the royal road of virtue.[245] The way of virtue (*tarmavaḻi*) is suffering for the sake of the Lord.[246] Dying for the sake of the Lord is an act of love of God above all things which the incarnate Teacher Himself taught. It is the precious virtue (*arumaiyuḷḷa tarmam*).[247] The death of the divine Teacher could be an offence to the Hindus. But de Nobili explains that if death ensues for the sake of righteousness, there can be no offence.[248] Moreover, the divine Teacher in His death for the sake of righteousness showed what it means to love God above all loves.[249] Dying for the love of God and suffering for His sake come to be the perfect reason, the right order and the way taught for slvation.[250] De Nobili's adoption of the use of *kuru* for Christ was to express the idea that Christ was the Teacher of the way of salvation. The incar-

---

240 T.T. p. 143.

241 Ibid. p. 176.

242 Ibid. p. 136.

243 Ibid. pp. 212-213.

244 *Kāṇṭam* III, p. 147.

245 Ibid. p. 147.

26 T.T. pp. 185, 225. "The conduct of virtuous fortitude (*tarma taiyiriya carittiram*) to face death." It is fortitude of righteousness.

247 Ibid. pp. 166-167.

248 Ibid. p. 160. Cf. ch. VI on Suffering Saviour.

249 Ibid. p. 185.

250 Ibid.

nate Lord is the divine Teacher (*kuru*) who came to show the way of righteousness for salvation of man through His own life and death.[251]

d. *Christian Life and Dharma*

The Christian life is explained in the language of *dharma* by de Nobili. Holiness (*arcciyaciṣta tanam*) is called 'all righteousness (*cakalatarmam*).[252] The idea of righteousness is expressed also by *nīti*. The Christian religion is called the 'way of righteousness" *nītineṛi*) [253] or the 'all pure way of righteousness' (*cakalanirmala nītineṛi*).[254] The disciples of Christ suffer for the sake of justice (*nītiniyāya-nimittam*) [255] and they will be tempted to give up the faultless righteousness (*kuraiyaṛṛa nīti*).[256]

The theological virtues of faith, hope and love are necessary for salvation.[257] De Nobili speaks mostly of faith and love.[258] In his explanation of *bhakti* he makes faith itself an expression of it. The act of believing in God is done properly only through love.[259] When faith is considered distinct from *bhakti*, it has reference to knowledge and to the intellect. God who is the author of religion (*vētiyan*) writes the word (*vācakam*) of faith concerning truth on the living palm leaf of the intellect (*putti*).[260]

Speaking of the love of neighbour, de Nobili says that according to the order of creation itself all men should live in love for one another.[261] The order of creation means that God is the Father of all men.[262] That makes all men brothers. Thus fraternal love becomes universal. Such fraternal love based on the truth of creation is neces-

---

[251] *Kāṇṭam* III, pp. 96-97. Cf. ch. VI, subtitle "the use of *Guru* for God Incarnate" for the adoption of the Saivaite term Guru and Satguru for Christ.

[252] A.N. p. 598.

[253] T.T. p. 313.

[254] Ibid. p. 228.

[255] Ibid. p. 333. Ibid. p. 332. Here de Nobili uses *niyāyanīti* for 'righteousness'.

[256] Ibid. p. 228.

[257] KP, p. 50. *Kantam* III, p. 71. Hope is *dharma*.

[258] Cf. ch. VI on Theological virtue of *bhakti*.

[259] M.V. p. 59.

[260] Ibid.

[261] *Kāṇṭam* II, pp. 38-39; T.T. p. 150.

[262] Ibid. p. 38. Also T.T. p. 150.

sary for salvation.[263] The newness of the fraternal command given by the divine Teacher consists in loving one another as He loved his disciples.[264] His love for his disciples concerned supremely the salvation of men. The love of enemies and prayer for them are required of those who want to be the disciples of the divine Teacher.[265] The deeper meaning of the commandment "do not commit murder" of the Ten Commandmens is fulfilled only if one loves one's enemies.[266]

The acts of the virtue of religion are called *tarmam* and *tarmacarittiram.* Thus acts of prayer, meditation,[267] offerings by way of worship and sacrifice (*pūcai* and *naivēttiyam*) [268] are called righteous actions (*tarmaviruttis*). The worship of the divine Saviour by the Magi is an act of righteousness.[269] So too austerities, abstinence practised for the Lord are acts of righteousness (*tarmakariyam*).[270] All the acts of the virtue of religion are *dharma* because they are right expressions of man's relation to God and of his final end: salvation.

The virtue of humility is a specifically Judaeo-Christian virtue.[271] De Nobili explains this virtue as 'all righteousness' (*cakala nīti*). One who is humble is ready to obey the will of God.[272] One who is humble will observe all righteous conduct (*tarma ācāram*). Hence it is called the foundation of all virtues.

De Nobili speaks of the virtue of poverty as necessary for salvation.[273] The spirit of poverty is needed to hear the Gospel. The poor deserve the beatitude of heaven. Detachment from riches is needed for *bhakti* towards God above all things.[274] The virtue of purity is called *paricutta tarmakuṇam* (the purest virtue).[275] The virtue of

---

[263] *Kāṇṭam* II, p. 39.
[264] *Kāṇṭam* III, p. 327.
[265] T.T. pp. 317, 334.
[266] C.C. p. 33.
[267] *Kāṇṭam* III, p. 187.
[268] T.T. p. 72.
[269] *Kāṇṭam* III, pp. 170-171.
[270] T.T. p. 72.
[271] HÄRING, *La Loi du Christ*, tome I, pp. 330-331.
[272] *Kāṇṭam* III, pp. 66-67.
[273] T.T. pp. 164-166.
[274] Ibid. p. 305.
[275] Ibid. pp. 164-166, 218.

patience is another *dharma* that adorns the saints in their relation to those who persecute them.[276] The disciples of the divine Teacher must be adorned with the *dharma* of simplicity (*ārccavakuṇam*) along with wisdom (*paramārtam*).[277]

The meaning of suffering is explained in terms of *dharma*. De Nobili rejects the idea of suffering being punishment for sin, as in the theory of *karma* and rebirth in Hinduism.[278] Suffering is an act of virtue for the virtuous and a call to conversion for a sinner.[279] Though de Nobili speaks of suffering for the sake of the Lord, there is no idea of suffering being a participation in the suffering of Christ. Besides, suffering which comes from the following of the way of righteousness is called the 'divine way', since Christ himself went that way.[280] The disciples continued to preach the Ten Commandments revealed anew.[281] They are both the teaching of right reason[282] and the teaching of God.[283] They are religious commandments insofar as they are taught by religion.[284] All the commandments taught by religion are summed up in the commandment of love.[285] One must fulfil the *dharma* taught by the commandments.[286]

When we speak of *dharma* in religion, we must refer to a definition of sin which de Nobili found in Hinduism and his interpretation of it.[287] Though he defines *piramāṇam* in terms of right reason, when applied to religion, the righteous things (*piramāṇikka*) are not merely actions in harmony with right reason but "those things that have been effectively revealed in religion ordained for the salvation of men."[288] Therefore the righteous conduct taught by God is in

---

276 Ibid. pp. 213-214.

277 Ibid. p. 214.

278 P.J.A. Cf. *Callāpam* 5.

279 A.N. pp. 215-216.

280 T.T. p. 333.

281 M.V. pp. 108-109.

282 E. HAMEL, *Les dix paroles*, pp. 29-32. The Decalogue safeguards the humanity of man. The religious commandments do not empty man and they are not arbitrary imperatives originating from divine voluntarism.

283 M.V. p. 108.

284 Ibid.

285 Ibid. p. 170.

286 Ibid.

287 T.T. p. 400.

288 Ibid.

harmony with the understanding of right reason (*niyāyamulla putti*) and with the pure way of virtue (*nirmala puṇṇiya vaḷi*) which is the religion of God.[289] The relation of the ethical to the religious is clear but the ethical justification of the righteous conduct revealed in religion means this: that which has been revealed as proper conduct in religion must be in conformity with right reason. The religious law for salvation is justified by the will of God, who has ordained it as the way of salvation, since righteous conduct helpful to salvation is not merely the ethical effort of man but also something that is possible through the grace of God freely bestowed on him.

De Nobili adopts the terminology of *āśramadharma* for the two states of life, the state of renunciation and the state of married life. Life in the world, namely, life in the married state and family is called *camucāratarmam* [290] or *vivāka tarmam* (*dharma* of matrimony).[291] Life of renunciation is called *canniyācatarmam.*[292] *Tarmam* in these two expressions refers to the established and approved states of life, which two states of life were taught by the divine Teacher.[293] De Nobili uses the expression *āciramam* (*āśrama*) to signify the states of life. The basic obstacle to love of God and salvation comes from the inordinate desire (of pleasure, honour and riches).[294] Hence man must either give up desire for them completely or regulate them according to the order of right reason. The divine physician granted the means of the two fold 'aśramadharma of *canniyāca āciramam* and of *vivākatarmam.*[295]

e. *Dharma and Grace*

Grace offered by God for man's salvation is explained in the language of *dharma*. Grace is called virtuous quality (*cukirtakuṇam*).[296] Sanctifying grace (*tēvaiṣtappiracātam*) too is a virtuous

---

[289] Ibid.

[290] Ibid. p. 389. Cf. *Kāṇṭam* II, p. 87. The Tamil expression for *sannyāsa dharma* is *tuṟavaṟam* (*tuṟavu aṟam*) and *vivākadharma illaṟam* (*il aṟam*).

[291] T.T. p. 390.

[292] Ibid. p. 124.

[293] C.C. p. 33.

[294] T.T. p. 124.

[295] Ibid.

[296] *Kāṇṭam* III, pp. 404-405, 433.

quality (*tarmakuṇam*) because as a *habitus* of the soul it is the foundation of the theological virtues.

The initial offer of grace given to man by God is named *tarmavicāram* (desire of righteousness).[297] The use of *tarmavicāram* for the initial grace of God is significant. That God wants to save all means that He gives His grace of righteous desires to all men.[298]

The virtuous way to heaven is founded on sanctifying grace and it manifests itself in different manners according to the different virtues, such as poverty of spirit, patience, sorrow for sin, desire for justice.[299] Right living is, therefore, not mere human action but man's and God's action together. God gives not only the initial grace of desire of righteousness, but also all the riches of the virtues.[300] All righteous conduct helpful to salvation (*mōccacātakam*) is a supernatural grace of God.[301]

f. *Dharma and Beatitude of Heaven*

De Nobili presents the doctrine of forgiveness of sin as an important element of the content of the Christian religion. It is part and parcel of the spiritual teaching.[302] He stresses repentance as important for forgiveness. Repentance consists principally in turning one's will from sin.[303] God forgives only if man has repentance.[304]

In explaining the final beatitude and union of the human soul with God which is heaven, de Nobili uses the language of *dharma*. The final end of heaven consists in direct vision of God, love (*patti*) and bliss (*paramānantam*).[305] It is through the direct vision or contemplation of God that the supreme *dharma* of *bhakti* is born in the soul of the blessed. Such love leads to union of the blessed with God and communion and participation in the divine. The union of

---

[297] *Kāṇṭam* II, p. 58.
[298] *Kāṇṭam* III, p. 437.
[299] T.T. p. 332.
[300] Ibid. pp. 305-306.
[301] A.N. p. 471.
[302] 26 Serm. pp. 1-2.
[303] A.N. p. 218.
[304] P.J.A. pp. 64-65.
[305] A.N. pp. 219-220.

the soul with God is explained with the image of iron in the fire.[306] Love of the blessed is love of friendship (*cinēka paccam*).[307] In heaven the blessed have *bhakti* for God who deserves limitless love.[308] All the praises which the blessed give to God are expressions of *bhakti*.[309]

The bliss of heaven is called holy or righteous bliss (*tarmapākkiyam*). God gives this righteous bliss to those who walk according to His will.[310] The virtuous (*tarmapārakar*) in heaven are irreversibly fixed in righteousness (*tarmam*)[311] Their freedom is defined by its infallible orientation to *dharma*.[312] This is the righteous state of freedom as the name *mokṣa* means the state of being liberated. It is not only freedom from sin, but freedom for *dharma* in an irrevocable manner, especially for the supreme *dharma* of *bhakti*. The blessed are adorned with all the purest virtues (*cakalaparicutta tarmankaḷināl*).[313] All *dharma* is directed to the final end of man. The final end and salvation of man consists in reaching God in direct vision of Him, union in love and the enjoyment of bliss divine which is *mokṣa*.[314] Heaven is the good which is the form of the final end of all righteous conduct and its goal.[315]

CONCLUSION

De Nobili understands *dharma* in its different meanings in Hinduism under its social, ethical and religious aspects. In Christianity he comes to use it in its ethical and religious meanings. De Nobili's use of *dharma* for the Christian religion and the Christian way of life, as expressed in *tarmavaḻi* or *tarma neṟi*, or *nītineṟi* is a significant

[306] Ibid. pp. 395, 485. *Kāṇṭam* III, pp. 569, 576.

[307] A.N. pp. 513-514.

[308] Ibid. p. 518.

[309] Ibid.

[310] Ibid. p. 521.

[311] Ibid. p. 251.

[312] Ibid. p. 543.

[313] Ibid. p. 535.

[314] T.T. pp. 176-177. Also KP p. 2.

[315] T.T. p. 122. *Mōccam* as *avatirūpananmai* (heaven as the good in the form of the final end).

one. It is the way of salvation revealed by God in Jesus, the divine *guru*, for all men. The way of righteousness unites the ethical and the religious meanings of *dharma*. The goal of *dharma* is the salvation of man, and the way of salvation is the way of *dharma* (righteousness).

SECTION III

De Nobili in the light of Vatican II

De Nobili profoundly understood the socio-ethico-religious meaning of *dharma*. This understanding is an essential aspect of his method of adaptation, as we have shown in our study. His approach to the Hindus through the recognition of the valid socio-ethico-religious meanings of *dharma* has been abundantly confirmed by the doctrine of the Second Vatican Council on the salvation of non-Christians, non-Christian religions and the relation of the Church to non-Christians and that of non-Christians to the Church. His understanding of *dharma* in Hinduism and his use of it in Christianity is understood better as one of the first 'encounters' of Christianity with Hinduism. We show here what de Nobili did more than three hundred years ago anticipates in some way, though in an imperfect and incipient manner, what the Second Vatican Council has formulated in its different documents concerning non-Christians and non-Christian religions.[316] One finds in de Nobili's writings examined by us points in the context of an 'encounter' of Christianity with Hinduism which find a fuller development in the Council documents.[317]

---

[316] Cf. P. ROSSANO, "Quid de non Christianis Oecumenicum Concilium Vaticanum II docuerit", in *Bulletin*, (Secretariatus pro non-Christianis) I (1966) pp. 15-22. I have profited by this article, especially the five questions under which Rossano considers the doctrine of the Council on this point.

[317] Cf. E. HAMEL: 'Lumen rationis et lux Evangelii', *Periodica*, 59 (1970) pp. 215-249. He shows the progress of doctrine on this point from Vatican I to Vatican II. One could say the same of de Nobili's approach to non-Christians. Some of his insights and ideas concerning non-Christians find fuller development and more perfect expression in the Vat. II.

i. *According to the Council one could ask what the action and operation of the grace of God are in those who live outside the Church.*

The Council says in *Lumen Gentium* (16):

> Those also can attain to everlasting salvation who through no fault of their own do not know the Gospel of Christ or His Church, yet sincerely seek God and, moved by grace, strive by their deeds to do His will as it is known to them through the dictates of conscience.[318]

The same document continues:

> Nor does Divine Providence deny the help necessary for salvation to those who without blame on their part have not yet arrived at an explicit knowledge of God, but who strive to live a good life, thanks to His grace.[319]

In *Gaudium et Spes* (22) the Council says that the paschal mystery of Christ

> holds true not only for Christians, but for all men of good will in whose heart grace works in an unseen way. For, since Christ died for all men, and since the ultimate vocation of man is in fact one, we ought to believe that the Holy Spirit in a manner known only to God offers to every man the possibility of being associated with this paschal mystery.[320]

De Nobili discusses the theological opinions on the salvation of a non-Christian who has not known the Gospel through no fault of his own.[321] Such a non-Christian comes to recognise God to be the one

---

[318] W. ABBOT (ed.), *The Documents of Vatican II*, New York, 1966, p. 35. "Sincerely seek" in the latin text is "sincero corde quaerunt." For the English texts of Vat. II Council documents, we follow W. Abbot's translation. For the Latin text, we follow *Constitutionis Decreta Declarationes* cura et studio Secretariae Generalis Concilii Oecumenici Vaticani II, Vatican, 1966. The documents of Vat. II will be referred to in their Latin titles.

[319] W. ABBOT, op. cit. p. 35. The 'help' is plural in the latin text: auxilia.

[320] Ibid. pp. 221-222. The Latin text says that the ultimate vocation of a man is one, namely divine: "una sit, scilicet divina."

[321] T.T. pp. 413-420.

universal cause of the world. His genuine seeking of God is seen in his avoidance of sin, practices of austerity and virtues and in his love of God he knows through reason. This means he strives to do the will of God and lives a good life as the Council speaks of a good non-Christian who with a sincere heart seeks God.[322] The Council says that a non-Christian leads a good life, seeks God and fulfils God's will under the influence of grace or with the divine help.[323] De Nobili is silent on the need for actual graces but elsewhere he says that man needs grace for the practice of virtues.[324] The Council in *Lumen Gentium* and in *Gaudium et Spes*[325] says that such a good non-Christian can attain salvation.[326] To condemn such a man will not be in keeping with His infinite mercy.[327] When such a good non-Christian avoids sin, he does not create the obstacles of sin to (the justifying) grace of God.[328] If a good non-Christian does what he can to seek the way of salvation, God cannot but grant the saving truth (of the Gospel). De Nobili says that if a good non-Christian has done what he could, one can presume that God will grant him the saving grace of truth.[329] Speaking of bad non-Christians who turn to God with repentance and do good works, de Nobili says that God will necessarily grant His divine help for their salvation. Such an opinion is acceptable to all theologians.[330]

The Council speaks of the universality of redemption of Christ reaching all men and that there is one divine vocation for all men.[331] De Nobili is aware of the universal salvific will of God in his presentation of Christianity.[332]

---

322 *Lumen Gentium*, 16.

323 Ibid. "Sub gratiae influxu or auxilia." Cf. also *Gaudium et Spes*, 22.

324 A.N. pp. 86, 92-93, 466-467; T.T. pp. 435-436.

325 *Lumen Gentium*, 16, *Gaudium et Spes*, 22.

326 T.T. p. 414.

Cf. Hamel, art. cit. pp. 232-233. Hamel points out that the Council (*Gaudium et Spes*, 92) calls for a prudent dialogue even with atheists who cultivate the excellent qualities of the human spirit and speaks of those who have not yet come to an explicit knowledge of God but who lead a good life not without the grace of God. (*Lumen Gentium* 16). Hamel says that one could speak of *atheismus inculpabilis*.

327 T.T. p. 415.

328 Ibid. p. 417.

329 Ibid. p. 417.

330 Ibid. p. 419.

331 *Gaudium et Spes*, 22.

332 P.J.A. p. 92. Here de Nobili cites the text from I Tim. 2:4. Cf. also A.N. p. 124,

ii. *The Council speaks of the way and modes in which the salvific action of God reaches non-Christians.*

The Council says in its document *Dei Verbum*:

> God, who through the Word created all things (cf. Jn. 1:3) and keeps them in existence, gives men an enduring witness to Himself in created realities (cf. Rom. I: 19-20).[333]

The document *Gaudium et Spes* (36) says:

> all believers of whatever religion have always heard His revealing voice in the discourse of creatures.[334]

De Nobili recognises that men of other religions come to know the one universal cause of the world. The school of *jñānis* recognises the one and unique universal cause from the order and creation of the world.[335] While discussing the salvation of non-Christians, de Nobili observes that a good non-Christian comes to acknowledge the Creator of the world from the order of the world[336] This knowledge of God men come to have by the light of reason.[337]

The Council speaks of an inner law, in *Gaudium et Spes* (16):

> For man has in his heart a law written by God. To obey it is the very dignity of man; according to it he will be judged.

Kāṇṭam II, pp. 294, 98-100: God has ordained one and the same end to all men. Cf. FREDDY NIETLISPACH: "Le Religioni non Cristiane nella Riflessione del Vaticano II e della Nuova Teologia", in Il *Problema Teologico delle Religioni*, da P. Rossano, Catania, 1975, pp. 100-101.

333 Abbot, op. cit. p. 112.

334 Ibid. p. 234.

335 I.C. p. 30. De Nobili quotes Cittiar's poem in which the recognition of one cause, God is found from the way the world exists. In *Kāṇṭam* I, p. 18, de Nobili quotes the same poem. Cf. also KP. pp. 12, 13. *Tirukkuṛaḷ* is quoted to confirm the truth of the one cause of the world. Ibid. p. 14. There is a citation from *Paṭṭinattar* to the same effect. Cf. PIERRE DAHMEN - M. GLADBACH, "Le Votum de Pierre Lombard archeveque d'Armagh et la controverse autour de Robert de Nobili", *AHSI* 4 (1935) p. 76.

336 T.T. pp. 413, 418.

337 I.C. pp. 24-25. Cf. Hamel, pp. 217, 229. The Council speaks a different language (*Dei Verbum*, 3) about man's knowledge of God. God Himself gives testimony of Himself in creation. De Nobili is still in the framework of man coming to know God from creation, (anthroplogical) but the Council is more theocentric.

> Conscience is the most secret core and sanctuary of a man. There he is alone with God, whose voice echoes in his depths. In a wonderful manner conscience reveals that law which is fulfilled by love of God and neighbour.[338]

The Council, while speaking of the conscience of man, says in its declaration on religious freedom *Dignitatis Humanae* (3):

> On his part, man perceives and acknowledges the imperatives of the divine law through the mediation of conscience. In all his activity a man is bound to follow his conscience faithfully...especially in matters religious.[339]

The Council is cautious on its ignorance of the secret ways of God, as we read in *Ad Gentes* (7):

> God in ways known to Himself can lead those inculpably ignorant of the gospel to that faith without which it is impossible to please Him (Heb. 11:6).[340]

In the same document (9) the Council says:

> Whatever truth and grace are to be found among the nations, as a sort of secret presence of God...[341]

The Church knows that man is constantly worked upon by the Holy Spirit, and therefore man cannot be completely indifferent to the problems of religion.[342]

De Nobili considers the right reason (*ñāyaputti*) and, therefore, conscience indirectly, present in man to be God's "representative" (*piratāni*) through which man is expected to avoid the ways of sin.[343]

---

338 Abbot, pp. 213-214.

339 Ibid. p. 681.

340 Ibid. p. 593. Cf. also *Gaudium et Spes*, 22. God's grace works in the hearts of all men in unseen ways.

341 Ibid. pp. 595-596.

342 *Gaudium et Spes*, 41, also 36.

343 *Kāṇṭam* II, p. 119. The Second Vatican Council speaks of conscience in the language of personal encounter with God (*Gaudium et Spes* 16).

Speaking of the salvation of the good non-Christian, he says that such a person is understood to be guided by right reason in his avoidance of sin [344] which is an expression of the law written in the heart of man. It is the just order of reason. De Nobili observes in his *Narratio* that men (here non-Christians) are led by the natural light of reason (*lumen naturale*).[35] He says that the *jñānis* through the natural light of reason teach that good works and moral virtues are to be performed and sins to be avoided.[346] It is through natural law (*jure naturae*) gentiles come to have many good and legitimate customs.[347] The law of right reason or natural law, and therefore conscience, which is the vicar of God in man guide his actions, and they concern especially matters of religion as seen in the case of a good non-Christian who, led by the light of reason, comes to know the nature of sin and avoidance of sin.

The Council says that religious endeavours are not purely in the soul of man. De Nobili says that men in external acts of worship of one true God, of austerity and alms-giving begin to seek God.[348] The universal salvific will of God reaches men in different ways. These are religious attempts which are a receptable of God's action in non-Christians.[349] The action of God is seen also in those who reject idolatory, as those of the school of *jñānis*. They say that because God is spirit he should be adored in spirit.[350] Men through austerity and alms-giving seek ardently eternal salvation.[351] De Nobili mentions how the Hindus of Madurai spoke of a fourth spiritual law through which alone one could obtain the salvation of soul.[352] He recognises the serious desire of the Hindus for forgiveness of sin.[353] These practices become beneficial, if done for the sake of the

---

[344] T.T. pp. 413, 414.

[345] *Narratio*, p. 8.

[346] Ibid. p. 90.

[347] I.C. p. 107.

[348] T.T. pp. 413-420.

[349] Rossano, art. cit., p. 17.

[350] *Narratio*, p. 90; I.C. p. 30. Cf. PIERRE DAHMEN - M. GLADBACH, p. 88.

[351] Bertrand II, p. 21. Though de Nobili is not so explicit on the need of actual graces for the good deeds of non-Christians (the Council *Lumen Gentium*, 11; *Gaudium et Spes*, 22) yet it is implicit in what de Nobili says on grace in general. Cf. Hamel, p. 247.

[352] Bertrand II, p. 20.

[353] T.T. p. 339; *Kāṇṭam* I, p. 9.

one true God.[354] They are beneficial in the sense that they remove obstacles to God's grace and prevent sin. God continually grants His graces to all men in different ways.[355] But de Nobili is also fully aware of the unique mediatorship of Christ...[356]

iii. *What are the elements of truth and grace that exist in non-Christian religions?*

The Council speaks of the elements of truth and grace which are found already among the nations as it were a secret presence of God,[357] before the proclamation of the Gospel to them. The conduct of life rules and teachings proposed by non-Christian religions which frequently reflect the ray of truth that enlightens all men.[358] The document *Ad Gentes* (9) says:

> Whatever good is found to be sown in the hearts and minds of men, or in the rites and cultures peculiar to various peoples, is not lost.[359]

The same document (18) speaks of

> the ascetic and contemplative traditions whose seeds were sometimes already planted by God in ancient cultures prior to the preaching of the Gospel.[360]

The Council says in *Nostra Aetate* (2):

> The Catholic Church rejects nothing which is true and holy in these religions.[361]

---

[354] Ibid. pp. 414, 417-418.

[355] A.N. pp. 86, 92-93, 98-99, 110.

[356] *Kāṇṭam* III, p. 429.

[357] *Ad Gentes*, 9. The document says: "Quidquid autem veritatis et gratiae iam apud gentes... inveniebatur." The Council doesn't say that "good elements can be found" but "were already found."

[358] *Nostra Aetate*, 2.

[359] Abbot, p. 596. Cf. ibid. p. 598. "The seeds of the Word which lie hidden in them.

[360] Ibid. p. 607.

[361] Ibid. p. 662.

The reason for this attitude is because the Church considers it a sort of *preparatio evangelica.* The Council in *Ad Gentes* (3) says that the religious endeavours of men by which they may seek God:

> may sometimes serve as a guidance course towards the true God, as a preparation for the Gospel.[362]

The dogmatic constitution on the Church, *Lumen Gentium* (16) mentions the same idea:

> Whatever goodness or truth is found among them is looked upon by the Church as a preparation for the Gospel.[363]

Gaudium et Spes (57) says:

> Before he became flesh in order to save all things and to sum them up in Himself, 'He was in the world', already as 'the true light that enlightens every man' (Jn. 1:9-10).[364]

The Council in *Ad Gentes* speaks of the Holy Spirit as already at work in the world even before Christ was glorified.[365]

This doctrine of the Council is implicit in the works of de Nobili. He recognises the good moral and religious elements in Hinduism. The school of *jñānis* not only acknowledge the one supreme cause which is spirit. They say that sacrifices to idols must be given up and that God must be worshipped in spirit.[366] Almost all the at-

---

[362] Ibid. p. 586.

[363] Ibid. p. 35.

[364] Ibid. p. 263.

[365] *Ad Gentes*, 4.

[366] I.C. p. 30. Cf. also the poem of Cittiar on the one universal cause of the world. Ibid. p. 39. *Narratio*, p. 90. Bertrand II, pp. 210-211. Here Antonio Vico in his letter written to Fr. General in November, 1622, speaking of a particular *jñāni* defines what a *jñāni* in general is. A *jñāni is not an idolator; jñaṇi* adores only one God or he does not adore at all. He is proud because he displays sanctity. He possesses some portions of truth which he conceals like the ancient philosophers in the midst of more ridicules and more monstrous errors. Vico remarks that the particular *jñāni* about whom he speaks in the letter admits the unity, the spiritual nature, invisibility, infinity of one God, creator of the world. We mention Vico's understanding of the *jñānis* for that is also the understanding of de Nobili whose faithful collaborator Vico was.

tributes of God have been explained in the works of the *Vedānta.* That God is a being by Himself, that He is eternal, incorporeal, good by nature, omnipresent and that He is the universal cause are mentioned in them.[367] Such knowledge of God is found in the non-Christian scriptures.[368] De Nobili mentions a *smṛti* text in which he finds the idea that the world was created by the virtue of truthfulness.[369] In *Kalidasa* he finds the idea that God creates the world by knowledge, that He is the One worthy to be known that He is the One who knows, that He is worthy to be contemplated and the One who contemplates.[370] De Nobili finds some adumbration of the most recondite mystery of the Blessed Trinity which God allows through the mouth of some sage just like Sybillas and Trimagistus in the West.[371] If the sage here has an inkling into the mystery of the Trinity, it is through God's activity (*permittente...Deo*). De Nobili says that in the *Sikṣā Valli* of Taitt. Up there are teachings on truth, truthfulness, virtue to be practised, gratitude, just rendering to each one his due, and many other things on the unity of God and the true cause of the world.[372] In *smṛti* texts, there is a description of virtues and their relation to the final beatitude of man.[373] De Nobili finds the idea of St Thomas that the happiness of man consists in the contemplation of God and that practice of virtues prepares one for this end in *smṛti* works. He also mentions an upanisadic text in

---

[367] Ibid. p. 25. In N.C.C. (p. 107) the six attributes of God given in a skt. *sloka* as a help to examine the non-Christian concepts of God correspond to those found in the works of the school of *Vedānta.* Cf. I.C. pp. 34-35. Here de Nobili refers to Taitt. Up. where he finds texts which say that God is good by nature, that He is spirit, that He is knowledge and that He is truth.

[368] Cf. N.C.C. p. 110. It is said here that such attributes of God have been revealed to men by God in His religion.

[369] I.C. p. 75.

[370] Ibid. p. 76.

[371] Ibid. p. 35. De Nobili says that God permitting, a sage by a secret penetration has expressed an adumbration of the Trinity. The text quoted by de Nobili is from Taitt. Up. (1.6.1.). One may not agree with de Nobili's understanding of the text but his appreciation of the Upaniṣad is noteworthy. Cf. S.Th. on Sibyllas, 2,2, q. 172, a. 6 ad I; also 2,2, q. 2 a. 7, where St. Thomas says that Sibyllas prophesied about Christ. Cf. OHM, *Die Stellung der Heiden*, pp. 236, 231.

[372] I.C. p. 34.

[373] Ibid. pp. 8-10. De Nobili says this commenting on a text of Manu (I, 97).

which the idea that God is the true rewarder of the good is found.[374] It means that he who knows God (and leads a good life) attains to glory. De Nobili recognises the tradition of contemplation. Interpreting a text from Manu (1,97) he says that among those who act virtuously, perfect are those who contemplate the true God.[375]

De Nobili recognises the valid idea of God's descent into the world to help and save man in the idea of Viṣṇu *avatāras*. The use of the term *avatāra* for the incarnation of the Word shows that he was profiting by the idea, though in a critical way.[376] So too he recognises the idea of God as the divine *guru* of men, a Śaivite idea and used it of God, especially to signify Christ.[377] The school of *jñānis* teaches that good works and moral virtues are to be practised and sins to be avoided.[378] De Nobili says that he found a good definition of sin written by the wise men in India.[379] His appreciation of renunciation (*sannyāsa*) is clear in his explanation of the titles of the moral heroes in the Buddhist sect [380] and in his adoption of the life of a renouncer (*sannyāsin*).[381]

De Nobili observes their great desire for forgiveness of sin.[582] In one of his letters, he writes to his Provincial in 1609 about the desire of the Hindus to know what sin and virtue mean.[383] He finds the notion of final salvation expressed by the term *mokṣa* and adopts it to signify the Christian notion of heaven.[384] He also finds in Hin-

---

374 Ibid. p. 35. Taitt. Up. 2.1.1. From the same verse de Nobili quotes (p. 34): "jñānam anantam Brahma." (God is infinite knowledge.)

375 Ibid. p. 9.

376 T.T. pp. 116-118.

377 Cf. Pr.Ap. Introduction, pp. 25-26 and f. n. 46 on p. 26. Cf. SCHOMERUS, *Der Caiva-Siddhānta*, pp. 290-317. Cf. also Schomerus; *Indische Erlösungslehren*, Leipzig, 1919, pp. 198-199.

378 *Narratio*, p. 9.

379 T.T. p. 400.

380 I.C. pp. 27-28.

381 Pr.Ap. p. 59. Cf. A.N. pp. 386-387, on appreciation of austerity. Ibid. pp. 385-386: Austerity is considered acceptable virtuous conduct towards God.

382 *Kāṇṭam* I, p. 9. T.T. p. 399.

383 Bertrand II, p. 28.

384 Pr.Ap. pp. 154-155, for definition of *mokṣa*. A.N. pp. 10, 393, 404. The Hindus accept that "through *mokṣa*, the final end of man is realised."

duism the Christian notion of heaven as direct vision of God.[385] He avoided the use of *svarga* for the final beatitude.[386]

De Nobili says that the good things said or written on virtue and God in Hinduism cannot only be accepted but must be embraced.[387] But the Council speaks more positively of 'the true and holy' in non-Christian religions and of their being planted by God in ancient cultures.

The Council says in *Nostra Aetate* (2):

> Thus in Hinduism men contemplate the divine mystery and express through an unspent fruitfulness of myths and through searching philosophical inquiry. They seek release from the anguish of our condition through ascetical practices or deep meditation...[388]

Another text from the same document (1) of the Council says:

> Men look to the various religions for answers to those profound mysteries of the human condition...: What is man? What is the meaning and purpose of our life? What is goodness and what is sin? What gives rise to our sorrows and to what intent? Where lies the path to true happiness? What is the truth about death, judgement, and retribution beyond the grave? What finally is that ultimate and unutterable mystery which engulfs our being, and whence we take our rise, and whither our journey leads?[389]

De Nobili's approach to the Hindus shows that he was sensitive to these questions of the Hindus in their quest for salvation.[390] De

---

385 A.N. pp. 405-406, 405: "It is acceptable to all that it is God the Supreme Being who grants heaven" (*mokṣa*).

386 Cf. Pr.Ap. pp. 148-149, A.N. pp. 394-398. Cf. SCHOMERUS: *Indische Erlösungslehren*, pp. 179, 180. He says that one must avoid showing the highest good in Christianity in comparison with Indian teachings on salvation which might make the Christian idea as less valuable or as inferior as it would be the case if one were to use *svarga* (*Himmel*). De Nobili was explicit about avoiding this expression for the final goal of salvation. Christianity doesn't admit intermediate heaven.

387 I.C. p. 34.

388 Abbot, pp. 661-662.

389 Ibid. p. 661.

390 Bertrand II, pp. 6-8. De Nobili mentions the topics he discussed with the Hindus and

Nobili speaks of the few utterances of righteousness as stars though not the sun.[391] He speaks of the pearls which are found in the law-books of Brahmins which they should not reject when they become Christians. If accepted, they bring glory to them.[392] De Nobili does not say explicitly that the morally and religiously good elements are graces of God. But it is implicit in his theology of grace and of salvation of non-Christians. The simile that few good utterances are like stars implies that they have the light of truth however little that comes from God.

De Nobili in his work of evangelisation strove to preserve the good elements found in the rites and culture of the Indians as the Council wants the Church to preserve them.[393] In our study of *dharma* we have seen how de Nobili recognised the valid social *dharma* and justified its need and acceptance.[394] Concerning the many rites with religious invocations, he changed their intentions and preserved them quite in keeping with the tradition of the Church.[395] All this shows that the idea of *preparatio evangelica* was implicit in his approach to Hinduism.[396]

The Council in *Ad Gentes* (9) says that the missionary activity of the Church:

> frees from all taint of evil and restores to Christ its maker the elements of truth and grace.[306]

---

the qiuestions they had in their minds on God, the cause of suffering in the world, forgiveness of sin.

[391] T.T. p. 77.

[392] I.C. p. 37.

[393] *Ad Gentes*, 9.

[394] Cf. Chs. I-III.

[395] I.C. pp. 106-108. On p. 10 de Nobili says that he changed the meaning of the rites and adapted them to the piety of Christians. Cf. *Narratio*, p. 172. He changed the invocation during the baths. The changed rite of baths was called *Christuvandanam* (adoration of Christ). Cf. Pr. Ap. pp. 66-67, for the blessing of sandal paste. Cf. ibid. p. 183, for the prayer of blessing for the same. Cf. ibid. pp. 67-68, on the wearing of the thread. Religious rites and ceremonies were also considered *dharma*. De Nobili accepts this aspect of *dharma* though giving new intentions and meanings.

[396] Cf. Hamel, pp. 229-230. In de Nobili's approach, *preparatio evangelica* is more anthropological than theocentric whereas the Council's view of *preparatio evangelica* is more theocentric than anthropological.

The Church is aware of the errors that come from man's weakness and the Evil One.[307] The Council says also that one must carry on a prudent and loving dialogue.[308]

De Nobili knew that the law-books of the Hindus were mixed with good and bad elements.[399] In the first apology of his method, de Nobili explains how he was trying to steer a *via media* with regard to Hindu customs and practices.[400] There is a discerning judgement on the Hindu customs and practices.[401] He does not reject anything because it was gentile.

De Nobili has the idea of a primitive revelation which in course of time came to be lost through man's sin. In the minds of many men there remained only the knowledge that there is one original Lord, the cause of all things. Hence many men came to lose the knowledge of God's nature.[402]

Here we mention how de Nobili evaluates the non-Christian religions as the way of salvation. The different religious sects hold different views of God. They create difficulties about the correct knowledge of God since the different views of God are also contradictory to each other.[403] To claim that all these religious sects (*vētamatams*) were revealed by God cannot be a help to know God truly and determine the nature of *dharma* of salvation.[404] Therefore they cannot be the way (*neṟi*) to salvation. The idea that religion is the way (skt. *marga*, in Tamil, *mārkkam*, *vaḻi* and *neṟi*) is basic to the definition of religion.[405] Though de Nobili refrains from using *mārkkam* for the

---

[397] *Lumen Gentium*, 16; Gaudium et Spes, 13.

[398] I.C. pp. 25, 38-39. *Kāṇṭam* II, pp. 190-192. T.T. pp. 77, 399.

[399] *Nostra Aetate*, 2.

[400] Pr.Ap. pp. 90-148.

[401] I.C. Chs. 10-11, cf. *Narratio*, The whole treatise is a verification of a 'prudent and loving dialogue' with the social and religious customs of the Hindus.

[402] *Kāṇṭam* II, pp. 185-186. De Nobili understands that this primitive revelation was given at the beginning to the first parents. Cf. Bertrand II, p. 257 Antonio Vico echoes this idea of a sage who taught the attributes of God correctly which came to be later corrupted by idolatry and proposed as the doctrine of *trimūrti*.

[403] I.C. pp. 24, 26.

[404] *Kāṇṭam* II, p. 201.

[405] H.R. SCHLETTE, *Towards a Theology of Religions*, London, 1966, p. 64. He says that religion as the way of salvation has the means sanctioned for salvation and willed by God. Cf. ibid. p. 8. Cf. Y. CONGAR, 'Non-Christian Religions and Christianity', in *Service and Salvation*, ed. J. Pathrapankal, Bangalore, 1975, p. 172. "Religions are activities of men. Whether they be

Christian religion, he does not avoid its use completely.[406] Our purpose here is to show the normative character of religion as the way of salvation as indicated by the use of the expression the 'way'.

The religious scriptures are said to be utterances of God (*īcuraprōktankaḷ*) and the form of God (*parāpara vastu rūpam*). The different *purāṇas* are said to be uttered by great sages (*ṛṣis*) who were enlightened by God.[407] Hence they are accepted on this authorithy. Yet this alone is not to recognise the pearls (*margaritae*)[408] or the 'sweet utterances' (*maturavacanankaḷ*)[409] or utterances of dharma (*tarmavākkiyankaḷ*). But because they are mixed with other erroneous observations on the nature of God and virtue they lose their value in the religion considered as a whole.[410] Hence de Nobili tends to use sparingly the expression *vētam* for the Hindu religious sects since for him *vētam* is the religion that proposes the things of God and of virtue unmixed with error. Only this can be the way of salvation. In his view if non-Christian religions hold the same truth about God, they are valid, since different 'ways' look to the same truth. The different 'ways' would be the different ways of living

---

of divine origin or not, they propose a "way" — doctrines, rules of life, sacred rites — by which satisfaction may be given to the questions and demands which disturb men with regard to that which transcends them."

[406] T.T. pp. 513-514. For the use of *markkam* in a religious sense cf. A.N. pp. 81, 300.

[407] *Kāṇṭam* II, p. 212. T.T. p. 363. Cf. the expression like *tiruvāy moḻi* (utterance of the divine mouth), a term used for one of the Vaiṣṇavite Tamil scriptures. Cf. also ch. IV.

[408] I.C. pp. 36-37. The work *Ñānōpatēca Kuṟippiṭam* uses many poems from Hindu writers on the transitoriness of wealth (p. 9), on the one universal cause of the world (pp. 12-13), the only way of removing the anguish of the heart by reaching the feet of the Lord (p. 2), on that the human soul must desire only the feet of the excellent Teacher (*caṟkuru*). We are not sure if all the citations from the Hindu authors come from de Nobili or from one of his disciples who follows the example of his master in using the Hindu scriptures. It is significant that the author quotes them in the catechism, not in an apologetic work, to explain virtue and the idea of oneness of God. The same work also quotes the poems with wrong ideas. In I.C. p. 9 de Nobili quotes Manu on the qualities of the true Brahmin, one of which is to embrace truth whoever says it.

[409] K.N. p. 118.

[410] T.T. p. 77. De Nobili is still somewhat negative towards the 'few good utterances of *dharma*' which like stars lose their importance before the sun of the Christian religion. But the Council is not only positive in its approval of the good elements in non-Christian religions and peoples but it considers them not unrelated to the work of God among men (cf. esp. *Ad Gentes*, 18; *Nostra Aetate*, 2).

righteousness. Concretely *dharmas* are different.[411] For example the *dharma* of married life is different from the *dharma* of renunciation. De Nobili accepts the basic idea that all virtuous conduct is capable of being the way of salvation with the grace of God.[412] De Nobili has nothing in principle against the image that 'just as different rivers flow into the same ocean, so too different religions lead to the same goal of salvation.'[413] The problem is the nature of revealed religion. If God reveals His religion, he cannot reveal things that are contradictory to each. [414] De Nobili mentions the diferent words used for religion by the different sects.[415] He adopts the expression *vētam* for the Christian religion and the Christian scriptures.[416]

The Council, speaking of Hinduism, says that men express the divine mystery through inexhaustible fruitfulness of myths and through searching philosophical inquiry.[417] De Nobili speaking of the science of God says that one uses symbols, fables and numbers here in India in this science as did Pythagoras, Plato and other philosophers in the West.[418] In the part called *cintāmaṇi*, says de Nobili, the Hindu philosophers discuss the final end of the good and the bad and the beatitude of man and debate also if it consists only in action or also in action.[419]

iv. *The relation of non-Christians towards the Church of Christ.*

iv. The relation of non-Christians towards the Church of Christ.

The Council in *Lumen Gentium* (16) says that "those who have not received the Gospel are related in various ways to the People of God." [420] It mentions first the Israel, then the Moslems and "those

---

[411] N.C.C. pp. 34-36. In a religion that has the same truth, one can live in the *āśrama* of *sannyāsa*, or one can practise different *dharmas*.

[412] T.T. p. 127.

[413] N.C.C. p. 34.

[414] Ibid. pp. 32-34; T.T. p. 91.

[415] T.T. p. 363. For example, Śaivite scriptures called utterances of God (*īciraprōktankaḷ*), the utterance of the divine mouth (*tiruvāy moḻi*).

[416] Ibid. p. 364. Cf. I.C. p. 93. *Veda* is used in the sense of law besides meaning doctrine for living as the Hebrew *Torah* could mean either doctrine (or instruction for living) or law.

[417] *Nostra Aetate*, 2.

[418] I.C. p. 24.

[419] Ibid. p. 23.

[420] Abbot, p. 34.

who in shadows and images seek the unknown God" and "those who without blame on their part, have not yet arrived at an explicit knowledge of God, but who strive to live a good life, thanks to His grace." [421] The same document of the Council says:

> All just men from the time of Adam, 'from Abel, the just one, to the last of the elect', will be gathered together with the Father in the universal Church.[422]

The Church prays that "the entire world may become the people of God..." [423] The Church proclaims what was once preached by the Lord to the ends of the earth.

De Nobili mentions not only the great desire of the Hindus for salvation [42`] and for forgiveness [425] but also their desire to know the spiritual law of salvation.[426] He says that the Hindus in Madurai spoke of the fourth spiritual law by which one could attain salvation. They said a great part of it had been lost, though parts of it could be found mixed with the other three laws. They also said that never was man sufficiently holy and wise to recover that law. De Nobili says that he told them that he has come to teach this spiritual law. This he did in the manner of St Paul who preached to the Athenians the unknown God.[427] Moreover, de Nobili comes to be considered a *muniver* (a sage-ascetic).[428] He is the *guru* around whom disciples gather and receive his teaching as disciples get *dīkṣā* from a *guru* among the Śaivites.[429] He is also considered a *jñāni* who has come to teach the spiritual law of salvation.[430] When he met two al-

[421] Ibid. p. 35.

[422] Ibid. p. 16.

[423] Ibid. pp. 36-37.

[424] Bertrand II, pp. 20-21.

[425] *Kāṇṭam* I, p. 9. T.T. p. 399.

[426] Bertrand II, p. 21. Cf. *Narratio*, pp. 90-92, on what St. Clement, disciple of St Peter, says on Brahmins "who through tradition of ancestors, harmonious laws and conduct commit neither murder, nor adultery, nor do they worship idols. They do not have the habit of eating meat of animals, do not get drunk and do not do anything from malice. They always fear God."

[427] Bertrand II, p. 21. Cf. Acts, 17: 22-31.

[428] Ibid. p. 20.

[429] Ibid. p. 21. T.T. p. 41.

[430] Pr.Ap. pp. 138-139. Bertrand II, p. 17: He is considered a *jñāni* who is indifferent to riches and poverty like a dead body.

chemists, he spoke of the divine spiritual alchemy which changes sinners into just and perfect men, mortal men into immortals and communicates to the low creatures that men are the goodness and the glory of becoming living images of God Almighty.[431]

De Nobili also considers that the religion of God existed from the very beginning.[432] It continued to exist in Israel, now in the Church.[433] Christ is the unique mediator of all men.[434] The economy of salvation is one. All men come under the universal salvific will of God.

v. *The Council gives many directives as to how Christians should relate themselves to non-Christians.*

The way the Church should relate itself to non-Christian religions consists in this: to announce, to testify, to recognise, not to reject the true and the holy, to preserve and promote.[435] The Council exhorts Christians to example of life, testimony of the Word, esteem and charity, knowledge and familiarity, and finally study by which they reverently and gladly discover the hidden seeds of the Word in them. It exhorts them to know the national and religious traditions, learn of the riches which God has generously bestowed on them in sincere and patient dialogue. They must also illumine them with the light of the Gospel, liberate them and bring them under the Lordship of Christ.[436]

The Council desires anything in the way of life of the nations that is not inseparably connected with superstition and error be considered with sympathy and be preserved intact. Sometimes, the Church admits some things in so far as they harmonise with its true and authentic spirit.[437]

The Council in the document *Sacrosanctum Concilium* (123) says that the Church

> has admitted fashions from every period according to the

431 Bertrand II, p. 235.

432 Ibid. p. 21.

433 N.C.C. p. 9.

434 *Kāṇṭam* III, p. 429.

435 Nostra Aetate, 2.

436 Ad Gentes.

> natural talents and circumstances of peoples, and the needs of the various rites.[438]

The Council continues in the same document (40) that the bishops

> must, in this matter, carefully and prudently consider which elements from the traditions and genius of individual peoples might appropriately be admitted into divine worship.[439]

This way of acting is not new to the Church. This is what the Council in *Gaudium et Spes* (44) says:

> From the very beginning of her history, she has learned to express the message of Christ with the help of the ideas and terminology of various peoples, and has clarified with the wisdom of philosophers, too.[440]

The Council desires that the students for priesthood be introduced to a knowledge of other religions which are spread in different areas. They will be able to understand better the elements of goodness and truth in such religions, learn to disprove errors in them and share the fulness of light of truth with those who lack it.[441] In *Ad Gentes* (26), the Council expects from the missionaries

> a more thorough knowledge of the history, social structures, and customs of the people. They will ascertain their system of moral values, and their religious precepts, and the innermost ideas which, according to their sacred traditions, they have formed concerning God, the world, and man.[442]

---

[437] *Sacrosanctum Concilium*, 37.

[438] Abbot, p. 175.

[439] Ibid. pp. 151-152.

[440] Ibid. p. 246.

[441] *Optatam Totius*, 16. *Ad Gentes*, 16. This document says that the students be open and attuned that they can be versed in the culture of their people and evaluate it. In the study of philosophy and theology they must consider points of contact between traditions and religions of the homeland and the Christian religion.

[442] Abbot, p. 617.

De Nobili, in his new method of the Madurai Mission by careful and patient study tried to discover the national and religious traditions of India.[443] He began to study the customs of the Hindus from their own books.[444] It meant learning the *dharma* of the Hindus.

In the first defence of his method he opposed the idea that condemned all gentile customs *en masse* as superstitious.[445] In India all actions, be they religious, be they human or social are governed and regulated by the scriptures.[446] De Nobili read the scriptures and thus came to discover the good elements in them.[447]

The good elements he tried to preserve and promote, by adopting the ideas and the religious terminology in the presentation of Christianity. He is said to have introduced a new method of adaptation, which consisted in a few externals like the wearing of the thread, the wearing of the tuft of hair and the use of sandal paste. He is considered to have contributed nothing to an 'indigenous theology' using Hindu terminology.[448] De Nobili's method was also an "exterior adaptation of the Christian dogmas to the undestanding of those to be evangelised."[449] Here we may refer to our study of

---

[443] I.C. p. 16. Learning (or philosophy) among the Hindus is not fit to be rejected as some do through distorted prejudice thinking thar it is pernicious and that it turns one from God.

[444] Pr.Ap. p. 91. Here de Nobili remarks: "4um noto istorum etnicorum non omnium operum seu insignium finem reperiri in D. Th. nec in aliis scholasticis." Cf. *Robert Bellarmini S.R.E. Cardinalis e Societatis Iesu Epistolae Familiares*, Romae, 1650, pp. 395-396. It is a letter of Cardinal Bellarmine written to Archbishop of Goa on 22 Dec. 1620. He testifies in this letter that de Nobili had read carefully the books of Brahmins and had judged what others had considered to be rites of religion to be *ritus nobilitatis.* Hence he thinks that they must be allowed to Brahmins.

[445] Pr. Ap. pp. 90-111.

[446] Cf. 'La Congregazione de Nobili' in *La Revue d'Histoire des Missions*, (to be referred to as RHM) 12 (1935) p. 596.

[447] I.C. pp. 30, 34-36, *Narratio*, pp. 8, 90. Pr.Ap. pp. 54, 58, 59, 154-155. T.T. P. 400.

[448] R. BOYD, *An Introduction to Indian Christian Theology*, Madras, 1969, p. 13. The judgement of Boyd is not sufficiently founded for want of a better study of de Nobili's writings. Cf. Yesudas, art. cit. p. 52. His judgement on de Nobili is not fair for lack of evaluation of all his works.

[449] DANDOY: 'El problema de la adaptacion en el apostolado', in *Razon y Fe*, 88 (1929) p. 99. B. LONERGAN: Method in Theology, London, 1973, p. 276. Lonergan says on pluralism in religious language that "to preach the gospel to all men calls for at least as many as

dharma, the concept of *avatāra*,[450] *guru*, the terminology of grace, *mokṣa*, *veda*. De Nobili refers to the four fold means of knowledge of *nyāya*[451] and uses in his writings the three means of knowing: direct perception (*pratyakṣa*), inference (*anumāna*), and verbal authority (*śabda* or *āptavacanam*).[452] He does not reject the philosophy of the gentiles as some others who through perverse prejudice (*pravo iudicio*) consider all pagan learning (therefore their philosophy) as insidious, dangerous and bound to turn one far away from God.[453] De Nobili understands the positive elements in it in some way oriented to the salvation coming from God. Thus he finds that Brahmins consider the happiness of man to consist in contemplation. The practice of virtues help dispose man for happiness, as St. Thomas explains.[454]

De Nobili writes to Pope Paul V that the customs of the Hindus must be rid of impious and bad intentions attached to them, then purified and sanctified with the holy mysteries and sacred ceremonies.[455] He was aware of what the Church had done in the past with regard to adoption of pontifical stoles used once by the Roman priests.[456] De Nobili adopted a policy of tolerance and chari-

---

there are differing places, and times, and it requires each of them to get to know the people to whom he or she is sent, their ways of thought, their manners, their style of speech. There follows a manifold pluralism. Primarily it is a pluralism of communications rather than of doctrines." Cf. also pp. 362-363.

[450] Bertrand II, pp. 397-398. Emmanuel Martins in his letter to Fr. General of the Jesuits, Fr. V. Caraffa, in 1651 speaks of an extraordinary woman revered as being supernatural and divine. People believed that from her a new king had been born to save them from their condition of oppression. He was considered the tenth incarnation (*kalki*) of Viṣṇu. Fr. Martins commenting on these stories of the incarnation of Viṣṇu says that they have, however, some traits of truth. They are a grotesque imitation and a corruption of the truth. Martins who was a co-worker of de Nobili considers the stories of the incarnations of Viṣṇu to be pointers to the Christian mystery of incarnation.

[451] I.C. p. 20. Cf. Monier-Williams, p. 685. Also Bertrand II, p. 90.

[452] N.C.C. p. 3. De Nobili calls religion (*vētam*) as reliable word (*āptavākkiyam*). This is the *śabda* or *āpta vacanam* of the *nyāya* system. Cf. ibid. pp. 14, 15 and 21 for the use of *pratyakṣa darśana, anumāna darśana* and *śabda darśana*.

[453] I.C. p. 16. De Nobili refers to St. Gregory who says: "plerique Christiani pravo iudicio ut insidiosam, et perniciosam, et procul a Deo aversantem repudiant."

[454] Ibid. pp. 9-10. Cf. S.Th. 1,2, q. 3, a. 5; 2,2, q. 180; 1,2, q. 3, a. 5,6; 2,2, q. 18, a. 2.

[455] *RHM* 12 (1935) p. 602. *Sacrosanctum Concilium* (Vat. II), 37.

[456] *Narratio*, pp. 135-136.

ty, an attitude the Council recommends to the missionaies of today.[457]

In the Church's approach to non-Christians a great respect for the rights of the human person must be shown.[458] De Nobili defended the freedom in which the evangelised must hear the Gospel.[459] He understood the social structure of the people and would not violate it. He defended it in its legitimate aspects.[460] De Nobili held the principle that the preacher of the Gospel must conform himself as far as he can to the social customs of the people whom he evangelises. This principle of adaptation de Nobili draws not only from the history of the Church but also from the *dharma* of the Hindus themselves.[461] The good customs (*sadācāra*) of each country must be respected. In this sense, de Nobili accepts the customs governing society and its structures, though in a critical manner. He would not reject that to which the Hindus owe so much as their civilization. It is the *dharma* which is at once social and religious.[462] Concerning religious practices, de Nobili adopted a discerning ap-

---

[457] Ibid. pp. 132-138; T.T. pp. 478-479; *RHM* 12 (1935) p. 602, on facilitating conversion. Cf. also Pr.Ap. pp. 91-111.

[458] *Dignitatis Humanae*, 14. RHM 12 (1935) p. 606. I.C. pp. 113-114, 108. *Narratio*, p. 14-16. On p. 14: *charitatis norma*.

[459] *Narratio*, pp. 8-13, 32. T.T. pp. 506-507. Here de Nobili condemns the custom that a Christian *guru* gives the fruit of which he has had a bite to the disciple newly converted so that he may not return to his pagan religion. Such a means is humiliating and therefore evil. De Nobili recalls St. Paul (R. 3:8) that one may not do evil that good may come out of it.

[460] I.C. pp. 5, 81, 105-107, 113-114. Cf. P.J.A. pp. 82-86. A.N. pp. 277-286. This does not mean that de Nobili was unaware of the discriminatory aspect of caste system. Cf. T.T. pp. 59-60, 513. Pr.Ap. p. 189. Pope Gregory XV in his bull Romanae Sedis Antistes (1623) approving of the method of de Nobili exhorts the Indian converts from higher castes not to look down upon those of lower castes mindful of the truth that they too are members of that Head (Christ) who is humble of heart and who is no respector of persons and that they are nourished by the same word and bread and destined for the same heavenly kingdom.

[461] Pr. Ap. pp. 105-106. De Nobili refers to a passage from 'De vita et honestate clericorum,' cap. IX in *Decretalium Gregorii*, IX, lib. III, tit. I. The preachers of the gospel wear the dress of the people whom they evangelise to avoid their aversion. Then de Nobili cites a gloss to the passage of Gregory: "quia quilibet, inquit, se conformare debet moribus eorum inter quos vivit." (p. 106). De Nobili then quotes from *smṛti* (Manu): "Unusquisque in regione, in qua vivit, ad illius mores ex antiquitate protractos se effingere justum est." (ibid.) In I.C. p. 113, he quotes Manu (2, 18) whose meaning corresponds to that of the above-mentioned passage from *smṛti*. *Narratio*, pp. 36-42. Here reference is made to the Church's practice to allow the nations to keep their customs.

[462] Dandoy, art. cit., p. 102.

proach. Only that which is by its nature constituted for the cult of false gods must be rejected. All else could be transformed into Christian piety with new meanings given to them.

In our own time, the great Bengali Brahmin convert Brahmabandhav Upadhyay was inspired by the example of de Nobili. He has this to say:

> By birth we are Hindus and shall remain Hindu till death. But as *dvija* (by virtue of our sacramental rebirth), we are Catholic; we are members of an indefectible communion embracing all ages and climes. In customs and manners, in observing caste and social distinctions, in eating and drinking, in our life and living, we are genuine Hindus; but in our faith we are neither Hindus, nor Europeans nor American, nor Chinese but all-inclusive. Our faith fills the whole world, and is not confined to any country or race; our faith is universal and consequently includes all truths.[463]

---

[463] Quoted in *The Light of the East*, n. 5 (Feb. 1924), Calcutta, p. 8. Cf. H. STAFFNER, "Conversion to Christianity — From the Hindu Point of View," *Clergy Monthly*, 36 (1972) pp. 3-15; H. STAFFNER, "May a Convert Retain his Spiritual Identity?" *Vidyajvoti*, 40 (1976) pp. 356-362. Today one would not appreciate B. Upadhyay's idea of observing caste distinctions amongst Indian Christians purely as an expression of culture.

ABBREVIATIONS

AHSI = Archivum Historiae Societatis Iesu

ZMR = Zeitschrift für Missionswissenschaft und Religionswissenschaft

RHM = La Revue d'istoire des Missions

SELECT BIBLIOGRAPHY

I. SOURCES

A. *Latin Works.*

NOBILI, Roberto de, *Responsio ad ea quae contra modum quo nova Missio Madurensis utitur ad ethnicos Christo convertendos obiecta sunt* in: 'Roberto de Nobili. L'Apôtre des Brahmes, Première Apologie. 1610,' ed. Pierre Dahmen, S.J., Paris, 1931.

—, *De Linea Bracmanum* in: 'Roberto de Nobili on Adaptation', ed. S. Rajamanickam, S.J., Palayamkottai, 1971, pp. 176-192.

—, *Informatio de quibusdam moribus Nationis Indicae* in: 'Roberto de Nobili on Indian Customs', ed. S. Rajamanickam, S.J., Palayamkottai, 1972. The Latin text is given in the second half of the book with its own pagination.

—, *Narratio Fundamentorum quibus Madurensis Missionis Institutum Caeptum est, et hucusque Constitit* in: 'Roberto de Nobili on Adaptation', ed. S. Rajamanickam, S.J., Palayamkottai, 1971. Though this work was composed by de Nobili, it appeared under the name of Francis Ros, his ordinary for the sake of unprejudiced hearing at the Council of Goa in 1619.

B. *English Translations.*

RAJAMANICKAM, S., 'De Nobili's Reply to Buccerio', *Archivum Historiae Societatis Iesu*, 39 (1970) pp. 252-264. This is a translation into English of the Latin text of de Nobili's answer to Andrea Buccerio's objections: *Responsio quibusdam a P. Andrea Buccerio obiectis contra meam Informationem* (29.12.1615). With the help of Fr. Hambye I checked the passage in Latin in which de Nobili refers to the different meanings of the term *dharma* in the MSS in the Jesuit archives in Rome (ARSI: Goa 51, f. 214).

—, 'A Reply to Fr. Buccerio's objections', in: *Roberto de Nobili on Adaptation*, Palayamkottai, 1971. This is only a summary of de Nobili's *Responsio*.

C. *Letters of .*

BERTRAND, J., *La Mission de Maduré*, Tome 2, Paris, 1948. Bertrand has translated many letters of de Nobili into French from the original Latin, Italian and Portuguese, though he has put under one title many letters for the sake of conveniente.

DAHMEN, Pierre, 'La Correspondance de Roberto de Nobili' (1606, 1619) *La Revue d'Histoire des Missions* (RHM), 12 (1935), pp. 579-607. Dahmen has translated five letters into French.

—, 'Trois Lettres Spirituelles inédites de Roberto de Nobili' (1610, 1615, 1649), *Reuve d'ascétique et de mystique* (RAM), 16 (1935), pp. 180-185.

RAJAMANICKAM, S., 'The Goa Conference', *Indian Church History Review*, 2 (1968), pp. 81-96. It contains the letter of de Nobili to Pope Paul V (15-2-1619) in English translation.

WICKI, Josef, ed., Sei Lettere inedite del P. Roberto Nobili S.I., *Archivum Historiae Societatis Iesu*, 37 (1968), pp. 129-144. Here all the six letters have been edited in the original Italian text.

D. *Tamil Works.*

Tamil works of de Nobili appear under his Indian name Tattuva Pōtakar (Teacher of Truth). They have been edited by Fr. S. Rajamanickam, S.J. and published by the Tamil Ilakkiyak Kaḷakam (Tamil Literature Society) Tuticorin.

TATTUVA PŌTAKAR, *Ñāna Upatēcam, Kāṇṭam* I, 1966.

—, *Ñāna Upatēcam, Kāṇṭam* II, 1966.

—, *Ñāna Upatēcam, Kāṇṭam* III, 1968.

The first three *Kāṇṭams* of *Ñāna Upatēcam* are referred to in the thesis as *Kāṇṭam I, Kāṇṭam II* and *Kāṇṭam III.*

TATTUVA POTAKAR, *Mantira Viākkiyānam* (*Kantam IV*), 1963. This work is referred to in the thesis as M.V. With this the four *Kāṇṭams* of the five-part Catechism of de Nobili are available in the original Tamil text. The fifth *Kāṇṭam* in tamil has not yet been found. We have it only in Portuguese traslation. 'Quinta Parte do Catechismo in Catecismo Em Q Se Explicao Todas as Verdades Catholicas, Tradusido em lingoa Portuguesa pello P. Balthazar da Costa, 1662. (A la Bibl. de l'Académie des Sciences de Lisbonne, Gal. 5a. 2a, n. 13, ff. 198-224). This is the fifth *Kāṇṭam* of *Ñāna Upatēcam* which deals with the signs of the true Religion.

—, *Attuma Nirṇayam* (Science of the Soul), 1967.

—, *Nittiya Cīvana Callāpam* (Dialogue on Eternal Life), 1964.

—, *Punar Jenma Accēpam* (Objection to Rebirth), 1963.

—, *Tūṣaṇa Tikkāram* (Refutation of Calumnies), 1964.

Tamil works attributed to de Nobili with greater probability and used in our study:

—, *'Kaṭavuḷ Nirṇayam' in: Nittiya Cīvana Callāpam*, ed. S. Rajamanickam, S.J., 1964, pp. 106-122. In the thesis it is referred to as K.N.

—, *Ñānopatēcam (26 Piracankankaḷ*), 1963. This work is referred to in the thesis as 26 Sermons (26 Ser.).

—, *Cēsunātar Carittiram* (Story of Jesus), 1964. This work is referred to in the thesis as C. C.

—, *Tēvamāta Carittiram* (Story of Mary), 1964. It is referred to in the thesis as T.C.

—, *Ñānopatēca Kuṛippiṭam*, 1965. This work is referred to in the thesis as KP.

—, *Upatēcam*, 1965. Under this title appear two works: *Ñāna Upatēcam or 30 pātankaḷ* (30 Lessons and *Cinna Upatēcam*. These two works have been compiled from the works of de Nobili and those of another missionary writer (Tattuva Pōtaka Cuvāmy of the Region of Kannaṭa).

II. WORKS CITED OR USED IN THE THESIS

A. *Books.*

ABBOT, W.M., *The Documenta of Vatican II*, New York, 1966.

AIYER, Sivasamy, P.S., *Evolution of Hindu Moral Ideals*. The Calcutta University, 1935.

ANTRIKKES, Antrikku, S. (Henrique Henriques), 'Kiricittiyāni Vaṇakkam', in: *Vaṇakkam*, ed. S. Rajamanickam, S.J., Tuticorin 1963.

—, *Atiyār Varalaṟu*, ed. S. Rajamanickam, Tuticorin 1967.

AQUINAS, Thomas, *Opera Omnia*, ed. L. Vives, Paris, 1871-1880.

BACHMANN, Peter R., *Roberto Nobili 1577-1656. Ein Missionsgeschichtlicher Beitrag zum Christlichen Dialog mit Hinduismus*, Roma, 1972.

BANERJEE, N.V., *The Spirit of Indian Philosophy*, London, 1975.

BERTRAND, J., *La Mission du Maduré*, tome 2, Paris, 1848.

The Bhagavat-Gītā, ed. and tr. R.C. Zaehner, London, 1969.

BOYD, Robin, *An Introduction to Indian Christian Theology*, Madras, 1969.

BRANDOLINI, Broglio Antonio, *Giustificazione del praticato sin'ora da Religiosi della Compagnia di Gesù nelle Missioni del Madurey, Mayssur, e carnate*, Roma, 1724.

BROR, Tiliander, *Christian and Hindu Terminology. A Study in Their Mutual Relations with Special Reference to the Tamil Area*, Uppsala, 1974.

BURROW, T-Emeneau, M.B., *A Dravidian Etymological Dictionary*, Oxford, 1961.

CASTETS, *La Mission du Maduré*, Trichinopoly, 1924.

'Concilium Tridentinum Actorum, Tomus Quintus, Actorum Pars Altera, ed. Stephanus Ehses, Freibourg, 1911.

Constitutiones Decreta Declarationes. Sacrosanctum Oecumenicum Concilium Vaticanum II. Cura et Studio Secretariae Generalis Concilii Oecumenici Vaticani II, Romae, 1966.

CRONIN, V., *A Pearl to India: The Life of Roberto de Nobili*, London, 1959.

DAHMEN, Pierre, S.J., *Robert de Nobili.* L'apôtre des Brahmes. Première Apologie, Paris, 1931.

—, *Robert de Nobili, S.J.* Ein Beitrag zur Geschichte der Missionsmethode und der Indologie, Münster, 1924.

—, *Un Jesuite Brahme. Roberto de Nobili, S.J.*, Paris, 1924.

DANTO, C. Arthur, *Mysticism and Morality*, New York, 1922.

DHAVAMONY, M., S.J., *Love of God According to Śaiva Siddhānta*, Oxford, 1971.

—, *Phenomenology of Religion*, Roma, 1973.

DUBOIS, J.A., *Moeurs, Institutions et Cérémonies de Peuples de l'Inde*, tomes 1-2, Paris, 1825.

FUCHS, J., *Theologia Moralis Generalis* (ad usum privatum auditorum) Pars altera, Romae, 1968/69.

GILLEMAN, Gerard, S.J., *Le Primat de la Charité en Theologie Morale*, Paris, 1952.

GILSON, Etienne, *Saint Thomas Moraliste*, 2nde édition, Paris, 1952.

GISPERT-SAUCH, G., ed., *God's Word Among Men*, Delhi, 1973.

—, *Bliss in the Upaniṣads*, New Delhi, 1977.

GONDA, J., *Die Religionen Indiens*, 2 vols., Stuttgart, 1960.

—, *Viṣṇuism and Śivaism*, University of London, 1970.

HAMBYE, Edward, 'Robert de Nobili and Hinduism' in: *God's Word among Men*, ed. G. Gispert-Sauch, S.J., Delhi, 1973.

HAMEL, Edward, *Les Dix Paroles*, Bruxelles-Paris, 1969.

—, *Loi Naturelle et Loi du Christ*, Bruges-Paris, 1964.

HĀRING, Bernard, *La Loi du Christ*, 3 Tomes, Paris, 1955-1959.

HÖRMAN, Karl, ed. *Lexikon Der Christlichen Moral*, Innsbruck, 1976.

JOHNSON, Jean, *God and Gods in Hinduism*, New Delhi, 1972.

KANE, P.V., *History of Dharmaśāstras*, Vols. I-V, Poona 1941-1962.

KLAES, N., *Conscience and Consciousness*, Bangalore, 1975.

LONERGAN, Bernard, S.J., *Method in Theology*, 2nd edition, London, 1973.

MACDONNELL, Arthur Anthony, *A Practical Sanskrit Dictionary*, London, 1974.

MACQUARRIE, John, *Three Issues in Ethics*, London, 1970.

MAGISTRIS, Giacinto de, *Relatione della Christianità i Maduré fatta da Padri Missionarii della Compagnia di Gesù della Provincia del Malabar*, Roma, 1661.

MAHADEVAN, T.M.P., *Outlines of Hinduism*, 2nd edition, Bombay, 1960.

MAITRA, Susil Kumar, *The Ethics of the Hindus*, 3rd edition, Calcutta, 1963.

MEES, G.H., *Dharma and Society*, 'S-Gravenhage, 1935.

MIDGLEY, E.B.F., *The Natural Law Tradition and the Theory of International Relations*, London, 1975.

MONIER-WILLIAMS, M., *A Sanskrit-English Dictionary* (new edition enlarged and improved by E. Leumann and C. Capeller), Oxford, 1956.

NEUNER, J., ed., *Religious Hinduism*, 2nd edition, Allahabad, 1964.

OHM, Thomas, *Die Libe zu Gott in den Nichtchristlichen Religionen*, München, 1950.

—, *Die Stellung der Heiden zu Natur und Übernatur nach dem Hl. Thomas von Aquin.* Münster, 1927.

OTTO, Rudolf, *The Idea of the Holy*, Oxford University paperback, Oxford, 1973.

OUTKA, GENE and REEDER, John P. Jr., ed., *Religion and Morality*, New York, 1973.

PATHRAPANKAL, Joseph, *Service and Salvation.* Nagpur Theological Conference on Evangelisation, Bangalore, 1973.

PONNAIYA, V.A., *Kuntrilmel Itta Teepam*, Mathurai, 1980. It is one of the best biographies in Tamil.

Prima Testimonianza del P. Antonio de Vico, estratta da un suo trattato in: *Giustificazione del*

Praticato sin'ora da Religiosi della Compagnia di Gesù nelle Missioni del Madurey, Mayssur e carnate, ed. Brandolini, Roma, 1724, pp. 30-31.

POPE, G.U., ed. *Tiruvācagam*, Oxford 1900.

RADHAKRISHNAN, S., *The Principal Upaniṣads*, London, 1953.

Raguali d'Alcune Missioni fatte dalli Padri della Compagnia di Gesù nell'India cioe nella Provincia di Goa, e Coccino, nell'Africa in Capo verde, Roma, 1615.

RAJAMANICKAM, S., S.J., *The First Oriental Scholar*, Tirunelveli, 1972.

—, Treatise of Nicolas Godinho, S.J., in his *Adaptation*, Palayamkottai, 1971. It is a summary in English of the Latin treatise, "An probari (possit) debeat Modus quem servat P. Rub. de Nobilis et Ant. Viccus eius socius in conversione Brachmanorum urbis Madurai?"

Roberto Bellarmino S.R.E. Cardinalis Societatis Iesu Epistolae Familiares, Romae, 1650.

ROSSANO, Piero, *Il Problema Teologico delle Religioni*, Catania, 1975.

SCHELKLE, Karl Hermann, *Theology of the New Testament*, 3 Morality, Collegeville, 1973.

SCHLETTE, Robert Heinz, *Towards a Theology of Religions*, London, 1966.

SCHOMERUS, H.W., *Der Çaiva-Siddhānta, eine Mystik Indiens*, Leipzig, 1912.

—, *Indische Erlösungslehren*, Leipzig, 1919.

SOMMERVOGEL, Carlos S.J., *Bibliothèque de la Compagnie de Jésus*, Tome 5, 1814.

STELZEMBERGER, Johannes, *Moraltheologie. Die Sittlichkeitslehre der Königsherrschaft Gottes*, Zweite Auflage, Paderborn 1968.

TÄHTINEN, Unto., *Indian Philosophy of Value*, Turku, 1968.

'Testimonianza del P. Nicolò Godinho Revisore' in: *Giustificazione del Praticato sin'ora da Religiosi della Compagnia di Gesù Nelle Missioni Madurey, Mayssur et Carnate*, ed. Brandolini, Roma, 1724.

THAKUR, S.C., *Christian and Hindu Ethics*, London, 1960.

TORNESE, Nicolas S.J., *Roberto de Nobili*, Cagliari, 1973.

WEBER, Max, *The Religion of India* (A Free Press Paperback), New York, 1967.

WICKI, José, ed. *Tratado Do Pe Gonçalo Fernandes Trancoso sobre O Hinduismo* (Maduré 1616), Lisboa, 1973.

ZAEHNER, R.C., *Hinduism*, 2nd edition, Oxford, 1966.

ZALBA, Marcellino, *Theologiae Moralis Compendium I*, Matriti, 1958.

b. *Periodicals.*

CALAND, W., 'Roberto de Nobili and the Sanskrit Language and Literature', *Acta Orientalia*, 3 (1926), pp. 38-51.

DAHMEN, Pierre S.J., -Gladbach, M., 'Le Votum De Pierre Lombard', *Archivum Historiae Societatis Iesu*, 4 (1935), pp. 68-101.

DANDOY, G., 'El Problema de la Adaptacion en el Apostolado', *Razon y Fé*, 88 (1929), pp. 97-107.

DE SMET, Richard, 'Robert de Nobili and Vedānta', *Vidyajyoti* 40 (1976), pp. 363-371.

DHAVAMONY, M. S.J., 'Hindu Incarnations', *Studia Missionalia*, vol. 21 (1972), pp. 127-169.

—, 'Self-understanding of World Religions as Religion', *Gregorianum*, 54 (1973), pp. 91-130.

HAECKER, Paul, 'Dharma in Hinduism', *Zeitschrift für Missionswissenschaft und Religionswissenschaft* 49 (1965), pp. 93-106.

HAMEL, E., 'l'Ecriture, âme de la théologie morale?', *Gregorianum* 54 (1973), pp. 417-445.

—, 'Lumen rationis et lux Evangelii', *Periodica*, 59 (1970), pp. 215-249.

KUPPUSWAMY, B., 'A Modern Review of Hindu Dharma', *Journal of Dharma* I (1975), pp. 118-131.

The Light of the East, Calcutta, (1924) Feb.-Nov.

MANICKAM, T.M., 'Manu's Vision of the Hindu Dharma', *Journal of Dharma* I (1975), pp. 101-117.

RAJAMANICKAM, S. S.J., 'The Newly Discovered Informatio of Robert de Nobili' *Archivum Historiae Societatis Iesu* 39 (1970), pp. 221-267. This includes de Nobili's reply to Buccerio's objections and parts of a letter of Antonio Vico to Fr. Jerome Gomez, the Procurator of the Malabar Province on his way to the Procurators' Congregation in Rome. (The letter is dated 28.11.1613. Answer to Buccerio's objections and the letter of Vico are given in English translation).

—, *Robert de Nobili Presents Christ to the Hindus.* A paper read during the Triennial Conference of Indian History Association, Ranchi, 1968.

—, 'The Goa Conference' *Indian Church History Review* 2 (1968), pp. 81-96.

ROSSANO, P., 'Quid de non Christianis Oecumenicum Concilium Vaticanum II docuerit' *Bulletin* (Secretariatus pro non Christianis), Vol. I (1966), pp. 15-22.

SICKLER, Max, 'Das Heil der Nichtevangelisierten in Thomistischer Sicht'. *Theologische Quartalschrift* 140 (1960), pp. 38-69.

STAFFNER, H., 'Conversion to Christianity - From the Hindu point of view' *Clergy Monthly*, 36 (1972), pp. 3-15.

—, 'May a Convert Retain His Spiritual Identity?' *Vidyajvoti*, 40 (1976), pp. 356-362.

YESUDHAS, D., 'Indigenisation or Adaptation? A Brief Study of Roberto de Nobili's Attitude to Hinduism'. *Bangalore Theological Forum* I (1967), pp. 39-52.

INDEX

A

Abel, 351.
Absolute, 306.
ācai, 267, n. 316.
ācārams, 51, 54, 214, 315.
ācārikappuṇṇiyam, 242, n. 106.
ācāryas, 142.
acarīri, 137, 146.
āccariyam, 141, 309.
āciramam, 207, 333.
āciriya ātāram, 228 ch. 6.b.
ācīvitānta vivākam, 266.
actual grace, 317, n. 162, 338.
actus humanus, 159, 303.
Adam, 351.
adaptation, 15.
Ad Gentes, 340, 342, 343, 347, 353, cf Vatican Council II.
adhyātmika, 183, n. 326.
adhyātmika Śāstra, 133.
Advaita Vādi, 59, n. 184, cf *Vedāntins*.
Advaita Vedānta, 306, cf *Vedānta*.
Advaitin, 306, n. 96.
Advi Tipichei, 134.
āgamas, 46, 142, 179, 180, cf *Śiva āgamas*.
Āgama Purāṇa, 179.
agape, 246, n. 140.
ahankāra, 65, n. 7, 71, n. 45.
ahiṁsā, 57, 72, 108, 159, n. 160, 298, 299.
aiyyar, 50, n. 139.
ajnāna vēdam, 210, n. 133.
ākāca carīram piramam, 137, 148, 149, n. 102.
ākācacarīri, 146.
ākācam, 137.
akkiramam, 123, 305.
akkiyānam 203, cf añānam.
akkiyāna mārkkam, 183, n. 327.
alchemy, 352.
Alexander, 319, n. 169.
ālvars, 142.
Āmarasingha, 233, n. 40.
ambrosia, 238.
amirtam, 238.
amṛtatvam, 167.
amśa avatāra, 153, n. 125, cf *avatāara*.
añānis, 193.
añānam, 253.
añāna matams, 193.
anāti, 68.
anavastai tōṣam, 89, n. 128.
angels, 249.
aniyāyam, 118, 119, 213, 265.
antakaraṇa, 65, n. 7.
antakaranankaḷ, 151, n. 115.
aṇṭam, 95f, 126 n. 124; 165, 166.
antarhata avati, 166.
anugraha kāraṇa, 149 n. 101.
anukkirakam, 272, 273, cf grace.
anumāna (anumānam), 86, 174, 355.
anumāna darśana, 194, n. 24.
anumānapiramāṇam, 86, cf inferential knowledge.
anumānataricanam, 194.
anunayavirtutti, 242, n. 106, 257.
anurūpakāraṇam, 145, n. 80; 198.
anutāpam, 278, n. 413.
Āpastamba Gṛhya sūtra, 52, n. 150; 105, n. 16.
Āpastamba Sūtra, 102, 105, 297.
apocalyptic, 234.
apokatastasis, 173.
Apollo, 107.
appiramāṇikkaccuvikāram, 279, cf sin.
appiramāṇikkam, 117, 118, 120, 160, 212, 302, cf sin.
appiramānikkapparittiyākam, 118, 280, cf virtue.

āptan, 197, 208, 209, 218.
āptavākkiyam, 208, 323.
Āraṇyaka 56, 94 n. 150, 136.
ārccavakuṇam (*skt ārjava guṇa*), 259, 260, 332.
Arcciyam, 243 n. 109, cf holiness, saints.
aṛiār (cf *aṭiār*), 246, n. 142.
aṛikkai, 260, 287.
ārjava, 260, n. 254.
artha, 127, n. 127; 225, 265 n. 300.
aruḷ, 205, cf grace.
Aruḷnanti, 199, n. 58.
asatya vēdam, 210, n. 133.
āśrama, 47, 49, 50, 268, 293, 297 n. 44.
āśrama dharma, 17, 19, 47, 265-267, 290, 293, 333.
Assembly, 236.
aśvamedha, 45, n. 115.
atatai, 41, 107 n. 24.
atatayin, 41 n. 97.
Atharva Veda, 179.
Athenians, 351.
Aṭiār, 246, n. 142, 250.
aticayam, 141, n. 54.
ātikāraṇam, 192, 210, 254.
ātipitā, 254.
ātman, 252 n. 190.
Attributes of God 18, cf *kaṭavuḷ nirṇayam*.
Augustine St., 131.
austerity, 82.
avatāra (incarnation), 18, 142, 145, 150-155, 180, 227, 229-232, 235, 237-239, 241-242, 310, 355.
  avatāras, different 153 n. 125.
  jaṭa, 151f, 227.
  kāla, 153 n. 125; *kārya*, 153, n. 125.
  Kṛṣṇa, 154, 239, n. 87; *śakti*, 153 n. 125; Viṣṇu, 345.
avati, 165, 166, 172, 211, 249, 253, 270, 278.
avatirūpam, 283 n. 447.
avināpūta (skt a-vinābhūta), 264.
Ayur Veda (Aiur), 178, n. 296, 179.

B

bagavani, 58, n. 178.
Bandinellus, Rolandus, 166, 318.
baptism, 193, 219, 220, 221, 222, 229, 234, cf Ch. X.
Baptist, John the, 243 n. 109, 287.
beatitude, 110, 126, 127, 238, 319, 326, 334, 346, 350.
Beda Ticcaram, 134, 136.
Bellarmine, 354 n. 444.
believer, 245.
Bertrand, J., 28, n. 33; 71 n. 43; 158 n. 156; 193 n. 16; 202 n. 80; 231 n. 25; 308 n. 107; 50 n. 139.
Beschi, 89 n. 128; 243 n. 109.
Bhagavad-Gītā, 34 n. 61; 142, 251 n. 180; 310 n. 116.
bhakta, 250, cf *aṭiār* and pattan.
bhakti, 164 n. 190; 219, 245, 246, 247, 248, 249, 250, 251, 253, 254, 258, 259, 260, 277, 280, 286, 310, 312, 327, 328, 334, 335, cf *patti*.
bhaktimārga, 247 n. 146, 248, 327.
Bhartrihari, 147, n. 88.
bhāṣyam, 142.
Bhatta, 138.
bhūta, 69 n. 31.
blasphemy, 239.
bliss, 240.
Boyd, 254 n. 448.
Brhadāranyaha Upaniṣad, 251 n. 186.
Brahma, 87, 91 n. 139, 144-147, 149, 201, 233 n. 40, 311, 252 n. 190.
Brahmabandhav Upādhyāy, 357.
brahmacārya, 47, 49, 290, cf *āśramas*.
brahmacārya āśrama, 265 n. 300, 47 n. 125.
brahmacārya karman, 47.
Brahmaṇa, 87, 92 n. 142, 106 n. 23, 290.
Brahmin, 24-27, 29, 33, 35-37, 73, 87-88, 91-98, 193, 222, 296, 315, 38-48, 55, 57.
Buccerio, A., 21 n. 2, 40 n. 91; 50 n. 139; 61 n. 198, 50 n. 139.
budhers, 299 n. 55.
buddhi, 65 n. 7.
Bühler, 26 n. 25; 53 n. 155; 92 n. 142; 93 n. 146; 106 n. 20; 41 n. 94; 51 n. 150.

C

cakalanīti, 158.
cakala punniyaneṛi, 324.
cakalanirmala puṇṇiyavaḻi, 327.
cakalatarmam, 243.
Caland, W., 281 n. 431, 51 n. 150, 52 n. 150.
cakala tarmamērai, 195 Chapter 2.
Calista 246 n. 142.

R

U

V

TIPOGRAFIA POLIGLOTTA DELLA PONTIFICIA UNIVERSITÀ GREGORIANA
PIAZZA DELLA PILOTTA, 4 - ROMA